THE
WESTERN HERITAGE
Brief Edition

VOLUME I: TO 1715
Third Edition

Donald Kagan
YALE UNIVERSITY

Steven Ozment
HARVARD UNIVERSITY

Frank M. Turner
YALE UNIVERSITY

A. Daniel Frankforter
PENNSYLVANIA STATE UNIVERSITY, BEHREND COLLEGE

Prentice Hall

UPPER SADDLE RIVER, NEW JERSEY 07458

Library of Congress Cataloging-in-Publication Data

Kagan, Donald.
    The western heritage/Donald Kagan, Steven Ozment, Frank M. Turner; with the
assistance of A. Daniel Frankforter.—3rd ed., brief ed.
        p. cm.
    "Combined volume."
    Includes bibliographical references and index.
    ISBN 0-13-041578-2 (pbk.)
    1. Civilization, Western. I. Ozment, Steven E. II. Turner, Frank M. (Frank Miller),
1944- III. Title
CB245.K28 2001b
909'.09812—dc21   00-066895

Editorial Director: Charlyce Jones Owen
Acquisitions Editor: Charles Cavaliere
Associate Editor: Emsal Hasan
Director of Production and Manufacturing: Barbara Kittle
Production Editor: Louise Rothman
Prepress and Manufacturing Manager: Nick Sklitsis
Prepress and Manufacturing Buyer: Lynn Pearlman
Creative Design Director: Leslie Osher
Interior and Cover Designer: Nancy Wells and Laura Gardner

Cover Art: *The Grape Harvest*, Tapestry/Textiles, Musèe De Cluny, Paris, France

This book was set in 10/12 Trump Mediaeval by Carlisle Communications
and was printed and bound by Webcrafters.
The cover was printed by Phoenix Color Corp.

 © 2002, 1999, 1996 by Pearson Education, Inc.
Upper Saddle River, New Jersey 07458

Printed in the United States of America

10 9 8 7 6 5 4 3 2 1

0-13-041576-6

Prentice-Hall International (UK) Limited, *London*
Prentice-Hall of Australia Pty. Limited, *Sydney*
Prentice-Hall Canada Inc., *Toronto*
Prentice-Hall Hispanoamerica, S.A., *Mexico*
Prentice-Hall of India Private Limited, *New Delhi*
Prentice-Hall of Japan, Inc., *Tokyo*
Pearson Education Asia Pte. Ltd., *Singapore*
Editora Prentice-Hall do Brasil, Ltda., *Rio de Janeiro*

Brief Contents

Detailed Contents

PART 2   THE MIDDLE AGES, 476–1300

PART 3 EUROPE IN TRANSITION, 1300–1750

Maps

Preface

The heritage of Western civilization is a major point of departure for an understanding of the modern world. The global context in which we now conduct our daily lives is unprecedented, and it has been shaped in large measure by Western technologies, economic systems, and political ideologies. From the sixteenth through the twentieth centuries the West had a tremendous influence, for both good and ill, on cultures scattered around the globe, and we live today in the wake of that impact. It is the goal of this book to help students become better informed and more culturally sensitive citizens of the emerging global age by introducing them to the West's legacy.

Since *The Western Heritage* first appeared, its authors have sought to provide their readers with a work that does justice to the scope of Western civilization. Their expectation is that accurate understanding of the West will foster useful debates about the West's character, values, institutions, and global influence. Since the authors believe that a critical attitude toward their own culture has always been a characteristic of Western peoples, it is hoped that this new brief edition of *The Western Heritage* will contribute to the on-going debate about the strengths and weaknesses of the West that has been a persistent feature of Western intellectual life.

In this edition as in earlier ones, the goal has been to present Western civilization fairly, accurately, and in a way that does justice to the immense diversity of the human enterprise. Since history is made, experienced, and recorded by a multiplicity of peoples, history has many facets, no one of which can account for all the others. Any attempt to tell the story of the West from a single overarching perspective, no matter how timely, is bound to neglect or suppress some important part of that story. The authors have had to make selections to bring the story of the West within the compass of an introductory text, but they have also tried to provide the broadest possible coverage of their subject.

They also believe that any book that addresses the experience of the West must look beyond Europe's borders. The students who will read this book are drawn from a wide variety of social contexts, and they live in a world characterized by highly interconnected economies and instant communication across cultural boundaries. It is important, therefore, to recognize the ways in which Western civilization has, throughout its history, engaged other cultures and been influenced by them. Examples of the two-way interaction between Western and non-Western societies appear throughout the text and are highlighted in a series of comparative essays entitled "The West & the World."

Goals of the Text

The primary goal of *The Western Heritage* is to present a strong, clear narrative that surveys key developments in Western history while paying special attention to several critical themes:

- The capacity of Western civilization to generate transforming self-criticism.

- The development of political freedom, constitutional government, and concern for the rule of law and the rights of individuals.

- The shifting relations among religion, society, and the state.

- The development of science and technology and their expanding impact on thought, social institutions, and everyday life.

- The major religious and intellectual influences that have shaped Western culture.

FLEXIBLE PRESENTATION *The Western Heritage* is designed to accommodate a variety of approaches to a course in Western civilization and to allow instructors to stress what is most important to them. The last two chapters (30 and 31) have been specifically reorganized and rewritten so that courses can conclude by emphasizing either social or political developments.

INTEGRATED SOCIAL, CULTURAL, AND POLITICAL HISTORY *The Western Heritage* provides one of the richest accounts of Western social history found in any current textbook. It provides strong coverage of family life, the changing roles of women, and the place of the family in relation to broader economic, political, and social developments. This reflects the explosive growth that has taken place in social historical research in the past quarter century and which has enriched virtually all areas of historical study. But the authors, while strongly believing in the value of social history, have also been sensitive to the needs of teachers who have repeatedly said that they believe that a political narrative provides students with the most effective tool for constructing an initial understanding of the past.

No other survey text presents so full an account of the religious and intellectual development of the West. People may be political and social animals, but they are also reasoning and spiritual beings. What past generations thought and believed are among the most important things we can know about them, and we cannot fully understand ourselves without understanding the intellectual currents of the past that have shaped our thoughts and conceptual categories.

CLARITY AND ACCESSIBILITY Good narrative history requires clear, vigorous prose. The goal of the authors was to produce a fully accessible text without condescending to readers by compromising vocabulary or conceptual level.

Changes in the Current Edition

ART & THE WEST A beautiful and important new feature enhances students' understanding of the artistic heritage of the West. In each chapter a work of art or architecture is highlighted to illustrate key developments from the era of its creation.

THE WEST & THE WORLD Sections of the text are supplemented by a series of extended essays that compare various Western institutions with those from other parts of the world or which discuss the ways in which developments in the West have influenced non-Western cultures.

RECENT SCHOLARSHIP The new edition has been revised to incorporate the most recent developments in historical scholarship and to address the current concerns of professional historians. Of particular interest are expanded discussions of:

- **Women in the history of the West** (see, especially, chapters 3, 4, 5, 7, 14, 30.)

- **The Scientific Revolution** (chapter 14 has been wholly revised and rewritten to explain the scientific theories that arose from the Copernican revolution, the current interpretation of the Galileo case, the role played by pioneering female scientists, and the social context for the development of early science).

- **The Dutch Golden Age** (chapter 15 contains a new section discussing the United Netherlands during the seventeenth and eighteenth centuries).

- **Africa and the transatlantic economy** (chapter 17 extensively explores the relationship of Africa to the transatlantic economy of the sixteenth through the eighteenth centuries, focusing on: the role of African society and politics in the slave trade, the experience of Africans forcibly transported to the Americas, and the incorporation of African elements in New World cultures).

- **Jewish thinkers in the Enlightenment** (chapter 18 contains a new section discussing the thought of Spinoza and Moses Mendelsohn as they relate to the role of Jewish religion and society in the wider European culture).

- **The Holocaust** (chapter 29 provides more analysis of the causes of the Holocaust, and chapter 30 includes an extensive new section on the destruction of the Jews of Poland).

- **Twentieth century social history** (*The Western Heritage* presents the most extensive treatment of modern social history available in a survey text; of particular significance is chapter 30 which treats the experiences of women under authoritarian governments, the collectivization of Soviet agriculture, the destruction of the Polish Jews, European migration, and the impact of computers and new technology on European life).

- **The history of the Cold War and Europe at the start of the twenty-first century** (chapter 31, which deals with the Soviet–American rivalry and the collapse of communism, has been wholly rewritten). Chapters 30 and 31 are designed so that instructors, though teaching both chapters, may choose to close their course with either one. Those who want to emphasize social history might end with chapter 30 and those who wish to emphasize political developments may choose to conclude with chapter 31.

MAPS AND ILLUSTRATIONS To help students understand the relationship between geography and history, relief features have been added to many of the maps. The text also contains numerous color illustrations.

PEDAGOGICAL FEATURES These include chronological tables, a list of key topics at the beginning of each chapter, chapter summaries, review questions, and bibliographies. This edition continues the practice of using B.C.E. (before the common era) and C.E. (common era) instead of B.C. (before Christ) and A.D. (anno domini, the year of the Lord) to designate dates. It also utilizes the most accurate currently accepted English transliterations of Arabic words.

Ancillary Instructional Materials

The ancillary instructional materials that accompany *The Western Heritage* include print and multimedia supplements that are designed to reinforce and enliven the richness of the past and inspire students with the excitement of studying the history of Western civilization.

Print Supplements for the Instructor

INSTRUCTOR'S MANUAL WITH TEST ITEMS   The Instructor's Manual contains chapter summaries, key points and vital concepts, and information on audiovisual resources that can be used in developing and preparing lecture presentations. Also included is a test item file that offers multiple-choice, identification, and essay test questions.

PRENTICE HALL CUSTOM TEST   This commercial-quality computerized test management program, for Windows and Macintosh environments, allows users to create their own tests using items from the printed Test Item File. The program allows users to edit the items in the Test Item File and to add their own questions. Online testing is also available.

TRANSPARENCY PACKAGE   This collection of full-color transparency acetates provides the maps, charts, and graphs from the text for use in classroom presentations.

Print Supplements for the Student

STUDY GUIDE, VOLUMES I AND II   The study guide includes commentaries, definitions, and a variety of exercises designed to reinforce the concepts in the chapter. These exercises include: identification, map exercises, and short-answer and essay questions.

DOCUMENTS SET, VOLUMES I AND II   This carefully selected and edited set of documents provides over 100 additional primary source readings. Each document includes a brief introduction as well as questions to encourage critical analysis of the reading and to relate it to the content of the text.

MAP WORKBOOK   This brief workbook gives students the opportunity to increase their knowledge of geography through identification and other map exercises. It is available free to students when shrink-wrapped with the text.

HISTORICAL ATLAS OF THE WORLD   This four-color historical atlas provides additional map resources to reinforce concepts in the text. It is available for a nominal fee when shrink-wrapped with the text.

UNDERSTANDING AND ANSWERING ESSAY QUESTIONS   Prepared by Mary L. Kelley, San Antonio College. This brief guide suggests helpful study techniques as well as specific analytical tools for understanding different types of essay questions and provides precise guidelines for preparing well-crafted essay answers. This guide is available free to students when shrink-wrapped with the text.

READING CRITICALLY ABOUT HISTORY: A GUIDE TO ACTIVE READING   Prepared by Rose Wassman and Lee Ann Rinsky. This guide focuses on the skills needed to learn the essential information presented in college history textbooks. Material covered includes vocabulary skills, recognizing organizational patterns, critical thinking skills, understanding visual aids, and practice sections. This guide is available free to students when shrink-wrapped with the text.

THEMES OF THE TIMES   *The New York Times* and Prentice Hall are sponsoring *Themes of the Times*, a program designed to enhance student access to current information of relevance in the classroom. Through this program, the core subject matter provided in the text is supplemented by a collection of current articles from one of the world's most distinguished newspapers, *The New York Times*. These articles demonstrate the vital, ongoing connection between what is learned in the classroom and what is happening in the world around us. To enjoy the wealth of information of *The New York Times* daily, a reduced subscription rate is available. For information call toll-free: 1-800-631-1222.

Prentice Hall and *The New York Times* are proud to co-sponsor *Themes of the Times*. We hope it will make the reading of both textbooks and newspapers a more dynamic, involving process.

Multimedia Supplements

HISTORY ON THE INTERNET   This guide focuses on developing the critical thinking skills necessary to evaluate and use online sources. The guide also provides a brief introduction to navigating the Internet, along with complete references related specifically to the History discipline and how to use the *Companion Website*™ available for *The Western Heritage*. This supplementary book is free to students when shrink-wrapped with the text.

COMPANION WEBSITE™
ADDRESS: WWW.PRENHALL.COM/KAGAN
Students can now take full advantage of the World Wide Web to enrich their study of Western Civilization through *The Western Heritage Companion Website*™. Features of the website include, for each chapter in the text, objectives, study questions, map labeling exercises, related links, and document exercises. A faculty module provides material from the Instructor's Manual and the maps and charts from the text in Powerpoint™ format.

POWERPOINT™ IMAGES CD ROM   Available for Windows and Macintosh environments, this resource includes the maps, charts, and graphs from the text for use in Powerpoint™. Organized by chapters in the text, this collection of images is useful for classroom presentations and lectures.

IRC WESTERN CIVILIZATION CD ROM   Available for Windows 95 and 3.1, this lecture and presentation resource includes a library of over 3000 images, each with a descriptive caption, plus film clips, maps, and sound recordings. A correlation guide lists the images as they correspond to the chapters of *The Western Heritage*. Contact your local Prentice Hall representative for information about the adoption requirements for this resource.

DOCUMENTS CD ROM   Functional in both Windows and Macintosh environments, this resource contains all the primary source readings from the print Documents Set in easy-to-read Adobe Acrobat™. Additionally, all the document questions are linked directly to the *Companion Website*, enhancing an already useful study tool. This CD ROM comes packaged free with all new copies of *The Western Heritage, Brief Third Edition*.

Acknowledgments

We are grateful to the scholars and teachers whose thoughtful and often detailed comments helped shape this revision:

Lenard R. Berlanstein, University of Virginia, Charlottesville

Stephanie Christelow, Idaho State University

Samuel Willard Crompton, Holyoke Community College

Robert L. Ervin, San Jacinto Community College

Benjamin Foster, Yale University

Joseph Gonzales, Moorpark College

Victor Davis Hanson, California State University, Fresno

James Halverson, Judson College

Mark C. Herman, Edison Community College

William I. Hitchcock, Wellesley College

Pardaic Kenny, University of Colorado, Boulder

Raymond F. Kierstead, Reed College

David Lindberg, University of Wisconsin, Madison

Eleanor McCluskey, Palm Beach Atlantic College and Broward Community College

Robert J. Mueller, Hastings College

John Nicols, University of Oregon, Eugene

Sandra J. Peacock, State University of New York, Binghamton

John Powell, Cumberland College

Robert A. Schneider, Catholic University

Hugo Schwyzer, Pasadena City College

Sidney R. Sherter, Long Island University

Roger P. Snow, College of Great Falls

Finally, we would like to thank the dedicated people who helped produce this revision. Our acquisitions team of Charlyce Jones Owen, Charles Cavaliere, and Emsal Hasan; our development editor, Roberta Meyer; our production editor, Louise Rothman; Nancy Wells and Laura Gardner, who created the handsome new design of this edition; Lynn Pearlman, our manufacturing buyer; and Barbara Salz, photo researcher.

D.K.
S.O.
F.M.T.

About the Authors

DONALD KAGAN is Hillhouse Professor of History and Classics at Yale University, where he has taught since 1969. He received the A.B. degree in history from Brooklyn College, the M.A. in classics from Brown University, and the Ph.D. in history from Ohio State University. During 1958–1959 he studied at the American School of Classical Studies as a Fulbright Scholar. He has received three awards for undergraduate teaching at Cornell and Yale. He is the author of a history of Greek political thought, *The Great Dialogue* (1965); a four-volume history of the Peloponnesian war, *The Origins of the Peloponnesian War* (1969); *The Archidamian War* (1974); *The Peace of Nicias and the Sicilian Expedition* (1981); *The Fall of the Athenian Empire* (1987); and a biography of Pericles, *Pericles of Athens and the Birth of Democracy* (1991); and *On the Origins of War* (1995). He is coauthor, with Frederick W. Kagan of *While America Sleeps* (2000). With Brian Tierney and L. Pearce Williams, he is the editor of *Great Issues in Western Civilization*, a collection of readings.

STEVEN OZMENT is McLean Professor of Ancient and Modern History at Harvard University. He has taught Western Civilization at Yale, Stanford, and Harvard. He is the author of ten books. *The Age of Reform, 1250–1550* (1980) won the Schaff Prize and was nominated for the 1981 American Book Award. *Magdalena and Balthasar: An Intimate Portrait of Life in Sixteenth Century Europe* (1986), *Three Behaim Boys: Growing Up in Early Modern Germany* (1990), *Protestants: The Birth of a Revolution* (1992), and *The Burgermeister's Daughter: Scandal in a Sixteenth Century German Town* (1996) were selections of the History Book Club, as is his most recent book, *Flesh and Spirit: Private Life in Early Modern Germany* (1999).

FRANK M. TURNER is John Hay Whitney Professor of History at Yale University, where he served as University Provost from 1988 to 1992. He received his B.A. degree at the College of William and Mary and his Ph.D. from Yale. He has received the Yale College Award for Distinguished Undergraduate Teaching. He has directed a National Endowment for the Humanities Summer Institute. His scholarly research has received the support of fellowships from the National Endowment for the Humanities and the Guggenheim Foundation and the Woodrow Wilson Center. He is the author of *Between Science and Religion: The Reaction to Scientific Naturalism in Late Victorian England* (1974), *The Greek Heritage in Victorian Britain* (1981), which received the British Council Prize of the Conference on British Studies and the Yale Press Governors Award, and *Contesting Cultural Authority: Essays in Victorian Intellectual Life* (1993). He has also contributed numerous articles to journals and has served on the editorial advisory boards of *The Journal of Modern History, Isis,* and *Victorian Studies.* He edited *The Idea of a University,* by John Henry Newman (1996). Since 1996 he has served as a Trustee of Connecticut College.

A. DANIEL FRANKFORTER is Professor of Medieval History at the Pennsylvania State University. He holds degrees from Franklin and Marshall College, Drew University, and the Pennsylvania State University, where he has taught since 1970. His books include: *A History of the Christian Movement; Civilization and Survival; The Shakespeare Name Dictionary, The Medieval Millennium, An Introduction;* an edition and translation of Françoise Poullain de la Barre's *De l'Égalité des Deux Sexes,* and *Stones for Bread: A Critique of Contemporary Worship.* He has received four awards for excellence in teaching and research from the Pennsylvania State University.

Chapter 1

The Birth of Civilization

K E Y   T O P I C S

- ❂ The earliest history of humanity, the origins of human culture in the Paleolithic Age, the shift from food gathering to food production, and the emergence of civilizations in the Middle East and Africa
- ❂ The ancient civilizations of Mesopotamia and Egypt
- ❂ The great Middle Eastern empires, 1500–539 B.C.E.[1]
- ❂ The emergence of Judaism
- ❂ The different outlooks of the ancient Middle Eastern and Greek civilizations

For hundreds of thousands of years, human beings lived by hunting and gathering what nature provided. Only about 10,000 years ago did they begin to cultivate plants and domesticate animals. As they turned from harvesting food to producing it, settled life became possible. About 5,000 years ago the Sumerians, who lived near the confluence of the Tigris and Euphrates Rivers (a region the Greeks named "Mesopotamia," i.e., "between-rivers"), and the Egyptians, who dwelt in the Nile Valley, pioneered civilization. By the

---

[1]This book substitutes B.C.E. ("before the common era") and C.E. ("common era") for B.C. and A.D.

fourteenth century B.C.E. powerful empires had arisen and were struggling for dominance of the civilized world. But one of the region's smaller states, Israel, made the ancient Middle East's greatest contribution to civilization. It began the evolution of the modern West's major religions: Judaism, Christianity, and Islam.

Early Humans and Their Culture

Scientists estimate that Earth may be 6 billion years old and that its human inhabitants have been developing for 3 to 5 million years. Some 1 to 2 million years ago, erect, tool-using beings spread from their probable place of origin in Africa to Europe and Asia. Our own species, *Homo sapiens*, is about 200,000 years old, and fully modern humans have existed for about 90,000 years.

Humans are distinguished by a unique capacity to construct cultures. A *culture* may be defined as a way of life invented by a group and passed on by teaching. It includes both material things (tools, clothing, and shelter) and ideas, institutions, and beliefs. Because cultural behaviors are guided by learning rather than instinct, they can be altered at will to enable human beings to adapt rapidly to different environments and changing conditions.

The Paleolithic Age

Anthropologists identify prehistoric human cultures by the styles of their most durable and plentiful artifacts—stone tools. The earliest period in cultural development—the Paleolithic (Greek for "old stone") era—began with the first use of stone tools some 1 million years ago. It continued until about 10,000 B.C.E. Throughout this immensely long period of time, people were nomadic hunters and gatherers who depended for their food on what nature spontaneously offered. An uncertain food supply and vulnerability to wild beasts, accidents, and environmental disasters persuaded early humans that they occupied a world governed by superhuman powers. Cave art, ritual burial practices, and other evidences of religious or magical belief that appeared during the Paleolithic era bear witness to a suspicion as old as humanity itself that there is more to the world than meets the eye.

Human society in the Paleolithic Age was probably based on a division of labor by sex. Males ranged far afield on the hunt. Females, who were less mobile because of the burdens of childbearing and nursing, gathered edibles of various kinds in the vicinity of a base camp. The knowledge that people acquired as hunters and gatherers enabled them to develop agriculture and herding, food-producing technologies that drastically changed the human lifestyle.

The Neolithic Age

About 10,000 years ago people living in some parts of the Middle (or Near) East began to shift from hunting and gathering to agriculture. Only a few societies initially made the change, and anthropologists and archaeologists disagree as to what motivated them. Since the shift coincided with advances that promoted greater precision in chipping and grinding new styles of stone tools, this period is called the Neolithic (i.e., "new stone") Age. Neolithic peoples, who lived in the mountain foothills to which wild species of sheep, goats, wheat, and barley were native, began to domesticate these food sources. Once domesticated, species could then be transplanted to areas where they did not naturally occur.

Hunters and gatherers must wander from place to place to find food, but farmers have to stay with the fields they cultivate. Agriculture necessitated village life. That prompted the invention of techniques for constructing more permanent dwellings, and it encouraged the use of new materials such as pottery (in which to cook and store agricultural products). The earliest Neolithic dwellings were small, circular huts that clustered around a central storage facility. Later Neolithic people built larger rectangular homes with private storage places and enclosures for livestock. The similarity in size and equipment of these structures suggests that there were only minor differences in wealth and social status within Neolithic communities. There was some trade among them, but they were largely self-sufficient.

The two most exceptional Neolithic sites that have come to light are at Jericho (near the Dead Sea) and Çatal Hüyük (about 150 miles south of the capital of modern Turkey). Jericho was occupied as early as 12,000 B.C.E., and by 8000 B.C.E. it had a massive stone wall enclosing a space of more

In Chauvet cave, near Avignon, France, Paleolithic artists decorated the walls with exquisite drawings of animals. Jean Clottes/Corbis Sygma Photo News

than eight acres. (No other Neolithic site is known to have been fortified.) Çatal Hüyük was a somewhat later and larger community with a population well over 6,000. Its mud-brick dwellings were packed so tightly together that there were no streets between them and people entered them from ladders through roofs. Many interiors were elaborately and mysteriously decorated with sculptures and paintings that are assumed to have ritual significance.

In regions where agriculture and animal husbandry appeared, the relationship between human beings and nature was changed forever. Human population grew at an unprecedented rate, and people began to try to control nature, not just respond to what it offered. This was a vital prerequisite for the development of civilization, but it was not without cost. Farmers had to work harder and longer than hunters and gatherers. They faced health threats from accumulating wastes, and they had to figure out ways to live to-

gether permanently in one place. The earliest Neolithic communities appeared in the Middle East about 8000 B.C.E., in China about 4000 B.C.E., and in India about 3600 B.C.E.

The Bronze Age and the Birth of Civilization

As Neolithic villages and herding cultures were spreading over much of the world, another major shift in human lifestyles began on the plains along the Tigris and Euphrates Rivers and in the valley of the Nile River. Some villages grew into towns and cities and began to dominate the regions in which they evolved. These new urban centers usually had some monumental structures that could have been built only by the sustained effort of hundreds or thousands of people over many years. Social stratification appeared, and people were assigned to classes on the basis of wealth, family lineage, and religious and political authority. Writing was invented, probably to deal with urban problems of management and record keeping. Elaborate artwork was produced, and an important new technology for manufacturing tools and weapons appeared. It involved techniques for smelting metal ores and combining tin with copper to make a hard alloy called bronze. The prevalence of bronze has led scholars to call the period from 3100 B.C.E. to 1200 B.C.E. in the Middle East the Bronze Age. The characteristics of Bronze Age cultures (i.e., urbanism; technological, industrial, and social change; long-distance trade; and writing systems) are the hallmarks of *civilization*.

Early Civilizations to About 1000 B.C.E.

During the fourth millennium, populations of unprecedented density began to develop along Mesopotamia's Tigris and Euphrates Rivers and Egypt's Nile River. By about 3000 B.C.E., when the invention of writing gave birth to history, urban life had spread throughout these regions and centralized states had begun to develop. Since city-dwellers do not grow their own food, they need to establish some system to promote, collect, and disburse surpluses produced by rural farmers and herders. The arid climates of Mesopotamia and Egypt meant that farmers could meet the demands of urban populations for their products only with the help of extensive irrigation systems. Irrigation technology was more elaborate in Mesopotamia than in Egypt. In Egypt the Nile flooded at the right moment for cultivation, and irrigation simply involved channeling water to the fields. In Mesopotamia, however, the floods came at the wrong season. Dikes were needed to protect fields where crops were already growing and to store water for future use. Mesopotamian towns and villages were strung along rivers, streams, and canals. These were their lifelines, and control of the water they supplied was a contentious issue that could lead to war. Mesopotamia was a flat plain. The terrain provided little protection from floods and allowed swollen rivers and streams to carve new channels and change their courses. Cities were sometimes severely damaged or even forced to relocate. Archaeologists once believed that the

This statue of Gudea, city ruler of Lagash after the fall of the Akkadian empire, shows him as a pious Sumerian ruler. It was carved of very hard imported black stone. A brief historical inscription is visible on his cloak. Gudea built a major temple to a local deity at Lagash, Ningirsu, and describes the work, step by step, in one of the longest Sumerian poems known today. Scala/Art Resource, NY

need to construct and manage irrigation systems caused the development of cities and centralized states, but they now know that large-scale irrigation appeared long after urban civilization was established.

Mesopotamian Civilization

Civilization probably made its first appearance in Mesopotamia in Babylonia, a zone of arid ecology that stretches from modern Baghdad to the Persian Gulf. The first cities seem to have been founded in Sumer, the southern half of Babylo-

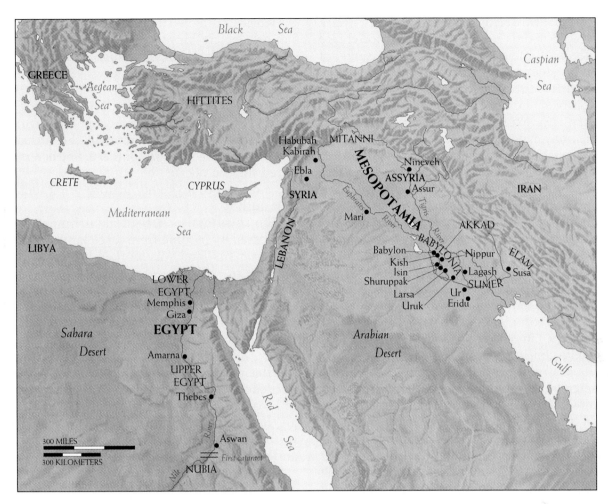

MAP 1–1   THE ANCIENT MIDDLE EAST   *The West's two premier civilizations were both dependent on unique, annually flooding rivers. Egypt was united as a single state at a very early period, but Mesopotamia was long divided into a number of city-states.*

nia, during the fourth millennium B.C.E. The earliest urban center may have been at Uruk, a city that established outposts of its culture as far afield as Syria and southern Anatolia. During the Early Dynastic Period (i.e., 2800–2370 B.C.E.), Uruk was joined by a number of other city-states scattered along the banks of the Tigris and Euphrates. Competition for water and land led to wars among them. Leagues and alliances were formed, and the weaker cities became subject to kingdoms built by the stronger. Legend claims that history's first monarchs reigned in the city of Kish.

The Sumerian language is not related to any known language, and most of the Sumerians' neighbors spoke Semitic tongues (i.e., languages belonging to the same family as Hebrew and Arabic). Many of the Semitic peoples were influenced by Sumerian civilization and adapted the Sumerian writing system for their own use. Among these were the Akkadians, a people whose first king, Sargon, established his seat at Akkade (near Baghdad). Sargon created history's first empire by conquering all the Sumerian city-states and extending his authority into southwestern Iran and northern Syria. Memory of the dynasty's splendor led later Mesopotamians to think of the reign of Naram-Sin, his grandson, as the high point of their history. (See "Art and the West.")

External attack and internal weakness eventually combined to destroy the Akkadian state, but about 2125 B.C.E. the kings of the Third Dynasty of the ancient Sumerian city of Ur restored unity to a part of the old empire. Under the leadership of the Third Dynasty of Ur, Sumerian civilization had its final flowering. Great monuments were built, epic poems were composed to celebrate the deeds of ancient heroes, and thousands of surviving documents witness to the existence of a highly centralized administrative system. Ur survived, however, for little more than a century. An extended period of agricultural failure may have produced a famine that undercut its ability to defend itself. The Elamites invaded Sumer from the east and the Amorites invaded from the north. They brought an end to Sumerian rule and eventually absorbed the Sumerian peoples. The Sumerian language survived but only as a learned tongue studied by priests and scholars—much like Latin in the modern West.

New Amorite dynasties seated themselves at Isin and Larsa, but they were soon brought under the control of a powerful new dynasty that founded the famous city of Babylon. Babylon extended its control over most of Mesopotamia. Its empire and culture reached their peaks during the reign of Hammurabi (r. ca. 1792–1750 B.C.E.), a ruler who is best remembered for the collection of laws that was issued during his reign. Earlier kings had compiled lists of laws, but the so-called Code of Hammurabi is the earliest major collection to survive. It provides its readers with uniquely intimate insights into the values and institutions of an early civilization.

Amorite society was divided into classes of nobles, commoners, and slaves, each one of which was treated differently by the law. Crimes against highly ranked individuals were punished more severely than those against inferior persons, but even the poor and humble had some protection under the law. The principle of justice was retribution: "an eye for an eye, a tooth for a tooth." Professionally trained judges decided cases on the basis of evidence and the testimony of witnesses. When that was unavailable, accused persons might be compelled to prove their innocence by taking sacred oaths or undergoing physical ordeals.

Hammurabi's dynasty survived until about 1600 B.C.E. It collapsed in the face of invasions from the north that brought new peoples (i.e., the Hittites, Hurrians, and Kassites) into Mesopotamia.

GOVERNMENT   The earliest historical records document the existence of monarchy in ancient Mesopotamia. The type of monarchy, however, varied according to time and place. Early Sumerian art depicts kings leading armies, executing captives, and making offerings to gods. In the northern district of Assyria kings served as chief priests, but in the south, in Babylonia, the roles of kings and priests were kept separate. Kings often appointed their sons and daughters to priesthoods. Enheduanna, daughter of the Akkadian emperor Sargon, was one of these. She is remembered for the poetry she wrote, some of which has survived to make her history's first identifiable author.

The royal and priestly establishments were supported by income from large landed estates. Some of this land was worked by low-ranking laborers in exchange for food rations, and some of it was leased to citizen entrepreneurs who paid rent or farmed it for a share of the crop. The government and the temples also maintained large herds of animals, which supported, among other things, the large-scale manufacture of textiles. Exports of wool and textiles were needed to pay for metals that were not available in Mesopotamia. Priests and kings did not own all the land in a Sumerian city-state. Some was in the hands of private individuals who bought and sold it freely.

WRITING AND MATHEMATICS   The challenge of administrating a Sumerian city promoted the invention of the world's first system of writing. Modern scholars have named it *cuneiform* (from Latin *cuneus*, "wedge") after the wedge-shaped marks that the Sumerian scribe made by pressing a reed stylus into the common writing material, a clay tablet. Writing began with a few signs intended to help the reader remember something that he already knew. Gradually the system evolved to record all the elements of speech so that authors could use it to pass on new information to their readers. Sumerian scribes had to learn several thousand characters, some of which stood for words and others for sounds. Since it took considerable time and training to learn how to write, the skill was restricted to a tiny elite whose services were much in demand.

Before 3000 B.C.E. no one seems to have conceived of the concept of a number apart from the act of counting specific things. Scribes used different numerals for counting different things, and a single sign could mean, for example, either 10 or 18 depending on what was being counted.

A Monument to a King's Triumph: The Victory Stele of Naram-Sin

The Victory Stele of Naram-Sin King of Akkad, over the mountain-dwelling Lullubi, Mesopotamian, Akkadian Period, c. 2230 B.C.E. (pink sandstone). Louvre, Paris, France. The Bridgeman Art Library International Ltd.

The Akkadian ruler Naram-Sin erected a pillar (i.e., stele) to commemorate a victory over the Lullubi, a people who lived in the Zagros Mountains on Mesopotamia's eastern frontier. Steles were erected in temples to record the deeds of kings and on frontiers to frighten off potential invaders by advertising a king's military prowess. Naram-Sin's stele is a six-foot-high slab of limestone that was carted off as war booty in the twelfth century B.C.E. by the Elamites. Modern archaeologists discovered it (along with the stele on which the Code of Hammurabi was inscribed) in the ruins of the Elamite capital at Susa.

Naram-Sin's stele is one of the finest extant Akkadian sculptures, and it illustrates the novel imperialistic point of view that distinguished the Akkadians from the Sumerians. The figure of the king is larger than all the others in testimony to his dominance. He wears a horned helmet to symbolize his divine power, and he tramples on the bodies of his enemies. The composition strides diagonally up the stele, creating a sense of mounting, conquering energy. Landscape appears for the first time in Mesopotamian art, and figures are naturalistically modeled with the exception of the gods. They are symbolized by stars to prevent them from competing with the deified king for dominance of the scene.

Once numbers began to be thought of as entities in themselves, development was rapid. Sumerian mathematicians developed a sexagesimal system (i.e., based on the number 60). It survives today in our convention of the 60-minute hour and the circle divided into 360 degrees. Mathematics enabled the Mesopotamians to make great strides in the study of astronomy and to develop accurate calendars.

RELIGION The Mesopotamians produced a large body of sacred literature, some of which influenced the composition of the Hebrew Bible. They worshiped many gods and goddesses, most of whom were deified natural phenomena (e.g., the powers behind storms, earthquakes, and the fecundity of nature). The Mesopotamians were religiously tolerant and accepted the fact that different people might have different gods. They assumed that the gods, although immortal and much greater in power than themselves, had the same needs as they did. Myths claimed that the gods had created humanity to do the work of food raising and housekeeping that otherwise the gods would have had to do for themselves. A temple served literally as a god's home. The image of the deity that it housed was provided with meals, draped in clothing, offered entertainment, and honored with ritual and ceremony. A garden was maintained for the god's pleasure and a bed for its nightly repose. Deities had universal authority, but each major god or goddess laid exclusive claim to a city of his or her own. The greater temples in the Sumerian cities were erected on the tops of huge terraced mounds of mudbrick called *ziggurats.* Poets sometimes described these structures as mountains linking earth with heaven, but their precise purpose and symbolism remain uncertain.

The gods were grouped into families, and heaven was assumed to be organized much like a human community. Each deity had its own area of responsibility. Gods presided not only over the processes of nature but also over human skills and crafts. The great gods who dominated heaven, like the kings who governed human affairs, were too remote to be approached by common people. Ordinary men and women took their concerns to minor deities whom they hoped would intercede for them in the courts of heaven.

Intercession was needed. The Mesopotamians had a keen sense of the fragility of human existence, and religion provided some of their most important tools for coping with life's crises and uncertainties. Mesopotamians believed that their world was full of omens that, if properly understood, would reveal the future. Knowledge of the future was important, for it was assumed that unfavorable developments could be headed off by appropriate rituals and careful planning. The Mesopotamians developed an elaborate science of divination that found meaning in everything from chance events to the shapes of the entrails of animals sacrificed to the gods. Temples kept extensive records of omens to enable priests to hone their skills at divining the meanings of portents. The Mesopotamians also believed that many of life's reverses could be blamed on black magic, and there were many rituals to provide protection against witchcraft.

The Mesopotamians did not hold out any hope for a better life after death. Death doomed spirits to a glum existence in a dusty, dark netherworld where they suffered hunger and thirst unless their living relatives continued to supply them with offerings. There was no reward in death for those who had led virtuous lives and no punishment for the wicked. Everyone was equally miserable. Since the desperate spirits of the dead might escape confinement to haunt the living, families took the precaution of burying their dead with offerings and holding ceremonies from time to time to placate departed kin. At the funerals of some of the early rulers, large numbers of their servants were sacrificed to provide them with retinues in the underworld.

SOCIETY Hundreds of thousands of cuneiform texts, dating from the early third millennium to the third century B.C.E., provide us with a detailed picture of life in ancient Mesopotamia. Evidence from the reign of Hammurabi is particularly abundant. In addition to his famous law code, there are numerous administrative documents and royal and private letters. The amount of space given to various topics in Hammurabi's code suggests the issues that were of chief concern to his subjects.

The code's third largest category of laws deals with commerce. Regulations governing debts, rates of interest, security, default, and the conduct of professionals (e.g., contractors, surgeons, etc.) testify to the complexity of Babylonian economic life. The second largest group of laws relates to land tenure and suggests that individual landholders feared that powerful officials would try to take their property from them. The largest collection of laws is devoted to family issues, that is, marriage, inheritance, and adoption. Parents arranged marriages for their children. The groom made a payment for his bride and her family provided her with a dowry. A marriage was expected to be monogamous unless it failed to produce offspring. In that case, a man whose wife was barren or sickly could take a second wife to provide him with the children he needed to care for them in their old age. Husbands were permitted extramarital affairs with concubines, slaves, and prostitutes, but wives were not granted comparable license. A married woman's place was assumed to be in the home, but wives could own property and run their own businesses—so long as they did not neglect the duties they owed to their husbands and families. A woman could initiate divorce and reclaim her dowry so long as her husband could not convict her of any wrongdoing. Single women sometimes supported themselves as tavern owners, moneylenders, midwives, nurses, priestesses, or temple servants.

SLAVERY: CHATTEL SLAVES AND DEBT SLAVES
There were two kinds of slavery in ancient Mesopotamia: chattel slaves and persons enslaved for debt. Chattel slaves were treated like pieces of property. They had no legal rights, for they were usually foreigners—prisoners of war or aliens bought from slave merchants. They were expensive luxuries and were used primarily as domestic servants. Debt slavery was more common. Individuals could pledge themselves or members of their families as security for loans, and extremely high interest rates made repayment difficult. Debtors who defaulted on their loans were enslaved to work off their debts, but they could not be sold. They could regain their freedom if they repaid their loan, and they could conduct businesses, own property, and marry free persons.

Egyptian Civilization

While Mesopotamian civilization evolved along the banks of the Tigris and Euphrates Rivers, an-other great civilization appeared in Egypt. It depended on the Nile, a river that flows from its source in central Africa some 4,000 miles north to the Mediterranean. The Nile divided Egypt into two geographically distinct districts. Upper (i.e., upstream) Egypt occupied a narrow valley and extended 650 miles from Aswan to Lower (downstream) Egypt, the Nile's 100-mile deep, triangularly shaped delta. Without the Nile, agriculture would have been impossible in Egypt's arid environment. Annually, rains in central Africa caused the river to flood, soaking Egypt's fields and depositing a new layer of fertile silt just in time for the autumn planting season. As the waters retreated, farmers sowed their crops, and relatively simple irrigation techniques were adequate to guarantee a level of prosperity that was unmatched in the ancient world.

Egypt was a long, narrow country. But since no one was ever far from the Nile, the river served as a kind of highway to tie the Egyptians together. As early as 3100 B.C.E., when the cities of Mesopotamia were still fighting among themselves, Upper and Lower Egypt had become a single state. It enjoyed remarkable stability, thanks in part to the security provided by its location. The cliffs and deserts that surrounded Egypt protected it from invasion. The valley sheltered its inhabitants from the violent storms that swept the Mesopotamian plain, and the river's annual flooding was predictable and minimally destructive. The peace and order that characterized life in Egypt produced an optimistic outlook that contrasts markedly with the pessimistic tone of so much Mesopotamian literature.

Events in the more than 3,000-year span of ancient Egyptian history are traditionally dated by reference to the reigns of thirty-one dynasties of pharaohs beginning with Menes, the king who united Upper and Lower Egypt, and ending with the death of Cleopatra (30 B.C.E.), the last ruler from a dynasty founded by one of Alexander the Great's Greek generals. Egypt was then absorbed into the Roman empire and ruled by a Roman provincial governor. This very long history spans three lengthy eras of stability and creativity (the Old, Middle, and New Kingdoms) separated by relatively brief episodes of confusion (the Intermediate Periods).

THE OLD KINGDOM (2700–2200 B.C.E.) Egypt's first two dynasties, the rulers of the Early Dynastic

Period (3100–2700 B.C.E), unified the country and paved the way for the brilliant achievements of the Old Kingdom. The Old Kingdom provided Egypt with over 400 years of stability and prosperity and fostered the development of many of the institutions, monuments, and arts that are most characteristic of Egyptian civilization.

The land and people of Egypt were the property of an absolute ruler, the pharaoh (i.e., "the great house"). He was considered to be a god on whom the safety and prosperity of his people depended. By building temples and honoring his fellow gods with rituals and offerings he maintained *maat*, the equilibrium of the universe. His word was law, and an elaborate bureaucracy of officials existed to help him enforce it. Pharaoh's officials exercised centralized control over granaries, land surveys, assessments, tax collections, and disbursements from the royal treasury. In addition to these agents of the central government, there were also governors of regional districts (i.e., *nomes*) called *nomarchs* who dealt with important local issues such as water management.

The power and resources of the Old Kingdom pharaohs are clearly revealed by their greatest monuments, the pyramids, which were built to serve as their tombs. The first experiments in pyramid construction were carried out by Djoser, a pharaoh of the Third Dynasty. He erected history's first major stone building, a great solid pyramid composed of six layers, or steps, and surrounded by an elaborate funeral complex. Snefru, founder of the Fourth Dynasty, built the first true (i.e., smooth-sided) pyramid, and his son Khufu (Cheops, in Greek sources) commissioned the largest pyramid every constructed. It rose on the desert plateau of Giza opposite Memphis, the Old Kingdom capital on the border between Upper and Lower Egypt. It covered 13.1 acres, soared to a height of 481 feet, and was composed of 2.3 million blocks of stone, each averaging 2.5 tons. It is extraordinary not only for its size, but for the precision of its engineering. Khufu's successors built additional pyramids at Giza, and the pharaoh Khafre added the famous Sphinx, a huge version of the enigmatic half-lion, half-human creature that was a common subject for Egyptian sculptors. The pyramids and their temples were originally provided with lavish offerings to support the pharaoh in the afterlife, but they were stripped of their contents by ancient grave robbers. The only major artifacts the thieves missed were two full-sized wooden boats that were buried at the base of the pyramids. These were intended to convey the pharaoh on his journeys in the next world.

THE FIRST INTERMEDIATE PERIOD AND THE MIDDLE KINGDOM (2200–1630 B.C.E.)   The Old Kingdom came apart when, for political and economic reasons, the power of the pharaohs declined and the nomarchs and other officials established their independence. Decentralization introduced an era of confusion and disorder (i.e., the First Intermediate Period) that lasted until about 2025 B.C.E. At that point, Amunemhet I, a vizier (i.e., chief minister) to a dynasty of pharaohs seated in the Upper Egyptian city of Thebes, seized control, reunited Egypt, and inaugurated the Middle Kingdom.

The confusion of the First Intermediate Period may have undercut some of the traditions that supported the pharaoh's authority. The rulers of the Middle Kingdom were regarded as less distant and godlike than their predecessors, and they seem to have been more directly concerned with the affairs of their subjects. The nomarchs who served them had more autonomy, and to secure an uncontested succession to the throne pharaohs found it wise to establish their heirs as co-regents during their lifetimes.

Egypt began to emerge from its isolation during the Middle Kingdom and to pay more attention to foreign affairs. The pharaohs pushed up the Nile into Nubia and built fortresses to guard the trade routes that brought African goods to Egypt. Syria and Palestine also became areas of concern, and fortifications were built to staunch the flow of eastern migrants into the delta.

THE SECOND INTERMEDIATE PERIOD AND THE NEW KINGDOM (1630–1075 B.C.E.)   For unknown reasons the crown passed rapidly from hand to hand during the Thirteenth Dynasty, and weak pharaohs were unable to prevent the rise of rivals in the western delta. In the eastern delta, Asiatic migration continued, and the region passed into the hands of pharaohs whom the native Egyptians called the Hyksos (i.e., "chiefs of foreign lands"). Archaeological remains suggest that these rulers were probably Amorites who had infiltrated the

Major Periods in Mesopotamian and Egyptian History

Mesopotamia

ca. 3500 B.C.E.	Cities appear
ca. 2800–2370 B.C.E.	First Dynasties
2370–2205 B.C.E.	Sargon's empire
2125–2027 B.C.E.	III Dynasty of Ur
Hammurabi (r. 1792–1750 B.C.E.)	
ca. 1600, fall of Amoritic Babylon	

Egypt

ca. 3100–2700 B.C.E.	Early Dynastic Period (dynasties I–II)
ca. 2700–2200 B.C.E.	The Old Kingdom (dynasties III–VI)
2200–2025 B.C.E.	I Intermediate Period (dynasties VII–XI)
2025–1630 B.C.E.	The Middle Kingdom (dynasties XII–XIII)
1630–1550 B.C.E.	II Intermediate Period (dynasties XIV–XVII)
1550–1075 B.C.E.	The New Kingdom (dynasties XVIII–XX)

delta during the Middle Kingdom. They became the dominant power in Egypt for about a century until they were driven out by Ahmose, first king of the Eighteenth Dynasty and founder of the New Kingdom.

The pharaohs of the New Kingdom had imperialistic aspirations. Their armies reached the Euphrates in the east and drove deep into Africa—extending Egyptian influence 1,300 miles south from Memphis. The Egyptian empire provided the pharaohs with unprecedented wealth and subjected them to numerous foreign influences. The result was the establishment in Thebes of a cosmopolitan court of extraordinary splendor and sophistication and a spate, throughout Egypt, of monumental building projects. The pharaohs of this era, hoping perhaps to safeguard the vast treasures they accumulated for the afterlife, ceased to erect pyramids that advertised the sites of their graves. They chose instead to be buried in cavelike tombs cut into the walls of the desolate "Valley of the Kings" near Thebes. Despite elaborate precautions, however, they failed to secure their final resting places. Only one pharaonic tomb (that of a young Eighteenth Dynasty ruler named Tutankhamun) escaped looting by ancient grave robbers. He was a fairly minor king who died prematurely and was buried in haste. His grave was doubtless less lavishly equipped than those of the more prominent pharaohs, but its treasures are truly awe-inspiring.

Tutankhamun was succeeded by a line of solider-pharaohs who erected some of Egypt's most imposing monuments. They fought numerous battles in Syria and Palestine where their chief opponents were the Hittites whose powerful empire was based in Asia Minor. The later New Kingdom pharaohs fended off attacks on the delta from the Libyans and from Mediterranean raiders called the Sea Peoples, but an increasingly volatile international situation gradually eroded their position. By 1075, Egypt was no longer an imperial power. It was weakened by internal divisions and succumbed to a succession of foreign conquerors—Assyrian, Persian, Greek, and ultimately Roman.

LANGUAGE AND LITERATURE   The Egyptians began to write about 3000 B.C.E. They may have been inspired by the example of Mesopotamia, but they invented their own writing systems. The Greeks called formal Egyptian writing *hieroglyphs* (i.e., "sacred carving"), for it was used to engrave holy texts on monuments. For business and general purposes there was an alternative cursive script that could be written much more rapidly and easily. It used pen and ink and a sheet of paperlike material made from the papyrus reed. Texts were usually written horizontally from right to left, but they could also be written from left to right and up and down in horizontal columns. The Egyptian writing system was very complex, for some hieroglyphic symbols represented syllables, others words, and still others categories of words.

The Egyptians produced a large and varied body of literature encompassing religious myths, entertaining stories, collections of proverbs, how-to advice for aspiring bureaucrats, love poems, personal letters, medical texts, astronomical observations, calendars, autobiographies, judicial records, and administrative documents. Curiously missing are any traces of epic poetry or of dramas, although the latter, at least, are known to have been performed as parts of some cult rituals.

RELIGION: GODS, TEMPLES, AND THE AFTERLIFE   The Egyptians never found it necessary to impose consistency on their religious beliefs. Three different myths arose in different parts of Egypt to explain the creation of the world, and each credited that achievement to a different god. Since gods sometimes had overlapping functions, they tended to blend into one another. Some were known by a variety of names. Gods were usually depicted as having human or animal form or an animal head on a human body. As in Mesopotamia they were believed literally to inhabit their temples. These structures became increasingly elaborate as time passed. The sacred complex at Karnak (near Thebes) was under construction for over 2,000 years. Armies of full-time priests tended the gods with elaborate rituals and managed their temple endowments. Ordinary people did not worship in the great temples, but they did attend festivals in which the images of the gods were brought out for the public to view.

Egyptian religion was the product of very ancient, enduring traditions. But during the reign of the Eighteenth Dynasty, a pharaoh named Amunhotep IV attempted suddenly to impose a new faith on his people. Amunhotep declared an aspect of the sun, the Aten (i.e., "disk"), to be the supreme god. He claimed that the Aten was the creator and sustainer of life and that he and his queen Nefertiti were the sole mediators between the Aten and the Egyptian people. To honor his god, Amunhotep changed his name to Akhenaten (i.e., "the effective spirit of the Aten") and built a new capital called Akhetaten (i.e., "the horizon of the Aten") near Amarna north of Thebes. Akhenaten's religious reforms failed to take hold, and after his death the court returned to Thebes. Akhetaten was dismantled. The Aten cult was suppressed, and the worship of the older sun-god, Amun, was restored. Alone among the Egyptian gods, the Aten was represented by an abstract symbol, not a human or animal form. The art of the Amarna period is also noteworthy for a degree of abstraction that marked a radical, if brief, departure from the traditional conventions of Egyptian painting and sculpture.

Most Egyptians worshiped at small local shrines, and many householders had private collections of sacred objects. Belief in magic, oracles, and amulets to ward off evil was strong, and magic was the primary tool on which the Egyptians relied for coping with the dangers that the soul presumably faced as it made its transition to the afterlife. Originally only the pharaoh was assumed to be able to survive death and join the immortal gods, but gradually the belief spread that all persons who could make the necessary preparations might enjoy this privilege. The spells needed to pass the various tests and fend off the monsters of the underworld were preserved in the *Book of the Dead*, which was often inscribed on tombs. The dead were assumed to want and need the same things as the living, and persons who could afford to do so loaded their tombs with provisions and equipment for life after death. It was the duty of their descendants to make occasional offerings at their tombs to replenish their supplies.

WOMEN IN EGYPTIAN SOCIETY   The Egyptian woman's primary duty was the management of a household. She could not study in scribal schools, become an artisan, or hold a government office, but she could own and manage property, sue for divorce, and claim the same legal protections as a man. Royal women were, of course, an exception. They often wielded considerable influence, and a few, such as Thutmosis I's daughter Hatshepsut, governed either as regents for dependent males or in their own names. Women are often depicted in art in scenes in which they make and receive offerings and enjoy the pleasures of banqueting and hunting with their husbands.

SLAVES   Slaves did not become common in Egypt until the foreign campaigns of the pharaohs of the Middle Kingdom began to produce Nubian and Asian prisoners of war. The successful imperialistic ventures of the New Kingdom vastly increased the number of captives who became slaves. Sometimes entire peoples were enslaved.

Slaves were assigned all kinds of tasks. Some worked in the fields alongside the native peasants. Some were domestic servants. Some were trained as artisans. A few even exercised authority as police or soldiers. They could be freed, but manumission was rare. There were no racial or other obstacles, however, to their gradual assimilation into the mass of the population.

Ancient Middle Eastern Empires

While Egypt was organizing the New Kingdom, new states and peoples were carving out domains for themselves in the Middle East.

This painting from the Theban tomb of a high-ranking Eighteenth Dynasty official shows him, accompanied by his wife and daughter, on a hunting trip through the papyrus marshes, an activity the family enjoyed during their lives on earth and would continue in the afterlife. Courtesy of the Trustees of the British Museum. Copyright The British Museum

The Hittites

The Hittites were an Indo-European people. That is, their language (which belonged to the same family as Greek, Latin, and Indian Sanskrit) set them apart from the older Middle Eastern peoples, most of whom favored Semitic tongues. The Hittites built a strong, centralized kingdom with its seat at Hattusas (near modern Turkey's capital, Ankara). From 1400 to 1200 B.C.E. they grew to become the dominant power in the Middle East. They destroyed their neighbors, the Mitannians, and contested control of Syria and Palestine with Egypt. An indecisive battle in 1285 B.C.E. culminated in a truce between these two superpowers. About 1200, the Hittite kingdom collapsed. It was one of the many victims of the confusion created by the invaders whom the Egyptians called the Sea Peoples.

The Hittites adopted the cuneiform script and many aspects of Mesopotamian culture, but their political institutions were their own. Their kings did not claim to be divine or even to be representatives of the gods. The king was advised by a council of nobles who limited his power, and an heir's succession to the throne required ratification by the army. One thing that may have contributed to Hittite success was the development in their region (a bit before the rise of their kingdom) of techniques for smelting iron and forging it into weapons. Iron was more plentiful and, therefore, more economical than bronze, and its spreading use merits designating the period after 1100 B.C.E. the Iron Age. Clay tablets from the Hittite archives are particularly interesting because they provide the earliest information about the Greeks, the Hittites' western neighbors.

The Kassites

The Kassites emerged from obscure origins to replace the Amorites as the rulers of Babylonia and to found a dynasty that endured for nearly half a millennium. They adopted, preserved, and promoted Babylonian culture and made Babylonia one of the major nation-states of the late Bronze Age. Their kingdom was tribally organized and supported by a military aristocracy skilled in the use of the most prestigious military equipment of the day, the horse and chariot. The Kassites engaged in frequent, but usually inconclusive, wars with their neighbors on a variety of fronts and were treated with respect by both the Hittites and Egyptians.

MAP 1–2 THE MIDDLE EAST AND GREECE ABOUT 1400 B.C.E. About 1400 B.C.E., the Middle East had been divided among four empires: Egypt, which extended south to Nubia and north to Phoenicia, Kassite Babylonia, Hittite Asia Minor, and Mitannian Assyria. Much of the Aegean was under the control of an assortment of Mycenaean Greek kingdoms.

The Mitannians

The Mitannians were part of a large group of people called the Hurrians whose Mesopotamian roots went back to the era of Akkad and the Third Dynasty of Ur. They remain something of a mystery, for their language is imperfectly understood and the location of their capital is unknown. They provided an important service by helping to spread Mesopotamian civilization throughout Syria and into Anatolia. They were masters of chariot warfare and used their military skills to build a large state between the Euphrates and the mountains of Iran. It was eventually overwhelmed by the Hittites.

The Assyrians

The Assyrian homeland was centered at Assur, a city on the Tigris River in northern Mesopotamia. The Assyrians spoke a Semitic language related to Babylonian and ancient trading ties with Babylonia imbued them with its cultural influences. When the Mitannian kingdom collapsed during the fourteenth century B.C.E., Assyria began to push out its northern and western frontiers. In the general confusion that descended on the Middle East at the end of the second millennium, an invasion by the Arameans brought an end to this first Assyrian empire. The Arameans originated in northern Syria, and they spread widely throughout the Middle East. Their language, Aramaic, is still a living language, and it played a role in the development of the biblical tradition.

About 1000 B.C.E. the Assyrians recovered and began to expand again. By 665 B.C.E. they had won control of Mesopotamia, southern Asia Minor, Syria, Palestine, and Egypt. They were famous for their innovative military technology and their willingness to commit atrocities to frighten their opponents into submission. The Assyrian empire was divided into provinces headed by military governors and kept in line by garrisons. Defeated peoples were often evicted from their homes and resettled elsewhere in order to break up potential pockets of resistance to Assyrian rule. Agricultural colonies were established to populate unused land and to maintain caches of supplies for the army. Great palaces were erected at Nineveh and Nimrud and ornamented with superb stone carvings in bas relief. They were meant to intimidate the vassal kings who annually brought their tribute to the Assyrian capital.

The Assyrian empire may have been a victim of its own success—becoming too large, given the communications available, to govern. Squabbling among its leaders also set it up for disaster, particularly once the Medes, an Indo-European people who settled in Iran, perfected a lethal, new style of fighting utilizing mounted archers. When the Medes attacked Assyria, the Babylonians seized the opportunity to rebel, and by 612 B.C.E., the Assyrian empire had collapsed.

This eighth-century B.C.E. relief of a hero gripping a lion formed part of the decoration of an Assyrian palace. The immense size of the figure and his powerful limbs and muscles may well have suggested the might of the Assyrian king. Giraudon/Art Resource, NY

The Neo-Babylonians

The Medes failed to exploit their victory, and this gave Nebuchadnezzar, king of Babylon, the chance to extend his authority over much of the old Assyrian empire. Babylon became a center of world trade and quickly developed into a city filled with monuments and wonders. Nebuchadnezzar's dynasty was, however, short-lived. The throne passed rapidly through a number of hands, and its last heir alienated his subjects by permitting graft and gross mismanagement and by imposing a new religion. They failed to put up much resistance when a conqueror from Persia descended on them in 539 B.C.E., and Babylon survived to enjoy even greater prosperity as a province within his empire.

Palestine

Many great kingdoms rose and fell in the ancient Middle East, but none had as much influence on Western civilization as a tiny state that began to develop in Palestine about 1200 B.C.E. Three of the world's great religions (Judaism, Christianity, and Islam) trace their origins, at least in part, to this region, and the history of its peoples inspired the Hebrew Bible.

The Canaanites and the Phoenicians

The original inhabitants of Palestine spoke a Semitic language called Canaanite. They lived in walled cities and were farmers and seafarers. Their most influential achievement was a highly simplified writing system. Instead of the hundreds of characters found in cuneiform and hieroglyphic scripts, it used a brief alphabet of twenty to thirty symbols. This made learning to read and write much easier and allowed the skill to spread more broadly.

The Canaanites of the Palestinian interior were forced out or absorbed by invading tribes of Israelites, but those on the northern coast, the Phoenicians, hung on to their territory. They became a seafaring people and developed a trade network that spanned the length of the Mediterranean Sea. They scattered colonies as far west as Spain, the most famous of which was the north African port of Carthage (near modern Tunis). Phoenician trade spread culture as well as goods. It acquainted the Greeks with the alphabet, which they adopted and passed on to us.

The Israelites

Since there are few references to the Israelites in records compiled by their neighbors, knowledge of them must be inferred from their chief literary monument: the Bible. Although the Bible contains some historical narratives (as well as collections of laws, ritual instructions, wisdom literature, poetry, and prophecy), it was not meant to be read simply as history. Scholars have developed all sorts of techniques to extract objective information from it, and there are many disputes about their findings.

According to tradition, the family of Abraham, the patriarch (i.e., founding father) of the Hebrew (or Israelite) nation, originated in Ur. He himself was, however, a homeless nomad who, about 1900 B.C.E., wandered into the land of the Canaanites. Some of his descendants later drifted into Egypt, perhaps in the wake of the Hyksos who were their fellow Semites. By the thirteenth century B.C.E., they had left Egypt under the leadership of a man named Moses. They spent some time wandering in the Sinai desert and then returned to Canaan where they settled down. They conquered their neighbors and established a monarchy that reached its peak in the tenth century B.C.E. under King David and his son and heir Solomon. At Solomon's death, the kingdom split in two. Israel, the northern section, was the larger and more advanced. Judah, the southern portion, was less populous and more rural, but it was the location of the old capital of Jerusalem, the site of the Israelites' most important temple.

In 722 B.C.E. Assyria conquered Israel and dispersed its people. The disappearance of the "ten lost tribes of Israel" left only the people of Judah (i.e., the Jews) to maintain their country's traditions, culture, and literature. But in 586 B.C.E. Judah was conquered by the Neo-Babylonian ruler Nebuchadnezzar II. He destroyed Jerusalem and its temple and resettled many of the Jews in distant lands. This period of exile or Babylonian captivity did not last long. When Babylon fell to Persia in 539 B.C.E., the new emperor permitted some Jews to return to rebuild Jerusalem and the temple. With only brief exceptions, the tiny Jewish homeland remained under the dominance of foreign powers until 70 C.E., when the Romans once again destroyed Jerusalem and dispersed its people. The Jews did not return to reestablish a state of Israel until 1948 C.E.

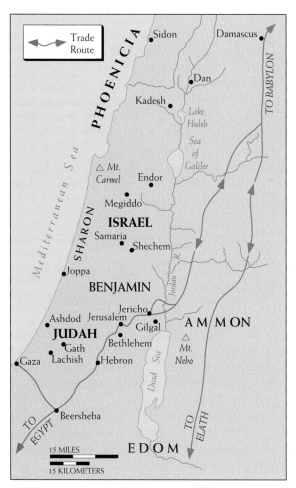

MAP 1–3   ANCIENT PALESTINE   *The Hebrews established a unified kingdom in Palestine under Kings David and Solomon in the tenth century B.C.E. After the death of Solomon, however, the kingdom was divided into two parts—Israel in the north and Judah, with its capital, Jerusalem, in the south. Along the coast, especially to the north, were the great commercial cities of the Phoenicians, such as Sidon and Tyre.*

The Jewish Religion

The fate of the tiny nation of Israel would be of little interest were it not for its unique religious achievement. The Jews' belief in a single universal God—in an all-powerful creator who loves humankind but demands righteousness and obedience to his laws—may be as old as Moses' generation and certainly dates back to the preaching of the major prophets in the eighth century B.C.E. The Jewish God is not thought of as a force of nature or a superhuman being. He is so transcendent that He cannot be pictured in any way. These beliefs have become fundamental to the religions that helped form the Western heritage.

Unlike most other ancient peoples, the Jews believed that there was a link between ethics and religion. They were a unique people because their ancestor Abraham had made a covenant (i.e., a contract) with God. God promised to preserve them so long as they accepted the burden of revealing Him by living according to the principles He established. The Jewish prophets described God as a severe but just judge who was not content with mere ritual and sacrifice. God is righteous and expects His people to live righteously. Although the prophets assured their followers that God dealt mercifully with repentant sinners, they explained the misfortunes that befell their country as a just God's necessary interventions in history to correct the people when they went astray. Confidence that God would fulfill His promise to deliver them from their enemies gradually persuaded the Jews that God intended to send them a special leader, a messiah (i.e., "annointed one") who would have the power to enable them fulfill their mission in history. Christianity diverges from Judaism in maintaining that Jesus of Nazareth was that messiah.

General Outlook of Middle Eastern Cultures

There were differences among the various cultures of the Middle East, but all of them taken together contrast significantly with the outlook of the ancient people who exerted the greatest influence on the Western tradition, the Greeks. This becomes clear when we compare the assumptions that the Greeks and other ancient peoples made about fundamental human concerns.

HUMANS AND NATURE   The peoples of the Middle East did not envision an absolute gulf between animate beings and inanimate objects. They believed that all things took part in life and the spirit and that the universe was an arena for a war of supernatural wills. They concluded that because nature seemed chaotic from the human perspective, the gods who governed it must be capricious. The Babylonian creation myth claimed that humanity's chief purpose was to serve the gods. In a world that powerful deities ran for their own benefit and with little concern for their human servants, existence was precarious. Even disasters, like wars, which we would see as the result of human decisions, were assumed to be the products of divine wills.

The helplessness of humankind in the face of irrational divine powers is the point of the story of a great primeval flood that is found in one form or another in Babylonian, Egyptian, and Hebrew sources. In the Egyptian tale the god Re, who created human beings, comes to believe that they are plotting against him and sends the vicious goddess Sekhmet to destroy them. Humanity is saved only when the god has a last minute, unexplained change of heart. In the Babylonian version of the story it is the noise made by an increasing human population that annoys the gods and determines them to destroy humanity. The species is saved only because one man wins the favor of the god Enki who helps him and his wife survive. In a world governed by such quixotic principles, human beings could not hope to control events by understanding them. At best, they might try to pit one mysterious force against another by means of magical spells.

Humans and the Gods, Law, and Justice

Since the gods could destroy humankind—and might do so at any time for no apparent reason—people tried to win the gods over by offering prayer and sacrifice. There was, however, no guarantee of success, for gods were capricious beings who were not bound by reason or conscience.

In areas that were more or less under human control, people attempted to establish more orderly and consistent principles to guide their lives. In the earliest civilized societies rulers decreed laws to govern human relations. The problem was to find some justification that would impart authority to laws. Why, apart from a lawgiver's power to coerce obedience, should anyone obey the law? The Egyptians simply assumed that since the king was a god, he had the right to establish whatever rules seemed best to him at the moment. The Mesopotamians believed that the gods commissioned their kings and gave them divine authority to keep order among the human herd. The Hebrews had a more subtle understanding of

law. Their God was capable of destructive rages, but He was open to rational discussion and imposed certain moral standards on Himself. In the biblical version of the flood story God is wrathful but not arbitrary. His creatures deserve destruction as punishment for their sins. When God decides to save Noah, He does so because Noah is a good man who merits God's protection. The Hebrews believed that God wanted human beings to live in just relationships with one another and that He Himself was an advocate for human justice.

Toward the Greeks and Western Thought

Many, if not most, Greeks in the ancient world must have thought about life in much the same way as their neighbors in the Middle East. Their gods were assumed to behave like Mesopotamian deities; they trusted in magic and incantations to manage life's uncertainties; and they believed that laws were to be obeyed simply because the gods decreed them. The surprising thing is that some Greeks were exceptions. They conceived strikingly original ideas that charted a different path for the West.

As early as the sixth century B.C.E., an intellectual revolution had begun among thinkers who lived on the Aegean coast of Asia Minor. Thales, the first Greek philosopher, taught his followers to explain natural events by referring them to other natural events, not to unknowable supernatural causes. His search for naturalistic explanations for phenomena launched Western science.

Rationalism of this kind characterized the approach major Greek thinkers took to exploring all kinds of issues. Xenophanes of Colophon, Thales's contemporary, pointed out that people had no grounds for imagining gods in human form. He argued that if oxen could draw, they would sketch gods who looked like oxen. Comments like this might promote skepticism, but they could also produce valuable insights. In the fifth century B.C.E., Thucydides of Athens wrote a history that made no reference to the gods, but explained events as the result of human decisions and chance. Similarly, Hippocrates of Cos founded a school of medicine that diagnosed and treated disease without invoking the supernatural. The same absence of interest in divine causality characterized Greek attitudes toward law and justice.

In Perspective

Although the Greeks' original insights account for much of the uniqueness of Western civilization, we should not forget that they were built on a foundation of lore that people in the Middle East had accumulated over millennia. Phoenicia gave the Greeks a writing system, and from ancient Mesopotamia and Egypt the Greeks acquired vital technical information and models that stimulated the development of mathematics, astronomy, art, and literature. The discontinuities between the cultures of the Greeks and their eastern neighbors are, however, more striking than the continuities.

A secular, reasoned quest for an understanding of the world that proceeded by seeking explanations for events in the natures of things rather than in the supernatures of gods was not characteristic of pre-Greek cultures. Nor would it appear in similar societies at other times in other parts of the world. This raises the issue of whether there was something special in the Greek experience that caused fundamental questions to be pondered in strikingly original ways.

REVIEW QUESTIONS

1. How was life during the Paleolithic Age different from life during the Neolithic Age? What advances account for the difference? Were there advances so major that they warrant referring to the Neolithic as a revolutionary era?
2. What differences do you see in the political and intellectual outlooks of the Egyptian and Mesopotamian civilizations? How do their religious views compare? What influence did geography have on religious outlooks?
3. How did religious faith help to bind the Hebrews together politically? Why did Middle Eastern civilizations regard the concept of monotheism as a radical idea?
4. Why were the Assyrians so successful in building an empire? How did their empire differ from those of the Egyptians and Hittites? What caused its failure? What might it have contributed to the civilization of the Middle East?
5. How did Greek thinkers depart from the assumptions that guided the work of Middle Eastern intellectuals?

SUGGESTED READINGS

M. EHRENBERG, *Women in Prehistory* (1989). An account of the role of women in early times.

H. FRANKFORT ET AL., *Before Philosophy* (1949). A brilliant examination of the mind of the ancients from the Stone Age to the Greeks.

O. R. GURNEY, *The Hittites* (1954). A good general survey.

W. W. HALLO AND L. YOUNGER, EDS. *The Context of Scripture, Canonical Compositions from the Biblical World* (1997). A good collection of literary works translated from ancient Middle Eastern sources, complete with introductions and explanatory notes.

G. HART, *Egyptian Myths* (1990). A clear presentation of major myths and religious literature.

D. C. JOHNSON AND M. R. EDEY, *Lucy: The Beginnings of Mankind* (1981). A study of the first human creatures based on remains found in Africa.

B. J. KEMP, *Ancient Egypt: Anatomy of a Civilization* (1989). A thought-provoking assessment of Egypt's social and intellectual history.

A. KUHRT, *The Ancient Near East, c. 3000–330 B.C.* (1995). The best compact and reliable history of the ancient Middle East, including Egypt and Israel.

S. LLOYD, *The Archaeology of Mesopotamia*, rev. ed. (1984). An account of the material remains of Mesopotamia and their meaning from the Paleolithic Age to the Persian Conquest.

K. R. NEMET-NEJAT, *Daily Life in Ancient Mesopotamia* (1998). An excellent introduction for the general reader.

J. N. POSTGATE, *Early Mesopotamia* (1992). An excellent study of Mesopotamian economy and society from the earliest times to about 1500 B.C.E.

D. B. REDFORD, *Akhenaten* (1987). A new study of the controversial pharaoh.

G. ROBINS, *Women in Ancient Egypt* (1993). A comprehensive study of the role of women in Egyptian society.

D. C. SNELL, *Life in the Ancient Near East, 3100–332 B.C.E.* (1997). Imaginative study focusing on social and economic history.

A. J. SPENCER, *Early Egypt: The Rise of Civilization in the Nile Valley* (1993). An up-to-date account of the latest research on the Predynastic and Early Dynastic periods.

M. VAN DE MIEROOP, *The Ancient Mesopotamian City* (1997). A concise survey of Mesopotamian urban life.

Chapter 2
The Rise of Greek Civilization

KEY TOPICS

- The Bronze Age civilizations that ruled the Aegean area before the development of Hellenic civilization
- The rise, development, and expansion of the *polis*, the characteristic political unit of Hellenic Greece
- The early history of Sparta and Athens
- The wars between the Greeks and the Persians

About 2000 B.C.E., Greek-speaking peoples settled the lands surrounding the Aegean Sea and established a culture that became one of the most powerful forces shaping Western heritage. The Greeks' location at the eastern end of the Mediterranean put them in touch, early in their history, with Mesopotamia, Egypt, Asia Minor, and Syria-Palestine. The Greeks acknowledged a debt to the cultures of these regions but were well aware of the uniqueness of their own contributions to civilization.

The Bronze Age on Crete and on the Mainland to About 1150 B.C.E.

Bronze Age civilizations developed in three parts of the Aegean world—on the island of Crete, on the smaller islands of the Aegean Sea, and on the mainland of Greece. Crete provided the bridge that linked these new cultural centers with the older civilizations of the East.

The Minoans

Historians have named the Aegean's first civilization—that of Crete—for Minos, a legendary king of the island. From 2100 to 1150 B.C.E. (the Middle and Late Minoan periods) Crete evolved a unique way of life. The palace sites that modern archaeologists have excavated at Phaestus, Haghia Triada, and especially Cnossus are its most striking remains. Cnossus was a labyrinth of rooms organized around great courtyards and rising in sections to a height of four stories. The main and upper floors contained living quarters as well as workshops for making pottery and jewelry, and the cellars had elaborate storage facilities for oil and grain. There were richly decorated reception rooms and even bathrooms to which water was piped. Roofs were supported by columns of a unique design that tapered from broad capitals down to narrow bases. Murals depicting landscapes, seascapes, festivals, and sports in a unique style reflected some Eastern influences.

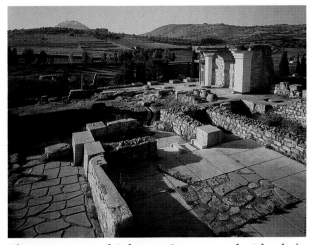

The Minoan-period Palace at Cnossus on the island of Crete. D. A. Harissiadis Photography, Benaki Museum, Photographic Department.

Chronology of the Rise of Greece	
ca. 2900–1150 B.C.E.	Minoan period
ca. 1900 B.C.E.	Arrival of the Greeks on the mainland
ca. 1600–1150 B.C.E.	Mycenaean period
ca. 1250 B.C.E.	Sack of Troy
ca. 1200–1150 B.C.E.	Fall of the Mycenaean kingdoms
ca. 1150–750 B.C.E.	The Greek Dark Ages
ca. 750–500 B.C.E.	Greek colonial expansion
ca. 725 B.C.E.	Homer flourished
ca. 700 B.C.E.	Hesiod flourished
ca. 700–500 B.C.E.	Ascendancy of the tyrants

Since Minoan palaces and settlements were wealthy, they would have been attractive targets for raiders. It is surprising, therefore, that the great Minoan structures lacked defensive walls. Minoan command of the sea may have made the fortification of buildings on Crete unnecessary.

The Minoans wrote on clay tablets similar to those found in Mesopotamia. Many of the extant specimens were preserved accidentally when they were baked into tiles by a great fire that destroyed the palace at Cnossus. The Cnossus tablets are inscribed with three distinct kinds of writing: hieroglyphic (picture writing) and two different linear scripts (A and B). Only Linear B, which records an early form of Greek, has been deciphered.

The Linear B tablets found at Cnossus are pedestrian documents. Most are inventories, the working papers of the kind of elaborate bureaucracy that was characteristic of the ancient Middle Eastern monarchies. However, they raise an intriguing question. The Minoans were not Greeks, so why were records at Cnossus being written in Greek?

The Mycenaeans

During the third millennium B.C.E. (the Early Helladic Period) the Greek mainland was occupied by non-Greek peoples. Some of the names they gave to places have survived, and these names do not fit the phonetic patterns of the Indo-European family of languages to which Greek belongs. Sometime after 2000 B.C.E., many of the Early Helladic sites were destroyed, abandoned, or occupied by a new people who were probably the Greeks. During the Late Helladic era (1580–1150 B.C.E.), the newcomers ruled the mainland and developed a civilization that historians have named for Mycenae, one of its cities. The Greek Linear B tablets found at Cnossus suggest that at the height of Mycenaean power (ca. 1400–1200 B.C.E.) the Mycenaeans conquered Crete.

The Mycenaean world contained a number of independent, powerful, and well-organized kingdoms. Their archaeological remains are those of a civilization that was influenced by, but very different from, that of the Minoans. Unlike the Minoans, the Mycenaeans were preoccupied with war. The walls of their palaces were decorated with paintings depicting scenes of battle and hunting, and they chose defensible sites for their cities. A need for protection probably promoted the development of strong, centralized monarchies.

By 1500 B.C.E. Mycenaean kings were constructing monumental *tholos* tombs that testify to the wealth and power of their governments. These great domed chambers were built of enormous blocks of dressed stones. They resembled

MAP 2–1   THE AEGEAN AREA IN THE BRONZE AGE   *Two civilizations flourished in the Aegean during its Bronze Age (1900–1100 B.C.E.): the Minoan (1900–1400 B.C.E.) and the Mycenaean (1600–1200 B.C.E.).*

beehives buried beneath artificial mountains. The wealth needed to finance the construction of such monuments probably came from raids and trade. Mycenaean ships visited the islands of the Aegean, the coast of Asia Minor, the cities of Syria, Egypt, and Crete, and ventured as far west as Italy and Sicily.

The Mycenaeans reached the height of their power from 1400 to 1200 B.C.E. They expanded their trade, established commercial colonies in the East, and began to be mentioned in Hittite and Egyptian archives. About 1250 B.C.E. the Mycenaeans probably sacked the city of Troy on the coast of northwestern Asia Minor. This campaign may have been the Mycenaeans' last great adventure, for by 1200 B.C.E. their world was in trouble, and by 1100 B.C.E. it was gone. Some memory of them survived, however, to give rise to the earliest monuments of Greek literature, Homer's epics, the *Iliad* and the *Odyssey*.

THE DORIAN INVASION   Many Mycenaean towns fell about 1200 B.C.E., but some flourished for another century, and some were never destroyed or abandoned. Ancient Greek legends imply that there may have been an attack on the Peloponnesus (the southern Greek peninsula) by Dorians, a rude people from the north whose Greek dialect was different from that of the Mycenaeans. Perhaps this set in motion a chain of events that undermined Mycenaean civilization. The development of rigid bureaucracies probably limited the flexibility of the Mycenaean kingdoms and increased their vulnerability to invasion. It is impossible, however, to say with any certainty what happened at the end of the Aegean Bronze Age.

The Greek "Middle Ages" to About 750 B.C.E.

The collapse of the Mycenaean world inaugurated a long period of depopulation, impoverishment, and cultural decline in the Aegean. The palaces of the kings and the bureaucratic governments of which they were the seats were destroyed. The wealth and social order that supported civilized life were swept away, and many villages were abandoned and never resettled.

Greek Migrations

The confusion that attended the Mycenaean decline caused many Greeks (including the Dorians who invaded the Peloponnesus) to emigrate from the mainland to the Aegean islands and the coast of Asia Minor. This turned the Aegean into a Greek lake, but trade and travel diminished with the fading of civilization. Each community was left largely to its own devices, and people turned inward. At the time, the Middle East was also in disarray, so no great foreign power was poised to take advantage of the Aegean's situation. The Greeks, therefore, had a chance to recover and the freedom to evolve a unique way of life. Little is known about this crucial era, for writing disappeared with the Mycenaeans. It was not reinvented until after 750 B.C.E., when architecture, sculpture, and painting also resume. This is for historians, therefore, a "dark age."

The Age of Homer

The *Iliad* and the *Odyssey* are our best sources of information about the Greek Dark Ages. They are the end products of a long tradition of oral poetry with roots in the Mycenaean era. For generations bards passed on tales of the heroes who fought at Troy. Since they used rhythmic formulas to aid the accurate memorization of their verses, some very old material was preserved. The poems, in the form in which they were ultimately written down, date from the eighth century B.C.E. and are attributed to an individual named Homer.

Although the poems narrate the adventures of Mycenaean heroes, the society they describe is not purely Mycenaean. Homer's warriors are not buried in *tholos* tombs but are cremated; they worship gods in temples, whereas no Mycenaean temples have been found; they have chariots but do not know their proper use in warfare. These inconsistencies arise because Homer's epics combine memories of the ancient Mycenaeans with material drawn from the very different world in which the poets of the tenth and ninth centuries B.C.E. lived.

GOVERNMENT AND SOCIETY   The kings Homer describes had much less power than Mycenaean monarchs. Homeric kings had to arrive at decisions in consultation with their nobles, and their nobles felt free to debate vigorously and to oppose a king's wishes. In the *Iliad*, Achilles does not hesitate to accuse Agamemnon, the "most kingly" commander of the Trojan expedition, of having "a dog's face and a deer's heart." This was impolite but apparently not treasonous.

The right to speak before a royal council was limited to noblemen, but the common people could not be ignored. If a king planned a war or a major change of policy, he would call all his soldiers together and explain his intentions. They expressed their feelings by acclamation, but they could not debate or propose ideas of their own. At a very early date, the Greeks seemed to have been accustomed to a very limited form of popular government.

Homeric society was sharply divided into classes. A hereditary aristocracy presided over three kinds of commoners: *thetes*, landless laborers, and slaves. The *thetes* may have owned the land they worked, or their fields may have been the property of their family clans and could not be sold. The landless agricultural laborer had the worst lot in life. Slaves who were attached to a household were guaranteed protection and food, but free workers were desperately vulnerable. They were loners in a society in which the only safety lay in belonging to a group that looked out for its members. There were few slaves. Most were women who served as maids and concubines. Some male slaves worked as shepherds, but throughout Greek history most farmers were free men.

HOMERIC VALUES The Homeric poems celebrated an aristocratic code that influenced all later Greek thinkers, for Greek education was based on Homer's works. The Greeks memorized Homer's texts and internalized respect for his values: physical prowess; courage; fierce protection of family, friends, and property; and, above all, defense of honor. The *Iliad* is the story of a dispute about honor. Agamemnon, the king who presides over the Greek army besieging Troy, wounds the honor of Achilles, his most important warrior. Achilles then refuses to fight and persuades the gods to avenge him by heaping defeat on the Greeks. When Achilles finally returns to the battlefield, he is brought back by a

personal obligation to avenge the death of a friend, not by a sense of duty to his country.

The highest virtue in Homeric society was *arete*—the manliness, courage, and excellence that enabled a hero to acquire and defend honor. Men demonstrated this quality by engaging in contests with worthy opponents. Homeric battles were usually single combats between matched competitors, and most Homeric festivals (even the funeral of Achilles' friend Patroclos, which ends the *Iliad*) featured athletic competitions.

Homer's view of life is summed up by the advice Achilles' father gave him when the young man left for the Trojan war: "Always be the best and distinguished above others." The father of another Homeric hero added a codicil to this prescription: "Do not bring shame on the family of your fathers." These admonitions articulated the ultimate concerns of the Homeric aristocrat: to vie for individual supremacy in *arete* and to enhance the honor of the family.

WOMEN IN HOMERIC SOCIETY The male-oriented warrior society that Homer describes relegated women to domestic roles. Their chief functions were to bear and raise children and to manage and safeguard their husbands' estates when the men were called away to battle. A husband might have sexual adventures, but a wife was expected to be unswervingly faithful. Homer's ideal woman was Penelope, Odysseus' wife. Her husband disappears for twenty years, but she does not give him up for dead. She refuses the many suitors who seek her hand (and his estate) and lives in chaste seclusion with her maids. She fills her days with the labor that Greeks associated with women of all classes: spinning and weaving. Penelope's opposite, the epitome of female evil, was Agamemnon's wife, Clytemnestra. While her husband leads the war at Troy, she takes a lover, and the two of them assassinate Agamemnon when he returns home. Homer's upper-class females were free to come and go as they wished. They attended banquets with their husbands and conversed with other men. No such privileges were enjoyed by their aristocratic sisters in later periods in Greek history. These women were expected to confine themselves to special women's quarters in their family homes.

The *Polis*

Classical Greek civilization emerged from an institution called the *polis* (plural *poleis*) that evolved during the Dark Ages. *Polis* is usually translated as "city-state," but that implies too much and too little. All Greek *poleis* began as agricultural villages, and many never grew large enough to be considered cities. All of them, however, were states in the sense that they were self-governing, but they were more than political institutions. The citizens of a *polis* viewed themselves as a kind of extended family based on descent from a common legendary ancestor, shared religious cults, and membership in a variety of hereditary subgroups (i.e., clans, tribes, and *phratries*—military fraternities).

In the fourth century B.C.E., hundreds of years after the *polis* came into existence, the philosopher Aristotle outlined the assumptions on which it was based. He argued that the human being was by nature "an animal who lives in a *polis*," for the attributes that define humanity—the power of speech and the ability to distinguish right from wrong—can be developed only when people live together.

Development of the Polis

Originally the word *polis* referred to a citadel, a defensible high ground to which the farmers of an area could retreat when attacked. (The most famous example is the Acropolis at the center of the city of Athens.) Unplanned, unfortified towns tended to evolve spontaneously at such sites. In contrast to Mesopotamian city-states, rivers or trade routes did not determine the location of Greek *poleis*. Proximity of farmland to a natural fortress was the decisive factor. Spots well back from the coast were popular, for they minimized the danger of pirate raids. Eventually an *agora*—a place for markets and political assemblies—would evolve beside the citadel to provide a center for community life.

Poleis probably appeared early in the eighth century B.C.E. and spread widely and quickly. All the colonies that the Greeks established in the years after 750 B.C.E. were *poleis*. Monarchy tended to disappear wherever *poleis* evolved. Sometimes vestigial kings survived as politically powerless figures whose functions were ceremonial. A *polis* was often founded as a republic dominated by an aristocratic class, but over time political participation tended to broaden. About 750 B.C.E., coincident with the development of the *polis*, there were other significant changes in Greek culture. A new style of pottery appeared, and the Greeks borrowed a script from the Phoenicians. By adding vowels to it, they created the first complete alphabet and invented a method of writing that was easy for the common person to learn. This empowered the ordinary man at a time when changes in military technology were also enhancing his importance.

The Hoplite Phalanx

Early Greek warfare was a disorganized free-for-all. Small troops of cavalry led by aristocratic "champions" cast spears at their enemies and then engaged individual opponents with swords at close quarters. Late in the eighth century B.C.E., a true infantry soldier called a *hoplite* began to dominate the battlefield. He was a heavily armed foot soldier, equipped with a spear and a large round shield (a *hoplon*), who fought in a tight formation called a *phalanx*—a company of men at least eight ranks deep. A phalanx that preserved its order on the field of battle could withstand cavalry charges and rout much larger armies consisting of less disciplined men. The phalanx reigned supreme in the ancient Mediterranean world until the more flexible Roman legion appeared.

A phalanx was effective only when all its members kept themselves in top physical condition, maintained their courage, and worked together as a team. *Hoplite* warfare favored brief, violent battles that resolved disputes quickly with minimal risk to the property on which citizen families depended for their survival. Its goal was to kill or drive off an enemy, not enslave him or hold him for ransom.

Greeks had traditionally thought of war as an aristocratic profession, but in the era of the *hoplite* no *polis* could afford to limit recruitment to a small group of nobles. The strength of an infantry depended on numbers. Farmers working relatively small holdings had to join aristocrats in defending their cities and could afford to do so. When they did, shared military responsibilities led inevitably to demands for shared political privileges.

A Funeral Scene in Eighth Century B.C.E. Greece:
The Dipylon Vase

The Dipylon Vase, c. 750 B.C.E. The Metropolitan Museum of Art, Rogers Fund, 1914. [14.130.14] Photograph © 1996 The Metropolitan Museum of Art. Sources: Janson, *History of Art*, (New York: Prentice Hall and Harry N. Abrams, 1997), 110–112; Marilyn Stokstad, *Art History*, rev. ed. (Upper Saddle River, NJ: Prentice Hall, 1999), pp. 152–161.

From 1100 to 700 B.C.E., a uniquely Hellenic civilization emerged from the more generally Mediterranean Bronze Age cultures of the Minoan and Mycenaean periods. Since writing had disappeared, this development is best documented by what happened in the arts—particularly the craft of pottery painting.

The potters and vase painters of this period broke with the past both in the shape and decoration of their work. The style they pioneered is called Geometric, for it is dominated by abstract forms (e.g., circles, rectangles, and triangles) arranged in parallel bands running around their vases. The earliest examples used simple schemes, but as the style developed designs became more complicated, and ultimately human and animal figures were added to the geometric patterns.

The *Dipylon Vase,* which was made about the time when Homer's poems were taking shape (ca. 750 B.C.E.), is an excellent example of the fully developed style. It is about 3 1/2 feet tall and was made to serve as a funeral monument in a graveyard outside Athens' Dipylon gate. It depicts a funeral. The top band or register shows the body of the deceased displayed on a high platform and surrounded by mourners. The lower register describes a funeral procession featuring horse-drawn chariots and soldiers equipped with shields. The vase was made with holes in its base to allow the libations that were poured into it to seep into the ground, but the Greeks did not share the Egyptian belief in an afterlife where the dead enjoyed the pleasures of this existence. The Greek view of what lay beyond the grave was much more grim.

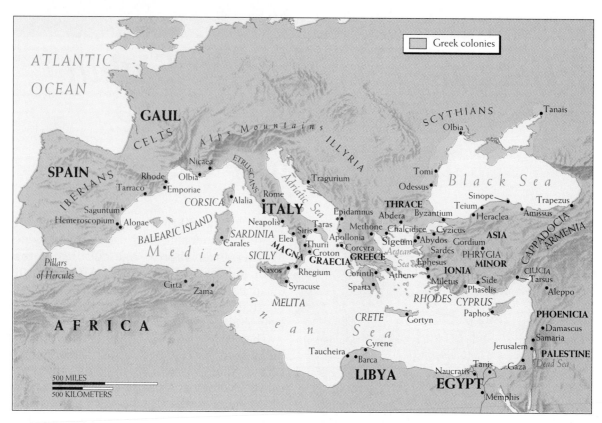

MAP 2–2   GREEK COLONIZATION   *Greek colonizing activity reached its peak between 750 and 550 B.C.E. and scattered colonies from the Black Sea and Asia Minor across Italy and Sicily to France and Spain.*

Expansion of the Greek World

About the middle of the eighth century B.C.E., the Greeks launched a colonization movement that planted *poleis* from Spain to the Black Sea. They avoided the eastern end of the Mediterranean, which was well populated and defended, and searched for western sites that were sparsely settled or whose natives were not well organized to resist. So many Greek colonies were established in southern Italy and Sicily that the Romans named the region *Magna Graecia*, "Great Greece."

The Greek Colony

The pressures of overpopulation probably explain why thousands of Greeks left the cities of their birth to found new *poleis*. Emigration was difficult but potentially rewarding. Colonies were carefully planned, and most had excellent prospects as centers of trade. Many copied the constitutions and the religious rites of the cities that founded them, but they were not controlled or exploited by those cities and their wealth was not siphoned off for the homeland. Colonies governed themselves. They usually maintained friendly relations with their mother-cities and each might ask the other for help. Occasionally, a city might try to impose its will on one of its colonies, and this could provoke a war.

Colonization added greatly to the material and cultural resources of Greek civilization. Over 1,000 *poleis* were established. This helped the Greeks of the mainland maintain peace among themselves by providing outlets for excess population. It also heightened the Greeks' sense of their unique identity by bringing them into contact with different cultures. *Poleis* across the Mediterranean sponsored festivals such as the Olympic Games to promote and keep alive their memory of their common heritage.

The colonies transformed life in the Greek homeland. The new markets they created had great economic and sociopolitical impact. Farmers on the Greek mainland began to concentrate less on local consumption and more on producing specialized crops (e.g., olives and wine) for export. Demand also increased for manufactured goods such as pottery, tools, weapons, and fine artistic metalwork. Expanding commercial opportunities enlarged the class of independent commoners, and their increasing prosperity led them to resent the aristocrats' traditional monopoly of governmental authority. The political turmoil this generated brought tyrants to power in some *poleis*.

The Tyrants (ca. 700–500 B.C.E.)

A tyrant, in the ancient Greek sense, was a ruler who ignored legal niceties and simply seized power. He often did so with widespread popular support. A typical tyrant was an aristocrat who broke with his class and took control of a city by appealing to the masses of its poor and politically disenfranchised. He usually expelled his aristocratic opponents, distributed their land among his followers, and instituted economic programs that benefitted the city at large.

A tyrant's authority was backed up by a personal bodyguard and troops of mercenary soldiers, but his rule was not necessarily oppressive. Tyrants preferred to concentrate on domestic development and to avoid wars. Aggression against a neighboring state would require fielding a citizen army that might turn on its tyrant. Tyrants courted the masses by financing public works projects that were popular and provided employment for the poor. They also promoted civic pride by sponsoring festivals and supporting the arts.

Despite the positive effect tyranny had on the evolution of some *poleis*, tyrannies faded away during the sixth century B.C.E. There was something about tyranny that was inconsistent with the forces that created the *polis*. The institutions of a *polis* were shaped by the responsibility all its citizens bore for its defense. Since they shared this traditional responsibility of the military aristocracy, they felt entitled also to share the customary aristocratic political prerogatives. The rule of a tyrant, no matter how beneficent, was unacceptable, for it was arbitrary and could not be held accountable. Tyranny did, however, contribute to the growth of popular government by breaking the monopoly aristocracies had on political power.

The Major States

There were many *poleis* and much diversity in their organization, but two—Sparta and Athens—were of such importance that they merit special attention.

Sparta

About 725 B.C.E., Sparta embarked on a path that made it Greece's most respected military power. It invaded Messenia, its western neighbor, to acquire more land to support its growing population. The conquest and enslavement of the Messenians solved Sparta's economic problems but created a difficulty of a different kind. The Spartans found themselves outnumbered ten to one by Helots, the Spartan term for slaves. A crisis was reached about 650 B.C.E. when a slave revolt nearly destroyed Sparta. The Spartans concluded that in order to survive they had to live constantly in a state of total military mobilization.

SPARTAN SOCIETY   The Spartan system subordinated the natural feelings of devotion to self and family interests to the needs of the state. The state needed all its men to be superb soldiers, and it persuaded them to sacrifice privacy and comfort to physical conditioning, military training, and discipline. The Spartans allowed nothing to distract them from their goal of becoming the best warriors in the world.

The Spartan *polis* controlled the life of each of its members from birth to death. Only infants whom officials of the state judged to be physically fit were raised. At the age of seven boys left their mothers to begin training at military camps. They learned to fight, to endure privation, to bear physical pain, and to live off the land. At twenty they joined the army in the field, and they lived in barracks until the age of thirty. They were allowed to marry but not to live at home. Young Spartan husbands had to steal away from camp to visit their wives. Only after a man acquired full citizen rights at the age of thirty could he maintain a home. But even then he took his meals at a public mess with other members of his military unit. His sparse diet included little meat or wine, and he eschewed all luxuries. His financial future was, however, secure, for he was supported by a grant from the state—a plot of land worked by Helots.

He remained on active military duty until the age of sixty.

Sparta prepared its females as well as its males to serve the state. Female infants were examined for fitness in the same way as males, and young girls, like boys, were given athletic training. Because Spartan men concentrated on military affairs and were often absent from home, Spartan women had much greater freedom and responsibility than other Greek females.

SPARTAN GOVERNMENT   The Spartan constitution mixed elements of monarchy, oligarchy, and democracy. Sparta acknowledged two royal families; the functions of the kings who headed them were chiefly religious and military. The Spartan army was usually commanded by one of its kings when it was in the field, but kings did not govern Sparta. An oligarchic council composed of the kings and twenty-eight men (aged sixty or more and elected for life) devised policy and sat as a high court. All Spartan males over the age of thirty could take part in a democratic assembly that, in theory, had final authority. The assembly, however, could only consider proposals referred to it by the council. Since it voted by acclamation rather than by counting ballots, it was limited to ratifying decisions already taken or deciding between alternative proposals.

The administration of Sparta's government was the duty of a board of five executives called *ephors*. The ephors were elected annually by the assembly. They controlled foreign policy, oversaw the generalship of the kings, presided at the assembly, and policed the Helots.

THE PELOPONNESIAN LEAGUE   Suppression of the Helots required all the energy Sparta had, and the Spartans did not want to overextend themselves by conquering and assimilating potentially troublesome neighbors. They preferred to force these people into alliances that left them free internally but subservient to Sparta's foreign policy. Sparta eventually enrolled every southern Greek state except Argos in its Peloponnesian League and became the most powerful *polis* on the Greek mainland before the rise of Athens.

Athens

Athens evolved more slowly than Sparta. Since Attica, the region Athens dominated, was large

Aristogeiton and Harmodius were Athenian aristocrats slain in 1514 B.C.E. after assassinating Hipparchus, brother of the tyrant Hippias. After the overthrow of the Pisistratus in 510 B.C.E., the Athenians erected a statue to honor their memory. This is a Roman copy. Scala/Art Resource, NY

by Greek standards (about 1,000 square miles), it was able to absorb a growing population. But size slowed its consolidation as a *polis* until the seventh century B.C.E., and its economic development was hampered by the fact that it was not situated on the trade routes most traveled during the eighth and seventh centuries B.C.E.

POLITICAL TENSIONS   In the seventh century B.C.E., aristocratic families held the most and the best land around Athens. They also dominated Attica by controlling the tribes, clans, and military fraternities that structured Athenian society. Athens' government was headed by the

Council of the Areopagus, a group of nobles that annually chose the city's nine *archons*, the magistrates who administered the *polis*. Since there was no formal law, leaders were guided primarily by custom and tradition.

Athens' political evolution was accelerated by an agrarian crisis that developed during the seventh century B.C.E. Many Athenians depended on small family farms that grew wheat, the staple of the ancient diet. Years of consistent cultivation diminished the fertility of their fields and the size of their harvests, but few could afford to shift to more profitable crops such as olives (for oil) and grapes (for wine). A lot of capital was needed to bring a vineyard or olive grove into production. In bad years the poorer farmers were forced to borrow from their wealthier neighbors—mortgaging future crops and, therefore, their own labor as surety for their loans. Eventually this reduced them to slavery, and some of them were even exported for sale outside Attica. The poor came to resent this and began to agitate for the abolition of debts and the redistribution of the land.

In 632 B.C.E., a nobleman named Cylon tried to exploit this situation to establish a tyranny. He failed, but his attempt frightened Athens' aristocratic leaders into taking steps to head off future coups. In 621 B.C.E., they commissioned a man named Draco to codify and publish Athens' laws. Draco decreed extremely hard punishments for crimes in hopes of deterring the blood feuds that resulted when victims sought revenge for wrongs done them. The establishment of a common standard of justice for all Athenians was meant to dissuade individuals from taking things into their own hands.

In the year 594 B.C.E., the Athenians instituted a more radical reform. They empowered a single *archon* (a man named Solon) to reorganize the *polis* as he saw fit. Solon attacked agrarian problems by canceling debts and forbidding loans secured by the freedom of the borrower. He emancipated people who had been enslaved for debt and brought home many of the Athenians who had been sold abroad. Instead of alienating the rich by redistributing their land to the poor, he tried to expand Athens' economy to create more opportunities of employment for the poor. He forbade the export of wheat (which might create shortages and drive up the price of the common person's food) but not olive oil (one of Attica's

cash crops). He facilitated trade by conforming Athenian weights and measures to standards used by Corinth, Euboea, and other commercial centers. And he developed industries by offering citizenship to foreign artisans who agreed to set up shop in Athens.

Solon also reformed Athenian political institutions. He divided Athens' citizens into four classes on the basis of wealth. Members of the two richest classes qualified for *archonships* and membership in the Council of the Areopagus. Men of the third class could serve as *hoplites* and be elected to a council of 400 chosen by the citizens. Solon intended this council to serve as a check on the Council of the Areopagus, and he gave it the power to decide what business was to be set before the popular assembly, the political organization to which all adult male citizens belonged. The poorest class, the *thetes*, voted in this assembly, participated in the election of *archons*, and sat on a popular new court that heard appeals from other jurisdictions. Women from citizen families were granted no role in the political process.

THE TYRANNIES Since the beneficial effects of Solon's reforms were slow to be felt, tensions continued to mount in Athens. On several occasions fighting was so bad that no *archons* could be elected. Twice (in 560 B.C.E. and 556 B.C.E.) a military hero named Pisistratus tried and failed to establish a tyranny, but in 546 B.C.E. his third attempt succeeded. Pisisitratus remained in power until his death in 527 B.C.E., and his son Hippias continued the tyranny until a competitor drove him from the city in 510 B.C.E.

Like the tyrants of other Greek cities, Pisistratus dominated his subjects by courting them. He sponsored public works programs, urban development, and civic festivals. He employed poets and artists to add luster to his court. And he secured his power by hiding it behind the facade of Solon's constitution. All the councils, assemblies, and courts continued to meet, and all the magistrates were elected. Pisistratus merely saw to it that his supporters won the key offices and dominated the important meetings. The constitutional cloak he spread over his tyranny won him a reputation as a popular, gentle ruler, but it also gave his people more experience with (and a greater appetite for) self-government.

Pisistratus's elder son, Hippias, began by imitating his father's gentle style, but in 514 B.C.E., the murder of his brother, Hipparchus, made him fearful for his own saftey. He began to impose harsh measures that lessened popular support for his rule and created opportunities for his opponents. In 510 B.C.E. the Alcmaeonids, a noble family that had been exiled from Athens, persuaded the Spartans to help them overthrow Hippias. Hippias fled, and the Spartans set a man named Isagoras over Athens. Isagoras believed that returning aristocrats to power would stabilize Athens, and he purged the citizen lists to remove the commoners whom Solon and Pisistratus had enfranchised. This was unpopular, and it created an opportunity for the Alcmaeonid leader, Clisthenes.

Clisthenes mobilized the masses against his political opponents, and Isagoras responded by calling on his Spartan allies. This time the Athenians resisted Spartan intervention in their affairs and helped Clisthenes drive out Isagoras.

DEMOCRACY Clisthenes set about destroying the regional political machines that were the bases for the aristocracy's power. In 508 B.C.E., he divided Attica into small political units called *demes*. The demes were then grouped together to create the tribes that composed Athens' army and elected its government. Care was taken to make sure that each tribe was made up of demes from different parts of Attica. This prevented the wealthy aristocratic families, whose large estates gave them control of local governments, from dominating the new tribal organizations. Aristocrats now found themselves voting with men who were strangers to them and not economically dependent on them.

Clisthenes increased Solon's council from 400 to 500 members and gave it authority to receive foreign emissaries and manage some fiscal affairs. Its chief responsibility was to prepare legislative proposals for discussion by the popular assembly in which ultimate authority was vested. All adult male Athenians were members of this assembly and had the right to propose legislation, to offer amendments, and to debate freely. Thanks to Solon, Pisistratus, and Clisthenes, Athens entered the fifth century B.C.E. well down the path to prosperity and democracy and prepared to claim a place among Greece's leading *poleis*.

Life in Archaic Greece

Society

Greek society's unique features began to become visible at the end of the Dark Ages. The vast majority of Greeks made their living from the land, but artisans and merchants acquired greater importance as contact with the non-Hellenic (i.e., non-Greek) world increased.

FARMERS Ordinary country folk rarely leave any record of their thoughts or activities, but the poet Hesiod (ca. 700 B.C.E.), who claimed in his *Works and Days* to be a small farmer, described what life was like for members of his class in ancient Greece. The crops farmers usually cultivated were barley, wheat, grapes for wine, olives for oil (for cooking, lighting, and lubrication), green vegetables, beans, and fruit. Sheep and goats provided milk and cheese. Since land that was fertile enough to grow fodder for cattle was better used to grow grain for human consumption, most people only dined on meat at religious festivals where they feasted on the animals sacrificed to the gods.

Hesiod had the help of oxen and mules and occasional hired laborers, but his life was one of continuous toil. The toughest season began with October's rains, the time for the first plowing. Plows were iron-tipped but light and fragile. Even with the aid of a team of animals it was difficult to break the sod. During autumn and winter, wood was cut and repairs were made to buildings and equipment. Vines needed attention in late winter. Grain was harvested in May. At the height of summer's heat there was time for a little rest. In September grapes had to be harvested and pressed, and then the round of yearly tasks began again. Hesiod says nothing about pleasures or entertainments, but the existence of his poetry witnesses to the presence in Greece of a more dynamic rural population than we know of anywhere else in the ancient world.

ARISTOCRATS Wealthy aristocrats worked their extensive lands with hired laborers, sharecroppers, and slaves. This gave them leisure for other kinds of activities. The centerpiece of aristocratic social life was the symposium, a men's drinking party. A symposium was sometimes only a pursuit of inebriation, but it could be

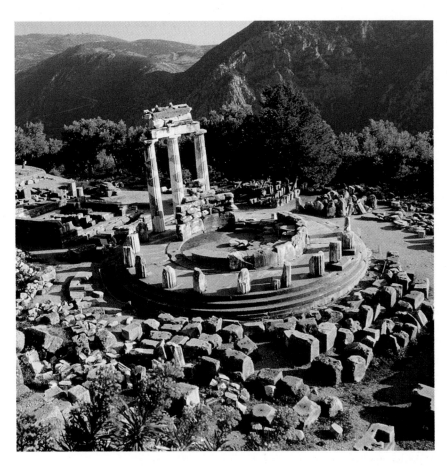

The ruins of the sanctuary of Apollo at Delphi, dating from the sixth century B.C.E. Greeks and foreigners traveled great distances to worship Apollo and to consult the famous Delphic oracle for clues to the future. Josè Fuste Raga/The Stock Market

more. It began with prayers and libations to the gods. There were usually games such as dice or *kottabos* (a contest in which wine was flicked from cups at a target). Sometimes dancing girls or flute girls offered entertainment. Frequently guests amused themselves with songs, poetry, or philosophical discussions. These activities were structured as contests, for aristocratic values put a premium on competition and the need to excel.

Athletic contests spread widely early in the sixth century B.C.E. They usually included foot races, long jumps, discus and javelin events, boxing, wrestling, and chariot races. Since the rich were the only ones who could afford horses, the chariot race was the special preserve of the nobility. Wrestling was also favored by the upper classes, and the *palaestra* where they practiced was an important gathering place. There was a great contrast between the drab lives of simple farmers and the cultivated pursuits of leisured aristocrats.

Religion

OLYMPIAN Religion permeated every aspect of Greek life. The Greeks were polytheists whose official pantheon centered on the twelve major deities who resided on Mount Olympus. Zeus, a sky god, exercised a kind of patriarchal authority over the other gods. He had three sisters: Hera, who was also his wife; Hestia, goddess of the hearth; and Demeter, goddess of agriculture and marriage. Zeus's brother Poseidon was god of the seas and earthquakes. By various mates he had an assortment of children: Aphrodite, goddess of love and beauty; Apollo, god of the sun, music, poetry, and prophecy; Ares, god of strife; Artemis, goddess of the moon and the hunt; Athena, goddess of wisdom and the arts; Hephaestus, god of fire and metallurgy; and Hermes, a cunning messenger-god who was the patron of traders.

Gods were believed, apart from their superhuman strength and immortality, to resemble mortals. Zeus, the defender of justice, presided over the cosmos, but he and the other gods were not omnipotent. They operated within limits set by the Fates who personified the inviolable order of the universe. Olympian religion was Panhellenic (i.e., shared by all the Greeks), but each *polis* chose one of the gods as its special guardian, and in the eighth and seventh centuries B.C.E., shrines honored by all Greeks were established at Olympia (to Zeus), Delphi (to Apollo), Corinth (to Poseidon), and Nemea (also to Zeus). Each of these sanctuaries staged athletic games in honor of its god, and all Greeks were invited to attend them. During the games, sacred truces suspended wars so that all parties could safely participate.

In the sixth century B.C.E., the shrine of Apollo at Delphi became famous for its oracle, the most important of several that the Greeks looked to for guidance. Delphian Apollo endorsed the pursuit of self-knowledge and self-control. "Know thyself" and "Nothing in excess" were Apollo's mottos. *Hubris*, the arrogance produced by excessive wealth or good fortune, was believed to be the most dangerous of human failings. It created moral blindness and tempted the gods to take vengeance. The moral order the gods enforced was simple. Virtue consisted of paying one's debts, doing good to one's friends, and attacking one's enemies. Civic responsibility involved taking part in the cult of the state deities, performing public service, and fighting in the state's army.

THE DIONYSIAN AND ORPHIC CULTS   The worship of the Olympian gods was a state religion that was not meant to address the concerns of private individuals. For their personal needs the Greeks practiced a religion of a different kind. They worshiped countless lesser deities associated with local shrines. Some were human heroes, both real and legendary, whose deeds had won them divine status. Ordinary people had no such grandiose aspirations. The cults that appealed to them offered divine help for this life.

The worship of Dionysus, a fertility deity associated with the growing of grapes, was very popular—particularly with women. Dionysus was a god of drunkenness and sexual abandon. His female devotees (the *maenads*) cavorted by night and were reputed, when possessed by their god, to tear to pieces and devour any creatures they encountered. The cult of Orpheus, a mythical poet, taught respect for life and offered the prospect of some kind of triumph over the grave—perhaps a transmigration of souls.

Poetry

A shift from epic to lyric poetry reflected the great changes that swept through the Greek world in the sixth century B.C.E. The poems of Sappho of Lesbos, Anacreon of Teos, and Simonides of Cos were intimately personal—often describing the pleasure and agony of love. Alcaeus of Mytilene, an aristocrat driven from his city by a tyrant, wrote bitter invectives, and from a political point of view the most interesting poet of the century may be Theonis of Megara. He spoke for the aristocrats whose power over most *poleis* was waning. He insisted that only nobles could aspire to true virtue, for only nobles possessed the crucial sense of honor. Honor, he claimed, could not be taught; it was innate, and noble families lost it if they debased their lines by marrying commoners. Although the political privileges of the old nobility were reduced in most Greek states, traditional assumptions of aristocratic superiority continued to influence important thinkers such as Plato.

The Persian Wars

The Greeks' era of freedom from interference from the outside world came to an end in the middle of the sixth century B.C.E. First, the Greek colonies, which had flourished on the coast of Asia Minor since the eleventh century B.C.E., came under the control of Croesus (ca. 560–546 B.C.E.), king of the Anatolian nation of Lydia. Then in 546 B.C.E., Lydia and its dependencies passed into the hands of the Persians.

The Persian Empire

The Persian Empire was created in a single generation by Cyrus the Great, founder of the Achaemenid dynasty. When Cyrus became the ruler of Persia in 559 B.C.E., it was a small kingdom well to the east of lower Mesopotamia. He steadily expanded his domain in all directions, conquered Babylon, and ultimately reached Asia Minor where he defeated Croesus and occupied Lydia. Most of the Greek cities of Asia Minor resisted the Persians, but by 540 B.C.E. they had all been subdued.

The Ionian Rebellion

The Greeks of Ionia (i.e., the western coast of Asia Minor) had been developing democratic governments, and they were restive under Persian rule. But the Persians were clever empire builders. They appointed Greek tyrants to govern Greek cities. Since these native leaders usually governed benignly and Persian tribute was not excessive, many Greeks were soon reconciled to life in Persia's empire. Neither the death of Cyrus in 530 B.C.E., nor the suicide of his successor Cambyses, nor the civil war that followed that event in 522–521 B.C.E. prompted the Greeks to revolt. In 521 B.C.E. when Darius became Great King (the Persian royal title), Ionia submitted to him as to his predecessors.

Aristagoras, an ambitious tyrant of Miletus, was responsible for ending the era of peaceful cooperation between Ionia and Persia. To escape punishment for having committed the Persians to an unsuccessful campaign against the island of Naxos, he persuaded the Ionian cities to join him in a rebellion in 499 B.C.E. He won support by helping to overthrow unpopular fellow tyrants and by endorsing democratic constitutions for some cities. He also sought help from the mainland states. The Spartans declined to become involved. They had no ties with the Ionians, no national interest in the region, and could not risk weakening their hold over their slaves by sending their army abroad.

The Athenians were more sympathetic toward Aristagoras. They were related to the Ionians and had reasons of their own to fear the Persians. Hippias, the deposed tyrant of Athens, was an honored guest at Darius's court, and the Great King supported Hippias's plans to restore his tyranny in Athens. The Persians also held both shores of the Hellespont, Athens' route to the grain fields surrounding the Black Sea. For all these reasons, the Athenian assembly decided to send a fleet of twenty ships to help the rebels.

In 498 B.C.E. the Athenian and Ionian armies overwhelmed Sardis, the capital of Lydia and the seat of the Persian *satrap* (i.e., governor). The sack of Sardis encouraged others to join the rebellion, but the Greeks did not follow up their victory. Athens withdrew, and the Persians gradually recovered the ground they had lost. In 495 B.C.E. they defeated the Ionian fleet at Lade, and a year later they leveled Miletus.

A Greek hoplite attacks a Persian soldier. The contrast between the Greek's metal body armor, large shield, and long spear and the Persian's cloth and leather garments indicates one reason the Greeks won. This Attic vase was found on Rhodes and dates from ca. 475 B.C.E. Greek vase, Red-figured. Attic.ca. 480–470 B.C. Neck amphora, Nolan type. Side 1: Greek warrior attacking a Persian. Said to be from Rhodes. Terracotta H. 13–11/16 in. The Metropolitan Museum of Art, Rogers Fund, 1906. (06.1021.117) Photograph © 1986 The Metropolitan Museum of Art.

The War in Greece

In 490 B.C.E. the Persians launched an expedition to punish Athens, to restore Hippias, and to gain control of the Aegean Sea. They first attacked Naxos and destroyed it as punishment for its resistance in 499 B.C.E. Then they conquered Eretria and deported its people, for the Eretrians had sent help to Miletus.

Despite the failure of their neighbors to withstand Persia's assault, the Athenians refused to submit to the invader. They chose Miltiades, an Athenian with a personal grudge against the Persians, to lead them and marched out to Marathon, the plain north of Athens where the Persians had made their landing. Although the odds were against them, the Athenians defeated the Persians and forced them to retreat. Victory

The Rise of the *Polis*

ca. 725 B.C.E.	Sparta conquers Messenia
ca. 650 B.C.E.	Spartan constitution militarizes the state
594 B.C.E.	Solon reforms the Athenian constitution
546–510 B.C.E.	Athenian tyranny of Pisistratus and Hippias
521 B.C.E.	Ionia submits to Persian rule
508 B.C.E.	Clisthenes inaugurates Athenian democracy
499 B.C.E.	Miletus rebels against Persia
490 B.C.E.	Darius's invasion, the battle of Marathon
480 B.C.E.	Xerxes' invasion, the battles of Thermopylae and Salamis
479 B.C.E.	Battles of Plataea and Mycale, Greek victory over Persia

enhanced their pride in themselves and their confidence in the fledgling democracy they had recently invented to govern their *polis.*

THE GREAT INVASION Internal troubles prevented the Persians from taking swift revenge for their loss at Marathon. Almost ten years elapsed before Darius's successor, Xerxes, turned his attention to the Greeks. In 481 B.C.E. he assembled an army of at least 150,000 men and a navy of more than 600 ships and set out to conquer the Aegean.

By then Athens had changed significantly. Themistocles, the city's leading politician, had begun to turn the *polis* into a naval power. During his *archonship* in 493 B.C.E., Athens built a fortified port at Piraeus, and a decade later the Athenians used the income from a rich vein of silver discovered in the state mines to finance the construction of a fleet. By 480 B.C.E., Athens had over 200 ships. They proved to be the salvation of Greece.

Of the hundreds of Greek states, only thirty-one (led by Sparta, Athens, Corinth, and Aegina) were willing to commit to fighting the vast Persian army that gathered south of the Hellespont in the spring of 480 B.C.E. Xerxes' strategy was to overwhelm the Greeks with superior numbers,

but Themistocles perceived a weakness in the emperor's plan. The Persian army had to stay in touch with the fleet that carried its supplies. If the Persian ships were destroyed, the army would have to retreat. Themistocles, therefore, argued that a naval engagement could win the war for the Greeks.

The Greek League, which was organized specifically to deal with the Persian invasion, met at Corinth as the Persians prepared to cross the Hellespont. Sparta was chosen to lead the Greeks, and the Greeks decided to take their stand at Thermopylae (i.e., the "hot gates"). The Persian army had to stay near the coast to maintain contact with its fleet, and at Thermopylae the coast was extremely narrow for the mountains came nearly to the sea. It was possible for a small force to stop the Persians here by blocking the narrow strip of beach at the foot of the mountains. The Greek army with which the Spartan king, Leonidas, hoped to hold this spot numbered only about 9,000—of which 300 were Spartans.

The Greeks had some luck, for storms wrecked a large number of Persians ships before Xerxes attacked Thermopylae. For two days the Greeks stood their ground and butchered the troops he threw at them. On the third day, however, a Greek traitor showed the Persians a trail through the mountains, and a company of Xerxes' men outflanked the Greek army and attacked it from the rear. Leonidas realized that the situation was hopeless. He discharged his Greek allies, but he and his 300 Spartans chose to stay and to die fighting. The way was now clear for the Persian army to invade Attica and burn Athens. If an inscription discovered in 1959 is authentic, Themistocles had foreseen this possibility and begun the evacuation of the city while the Greek army was still at Thermopylae.

The fate of Greece was decided by a sea battle fought in the narrow straits between Attica and the island of Salamis. The Spartans wanted the Athenian fleet to retreat from Salamis and move south to guard the coast of the Peloponnese, but Themistocles forced them to change their minds by threatening to abandon the war and use the fleet to carry the Athenians to new homes in Italy. In the battle that followed at Salamis the Persians lost more than half their ships. This forced Xerxes to return to Persia, but he left a large portion of his army behind to continue the war under a general named Mardonius.

While Mardonius went into winter camp in central Greece, Pausanias, a Spartan leader, assembled the largest army the Greeks had ever fielded. In the summer of 479 B.C.E. it decisively defeated Mardonius's forces at a battle near Plataea in Boeotia. At the same time, the Ionian Greeks persuaded Leotychidas, the Spartan commander of the Greek fleet, to take the offensive against a key Persian naval base at Mycale on the coast of Asia Minor. Leotychidas routed the enemy, and the Persians retreated from the Aegean and Ionia. Greece was safe, but no one knew for how long.

In Perspective

The Hellenic civilization that has so powerfully influenced the modern West was itself influenced by the Bronze Age cultures of Minoan Crete and Mycenae. But these early Aegean states more closely resembled Egypt, Mesopotamia, and Palestine-Syria than the Hellenic poleis. They were urbanized societies with systems of writing, centralized monarchies, large administrative bureaucracies, hierarchical social systems, professional standing armies, and systems of taxation. The Hellenic civilization that slowly emerged from the rubble of the Mycenaean kingdoms was quite different.

The Mycenaean collapse inaugurated an era of cultural decline for the Greeks. Villages replaced cities. Trade all but ended. Communication was curtailed. The art of writing was lost, and a "dark age" descended on the Aegean during which the Greeks were largely forgotten by the outside world. During this period (1100–750 B.C.E.), however, the Greeks laid foundations for a new civilization based on the polis, the Hellenic city-state.

Monarchy faded with the passing of the Mycenaean kingdoms, and several factors encouraged the development of republican governments in the new poleis. Because Greece was poor, distinctions of wealth between social classes were less dramatic than in other societies. Reliance on infantry—the hoplite phalanx—further narrowed the gap between aristocrat and commoner. A city that depended on its citizen-soldiers for its defense could hardly deny them some role in its government. Most poleis also had no need to impose regular taxation, for they did not have to hire professional soldiers or administrators. These services were duties citizens were expected to volunteer to the state. There were, therefore, no professional bureaucracies to stifle individual initiatives and no castes of priests to enforce religious orthodoxy. A polis was a dynamic, secular, and remarkably free community that created the kind of cultural environment in which speculative thinking (the basis of science) could thrive.

REVIEW QUESTIONS

1. What are the similarities and the differences between the Minoan and the Mycenaean civilizations?
2. What are the sources from which historians can derive information about the Aegean Bronze Age? What is Linear B and what can be learned from it? What are the difficulties in using the Homeric epics as historical sources?
3. What was a Greek *polis*? What role did geography play in the development of the Greek *poleis*? What contribution did the *polis* make to the development of Hellenic civilization?
4. How did the political, social, and economic institutions of Athens and Sparta compare around 500 B.C.E.? What explains Sparta's uniqueness?
5. What transpired in Athens between 600 and 500 B.C.E. to help it make the transition from aristocracy to democracy? What did Draco, Solon, Pisistratus, and Clisthenes each contribute to the process?
6. Why did the Greeks and Persians go to war in 490 and 480 B.C.E.? What motivated the Persian attempt to conquer Greece? Why were the Greeks victorious over the Persians? What were the effects of victory on the victors?

SUGGESTED READINGS

J. CHADWICK, *The Mycenaean World* (1976). A readable account by a man who helped decipher Mycenaean writing.

J. M. COOK, *The Persian Empire* (1983). A valuable study of Persian history based on archaeological and literary evidence.

O. DICKINSON, *The Aegean Bronze Age* (1994). A fine survey of Bronze Age culture in the Aegean region.

R. DREWS, *The End of the Bronze Age: Changes in Warfare and Catastrophes ca. 1200 B.C.* (1993). An examination of the theories explaining the fall of the late Bronze Age civilizations.

V. EHRENBERG, *From Solon to Socrates* (1968). An interpretive history that uses literature to illuminate politics.

J. V. A. FINE, *The Ancient Greeks* (1983). An excellent survey that discusses historical problems and the evidence that gives rise to them.

M. I. FINLEY, *World of Odysseus,* 2nd. ed. (1978). A fascinating attempt to reconstruct Homeric society.

W. G. FORREST, *The Emergence of Greek Democracy* (1966). An interpretation of social and political developments in the archaic period.

P. GREEN, *The Greco-Persian Wars* (1998). A stimulating history of the Persian wars.

V. D. HANSON, *The Western Way of War* (1989). A brilliant description of the *hoplite* phalanx and its influence on Greek society.

V. D. HANSON, *The Other Greeks* (1995). A revolutionary account of the invention of the family farm by the Greeks and the role of agrarianism in the *polis*.

J. M. HURWIT, *The Art and Culture of Early Greece* (1985). A fascinating study of the art of early Greece in its cultural context.

D. KAGAN, *The Great Dialogue: A History of Greek Political Thought from Homer to Polybius* (1965). A discussion of the relationship between historical experience and political theory.

P. B. MANVILLE, *The Origins of Citizenship in Ancient Athens* (1990). An examination of the concept of citizenship in Solon's generation.

L. G. MITCHELL and P. J. RHODES, eds., *The Development of the* Polis *in Archaic Greece* (1997). A collection of articles on the early development of the *polis*.

R. SALLARES, *The Ecology of the Ancient Greek World* (1991). A valuable study of the Greeks and their environment.

Chapter 3
Classical and Hellenistic Greece

KEY TOPICS

- The Peloponnesian War and the struggle between Athens and Sparta
- Democracy and empire in fifth-century B.C.E. Athens
- Culture and society in Classical Greece
- The struggle for dominance in Greece after the Peloponnesian War
- The Hellenistic world

The Greeks' victory over the Persians in 489–479 B.C.E. marked the start of an era of great achievement. Fear of another Persian incursion into the Aegean led the Greeks to contemplate some kind of cooperative defense. The Spartans refused to make commitments that would take them away from their homeland, but the Athenians were eager for opportunities to increase their influence. They negotiated a military alliance called the Delian League. As it developed into an Athenian empire, fear of Athenian expansion led other states to ally with Sparta. The polarized Greek world erupted in a civil war that weakened everyone, and in 338 B.C.E. Philip of Macedon imposed his will on the Greeks and brought the era of the polis *to an end.*

Aftermath of Victory

The Greek *poleis* had found it hard to cooperate even in the face of Persian invasions of their homeland. Within two years of Persia's retreat, divisions had emerged among the Greeks that threatened to involve them in serious civil conflict.

The Delian League

The Spartans led the Greeks to victory against the Persian invaders of the Greek mainland, but they were not prepared to assume responsibility for de-

fending the Aegean against the return of the Persians. Sparta could not risk stationing its troops far from home for long periods lest its slaves rebel. A *polis* with a navy was also better equipped to defend the Aegean than the Spartan army.

Athens was Greece's leading naval power, and it was an Ionian state with ties to the Greeks whom the Persians still threatened on the Aegean islands and the coasts of Asia Minor. In the winter of 478–477 B.C.E., the Athenians joined other Greeks on the sacred island of Delos to swear oaths of mutual assistance in a continuing struggle with Persia. The purpose of the Delian League they formed was to free Greeks still under Persian rule, to defend against a Persian return, and to obtain compensation from the Persians by raiding their lands.

The league succeeded in driving back the Persians and clearing the Aegean of pirates. In 467 B.C.E., it won a great victory over the Persians at

MAP 3–1 CLASSICAL GREECE *The history of Greece in the Classical Period (ca. 480–338 B.C.E.) centers on the Aegean, although Greek cities in Italy, Sicily, and the Black Sea also made important contributions.*

the Eurymedon River in Asia Minor, and some cities concluded that the alliance had served its purpose. When they tried to withdraw from the league, however, Athens forced them to continue their contributions. What had begun as a voluntary association of free states became an empire dominated by Athens.

The Rise of Cimon

Themistocles fell from power at the end of the Persian Wars, and for two decades leadership of Athens was exercised by Cimon, son of Miltiades, the general who triumphed at Marathon. At home, Cimon defended a limited version of Clisthenes' democratic constitution. Abroad he maintained pressure on Persia and cultivated friendly relations with Sparta.

The First Peloponnesian War: Athens Against Sparta

The Thasian Rebellion

In 465 B.C.E. the island of Thasos rebelled against the Delian League. During the two years it took to put down the revolt, Cimon was absent from Athens. When he returned, his political opponents tried to bring him down by charging him with taking bribes. He was acquitted, but a radically democratic faction led by a man named Ephialtes (and his young protégé, Pericles) continued to attack Cimon for his pro-Spartan, proaristocratic policies.

The Breach with Sparta

At the start of the Thasian rebellion, Thasos had asked Sparta to assist it by invading Athens. Sparta agreed, but an earthquake sparked a Helot revolt that kept the Spartan army tied up at home. Instead of attacking Athens, Sparta asked the Athenians for help. Cimon's fatal mistake was to talk the Athenians into sending it. The Spartans soon reconsidered the wisdom of letting an Athenian army into their land and ordered Cimon to retreat. The humiliated Athenians blamed Cimon, exiled him (461 B.C.E.), and allied with Argos, Sparta's enemy. A radical democratic faction under the leadership of Pericles emerged triumphant in Athens.

The Division of Greece

Since Sparta had been willing to help Thasos break up the Delian League by rebelling from Athens, Pericles persuaded Athens to back the city of Megara when it withdrew from Sparta's Peloponnesian League. (Since Megara was a key spot on the road that linked Attica with the Peloponnesus, Athens also understood the strategic importance of an alliance with Megara.) Sparta's vigorous objection led to the outbreak of the First Peloponnesian War. The Athenians maintained the upper hand until about 455 B.C.E., when they lost a fleet that they had sent to Egypt to harrass the Persians. Some members of Athens' empire seized the opportunity this gave them to rebel, and Athens was compelled to disentangle itself from war with Sparta. A truce was arranged, and in 449 B.C.E. Athens also made peace with Persia.

In 446 B.C.E., war again broke out between Sparta and Athens, but Pericles soon ended it by negotiation. Sparta recognized the Athenian empire in exchange for Athens ending its drive to win control of more of the Greek mainland, and the two *poleis* pledged to keep the peace for thirty years. This effectively divided Greece into two power blocs: Sparta dominating the Greek mainland and Athens ruling the Aegean Sea.

Classical Greece

The Athenian Empire

The Athenians used the failure of their Egyptian campaign as an excuse to move the league's treasury from the island of Delos to the greater security of Athens, and they began to keep one-sixtieth of its annual revenues for themselves. By 445 B.C.E. only Chios, Lesbos, and Samos maintained a semblance of equality with Athens by contributing their own ships to the league's navy. All the other states paid tribute like subject states, and they resented doing so. The fading of the Persian threat had removed the rationale for the league, but Athens profited too much from it to allow it to dissolve. Although the league became an Athenian empire, it was not unpopular with everyone. Democratic factions in its subject cities supported it, and Athens did what it could not to look like an oppressor but like a mother-city to

The Acropolis was both the religious and civic center of Athens. In its final form it is the work of Pericles and his successors in the late fifth century B.C.E. This photograph shows the Parthenon and to its left the Erechtheum. Meredith Pillon, Greek National

which allies were bound, like colonies, by ties of good feelings and shared religion.

Athenian Democracy

DEMOCRATIC LEGISLATION The Athenians sensed no inconsistency in demanding more democratic privileges for themselves while they pursued greater imperial dominance over others. The property qualification for holding high office was virtually suspended, and the Athenian *hoplite* class became eligible for the *archonship*. Pericles sponsored a law providing pay for jury members, which made it possible for the poor, who could not afford to take unpaid leave from their jobs, to serve. He revived the custom of sending circuit judges into the countryside to make justice readily available to the rural poor. He also persuaded the electorate to limit citizenship to men whose parents both descended from citizen families. Democracy made citizenship a valuable commodity, and it was in the self-interest of the electorate to increase the value of each vote by limiting the number of voters. All the Greek states denied participation in government to large segments of their populations—resident aliens, women, and slaves.

HOW DID THE DEMOCRACY WORK? Athenian democracy gave citizens extensive powers. Every decision of the state had to be approved by the popular assembly—by the voters themselves, not their representatives. Every judicial decision was subject to appeal to a popular court composed of not fewer than 51 and possibly as many as 1,501 citizens selected from the Athenian population at large. Most officials were chosen by casting lots, and their class status was unimportant. Successful candidates for the chief offices—for example, the imperial treasurers and the city's ten generals (who had both political and military authority)—were usually wealthy aristocrats. But the voters could, in theory, elect anyone. All public officials had to submit to examination before taking office. They could be removed from office and were called to account at the end of their term for the uses they had made of their authority. Since there was no standing army and no police force (public or secret), the city's leaders could not coerce or intimidate voters.

Pericles was elected to the generalship fifteen years in a row and thirty times in all, not because he was a dictator but because he was a persuasive speaker and a respected leader. On the few occasions when he lost the people's confidence, they did not hesitate to remove him from office. Pericles had been an imperialist, but after the defeat of the fleet Athens sent to Egypt and the failure of Athens' plans to win control over more of the mainland, he advocated a more conservative policy that was designed to preserve the empire Athens already had and peace with Sparta. By 443. B.C.E., when the First Peloponnesian War ended, he was at the height of his power as the guardian of Athens' imperial democracy.

Athenian Women: Legal Status and Everyday Life

Greek society, like most others throughout history, was dominated by men, and democratic Athens was no exception. Women from citizen families were excluded from most aspects of public life. They could not debate, vote, or hold office and were subject all their lives to the authority of a male guardian—a father, a husband, or other male relative. They married young, usually between the ages of twelve and eighteen. Since men often did not marry until they were in their thirties, husbands probably treated wives like dependent children. Marriages were arranged—often without consulting the bride. Woman were assigned dowries, but they had no control over them or any other property. Divorce was difficult for a woman to obtain, for she had to find a male relative who was willing to take responsibility for her after the dissolution of her marriage.

The chief function of an Athenian woman from a citizen family was the production of male heirs to perpetuate her husband's *oikos* (i.e., "household"). If a woman's father died without leaving a male heir, she became an *epikleros*, an heiress. If such a woman was married, she was required to separate from her husband and wed one of her father's relatives to bear a son who would reestablish the male line for her father's *oikos*.

Because citizenship was inherited, the legitimacy of children was important. Athenian males consorted freely with prostitutes and concubines, but citizen women were denied contact with any men but close relatives. Women spent their days confined to special women's quarters in their homes raising children, cooking, weaving, and managing their households. Occasionally they emerged in public to take part in the state religion. But for the most part, Athenian women were expected to be invisible. In a frequently quoted speech, Pericles declared that

Greek Women at Leisure. Most Greek women of the upper classes appear to have led a secluded and confined existence, but there is some evidence that suggests a somewhat richer social and cultural life. The picture of these women comes from a water-jar of the mid-fifth century B.C.E. Women used them to bring water into the house from wells or fountains, where ancient comedies portray them as gathering and conversing. This scene, however, is indoors, in the women's quarters of the house. The seated woman reads from a scroll; another holds a chest containing other works of literature on scrolls while the remaining two listen attentively. The British Museum

"the greatest glory of women is to be least talked about by men, whether for good or bad."

Evidence from myths and from the works of the great Athenian dramatists (who often featured women in their plays) suggests that the roles played by Athenian women may have been more complex than their legal status implies. Only the rich could have afforded to lock their women up at home. The poor needed the labor of their women in fields and shops, and such women had often to move about in public. Fetching water from the town wells and fountains was also women's work, and vase paintings and literature depict women gathering at these places. The opinions historians form about the place of women in Greek society depend on the kinds of sources they choose to emphasize. Consequently, woman's place in the Greek world remains a topic for debate.

AN EXCEPTIONAL WOMAN: ASPASIA The woman Pericles cared most for did not cultivate the invisibility that he said was "the greatest glory of women." Her name was Aspasia, and she was a *hetaira*, a high-class courtesan. Aspasia was not an Athenian. She came from Miletus, where Greek philosophy got its start. She was evidently very intelligent and apparently well educated. Socrates enjoyed her conversation, and in one of his dialogues Plato jokingly credits her with writing Pericles' speeches. There is no doubt that Pericles loved her. After divorcing his first wife, he took Aspasia into his home and treated her better than many Athenian men may have treated their wives. He lavished affection on her, involved her in conversations with his friends, discussed important issues with her, and respected her opinions. Athens was scandalized—not because Pericles kept a *hetaira* but because he held one in such high regard.

Slavery

The Greeks always had some form of slavery, but the earliest forms of bondage resembled serfdom more than chattel slavery. When the Spartans, for instance, conquered a people, they reduced them to the status of Helots—peasants who were bound to the state-owned farms that supported the Spartan soldiers. Until Solon put an end to the practice in Athens about 600 B.C.E., default on a debt could lead to temporary bondage for an Athenian citizen or even sale into permanent slavery outside Attica.

Chattel slavery proper began to increase about 500 B.C.E. and remained important to Greek society thereafter. Most slaves were prisoners of war or persons abducted by pirates. Like other ancient peoples, the Greeks regarded foreigners as inferior, and most slaves were foreigners. They were sometimes employed as shepherds, but Greek farms were often too small to support more than one enslaved agricultural worker. The upper class had more land, but it was usually worked by free tenant farmers. The estates of wealthy men usually consisted of small farms scattered about the *polis* rather than large, consolidated plantations. They had no use for the hordes of slaves associated with plantation economies. Slaves were used in greater numbers in some industries, especially mining. They worked as craftsmen in almost every trade, where, like slaves on small farms, they labored alongside their masters. Slaves were also used as domestic servants, and publicly owned slaves served as prison attendants, clerks, and secretaries.

The numbers of slaves and their importance to ancient Greek society are debated issues. Reliable statistics are hard to come by. During the fifth and fourth centuries B.C.E., there may have been anywhere from 20,000 to 100,000 slaves in Athens. If the accurate number is the mean between these extremes—60,000—and the city had about 40,000 households, there were fewer than two slaves per family. Only a quarter to a third of free Athenians may have owned slaves. This is comparable to the situation that existed in the American South prior to the Civil War, but unlike the South the Athenian economy did not depend on a single cash crop produced by slave labor. Greek slaves also did not differ from their masters in skin color, and slaves walked the streets of Athens with such ease as to offend class-conscious Athenians. The emancipation of slaves was rare in America but common in Greece.

The Great Peloponnesian War

The thirty years of peace that Sparta and Athens pledged to maintain in 445 B.C.E. ended prematurely. About 435 B.C.E., a dispute began in a remote part of the Greek world that escalated into a war that shook the foundations of Greek civilization.

Causes

The conflict began with a quarrel between Corinth and Corcyra, an island at the entrance to the Adriatic Sea. The Athenians decided to intervene because the Corcyraean fleet was second in size only to that of Athens. Its capture by Corinth would have upset the balance of power and threatened Athens' interests. This infuriated Corinth, a member of Sparta's Peloponnesian League. Corinth appealed to Sparta for help, and in the summer of 432 B.C.E., the Spartans convened a meeting of their allies to discuss the situation. The Corinthians persuaded the league to declare war on Athens, and in the spring of 431 B.C.E. Sparta marched into Attica.

Strategic Stalemate

The Spartan strategy was traditional—invade the enemy's territory, threaten his crops, and force him to defend them in a *hoplite* battle. Since the Spartans and their allies had the better army and outnumbered the Athenians by more than two to one, they were confident of victory.

Any ordinary *polis* would have yielded, but Athens had unique resources—the income from an empire, a vast reserve fund, and the Long Walls (a fortified highway that connected the inland city to its port at Piraeus). So long as the Athenians maintained their enormous navy, they could ride out a siege by supplying themselves from the sea. And if they remained secure behind their walls and ignored the Spartan invasion, they could demonstrate to the world that the Spartan army was no threat to them. Meanwhile the Athenian fleet could raid the Peloponnesian coast to frighten Sparta's allies. Pericles believed that this strategy would force the Peloponnesians to recognize the hopelessness of the situation and sue for peace. The plan was intelligent but difficult to implement. It required Athens' voters to exercise great self-control while Sparta destroyed their farms and taunted them, but Pericles' inspired leadership helped the democracy stay the course. In 429 B.C.E., however, plague swept the crowded city. Pericles died, and the politicians who succeeded him were unable to stick to a consistent plan of action.

Two factions appeared. The one led by a man named Nicias wanted to continue Pericles' defensive strategy; the other, which was headed by a certain Cleon, favored launching an offensive. In 425 B.C.E. Athens captured 400 Spartans in a skirmish in the Peloponnese, and Sparta offered peace in exchange for the return of its men. Cleon's party persuaded the Athenians to pass up this opportunity and to continue the war. The failure of two campaigns the following year shook the Athenian electorate's confidence in his aggressive policy—particularly after the Spartan general, Brasidas, captured Amphipolis, a port on which Athens depended for the protection of its grain imports. In 422 B.C.E., Cleon led an assault on Amphipolis in which both he and Brasidas were killed. The deaths of the leaders of the aggressive factions paved the way in the spring of 421 B.C.E. for a truce. There was also another outcome of the struggle over Amphipolis.

The Athenian admiral who failed to arrive in time to save the city was named Thucydides. Athens punished him with exile, and he used his enforced leisure to write a masterful account of the war—which, as it turned out, was far from over.

The Fall of Athens

The agreement between Athens and Sparta (the Peace of Nicias) was supposed to guarantee peace for fifty years, but neither side honored all its commitments. Despite the likelihood that hostilities would break out again, in 415 B.C.E. an ambitious young politician named Alcibiades persuaded the Athenians to send an army to intervene in the complicated affairs of Sicily. Two years later the entire expedition was destroyed. Athens lost 200 ships and 4,500 men, and the huge loss borne by its allies sparked rebellion in its empire. Persia sized up the situation and saw an opportunity to help the Greeks destroy themselves. It offered aide to Sparta.

Remarkably, the Athenians found the strength to continue fighting, but their resources were no match for the support Spartans received from Persia. In 405 B.C.E., Athens' fleet was caught at Aegospotami and destroyed. Since the city could not afford to replace it, Lysander, the Spartan commander, was able to cut off Athens' food supply and starve the city into submission (404 B.C.E.). Athens was allowed to survive but was stripped of its fleet and empire.

Competition for Leadership in the Fourth Century B.C.E.

Sparta tried, but failed, to take Athens' place as leader of the Greek world. Its limited population, restive slaves, conservative traditions, and indebtedness to Persia prevented it from devising means to govern and protect the Aegean. From 404 B.C.E. until 338 B.C.E., the Greeks squandered their resources fighting among themselves.

The Hegemony of Sparta

Sparta quickly alienated the Greeks by ceding the cities of Ionia to Persia as repayment for the help it had received during the war. Lysander then made a mockery of Sparta's claim to have freed the Greeks from Athenian dominance by attempting to make them part of a new Spartan empire. He installed oligarchies that were loyal to him in the Greek cities and deployed Spartan garrisons to back up his puppet governments. The tribute he demanded was no less than what Athens had collected.

In 404 B.C.E. Lysander installed an oligarchic government in Athens. It became so unpopular that its members were known as the Thirty Tyrants. When persecution prompted Athens' democratic leaders to flee to Thebes and Corinth and to begin to raise an army with which to retake their city, Sparta's cautious king, Pausanias, intervened. He prevented an outbreak of fighting by recalling Lysander and allowing Athens to revert to democracy. So long as Athenian foreign policy remained under Spartan control, Sparta could afford to allow Athens to have any kind of government it wanted.

Persia was distracted from further intervention in Greek affairs by an internal power struggle. In 405 B.C.E. the emperor Darius II died, and a young prince named Cyrus recruited a Greek mercenary army to contest the succession to the throne of his brother, Artaxerxes II. In 401 B.C.E., the Greeks defeated the Persians at Cunaxa in Mesopotamia, but Cyrus was killed in that battle. The Greeks suddenly found themselves stranded without a leader or a purpose deep in enemy territory. They succeeded in fighting their way back to the Black Sea and safety, but the cities of Asia Minor that had supported Cyrus now faced the threat of Artaxerxes' revenge.

In 396 B.C.E. the Spartans sent an army under the command of their king, Agesilaus, to defend Greek interests in Asia Minor. The Persians countered by offering aid to any Greek state willing to rebel against Sparta. Thebes was willing, and in 395 B.C.E. it created an alliance that included Argos, Corinth, and a resurgent Athens. The Corinthian War (395–387 B.C.E.) that ensued forced the Spartan army to evacuate Asia Minor, and in 394 B.C.E. the Persian fleet destroyed Sparta's navy. The Athenians seized the opportunity to rebuild their walls, enlarge their navy, and recover some of their foreign possessions.

The Persians believed that Athens was potentially a greater threat than Sparta, and they were willing to support Sparta so long as its ambitions were confined to the Greek mainland. In 382 B.C.E. Agesilaus seized Thebes in a surprise attack. A Spartan attempt to occupy Athens failed, and by 379 B.C.E. the Thebans had regained their independence. In 371 B.C.E. the great Theban general, Epaminondas, gave the Spartans a crushing defeat at Leuctra. He then freed the Helots and helped them found a city of their own. This deprived Sparta of much of its land and its slave labor force and hemmed it in with hostile neighbors. Sparta was never again to be a major power.

The Hegemony of Thebes: The Second Athenian Empire

Epaminondas's victory over Sparta opened the way for Thebes to become the dominant power in Greece, and Thebes took control of all the Greek states north of Athens and along the Corinthian Gulf. Theban expansion, however, threatened many Greeks, and Athens was able to recruit their help in opposing it. In 362 B.C.E. Epaminondas led an army into the Peloponnesus to confront Athens and its allies. His men routed their opponents at the battle of Mantinea, but he was killed. When no comparable leader arose to

The Competition for Leadership of Greece	
479 B.C.E.	Battles of Plataea and Mycale
478–477 B.C.E.	Formation of Delian League
465–463 B.C.E.	Thasos attempts to leave the league
462 B.C.E.	Pericles begins to lead Athens
460–445 B.C.E.	First Peloponnesian War
454 B.C.E.	Athens defeated in Egypt
449 B.C.E.	Peace with Persia
435 B.C.E.	Corinth attacks Corcyra
432–404 B.C.E.	Great Peloponnesian War
421 B.C.E.	Peace of Nicias
415–413 B.C.E.	Athens' Sicilian campaign
404 B.C.E.	Sparta victorious over Athens
404–403 B.C.E.	Thirty Tyrants govern Athens
382 B.C.E.	Sparta seizes Thebes
378 B.C.E.	Second Athenian Confederation
371 B.C.E.	Thebes defeats Sparta at Leuctra
362 B.C.E	End of Theban hegemony
338 B.C.E.	Philip of Macedon dominates Greece
336–323 B.C.E.	Reign of Alexander the Great

take his place, the era of Theban dominance came to an end.

Sixteen years earlier (in 378 B.C.E.), an alliance known as the Second Athenian Confederation had been organized to guard against Spartan aggression in the Aegean. Although its constitution was designed to prevent Athens from exploiting this alliance as it had the Delian League, Athens soon alienated its confederates. The collapse of Sparta and Thebes and Persia's lack of aggressive behavior convinced some of Athens' allies that the confederation was unnecessary. They rebelled, and by 355 B.C.E., Athens had once again lost an empire. Two centuries of almost continuous warfare had failed to bring order to the Greek world.

The Culture of Classical Greece

The Greeks' early victories in the Persian Wars inspired them with tremendous self-confidence and unleashed a flood of creative activity that was rarely, if ever, matched anywhere at any time. The result was the development of the Classical Period in the history of Western civilization.

The Fifth Century B.C.E.

The term *classical* often invokes the idea of calm and serenity, but the products of Greece's Classical Period are filled with tension. There were two reasons for this. One was the incompatibility between the private ambitions of individuals and the self-restraint imposed by the duties of *polis* citizenship. The other was the conflict between the Greeks' competitive drive and their fear that the gods punished excessive striving. The Greeks' faith in themselves had been strengthened by their victory over Persia, but they knew that they were not exempt from the kind of punishment Xerxes had received for his overreaching ambition. The Greek playwrights pondered this just as Athens and Sparta teetered on the brink of self-destructive war.

ATTIC TRAGEDY Greek plays were staged as competitions among playwrights at festivals honoring the god Dionysus. Poets competed by submitting three tragedies (which might or might not have a common subject) and a satyr play (a concluding comic choral dialogue with Dionysus). An *archon* chose three competitors for each festival and assigned each of them three actors and a chorus. The actors were paid by the state, and the chorus was sponsored by a donation from a wealthy citizen. Most plays were performed in the temple of Dionysus, an amphitheater of 30,000 seats on the south side of the Acropolis. A jury of Athenians, chosen by lot, awarded prizes for the best author, actor, and sponsor.

Attic theater provided poets with opportunities to challenge their fellow citizens to ponder vital issues of the day. On rare occasions the subject of a play might be a contemporary or historical event, but usually a playwright chose a tale from mythology that illuminated current affairs. The plays of Aeschylus and Sophocles, our earliest extant examples, deal with religion, politics, and ethics. The plays of Euripides, which were written a little later, show a greater interest in exploring the psychology of the individual.

OLD COMEDY Comedies were added to the Dionysian festival early in the fifth century B.C.E. The only complete comic plays to survive are those of Aristophanes (ca. 450–385 B.C.E.), who wrote humorously about serious political issues. He employed scathing invective and satire to lampoon his contemporaries—even powerful politicians such as Pericles and Cleon.

ARCHITECTURE AND SCULPTURE Like the plays that members of Pericles' generation witnessed, the buildings the city erected during this period reflect creative tension. In 448 B.C.E., Pericles inaugurated a great building program on the Acropolis (using income from the Delian League). The plan included new temples to honor the city's gods and an imposing gateway for the sacred precinct. Pericles' intent was to represent visually the political power and intellectual greatness of Athens—to make Athens, in his words, "the school of Hellas."

PHILOSOPHY The art of the fifth century B.C.E. tried to define humanity and illustrate its place in the natural world order. Similar concerns prompted the invention of philosophy in the sixth century B.C.E. Thales, the first philosopher, proposed a theory to explain how a world filled with

Art & the West

Victory and Nobility in Bronze:
The Charioteer of Delphi

This statue is one of the few full-scale bronze sculptures to survive from the fifth century B.C.E. It was a gift to the god Apollo at Delphi from Polyzalus, tyrant of Gela in Sicily, a thank offering for his victory in the chariot race at Delphi's Pythian games in 478 or 474 B.C.E. A victory in one of the greater Greek games (i.e., at Olympia, Delphi, Corinth, or Nemea) was one of the highest honors to which a Greek could aspire, and the deeds of such athletes were memorialized by major poets such as Pindar.

The statue represents the driver of a chariot sponsored by Polyzalus, not Polyzalus himself. It is the only surviving piece from a tableau that once included the chariot, horses, and possibly Polyzalus riding in a victory procession. It is an example of the "severe style" that characterized Greek art in the period after the Persian invasion (i.e., 480–479 B.C.E.). In contrast to earlier work, it is simple, serious, and austere. The expression on the charioteer's face is not the rigid smile typical of archaic sculpture. It projects a moody inwardness—the *ethos* (i.e., character) of a nobleman who takes justifiable pride in his achievements but eschews the arrogance that offends the gods.

Sources: J. J. Pollitt, *Art and Experience in Classical Greece* (Cambridge: Cambridge University Press, 1972), pp. 15–63. H. W. Janson and Anthony F. Janson, *History of Art*, 5th ed., rev. (Upper Saddle River, NJ: Prentice Hall, 1997), pp. 139–151.

The Charioteer of Delphi. c. 470 B.C.E.
Nimatallah/Art Resource, NY

changing phenomena could hang together as a stable, coherent whole. He suggested that the changes we see are nothing but alterations in the state of a single underlying universal substance. When attempts to identify this substance failed, later thinkers concluded that Thales had been naive in assuming that change and permanence could both exist in the same world.

Heraclitus argued that permanence was an illusion produced by our inability to perceive change that was very slow. Parmenides of Elea and his pupil Zeno countered that the concept of change was a logical absurdity, for it implied that something arose from nothing. Empedocles of Acragas suggested a compromise between these opposing points of view. He said that the world was composed of unchanging elements (e.g., fire, water, earth, and air) whose combinations changed. Similarly, Leucippus of Miletus and Democritus of Abdera imagined the world to be made up of innumerable tiny, solid, indivisible particles (*atomoi,* in Greek) that clump together and spin apart in the void of space. These philosophies endorsed materialism. That is, they assumed that spirit (or mind) was composed of matter and that physical laws, therefore, could explain everything. Anaxagoras of Clazomenae agreed that the universe was composed of tiny fundamental particles he called "seeds," but he claimed that it also contained another reality—a rational force, *nous* (i.e., "mind"), which controlled everything. These Greek thinkers began a debate between materialism and idealism that has yet to be resolved.

Most philosophical speculations were too abstract to interest many people, but the Sophists, a group of professional teachers who flourished in the mid-fifth century B.C.E., attracted a popular following. They were paid to develop and teach a practical skill: rhetoric. The arts of rhetorical persuasion were much valued in democracies in which many issues were resolved through public debate. Some Sophists also claimed to teach wisdom and virtue. They refrained from speculations about the physical universe but used reason to critique human beliefs and institutions. This led them to ponder a central issue of social life: the conflict between nature and custom. The more traditional among them argued that laws were of divine origin and in accord with nature, but others argued that

laws were merely conventions—arbitrary agreements among people. The most extreme Sophists maintained that law was contrary to nature—a device to reverse the natural order and enable the weak to dominate the strong. Critias, an Athenian oligarch, went so far as to claim that the gods themselves had been invented to deter people from doing what they wanted to do. Such speculations undermined the concept of justice on which the *polis* was founded, and the later giants of philosophy, Plato and Aristotle, worked hard to refute them.

HISTORY Herodotus—"the father of history," as he has been deservedly called—was born shortly before the outbreak of the Persian Wars. The account he wrote of those wars far exceeded attempts by earlier prose writers to explain human actions. Although his *History* was completed about 425 B.C.E. and shows a few traces of Sophist influence, its spirit is that of an earlier time. Herodotus accepted, although not uncritically, information taken from legends and oracles, and he often explained events as the result of divine intervention. But his work is typical of its time in celebrating the crucial role of human intelligence in determining the course of history. Herodotus was also aware of the importance of institutions. He credited Greece's victory over Persia to the love of liberty the *polis* instilled in its citizens.

Thucydides, the historian of the Peloponnesian War, was born about 460 B.C.E. and died a few years after the end of the war he spent his life studying. His thought was influenced by the secular, human-centered, skeptical rationalism of the Sophists of the late fifth century B.C.E., and he shared the scientific attitudes that characterized the work of contemporaries such as the physician Hippocrates of Cos. Thucydides took great pains to achieve factual accuracy, and he searched his evidence for significant patterns of human behavior. He hoped that by discovering these patterns people would be able to foresee events. Since human nature was, he believed, essentially unchanging, similar circumstances ought to produce similar responses. But Thucydides admitted that the lessons of history were not always enough to guarantee success. He believed that an element of randomness (i.e., chance) helps to shape human destiny.

The Fourth Century B.C.E.

The Peloponnesian War marked the passing of the *polis* as an effective form of government. The Greeks of the fourth century B.C.E. may not fully have grasped this fact, but they did realize that their traditional way of life was threatened. Some tried to shore up the weakened structure of the *polis;* others looked for alternatives to it; and still others averted their gaze from the public arena altogether.

DRAMA   The poetry of the fourth century B.C.E. reveals the disillusionment some Greeks felt with the *polis.* Its subjects are no longer drawn from politics and public life but from the private concerns of ordinary people—the family and the interior life of the individual. Old Comedy had focused on political issues and matters of public policy. Middle and New Comedy was devoted to a humorous-realistic depiction of daily life, to intrigue, and to mild satire of domestic situations. The role of the chorus, which in a way had represented the *polis* in the drama, was very much diminished. Menander (342–291 B.C.E.), the pioneer of New Comedy, wrote domestic tragicomedy: gentle satires of the foibles of ordinary people and tales of temporarily thwarted lovers—material such as is found in modern situation comedies.

Tragedy, which drew its inspiration from the robust political life of the *polis,* declined during the fourth century B.C.E. No plays from the period have survived. Theatrical producers may have sensed a decline in quaility, for they began to revive the plays of the previous century. Euripides' tragedies, which had rarely won top honors when first produced, finally found their audiences. More than the other great playwrights of his age, Euripides had explored the interior lives of individual human beings, and some of his late plays are more like fairy tales, fantasy adventures, or love stories than tragedies.

SCULPTURE   The same movement away from the grand, the ideal, and the general—and toward the ordinary, the real, and the individual—is apparent in the evolution of Greek sculpture. This becomes obvious when the work of Polycleitus (ca. 450–440 B.C.E.) is compared with that of Praxiteles (ca. 340–330 B.C.E.) or Lysippus (ca. 330 B.C.E.).

The striding god from Artemisium is a bronze statue dating from about 460 B.C.E. It was found in the sea near Artemisium, the northern tip of the large Greek island of Euboea, and is now on display in the Athens archaeological museum. Exactly whom he represents is not known. Some have thought him to be Poseidon holding a trident; others believe that he is Zeus hurling a thunderbolt. In either case, he is a splendid representative of the early Classical period of Greek sculpture. National Archaeological Museum, Athens

Philosophy and the Crisis of the *Polis*

SOCRATES   The life and teachings of Socrates (469–399 B.C.E.) reflect an early awareness of the crises that were developing for the *polis.* Socrates recognized the difficulties and criticized the shortcomings of the *polis.* He did not take an active role in politics, but he did not abandon the *polis* ideal. He fought as a soldier to defend Athens, obeyed its laws, and sought a sound, rational foundation for its values.

Since Socrates wrote nothing, our knowledge of him depends on the reports of his disciples, Plato and Xenophon, and on the work of later commentators. As a young man, he supposedly took an interest in the theories about the physical world developed by the first philosophers, but his concern soon shifted to the interior world—

to the explication of the processes of human understanding and decision making. Unlike some Sophists, he believed in the existence of truth and the power of reason to search it out.

Socrates sought truth by cross-examining people who were reputed to have it: that is, those who knew something—craftsmen, poets, and politicians. His conversations with them always ended the same way—by demonstrating that, apart from technical information and skills, they had little knowledge of the fundamental principles of human behavior. It is not surprising that Athenians, whose opinions were challenged by his rigorous logical critiques, concluded that he was trying to undermine their confidence in the beliefs and values on which the *polis* was based. Socrates also made enemies by failing to conceal his contempt for democracy—a system of government that he believed empowered the ignorant to make important decisions about things of which they knew nothing.

In 399 B.C.E. Athens, its confidence shaken by the loss of the Peloponnesian War, decided that it could no longer tolerate Socrates. He was condemned to death on charges that implied that he was undercutting the traditions on which the survival of the *polis* depended. He was given a chance to escape, but Plato says that he refused because of his respect for the laws of the city. In taking this stand Socrates demonstrated that he was not a Sophist or an irresponsible skeptic. He accepted that the laws of the *polis* were more than arbitrary human conventions that could be ignored whenever they proved inconvenient. What he had been unable to prove by rational argument he witnessed to by powerful example.

THE CYNICS Socrates had advocated concern with personal morality and the state of one's soul, disdain of worldly pleasure and wealth, and withdrawal from political life. After his death these ideas were developed as a program for a group of extremist philosophers called Cynics. Antisthenes (ca. 455–360 B.C.E.), a follower of Socrates, was the first, but the most famous was Diogenes of Sinope (ca. 400–325 B.C.E.), whom Plato described as Socrates gone mad.

Diogenes believed that happiness was achieved by satisfying natural needs in the simplest and most direct way. He dismissed all the constraints of civilized behavior as nothing more than arbitrary social convention and reveled in conduct that illustrated his contempt for the artifice of civilization and society. He begged for his bread, wore rags, lived in a tub, performed intimate acts of personal hygiene in public, and ridiculed religious observances.

Although the Cynics claimed to follow Socrates, they contradicted some of his beliefs. Socrates said that virtue was a matter of knowledge—that people do wrong only through ignorance of what is right. The Cynics, on the other hand, argued that wisdom and happiness derived from habits of living, not from knowledge. Where Socrates had criticized but ultimately defended the *polis*, the Cynics abandoned it. When Diogenes was asked about his citizenship, he answered that he was *kosmopolites*, "a citizen of the world."

PLATO Plato (429–347 B.C.E.), the most important of Socrates' associates, is the prime example of the pupil who becomes greater than his master. Plato was the first systematic philosopher—the first to lay out a consistent worldview that provided a context for all fundamental questions. He was also a brilliant writer. His twenty-six philosophical discussions—most cast in the form of dialogues—are artistic masterpieces that make the analysis of complicated philosophical ideas dramatic and entertaining.

Plato, like other members of his aristocratic Athenian family, planned a career in politics, but Socrates' execution discouraged him. He made two trips to Sicily, where he hoped that the tyrants of Syracuse (Dionysius I and II) would allow him to guide them in building a model state. When this project failed, he returned to Athens to found the Academy (386 B.C.E.), a center for research and a school for training statesmen and citizens. The Academy survived until a Christian government closed it in the sixth century C.E.

Like Socrates and unlike the radical Sophists, Plato believed in the *polis*. He thought that it was consistent with human nature and was an instrument for creating good people. Socrates' insistence that virtue was a kind of knowledge led Plato, however, to reject democracy as an ideal form of government for a *polis*. Justice, Plato said, consists in each man doing that to which he is best suited by nature. The true knowledge on which virtue is based is beyond most people. It is *episteme* (i.e., science), a wisdom achieved by only a few highly trained and specially gifted individuals. Plato believed that these persons should serve society as "philosopher kings." Only they could be trusted with political power, for only they were capable of subordinating private interests to the good of the community. Only they could restore harmony to the *polis* by eliminating the causes of strife: private property, the family, and every personal concern that distracts individuals from the public good.

Concern for the redemption of the *polis* was central to Plato's philosophy. Since he believed that the survival of the *polis* depended on its ability to produce good citizens, he felt that he had to define goodness—and since he believed that goodness was a kind of knowledge, he had to work out a theory of knowledge. This led him into the realm of metaphysics and culminated in the birth of systematic philosophy.

ARISTOTLE Aristotle (384–322 B.C.E.) was born at Stagirus in the Chalcidice, the son of the physician to the court of Macedon. As a youth he studied in Plato's Academy and remained in Athens until Plato's death. He then went to Assos and Mytilene in Asia Minor to conduct research in marine biology. In 342 B.C.E., he accepted an appointment as tutor to Alexander, son of King Philip of Macedon, and in 336 B.C.E., he returned to Athens to found his own school, the Lyceum or the *Peripatos*, a reference to a covered walkway on its grounds. (It was this that caused Aristotle's disciples to be dubbed the Peripatetics). After Alexander's death in 323 B.C.E., the Greeks turned against the Macedonians, and Aristotle found it wise to leave Athens. He died at Chalcis in Euboea a year later.

The program of the Lyceum was different from that of the Academy. Plato's students were preoccupied with mathematics; Aristotle was interested in gathering, ordering, and analyzing data relating to all fields of human knowledge. He and his students assembled collections of materials to support various scientific studies. The range of his interests is astonishing. He wrote on logic, physics, astronomy, biology, ethics, rhetoric, literary criticism, and politics.

Aristotle began the study of every subject the same way—by collecting empirical evidence. Sometimes the evidence was physical; sometimes it was anecdotal—a garnering of common opinions. The evidence was then rationally ana-lyzed to see if it could be consistently explained and if it revealed any general principles. Like Plato, Aristotle viewed things teleologically; that is, he explained things in terms of their ultimate ends or purposes. Plato described these ends as universal ideas or forms—transcendent realities that shaped the world but which people could not directly experience. Aristotle, however, inferred the purposes of most things from their behavior in the world. The most striking characteristic of his philosophy is its common sense. In his view, matter existed to achieve an end, and it evolved until it fully realized the form (i.e., the idea) that made it intelligible as what it was. Being was a constant process of moving from matter to form, from potentiality to actuality.

This metaphysical model is at the heart of Aristotle's thinking about the *polis*. He rejected the Sophists' claim that social life was a convention that frustrated the true nature of individuals. He believed that the *polis* was natural because it was necessary for the realization of human potential—that is, life as a social being. Since human survival and happiness depended on group life, the fundamental purpose of the *polis* was not economic or military. It was moral. It made life good.

Aristotle was less interested in theorizing about the perfect state than in designing the best state practically possible. To determine what this was, he assembled a collection of 158 constitutions. (Only the *Constitution of the Athenians* has come down to us.) He concluded that a *politeia*—not the best constitution but the one best suited to most states—was characterized by moderation. It was dominated neither by the rich nor the poor but the middle class. A large middle class was essential for political stability, for this class was not tempted to the arrogance of the rich nor infected by the malice that resentment of their circumstances creates in the poor. Stable constitutions were also usually "mixed"—that is, they blended aspects of democracy and oligarchy.

All the political thinkers of the fourth century B.C.E. recognized that the *polis* was in danger, and all hoped to save it. All recognized the economic and social troubles that threatened it, but few made such realistic proposals for its reform as Aristotle. It is ironic that the ablest defense of the *polis* came on the eve of its demise.

The Hellenistic World

The term *Hellenistic* was coined in the nineteenth century to describe the period in Greek history that began when a Macedonian dynasty conquered both Greece and the Persian Empire. This event brought elements of Greek and Middle Eastern cultures together to create a new, more cosmopolitan civilization.

The Macedonian Conquest

The quarrels among the Greeks made them vulnerable to conquest by Macedon, the northernmost of the mainland Greek states. By Greek standards Macedon was a backward, semibarbaric land. It had no *poleis* but was ruled by a king who, like Homer's Agamemnon, depended upon the cooperation of his nation's powerful aristocratic families. Hampered by constant wars with barbarian tribes on its northern frontier, internal strife, loose organization, and lack of money, Macedon played no great part in Greek affairs until the fourth century B.C.E.

PHILIP OF MACEDON   The Macedonian king who conquered Greece was Philip II (359–336 B.C.E.). As a youth, Philip had spent several years (367–364 B.C.E.) as a hostage in Thebes. There he learned much about Greek politics and warfare under the tutelage of Epaminondas, the general who defeated Sparta. Philip's talent and training made him the ablest king in Macedonian history. He solidified his hold on his throne, pacified the tribes on his frontiers, and challenged Athens' dominance of the northern Aegean. When the conquest of Amphipolis gave him control of the gold and silver mines of Mount Pangaeus, he used this wealth to elevate the level of Macedonian culture. He founded new cities, won friends abroad, and turned his army into the world's finest fighting force.

THE MACEDONIAN ARMY   Philip's army was more professional than the amateur armies of citizen-soldiers who fought for the individual *poleis*. Its infantry was recruited from Macedon's sturdy farming class and feisty hill people. Infantrymen were armed with thirteen-foot pikes instead of the *hoplite's* more common nine-foot weapon. This enabled them to spread out and form a more open, flexible phalanx than was customary. The Macedonian cavalry was recruited from the aristocracy. Its members, the "Companions," lived with the king and developed a special loyalty to him. Philip also employed mercenaries who knew the latest tactics and were familiar with the most sophisticated siege machinery. Altogether, he could field an army of about 40,000 men.

THE INVASION OF GREECE   The Greeks themselves gave Philip the excuse he needed to intervene in their affairs. The people of Thessaly invited Philip to assist them in a war against the Phocians. Philip won the war, treacherously occupied Thessaly, and marched on Thrace to take control of the Aegean's northern coast and the Hellespont.

These actions threatened the vital interests of Athens, but although Athens had a formidable fleet of 300 ships, it was not the Athens of 350 B.C.E. or the Athens of Pericles. Its population was smaller than in the fifth century B.C.E., and it had no empire from which to draw funds to support a major war. Consequently, the Athenians were uncertain how to respond to Philip.

Eubulus, a financial official and conservative political leader, favored a cautious policy of cooperation with Philip in the hope that his aims were limited and posed no real threat to Athens. Isocrates (436–338 B.C.E.), the head of an important rhetorical school in Athens, saw Philip as the savior of Greece. He believed that Philip could provide the unity and leadership the Greeks needed to launch a Panhellenic campaign against Persia and solve the economic, social, and political problems that had brought poverty and civil strife to Greece since the end of the Peloponnesian War. The leading opponent to appeasement of Macedon was Demosthenes (384–322 B.C.E.), one of the greatest orators in Greek history. He was convinced that Philip was a danger to Greece, and he ultimately persuaded Athens to join Thebes in opposing Macedonian expansion. In 338 B.C.E., a cavalry charge that Philip's eighteen-year-old son Alexander led in the battle of Chaeronea defeated the allied forces and made Philip master of Greece.

THE MACEDONIAN GOVERNMENT OF GREECE   The Macedonian settlement of Greek affairs was not as harsh as many had feared. Athens was spared on condition that it accept Macedonian leadership, and Macedonian garrisons were stationed around Greece to guard against rebellions. In 338 B.C.E. Philip called representatives of the Greek states to Corinth where he announced the formation of a federation, the League of Corinth. The constitution of the league promised autonomy, freedom from tribute and garrisons, and cooperation in suppressing piracy and civil war. This was an arrangement that enabled the Greeks to submit with dignity to Macedonian occupation. The defeat at Chaeronea had ended Greek freedom and the autonomy of the *polis.*

Philip chose Corinth as the seat of his new confederacy because it was at Corinth that the Greeks had gathered almost 150 years earlier to plan their strategy for the Persian Wars. It was there also, in 337 B.C.E., that Philip announced his intent to restore the glory of Greece by renewing war with Persia. This was a promise he failed to keep, for in the spring of 336 B.C.E., as he was about to launch this campaign, he was assassinated.

Alexander the Great

THE CONQUEST OF THE PERSIAN EMPIRE Alexander III (356–323 B.C.E.), who came to be known as "the Great," was only twenty when he ascended his father's throne, but he was determined to carry out his father's plan for invading Persia. The Persian Empire was vast and its resources enormous, but it was not an impossible target. Its size and the diversity of its subjects made it hard to control, and its rulers struggled constantly with threats to their far-flung frontiers and intrigues within their court. At the time of Philip II's death in 336 B.C.E., Persia's new king, Darius III, was inexperienced. But with a navy that dominated the sea, a huge army, and vast wealth, Darius was a formidable opponent.

In 334 B.C.E. Alexander crossed the Hellespont into Asia. His army consisted of only about 30,000 infantry and 5,000 cavalry. He had little money, and his opponents had command of the sea. He could not risk heading far inland until he had neutralized the Persian navy, but he needed a quick victory to inspire his men with confidence in his leadership and to win the booty needed to pay them. Memnon, the commander of the Persian navy, proposed an excellent strategy for defeating the Greeks: retreat, scorch the earth, avoid all but guerrilla engagements, and

deprive the enemy of supplies. Pride, however, led the Persians to reject his advice and give Alexander what he hoped for.

The Persians offered Alexander battle at the Granicus River on the coast of Asia Minor. Alexander led a cavalry charge across the river into the teeth of the enemy and nearly lost his life. His courage, however, inspired his soldiers, and the victory opened all of Asia Minor to conquest by the Greeks.

In 333 B.C.E., Alexander marched out of Asia Minor into Syria to meet the main Persian army under Darius. At Issus, Alexander led a cavalry charge that broke the Persian line, but instead of pursuing Darius as he retreated inland, Alexander continued south along the coast, taking Persia's naval bases. When he arrived in Egypt, he was greeted as liberator and proclaimed pharaoh. Like all of Egypt's divine kings, he was proclaimed a son of Re, the god who, as head of the Egyptian pantheon, the Greeks equated with Zeus.

In the spring of 331 B.C.E., Alexander marched into Mesopotamia to confront an army Darius had assembled at Gaugamela (near the ancient Assyrian city of Nineveh). Once again the Persian line broke, and Darius was forced to flee. Alexander occupied Babylon, and in January 330 B.C.E., he entered Persepolis, the Persian capital. Conquest of Persia's treasure cities ended Alexander's financial problems, and the gold he showered on his troops put vast sums of money into circulation—a development whose economic effects were felt for centuries.

Since the new regime could not be secure while Darius was at large, Alexander again set out to capture him. But the Persian nobles deprived the Greeks of that prize. Having lost faith in Darius, they killed him and proclaimed Bessus, one of his relatives, his successor. Alexander pursued Bessus into the east, captured him, and pushed on to the frontiers of India.

Near Samarkand, in the land of the Scythians, he founded the city of Alexandria Eschate ("Farthest Alexandria"), one of many cities Alexander created as part of a plan to secure the future of the empire. Alexander hoped to hold the empire he was winning by scattering Greeks through it and amalgamating its diverse peoples. To set an example, he took his first wife, a princess named Roxane from a remote province called Bactria. He also added 30,000 of her young countrymen to his army.

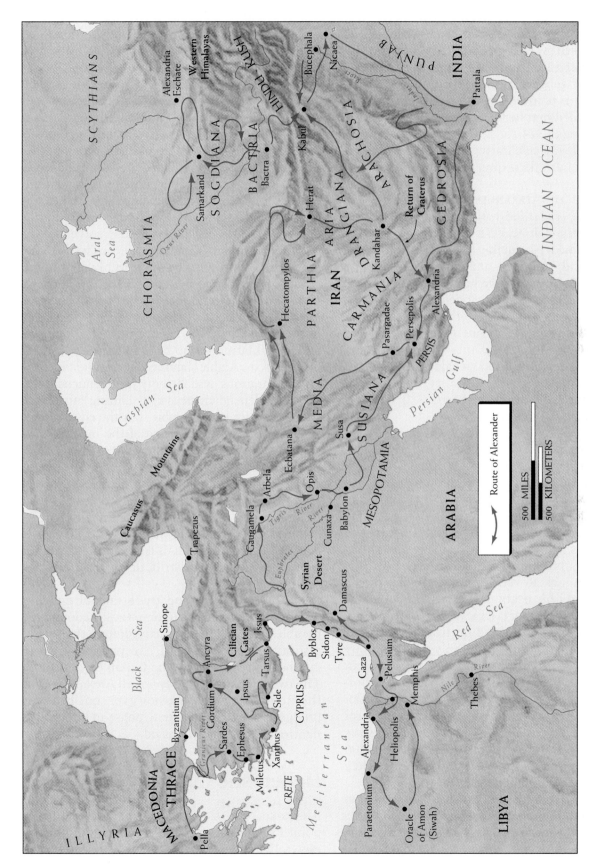

Map 3–2 ALEXANDER'S CAMPAIGNS *Starting from the Macedonian capital at Pella, Alexander marched his army to the Indus Valley before they persuaded him to return to Babylon where he died.*

In 327 B.C.E., the Greeks crossed the Khyber Pass and entered the territory of modern Pakistan. Porus, the native king, was subdued, but Alexander still was not content. He ordered the army farther east to find the river called Ocean that Greek geographers believed encircled the world. At this point his exhausted men mutinied and demanded that he take them home for a rest. By the spring of 324 B.C.E., they were back at the Persian Gulf and celebrating, in true Macedonian style, with a drunken spree.

THE DEATH OF ALEXANDER   Alexander, at age thirty-three, was filled with plans for the future, but in Babylon in June 323 B.C.E., he succumbed to a fever and died. He quickly became the subject of myth, legend, romance, and controversy among historians. Some have seen him as a man of grand and noble vision who transcended the narrow limits of Greek and Macedonian ethnocentrism, a visionary who sought to create a great world state based on the common humanity all peoples share. Others have depicted him as a calculating despot, given to drunken brawls, brutality, and murder. The truth probably lies in between.

The Successors

Nobody was prepared for Alexander's sudden death, and he had no obvious successor. He was one of history's greatest generals and a man of rare organizational talent, but even he would have had difficulty holding together the vast empire he had created. His nearest adult male relative, a weak-minded half-brother, could never have filled his shoes. Although Roxane, his queen, bore him a son soon after his death, an infant heir could not administer Alexander's legacy. The Macedonian generals, therefore, divided up responsibility for ruling the empire—allegedly only until the boy came of age. Conflicting ambitions soon had them at each other's throats, and in the battles that followed all of the direct members of the Macedonian royal house were destroyed. The deaths of Roxane and her son in 310 B.C.E. removed the last restraints on the surviving governors, and in 306 B.C.E. and 305 B.C.E. they declared the lands they ruled independent kingdoms.

Three Macedonian dynasties divided up Alexander's empire. Ptolemy I (ca. 367–283 B.C.E.) claimed Egypt and founded its thirty-first dynasty. (The famous queen Cleopatra, who died in 30 B.C.E., was the last of the Ptolemies.) Seleucus I (ca. 358–280 B.C.E.) created the Seleucid dynasty that ruled Mesopotamia, and Antigonus I (382–301 B.C.E.) established the Antigonid family that reigned over Asia Minor and Macedon.

For about seventy-five years after Alexander's death the world economy expanded. The money that Alexander had loosed to circulate increased the level of economic activity, and the opening of vast new territories to Greek trade, the increased demand for Greek products, the enhanced availability of goods, and the enlightened economic policies of the Hellenistic kings all helped the growth of commerce. Problems of overpopulation on the Greek mainland were also solved by opportunities to emigrate to new cities in the east.

The new prosperity was not evenly distributed. Urban Greeks, Macedonians, and Hellenized natives—the upper and middle classes—lived comfortable, even luxurious, lives, while the standard of living for rural laborers declined. The independent small farmers who had built the early *poleis* disappeared. Arable land was consolidated into large plantations, and farmers were reduced to the status of dependent peasants. During prosperous times their lot was bearable, but the costs of continuing wars and the effects of the inflation produced by the influx of Persian gold steadily eroded their position. Kings bore down heavily on the middle class, which shifted the burden to the peasants and the city laborers. These people responded by slowing their work and by striking. In parts of Greece, where economic pressures brought clashes between rich and poor and demands for the abolition of debt and the redistribution of land, civil war returned.

Internal tensions and the strain of endemic warfare rendered the Hellenistic kingdoms vulnerable to invasion. By the middle of the second century B.C.E. they had all, except for Egypt, succumbed to conquest by the Italian city of Rome. The two centuries that separated Alexander from the Roman Empire had, however, not been unproductive. A powerful new phase in Greek civilization had begun to unfold.

Hellenistic Culture

Alexander the Great's life marked a turning point in the history of Greek literature, philosophy, religion, and art. His empire and its successor kingdoms ended the role that the *polis* had played in shaping Greek culture. *Poleis* continued to exist throughout the Hellenistic period, but they were mere shadows of the vital *poleis* of the Hellenic era. Hellenistic cities were not free, sovereign states but municipal towns submerged within great military empires.

As the freedoms central to the life of the *polis* faded, Greeks lost interest in finding political solutions for their problems. They abandoned public affairs and resorted to religion, philosophy, and magic for help in dealing with their private hopes and fears. The confident humanism of the fifth century B.C.E. gave way to a kind of resignation to fate, a recognition of helplessness before forces too great for humans to manage.

Philosophy

Athens survived as the center of philosophical studies during the Hellenistic era. Plato's Academy and Aristotle's Lyceum continued to operate and were joined by new schools advocating the popular new philosophies of Epicureanism and Stoicism.

The Lyceum abandoned the scientific interests of its founder and became a center for literary and historical studies. The Academy was even more radically transformed. It endorsed Skepticism, a critique of the weaknesses of all schools of philosophy that led to the conclusion that nothing could be known. Skeptics urged their students, in lieu of better options, to accept conventional morality and not to try to change the world. The Cynics drew a more radical conclusion from the inevitability of human ignorance. They denounced convention and advocated a life in accordance with nature's cruder impulses. Neither of these views appealed much to the middle-class city-dwellers of the third century B.C.E. who were searching for the kind of dignity and meaning that the *polis* had provided for the lives of their ancestors.

THE EPICUREANS Like many thinkers of his day, Epicurus of Athens (342–271 B.C.E.) doubted that human beings could obtain knowledge. The atomists, Democritus and Leucippus, convinced him that the world was nothing more than a swirl of physical particles continually falling through a void. Knowledge was nothing more than a stream of impressions that atoms left on human sense organs. Since Epicurus believed that the atoms did not obey any laws of motion but swerved in arbitrary, unpredictable ways, he concluded that experience of their movements could not help anyone find truth or certainty. Philosophers, he argued, should abandon pursuit of knowledge of the world and seek insights that would promote human happiness. Epicurus believed that philosophy could free people from things like the fear of death. If people were helped to understand that death was merely the dispersal of the atoms of a body and soul, they would realize that nothing of themselves survived to suffer pain or loss. The proper pursuit of humankind, Epicurus argued, was pleasure—in the sense of *ataraxia*, a state of being undisturbed by any extreme feeling, either good or bad. The happiest people were those who withdrew from the world, avoided business concerns, and stayed free of the duties of family and public life. Epicurus's ideal was the genteel, disciplined selfishness of intellectual men of means. It was a dream not calculated to be widely attractive.

THE STOICS Soon after Epicurus began teaching in Athens, Zeno of Citium (335–263 B.C.E.) established the Stoic school, which was named for the *stoa poikile,* the Painted Portico in the Athenian marketplace where Zeno taught his disciples. Zeno and his successors owed much, by way of the Cynics, to Socrates and to Eastern thinkers.

Like the Epicureans, the Stoics sought the happiness of the individual, but Stoic philosophy relied more on religious images. Stoics believed that human fulfillment lay in living in harmony with nature, and Stoics claimed that nature was a manifestation of divine *logos,* an eternal principle of reason. Every human being had a spark of this divine "fire," and at death it returned to its source in the eternal spirit. Like individual living beings, the whole world was alive and faced periodic destruction and rebirth.

Stoics held that humans experienced happiness when they lived virtuous lives. A sense of fulfillment was produced by living in accordance with natural law. This required one to understand which things in life were good and evil and which were morally "indifferent." Things such as prudence, justice, courage, and temperance were good. Things such as folly, injustice, and cowardice were evil. Some things—such as life, health, pleasure, beauty, strength, and wealth—

were morally neutral, for by themselves they did not produce either happiness or misery. Misery was the result of passion, a disease of the soul that arose from attaching the self to the wrong things. Happy people achieved *apatheia*, freedom from passion.

The Stoics saw the world as a single *polis* in which all people were equally children of God. Despite the fact that politics invited preoccupation with things that were morally indifferent, many Stoics led active public lives. Their intent was to live in accordance with the divine will by fatalistically accepting their places in life and dispassionately playing out the roles in which they found themselves. This fit well with the reality of post-Alexandrian societies in which docile submission was more important than active participation.

Literature

Alexandria became the center of literary production in the third and second centuries B.C.E. Its intellectuals, unlike the creative thinkers who were citizens of a *polis*, were more preoccupied with past than current affairs, for they understood that they had little political influence. The Ptolemies supported a "museum," a great research institute that collected Greek literature of every kind for scholars to edit and interpret. Some of this work was dry and petty, but it helped to preserve the monuments of classical literature.

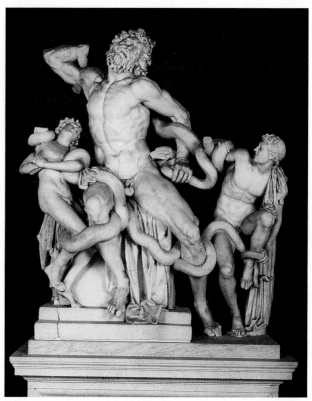

This is a Roman copy of one of the masterpieces of Hellenistic sculpture, the Laocoon. According to legend, Laocoon was a priest who warned the Trojans not to take the Greeks' wooden horse within their city. This sculpture depicts his punishment. Great serpents sent by the goddess Athena, who was on the side of the Greeks, devoured Laocoon and his sons before the horrified people of Troy. Musei Vaticani

Architecture and Sculpture

Hellenistic kings could afford to be lavish patrons of artists and architects as well as scholars. They built many new cities and rebuilt old ones, usually on the efficient grid plan introduced in the fifth century B.C.E. by Hippodamus of Miletus. The famous artists who traveled the world, fulfilling royal commissions, created a kind of uniform international style. It featured sentimental, emotional realism rather than the idealism that had been popular during the age of the *polis*.

Mathematics and Science

The most spectacular and remarkable intellectual achievements of the Hellenistic age were in mathematics and science. The scholars of Alexandria amassed the greater part of the scientific knowledge available to the Western world until the scientific revolution of the sixteenth and seventeenth centuries B.C.E.

Euclid's *Elements*, which was written early in the third century B.C.E., remained the standard textbook of plane and solid geometry until recent times. Archimedes of Syracuse (ca. 287–212 B.C.E.) explored the principles of the lever in mechanics and invented hydrostatics. Heraclides of Pontus (ca. 390–310 B.C.E.) advanced a heliocentric theory of the universe that was fully developed by Aristarchus of Samos (ca. 310–230 B.C.E.). Unfortunately, however, since Hellenistic technology could not provide data to confirm their intuitions, they did not take hold. A geocentric model advanced by Hipparchus of Nicaea (born ca. 190 B.C.E.) and refined by Ptolemy of Alexandria (second century C.E.) acquired currency and remained dominant until the work of Copernicus in the sixteenth century

C.E. The scholars of the age knew that Earth was round, and Eratosthenes of Cyrene (ca. 275–195 B.C.E.) calculated its circumference within about 200 miles. His maps were more accurate than those that were standard in the Middle Ages.

In Perspective

The achievements of Greece's Classical Period were unparalleled. To a great degree they sprang from the unique social environment created by the poleis, *the independent city-states. Democratic imperial Athens nurtured the greatest artists and intellectuals. The freedoms Athens gave its citizens bred respect for the human individual and curiosity about human potential. Philosophy, science, drama, and history were invented to explore this potential, and a naturalistic style of art was developed to celebrate the ideal human form.*

The Classical Period ended when the polis *was replaced by the great empires of the Hellenistic Age. Hellenistic civilization spread, assimilated influences from other cultures, and became a cosmopolitan phenomenon. By bringing diverse peoples together it prepared the way for Rome's empire.*

REVIEW QUESTIONS

1. How did Athens acquire an empire during the fifth century B.C.E.? Did Athens' empire offer any advantages to its subjects? Why was there resistance to Athens' efforts to unify the Greek world in the fifth and fourth centuries B.C.E.?
2. What caused the Great Peloponnesian War? What strategies did Athens and Sparta hope would bring them victory? Why did Sparta win?
3. What were the tensions that characterized Greek life in the Classical Period, and how were they reflected in its art, literature, and philosophy? How does Hellenistic art differ from art of the Classical Period?
4. Although Athens, Sparta, and Thebes each in turn tried to unite and rule the city-states of Greece, each failed. Why? What can you conclude from their examples that successful government requires?
5. How and why did Philip II conquer Greece? Why was Athens unable to stop him? Was his success due to Macedon's strength or to the weaknesses of the Greek city-states?
6. What were the consequences of Alexander the Great's early death? What were his lasting achievements? Did he consciously promote Greek civilization, or was he only an egomaniac devoted to endless conquest?

SUGGESTED READINGS

A. B. BOSWORTH, *Conquest and Empire: The Reign of Alexander the Great* (1988). An excellent, tough-minded account.

J. BUCKLER, *The Theban Hegemony, 371–362 B.C.E.* (1980). A study of Thebes at the height of its power.

W. BURKERT, *Greek Religion* (1985). A fine general study.

E. FANTHAM, H. FOLEY, N. KAMPEN, S. POMEROY, and H. A. SHAPIRO, *Women in the Classical World* (1994). A valuable survey based on written and visual evidence.

Y. GARLAN, *Slavery in Ancient Greece* (1988). An up-to-date survey.

P. GREEN, *From Alexander to Actium* (1990). A brilliant new synthesis of the Hellenistic period.

D. KAGAN, *Pericles of Athens and the Birth of Athenian Democracy* (1991). An account of the life and times of the great Athenian statesman.

D. KAGAN, *The Outbreak of the Peloponnesian War* (1969). A study of the period from the foundation of the Delian League to the coming of the Peloponnesian War that argues that war could have been avoided.

J. J. POLLITT, *Art in the Hellenistic Age* (1986). An extraordinary analysis that places the art in its historical and intellectual context.

S. POMERY, *Families in Classical and Hellenistic Greece* (1998). A valuable and thorough study of the Greek family.

B. S. STRAUSS, *Athens after the Peloponnesian War* (1987). An excellent discussion of Athens' recovery and history in the fourth century B.C.E.

G. VLASTOS, *Socrates: Ironist and Moral Philosopher* (1991). A study of the father of Western ethical philosophy.

F. W. WALBANK, *The Hellenistic World* (1981). A solid history.

Chapter 4

Rome: From Republic to Empire

KEY TOPICS

- The emergence of the Roman Republic
- The development of the republican constitution
- Roman expansion and imperialism
- The character of Roman society in the republican era
- The fall of the republic

The Romans, who started with nothing but a small village in central Italy, achieved remarkable things. They united the peoples of the Western world and maintained the longest period of peace in Western history. By adapting and spreading aspects of Greek culture through their empire, the Romans created a universal Graeco-Roman tradition that remains at the heart of Western civilization to this day.

Much of what we know of the Etruscans comes from their funerary art. This sculpture of an Etruscan couple is part of a sarcophagus. Erich Lessing/Art Resource, N.Y.

Prehistoric Italy

Italy's cultural evolution began slowly. The Paleolithic era lingered in Italy until 2500 B.C.E., and Italy did not feel the effects of the Bronze Age until 1500 B.C.E. About 1000 B.C.E., the Umbrians, Sabines, Samnites, and Latins—immigrants from the East whose Italic languages gave the peninsula its name—pioneered Italy's Iron Age. By 800 B.C.E., they had occupied the highland pastures of the Apennines, the mountain range that runs the length of Italy, and had begun to challenge earlier settlers for control of the western coastal plains.

The Etruscans

About 800 B.C.E., a mysterious people whose language was not Italic settled in Etruria (modern Tuscany) on a plain west of the Apennines between the Arno and Tiber Rivers. Although the origin of the Etruscan people is unknown, aspects of their civilization suggest Eastern roots. They had a powerful influence on the development of Rome.

Dominion

Etruscan communities were independent, self-governing city-states loosely linked in a religious confederation. Aristocratic landowners replaced kings in most cities and set up governments run by councils and annually elected magistrates. The Etruscans subjugated the peoples they conquered in Italy and became the militarized ruling class of their nation. They took to the sea as traders and pirates and competed with the other maritime powers of the western Mediterranean, the Carthaginians of north Africa and Italy's Greek colonists.

In the seventh and sixth centuries B.C.E., the Etruscans extended their power north to Italy's Po Valley and overseas to the islands of Corsica and Elba. They also moved south into Latium (a region that included the small town of Rome) and Campania (a plain that the Greeks of Naples had begun to colonize). These conquests were the work of independent Etruscan chieftains who rarely supported each other. As a result, they were short-lived.

Etruscan power peaked before 500 B.C.E. By 400 B.C.E., Celts from Gaul (modern France) had driven the Etruscans from the Po Valley, an area the Romans later called Cisalpine Gaul (i.e., "This-side-of-the-Alps" Gaul). Gradually the cities of Etruria lost their independence. Their language ceased to be a living tongue, but their culture was not forgotten. It had a profound effect on Rome.

Cultural Influences

Roman religion was powerfully influenced by Etruscan culture. The Romans, like the Etruscans, believed that innumerable supernatural beings had the power to intervene in human affairs. The Romans were convinced that human survival depended on understanding and placating these spirits—many of whom were evil. To divine the wills of these mysterious forces, they relied on Etruscan rites for interpreting the omens of the gods.

Roman society contrasted with Greek society in the greater freedom that it accorded women. This, too, may have been the result of Etruscan influences. Unlike Greek women, Etruscan wives appeared in public. They were guests at banquets with their husbands. They attended and participated in athletic contests. Many could read and write. Tomb inscriptions mention the mother as well as the father of the deceased, and Etruscan art depicts husbands and wives in poses that suggest respectful, loving relationships.

MAP 4–1 ANCIENT ITALY *This map indicates the geographical positions of Rome and its neighbors in the period before Roman expansion.*

Royal Rome

The Latin peoples who settled Rome may have been attracted by its location. Rome was established fifteen miles from the sea at the point where the Tiber River emerges from the foothills of the Apennines. Many trails converged here, for just southwest of Rome's Capitoline Hill an island made the Tiber fordable. Rome's site destined the city to become the center for Italy's inland communication and trade.

Government

Rome's potential was not realized until the sixth century B.C.E., when Etruscan kings established themselves in Rome and conquered most of Latium. Although one family monopolized the royal office, Roman kingship was technically elective. The Roman Senate, an aristocratic council, had to approve a candidate for the throne, and only the assembly of the Roman people could bestow on him his unique power—the *imperium*, the right to enforce commands by fines, arrests, and corporal or capital punishment. The king was Rome's chief priest, high judge, and supreme military leader.

According to legend, Rome's Senate originated when Romulus, Rome's founder, chose 100 of Rome's leading men to advise him. The early Senate had no formal executive or legislative authority. It met only when the king convened it to ask for advice. In practice, however, the Senate was very influential. It was composed of the most powerful men in the state—men a king could not safely ignore.

The curiate assembly, an organization to which all citizens belonged, was the third organ of government. It met only when summoned by the king, and he set its agenda and decided who could address it. Its job was to listen to and ratify the king's decrees. Romans voted, not as individuals, but as members of groups. Citizens were registered in thirty groups, and each group had a single vote that was cast according to the will of its majority.

The Family

Family organizations were the basic units of Roman society. The head of a family was its "king" in the sense that he held *imperium* over

Busts of a Roman couple from the period of the Republic. Although some have identified the individuals as Cato the Younger and his daughter Porcia, no solid evidence confirms this claim. Bust of Cato and Porcia. Roman sculpture. Vatican Museums, Vatican State. Scala/Art Resource NY

all its members. Like the king who presided over the state cult, a father supervised his family's most important religious rites, the daily worship of its ancestors. Like the king, a father had the power to execute his dependents (even his adult children) or sell them into slavery. The male head of a household had less authority over his wife, for she was protected by the family of her birth and could not be divorced unless convicted of certain serious offenses by a court of her male blood relatives. A Roman wife was greatly respected as the administrator of her husband's household. She controlled access to its storerooms, kept its accounts, supervised its slaves, and reared its children. She was also a respected adviser on all questions concerning the family.

Women

Roman society was male dominated and hierarchical. Throughout their lives women were required to have male guardians to conduct legal business on their behalf. Women could own and dispose of property and enter into contracts but only with the approval of these guardians. There were two forms of marriage in early Rome that transferred a woman from the *manus* (i.e., "hand") of her father to that of her husband. Gradually a third kind of marriage developed in which a bride's father retained his power of *manus* over her after her wedding. This gave a

woman more freedom from her husband and more inheritance rights from her father. To preserve the arrangement a woman had to spend at least three consecutive nights a year outside her husband's home.

Clientage

The head of a wealthy family could extend its influence by providing patronage to dependents called clients. Roman clientage was a formal, legally recognized institution. A patron provided a client with physical and legal protection and often with economic assistance. A client might subsist on daily handouts, receive a grant of land, become a tenant farmer, or labor on his patron's estate. In return a client fought for his patron, voted as his patron ordered, and did any jobs that were requested of him. Ambitious members of the upper classes might even become clients of great families with powerful political machines in order to further their careers.

Patricians and Plebeians

From the start of Rome's history, Roman families were divided into two hereditary classes. The patricians were the upper class, and they originally monopolized political authority. Only they could serve as priests, sit in the Senate, and hold office. The lower plebeian class may have sprung from families of small farmers, laborers, and artisans who were clients of the patricians. Wealth alone did not define the classes. Some plebeians were rich, and incompetence and bad luck sometimes impoverished patricians.

The Republic

According to Roman tradition, in 509 B.C.E. an atrocity committed by a member of the royal family sparked a revolt that drove the last Etruscan king from the city. The patricians chose not to appoint another king but to establish a republic.

Constitution

THE CONSULS   The Roman Republic had a very conservative unwritten constitution. At the start, it did little more than transfer many of the duties and trappings of monarchy to elected magistrates. Two patricians were annually chosen to be consuls and vested with *imperium*. Like the former kings, they led the army, oversaw the state religion, and sat as judges. They even used the traditional symbols of royalty—purple robes, ivory chairs, and lictors (guards who accompanied them bearing *fasces*, bundles of rods wrapped around an axe to signify the power to discipline and execute). A consul was, however, not a king, for he remained in office for only a year and had an equal, a colleague who could prevent him from taking independent action. Consular *imperium* was also limited. Consuls could execute citizens who were serving with the army outside the city, but in Rome citizens had the right to appeal all cases involving capital punishment to the popular assembly.

The checks on the consular office discouraged initiative, swift action, and change. This was what a conservative, aristocratic republic wanted. But since a divided command could create serious problems for an army in the field, the Romans usually sent only one consul into battle or assigned consuls sole command on alternate days. If this did not work, the consuls could, with the advice of the Senate, step down and appoint a single dictator. His term of office was limited to six months, but his *imperium* was valid everywhere and unlimited by any right of appeal.

These devices worked well enough for a small city whose wars were short skirmishes fought near home. But as Rome's wars grew longer and more difficult, adaptations had to be made. In 325 B.C.E. proconsulships were invented to extend the terms of consuls serving in the field. This maintained continuity of command during a long war, but it ran the risk of allowing ambitious men to monopolize political authority.

Consuls were assisted by financial officers called quaestors, and a need for more military commanders led to the introduction of other aides called praetors. A praetor's primary function was judicial, but he could also be granted a general's *imperium* and have his term of service in the field extended beyond a year. In the second half of the fifth century B.C.E., the consuls' responsibility for enrolling and keeping track of citizens was delegated to new officials, two censors. Since they determined the status and the tax liability of each citizen, they had to be men of unimpeachable reputation. They were usually senior senators who viewed the censorship as the pinnacle of their careers. By the fourth century B.C.E. censors had the right to expel from the Senate members whose conduct disgraced senatorial dignity.

THE SENATE AND THE ASSEMBLY   The Senate was the only deliberative body continuously in session in the Roman Republic. Senators were prominent patricians, often leaders of clans and patrons with many clients. The Senate controlled the state's finances and foreign policy, and its advice was not lightly ignored by magistrates or by popular assemblies.

The centuriate assembly—the name for the Roman army when it was convened to deliberate rather than fight—was the early republic's most important popular assembly. It elected the consuls and several other magistrates, voted on bills the Senate put before it, made decisions of war and peace, and served as a court of appeal for citizens convicted of serious offenses. The centuriate assembly was named for the "centuries" in which its members voted. A century was, in theory, a unit of 100 soldiers. Because each man bought his own equipment, centuries grouped citizens into classes according to wealth (i.e., according to the kind of weapons they could afford to buy). Each century cast a single vote, and votes were tallied beginning with the centuries that had the most expensive equipment, those of the cavalry.

Family Honor: A Roman Patrician with the Busts of His Ancestors

A Roman Patrician with the busts of his ancestors. First century C.E. Musei Capitolini, Rome/Scala/Art Resource NY

No large Roman sculptures survive much before the first century B.C.E., but literary sources suggest that long before then it was the custom to honor leaders by erecting statues of them in public places. This statue from the late first century C.E. is of an unknown aristocrat depicted with what are probably the busts of his father and grandfather.

When a nobleman died, his heirs had a likeness of his face made in wax. At funerals men marched in processions wearing all the masks in a family's collection so that the deceased's ancestors seemed literally to attend his burial rites. The oration at the funeral praised the achievements of each famous member of the departed's family in order to inspire the young men present to strive to equal the deeds of early generations.

Since wax images did not last, by the first century B.C.E. it was customary to have them copied in marble. Roman sculptors were heavily influenced by the Etruscans and later the Hellenistic Greeks, but these commemorative statues had a style of their own. They did not depict individual character and psychology but conformed to a cultural ideal of a stern, serious nobleman who was a responsible family man and a dutiful citizen.

Sources: Polybius 6.53, Janson; *Art History*, pp. 188–190. D. Kleiner, *Roman Sculpture* (New Haven: Yale University Press, 1992).

THE STRUGGLE OF THE ORDERS   Plebeians were barred from all political and religious offices in the early days of the republic. They could not serve as judges. They did not even know the law, for the law was an oral tradition maintained by patrician magistrates. When Rome acquired new land by conquest, patricians were situated to reward themselves most generously. They dominated the assemblies and the Senate, and they refused to sanction marriages outside their caste that would have permitted at least the most wealthy plebeian families to share their privileges.

The plebeians responded to the intransigence of the patricians by launching the "struggle of the orders," a fight for political, legal, and social equality that lasted for 200 years. Plebeians had a strong position from which to negotiate with the patricians, for plebeians made up a large part of the republic's army. According to tradition, the plebeians discovered early in the republic's history how to use this to their advantage. When danger threatened, they simply withdrew from the city and refused to fight until the patricians granted them concessions.

The plebeians made progress one step at a time. They won the right to form a political organization of their own, the plebeian tribal assembly, and to elect "tribunes," officials with the power to protect plebeians from abuse by patrician magistrates. Tribunes could veto any action of a magistrate or any bill in a Roman assembly or the Senate. The protection of plebeian rights required that Rome's laws be fixed and published, and in 450 B.C.E. the first attempt to codify Rome's harsh customs resulted in something called the Twelve Tables. In 445 B.C.E. plebeians won the right to marry patricians, but they were still barred from many public offices. It was not until 367 B.C.E. that one of the consuls was allowed to be of plebeian rank. Gradually other offices, even the dictatorship and the censorship, were opened to them, and in 300 B.C.E. they were admitted to the most important priesthoods. In 287 B.C.E. the plebeians completed their triumph by securing passage of a law that made decisions of the plebeian assembly binding on all Romans.

The plebeians' victory did not make Rome a democracy. It simply cleared the way for wealthy plebeian families to enter politics and share the privileges of the patrician aristocracy. The *nobiles*, a small group of rich and powerful families

of both patrician and plebeian rank, monopolized the republic's highest offices. Since there was no secret ballot, the numerous clients of the wealthy *nobiles* could easily be intimidated into voting as their patrons ordered. This permitted the great families to build political machines and maintain their holds on offices. From 233 to 133 B.C.E. twenty-six families produced 80 percent of the consuls, and ten of those families accounted for almost 50 percent of the successful candidates. Since the politically dominant families were all represented in the Senate, the Senate became the republic's chief deliberative body. The product of the struggle of the orders was, therefore, a republican constitution dominated by a senatorial aristocracy. Most Romans accepted it, for it led Rome well in the wars that won Rome an empire.

The Conquest of Italy

Not long after the birth of the republic in 509 B.C.E., a coalition of Romans, Latins, and Greeks defeated the Etruscans and drove them out of Latium. Rome's neighbor, the Etruscan city of Veii, continued to be a problem until 392 B.C.E. when Rome destroyed Veii and doubled its size by annexing Veii's territory.

Romans used both inducements and threats to come to terms with their foes and increase their military strength. If enemies could be turned into allies, their soldiers could be added to Rome's army. If they could not, their land could be annexed and redistributed to the Roman poor. This enabled them to equip themselves for military service and join the army. Thus, the Roman poor had a stake in their republic's success, which reconciled them to its aristocratic regime. When the long siege of Veii, which kept soldiers from working their farms, prompted the Romans to begin paying men for military service, this too pleased the poor and improved the quality of the army.

GALLIC INVASION OF ITALY AND ROMAN REACTION
Early in the fourth century B.C.E. Rome suffered a dramatic setback. In 387 B.C.E. the Gauls marched south from the Po Valley, defeated the Roman army, and burned Rome. The Romans, who had fled their city, had to pay a ransom to the Gauls to obtain its return. Rome quickly recovered from this humiliation, but in 340 B.C.E.

the city's Latin neighbors formed the Latin League to try to block its expansion. In 338 B.C.E. Rome defeated and dissolved the league. The terms Rome offered set a precedent for the eventual reorganization of Italy.

ROMAN POLICY TOWARD THE CONQUERED The Romans did not destroy any of the Latin cities, nor did they treat them all alike. Some were given full Roman citizenship. Others were granted municipal privileges (i.e., internal self-government, the right to intermarry and trade with Romans—but not to take part in Roman politics unless they moved to Rome and applied for citizenship). The treaties by which other states became allies of Rome differed from city to city. Some were given rights of intermarriage and commerce with Romans; some were not. (Allied states were always forbidden to exercise these rights with one another.) Some states, but not all, were allowed local autonomy. Land was taken from some but not from others. All allies supplied troops to serve in Rome's army under Roman officers, but they did not pay taxes to Rome.

The Romans planted colonies of veteran soldiers on some of the land they annexed. The colonists retained Roman citizenship and served as a permanent garrison to deter rebellion. A network of military roads was built to connect the colonies with Rome and guarantee that a Roman army could swiftly reinforce an embattled colony should it face an uprising.

The Roman settlement of Latium illustrates the strategy that led ultimately to Rome's dominance of Italy. Rome used diplomacy and force to separate enemies. It cultivated a reputation for harsh, speedy punishment of rebels. But it was also generous to those who submitted, and the status given a newly conquered city was not a permanent sentence. Loyal allies could improve their prospects and even achieve full Roman citizenship. This gave Rome's allies a sense of being colleagues rather than subjects. Consequently, most of them remained loyal even when put to severe tests.

DEFEAT OF THE SAMNITES After the struggle with the Latin League, Rome's next challenge was a series of wars with the tough mountain people of the southern Apennines, the Samnites. Some of Rome's allies joined the Samnites, as did various Etruscans and Gauls. But most of the allies remained loyal, and by 280 B.C.E. Rome's victories over these assorted opponents had won the city mastery of central Italy.

Rome's newly expanded territory brought it into direct contact with the Greek cities of southern Italy where Roman intervention in a quarrel between two of these cities led to a war with a Greek mercenary, Pyrrhus, king of Epirus. Pyrrhus, who was probably the best general of the day, defeated the Romans twice but suffered so many casualties that he decided that he could not afford to see the war through to its conclusion. Judging his a "Pyrrhic victory" (i.e., one not worth its cost), he withdrew, leaving his Greek employers no choice but to join the Roman confederation. By 265 B.C.E. Rome ruled all of Italy south of the Po River, an area of 47,200 square miles, and its defeat of Pyrrhus had won it international recognition as a power in the Hellenistic world.

Rome and Carthage

Late in the ninth century B.C.E. the Phoenician city of Tyre had planted a colony called Carthage ("New City") on the coast of northern Africa near modern Tunis. In the sixth century B.C.E. the conquest of Tyre by the Assyrians liberated the Carthaginians to develop the opportunities offered by their strategic location. Carthage had an excellent harbor and rich lands, which it worked with slave labor.

In the sixth century B.C.E. Carthage's domain expanded westward along the coast of northern Africa past Gibraltar and eastward into Libya. Parts of southern Spain, Sardinia, Corsica, Malta, the Balearic Islands, and western Sicily were also brought into the Carthaginian Empire. Their native peoples served in the Carthaginian army and navy and paid tribute to Carthage. Carthage also claimed exclusive rights to trade in the western Mediterranean.

Rome and Carthage became entangled when Hiero, tyrant of Syracuse, attacked the Sicilian city of Messana. Messana was strategically important, for it commanded the straits between Italy and Sicily. A band of Italian mercenaries who called themselves Mamertines ("Sons of Mars") had seized the city, and Hiero wanted to evict them. The Mamertines asked Carthage for help in fending him off, and Carthage agreed. But

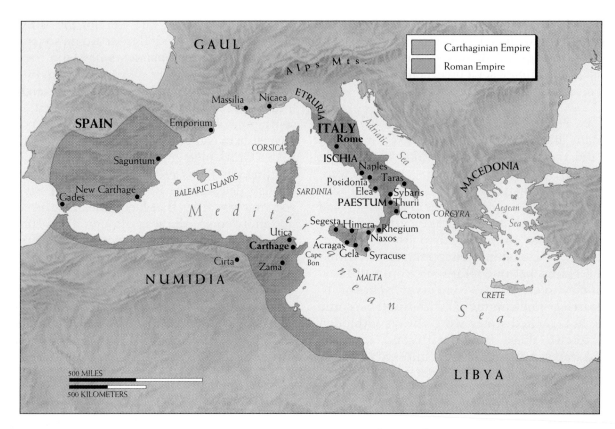

MAP 4–2   THE WESTERN MEDITERRANEAN AREA DURING THE RISE OF ROME   *This map illustrates the theater of conflict between Rome and Carthage in the third century B.C.E.*

the Mamertines then tried to check Carthage by also inviting the Romans to send them aid. Rome realized that if it did not intervene, it was ceding control of the straits and of Sicily to Carthage. Consequently, in 264 B.C.E. the assembly voted to send an army to Messana. Since the Roman term for the Carthaginians was *Poeni* or *Puni* (Latin for "Phoenician"), the ensuing conflict came to be known as the Punic War.

THE FIRST PUNIC WAR (264–241 B.C.E.)   The Romans made no progress against Carthage until they built a fleet to blockade the Carthaginian ports at the western end of Sicily. In 241 B.C.E., after a long war of attrition, Carthage capitulated. It surrendered Sicily and the islands between Italy and Sicily to Rome and agreed to pay a war indemnity. In 238 B.C.E., while Carthage struggled to put down a revolt led by mercenary soldiers whom it had failed to pay, Rome seized Sardinia and Corsica and demanded an additional indemnity. This was a provocative action that was to cost Rome a second war with Carthage.

It is hard to understand why Rome sought more territory, for the administration of lands outside of Italy created serious problems. Sicily, Sardinia, and Corsica became the first provinces in a Roman empire, for the Romans did not feel that it was possible to continue their traditional policy of extending citizenship or alliances beyond the borders of Italy. Rome turned its provinces over to military governors. And since there was no way to oversee the behavior of magistrates outside the city, there was nothing to prevent them from abusing their offices. The residents of the provinces were neither Roman citizens nor allies; they were subjects who paid tribute in lieu of serving in the army. Rome collected this tribute by "farming" out the right to gather money in the provinces to the highest bidder. Provincial governments soon became a source of corruption that undermined the machinery of the Roman Republic.

While Rome struggled to adjust to its new situation, Hamilcar Barca, the Carthaginian governor of Spain (237–229 B.C.E.), put Carthage on the road to recovery. His plan was to build a Punic empire in Spain that would make up for the lands Carthage had lost to Rome. Hasdrubal, Hamilcar's son-in-law and successor, continued his policies with such success that he alarmed the Romans. Rome reacted by imposing a treaty that obligated Carthage not to expand north of Spain's Ebro River. Hasdrubal doubtless assumed that if Carthage accepted the Ebro as its northern frontier, Rome would grant Carthage a free hand in the south. He was wrong. Within a few years the Romans had violated the Ebro treaty (at least in spirit) by accepting an offer of an alliance from the people of Saguntum, a town 100 miles south of the Ebro.

THE SECOND PUNIC WAR (218–202 B.C.E.) Hasdrubal was assassinated in 221 B.C.E., and the army chose Hannibal, the twenty-five-year-old son of Hamilcar Barca, to succeed him. Hannibal quickly consolidated and extended the Punic empire in Spain. At first, he avoided any action against Saguntum, but the Saguntines, confident of Rome's protection, began to stir up trouble for him. When Hannibal besieged and captured the town, the Romans sent an ultimatum to Carthage demanding Hannibal's surrender. Carthage refused, and Rome declared war (218 B.C.E.).

Rome had repeatedly provoked Carthage but had taken no steps to prevent Carthage from rebuilding its empire and made no plans to defend itself against a Punic attack. Hannibal exacted a high price for these blunders. In the fall of 218 B.C.E. he crossed the Alps into Italy with an army that the Gauls were eager to join. Hannibal first defeated the Romans at the Ticinus River and then crushed the joint consular armies at the Trebia River. In 217 B.C.E. he outmaneuvered and trapped another army at Lake Trasimene. He could not take Rome, however, without persuading its allies to abandon it. Despite his efforts to court them, most of them remained loyal.

Sobered by their defeats, the Romans suspended consular government and chose a dictator, Quintus Fabius Maximus. Since time and supplies were on Rome's side, his plan was to avoid pitched battles and wear Hannibal's army down by harassing its flanks. In 216 B.C.E. Hannibal tempted the Romans to abandon this strategy by attacking a grain depot at Cannae in Apulia. They took the bait, met him on the field, and suffered the worst defeat in their history. Eighty thousand Roman soldiers were killed.

The disaster at Cannae shattered Rome's prestige, and most of the allies in southern Italy (the crucial port of Syracuse in Sicily) went over to Hannibal. For the next decade no Roman army dared confront Hannibal directly. But Hannibal had neither the numbers nor the supplies to blockade walled cities, nor did he have the equipment to storm them. If the Romans refused to fight, there was little he could do to bring the war to an end.

The Romans devised a plan to defeat Hannibal by fighting him outside of Italy. Publius Cornelius Scipio (237–183 B.C.E.), whose Carthaginian victories earned him the title Africanus, set out to conquer Spain to deprive Hannibal of reinforcements from that quarter. Scipio was not yet twenty-five, but he was almost as talented a general as Hannibal. Within a few years he had taken Spain and won the Senate's permission to open a front in Africa. In 204 B.C.E. Scipio landed in Africa, defeated the Carthaginians, and forced them to order Hannibal to withdraw from Italy. Hannibal had won every battle but lost the war. His fatal error was to underestimate the determination of Rome and the loyalty of its allies. When Hannibal returned to Carthage, hostilities flared up again. In 202 B.C.E. he and Scipio met at the battle of Zama, and the day was decided by Scipio's generalship and the desertion of Hannibal's mercenaries. Rome, now the undisputed ruler of the western Mediterranean, reduced Carthage to the status of a dependent ally.

The Republic's Conquest of the Hellenistic World

THE EAST By the middle of the third century B.C.E. the three great Hellenistic kingdoms that dominated the eastern Mediterranean had achieved equilibrium. The balance of power among them was threatened, however, by the efforts of Philip V of Macedon (221–179 B.C.E.) and Antiochus III, the Seleucid ruler (223–187 B.C.E.), to expand their domains. Philip had allied himself with Carthage during the Second Punic War—provoking Rome to stir up a conflict in the Aegean called the First Macedonian War (215–205 B.C.E.). Once the Second Punic War was over, Rome determined to make sure that Macedon did not succeed Carthage as a threat to Italy. In 200 B.C.E. the Romans challenged Philip by ordering him to cease preying on the

Greek cities. Two years later the Romans demanded that Philip withdraw from Greece entirely. When Philip refused, Rome declared the Second Macedonian War. In 197 B.C.E. Flamininus, a gifted young Roman general, defeated Philip at Cynoscephalae in Thessaly, and the following year (196 B.C.E.) Flamininus surprised the Greeks by restoring the autonomy of the city-states and pulling Rome's troops out of Greece.

Philip's retreat offered Antiochus an opportunity to advance. On the pretext of freeing the Greeks from Roman domination, he invaded the Greek mainland. The Romans quickly drove him from Greece, and in 189 B.C.E., they crushed his army at Magnesia in Asia Minor. Antiochus was forced to relinquish his war-elephants and his navy and to pay a huge indemnity. Although the Romans again annexed no territory, they treated Greece and Asia Minor as protectorates in whose affairs they could freely intervene. This benign policy was to change as the influence of Cato, a conservative and ruthlessly businesslike censor, increased in Rome.

In 179 B.C.E. Perseus succeeded Philip V as king of Macedon. His popularity with democratic, revolutionary elements in the Greek cities convinced the Romans that he was a threat to the stability of the Aegean. The result was the Third Macedonian War (172–168 B.C.E.) and a harsher Roman policy. Macedon was divided into four separate republics whose citizens were forbidden to intermarry or do business with each other, and leaders of anti-Roman factions in the Greek cities were punished severely. Aemilius Paullus, the Roman general who defeated Perseus, brought so much booty home that Rome abolished some taxes on its citizens. Romans discovered that foreign campaigns could be profitable for the state, its soldiers, and its generals.

THE WEST Rome's worst abuses of power were directed not against the Greeks but against the people of the Iberian Peninsula whom the Romans considered barbarians. In 154 B.C.E. the natives of Iberia launched a fierce guerrilla campaign against their oppressors. By the time Scipio Aemilianus brought the war to a conclusion in 134 B.C.E. by taking the city of Numantia, Rome was having difficulty finding soldiers willing to go to Spain.

Significant Dates in Rome's Rise to Empire

509 B.C.E.	Republic founded
387 B.C.E.	Gauls sack Rome
338 B.C.E.	Rome defeats the Latin League
295 B.C.E.	Rome defeats the Samnites
287 B.C.E.	"Struggle of the Orders" ends
275 B.C.E.	Pyrrhus abandons Italy to Rome
264–241 B.C.E.	First Punic War
218–202 B.C.E.	Second Punic War
215–205 B.C.E.	First Macedonian War
200–197 B.C.E.	Second Macedonian War
189 B.C.E.	Rome defeats Antiochus
172–168 B.C.E.	Third Macedonian War
149–146 B.C.E.	Third Punic War
154–133 B.C.E.	Roman wars in Spain

Carthage fared much worse. Carthage scrupulously observed the terms of its treaty with Rome and posed no threat to Rome, but fear and hatred of Carthage were deeply ingrained in some Romans. Cato is said to have ended all his speeches in the Senate with a stern warning: "Besides, I think that Carthage must be destroyed." The Romans finally took advantage of a technical breach of the peace to declare war on Carthage, and in 146 B.C.E. Scipio Aemilianus destroyed the city. A province of Africa was then added to the five existing Roman provinces in Sicily, Sardinia-Corsica, Macedonia, Hither Spain, and Further Spain.

Civilization in the Early Roman Republic

The Roman attitude toward the Greeks ranged from admiration for their culture to contempt for their political squabbling and money grubbing. Conservatives such as Cato spoke contemptuously of the Greeks, but, as Roman life was transformed by association with the Greeks, even he learned Greek. The education of the Roman upper classes became bilingual, and young Roman nobles studied Greek rhetoric, literature, and sometimes philosophy. Greek refined the Latin language, and Greek literature provided models that inspired the birth and guided the development of Latin literature.

Religion

The Romans identified their ancestral gods with the Greek deities and worked Greek mythology into their own traditions. But Roman religious practice was little affected until new Eastern cults arrived in the third century B.C.E. In 205 B.C.E. the Senate approved the public worship of Cybele, the Great Mother goddess from Phrygia. But Cybele's cult involved rites that shocked and outraged conservative Romans, and the Senate soon reversed itself. For similar reasons, it banned the worship of Dionysus (i.e., Bacchus) in 186 B.C.E., and in 139 B.C.E. the Senate exiled Babylonian astrologers from Rome.

Education

In the early centuries of the Roman Republic, education was entirely the responsibility of the family. Fathers taught their sons at home. Daughters may not originally have been schooled, but they were at a later period in Rome's history. The curriculum was designed to provide males with vocational skills, to elevate their moral standards, and to inspire them with respect for Roman tradition. Boys were taught to read, write, calculate, and farm. They memorized the laws of the Twelve Tables, practiced religious rites, learned the legendary accounts of Rome's origin, and trained for military service.

HELLENIZED EDUCATION Contact with the Greeks of southern Italy in the third century B.C.E. produced momentous changes in Roman education. Greek teachers introduced the Romans to the study of language, literature, and philosophy—and to what the Romans called *humanitas,* the broad training and instruction in the critical habits of mind that are the characteristics of a liberal education.

Since Rome did not yet have a literature of its own, elementary education involved learning Greek as a preparation for the advanced study of rhetoric—the art of speaking and writing well. Philosophy was at the heart of Greek education, but the practical Romans preferred rhetoric. It was of great use in legal disputes and political life. Some important Romans were powerful advocates of Greek literature and philosophy. Scipio Aemilianus, the man who destroyed Carthage, was a patron of important Greek intellectuals—particularly the historian Polybius and the philosopher Panaetius. Conservative Romans, such as Cato the Elder, feared that Greek learning would weaken Roman moral fiber. On occasion the Senate was persuaded to expel philosophers and teachers of rhetoric from Rome, but Rome could not return to its simple agrarian past. If Romans were to deal with the sophisticated world of the Hellenistic Greeks, which they had come to dominate, they needed the new education.

In the late republic, Roman education, though still entirely private, became more formal and organized. From the ages of seven to twelve, boys went to elementary school accompanied by a Greek slave called a *paedagogus* (hence, our term *pedagogue*). He looked after them and helped them learn Greek by conversing with them. Boys learned to read, to write (on a waxed tablet with a stylus), and to do simple arithmetic with the aid of an abacus and pebbles (*calculi,* in Latin). From twelve to sixteen, boys studied Greek and Latin literature with a *grammaticus.* He gave them a liberal education that included dialectic, arithmetic, geometry, astronomy, music, and some elements of rhetoric. Some boys pursued advanced study in rhetoric. A few, such as the great orator Cicero, undertook what we might

This wall painting from the first century B.C.E. comes from the villa of Publius Fannius Synistor at Pompeii and shows a woman playing a cithera. Fresco on lime plaster. H. 6 ft. 1 1/2 in. W. 6ft. 1 1/2 in. (187 × 187 cm.) The Metropolitan Museum of Art, Rogers Fund, 1903. (03.14.5) Photograph © 1986 The Metropolitan Museum of Art call postgraduate study by traveling abroad to work with the great teachers of the Greek world.

EDUCATION FOR WOMEN   Though the evidence is limited, it is certain that girls of the upper classes received an education equivalent at least to the early stages of a boy's education. They were probably taught at home by tutors and not sent out to school as was increasingly common for their brothers in the late republican period. Young women did not study with philosophers and rhetoricians, for they were usually married by the age at which a man began this phase of his education. Still, some women found ways to continue their studies, and some became prose writers and poets. By the first century C.E. there were women in aristocratic circles who were famous or—as conservative males saw it—infamous for their learning.

Slavery

The Romans, like most ancient peoples, had always had slaves. But the simple family-farmers of early Rome owned few. Slavery became fundamental to the Roman way of life only during the second century B.C.E. in the wake of Rome's conquests. Between 264 B.C.E. and 133 B.C.E. the Romans enslaved some 250,000 prisoners of war. Slaves could marry, and their children increased the slave population.

In Rome as in Greece, domestic slaves and those engaged in crafts and commerce were allowed to earn money with which to purchase their freedom. The freeing of slaves was very common among the Romans. After a time, a considerable portion of the Roman population consisted of people who had been slaves or whose ancestors had been slaves. It was not uncommon to see a son or grandson of a slave become wealthy as a freedman and the slave himself or his son become a Roman citizen. By importing slaves from all over the Mediterranean world and freeing them, the Romans transformed the ethnic composition of their population.

Rome's unique contribution to slavery was the invention of an agricultural system employing vast numbers of unfree workers. At the end of the republic there were 2 to 3 million slaves in Italy, about 35 percent to 40 percent of the total population. Most belonged to great slave gangs working vast plantations called *latifundia.* These estates produced capital-intensive cash crops (wool, wine, olive oil, cattle) rather than the grain that small farmers raised. The lives of agricultural workers were harder than those of other kinds of slaves, for *latifundia* were designed to produce maximum profits. Slaves, who were simply a means to that end, were fed cheaply, treated like machines, and discarded when they were no longer productive.

Harsh treatment spawned slave rebellions of a kind unknown in other ancient societies. A rebellion in Sicily in 134 B.C.E. kept that island in turmoil for over two years. In 73 B.C.E. a gladiator named Spartacus raised an army of 70,000 fugitive slaves from the Italian countryside and repeatedly defeated the Roman legions. When the Romans finally subdued him, they crucified 6,000 of his men along the road from Capua to Rome.

Roman Imperialism: The Late Republic

Rome had no plan for building an empire. Territories were acquired as a result of wars that the Romans believed were either defensive or preventive. Roman foreign policy was designed to provide security for Rome on Rome's terms, not to acquire land. Since these terms were often unacceptable to other nations, conflicts arose—and, intentionally or not, Rome expanded.

The empire undercut the very republic it was built to protect. The constitution of the republic had been designed for a city-state. It could be adapted to rule Italy but not to handle the responsibility of governing an empire beyond the seas.

The Aftermath of Conquest

Before the Punic Wars most Italians owned their own farms and were largely self-sufficient. Some families had larger holdings than others, but they grew the same crops (mostly grain) and used free laborers rather than slaves. The Punic Wars changed this. For fourteen years Hannibal marauded through Italy, doing terrible damage to its farmland. Many veterans returned from the wars to find that they did not have enough capital to get their devastated farms back into production. Some moved to Rome seeking work as day laborers. Most stayed in the country and became ten-

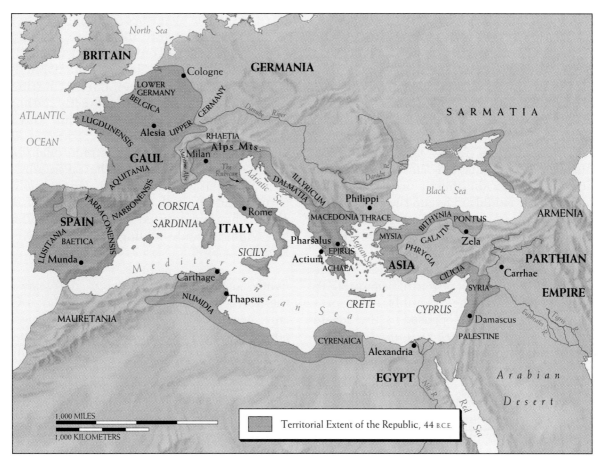

MAP 4–3 ROMAN DOMINIONS OF THE LATE ROMAN REPUBLIC *Depicted here are the Roman Republic's conquests until the death of Julius Caesar. Areas acquired before the tribunate of Tiberius Graccus (133 B.C.E.) are distinguished from later conquests and client states.*

ant farmers or hired hands. The land they abandoned was gathered into large parcels by the wealthy who had the capital to convert it to the crops (olives, grapes, and cattle) that were profitable on a world market. The upper classes had plenty of capital to invest, for the political offices they monopolized enabled them to win the governorships that allowed them to exploit Rome's new provinces. The economy that evolved within the empire separated the people of Rome and Italy more sharply into classes of rich and poor, landed and landless, privileged and deprived. The result was an increasingly tense situation that threatened the survival of the republic.

The Gracchi

By the middle of the second century B.C.E., perceptive Roman nobles were aware that institutions fundamental to the republic were collaps-

ing. The decline of the peasant farmer was shrinking the class from which Rome drew its soldiers, and the patron-client organizations that had structured Roman society were weakening. Patrons found it hard to control clients once the latter were no longer tied to the land. The introduction of the secret ballot in the 130s B.C.E. further weakened the traditional ties of clientage.

TIBERIUS GRACCHUS In 133 B.C.E. Tiberius Gracchus, a tribune, tried to solve these problems by proposing a program of land reform. He suggested reclaiming public land that was being held illegally. Current holders of this land were to be allowed to retain as many as 300 acres in clear title as private property, but the state would take the rest and redistribute it, at low rents and in small lots, to the poor. Those who received farms were not to be allowed to sell them.

There was much opposition to Tiberius's proposal. Many wealthy senators would be hurt by its passage. Others worried about the precedent set by any interference with property rights. Still others feared the political gains that Tiberius would make if the beneficiaries of his legislation were properly grateful to its drafter. When Tiberius put his land reform bill before the tribal assembly, one of his fellow tribunes, M. Octavius, vetoed it. This left Tiberius with the choice of dropping the matter or attempting a maneuver that would undercut the checks and balances of Rome's constitution. Tiberius opted for the later. He persuaded the assembly to remove the veto blocking discussion of his proposal by removing Octavius from office. At this point many of Tiberius's powerful senatorial allies deserted him. If the assembly could pass laws after they had been opposed by the Senate and vetoed by a tribune, then Rome would no longer be an oligarchical republic but a direct democracy (such as Athens).

Tiberius gave up hope of conciliating the Senate and passed a second bill that was harsher than the first one he had proposed—and, therefore, more appealing to the masses. It contained a scheme for funding a commission to carry out land redistribution. King Attalus of Pergamum had just died and left his kingdom to Rome. Tiberius's suggestion that revenue from this source be used to finance implementation of land reform was a second assault on the constitution. It ignored the Senate's traditional control of finances and foreign affairs.

Tiberius knew that he would be in great personal danger once he lost the protection of his tribunal office, so he announced his candidacy for a second successive term. This was another violation of custom, and his opponents feared that if he succeeded, he might hold office indefinitely and rule Rome as a demagogic tyrant. At the elections a riot broke out, and a mob of senators and their clients killed Tiberius and some 300 of his followers. The Senate had beaten back the threat to its rule but at the price of the first internal bloodshed in Rome's political history.

The tribunate of Tiberius Gracchus permanently changed the thinking of Roman politicians. Heretofore Roman politics had been a struggle among great families for honor and reputation. Fundamental issues were rarely at stake. Tiberius's revolutionary proposals and the sena-

torial resort to bloodshed created a new situation. Tiberius, despite his failure, had shown how the tribunate could be used to challenge senatorial dominance. He had demonstrated that a man could acquire power, not by courting the aristocracy, but by appealing directly to the people with a popular issue. Politicians who took this route came to be known as *populares.* Their opponents, who defended the traditional prerogatives of the Senate, were the *optimates* (i.e., "the best men"). These groups were not political parties with formal programs and party discipline. They represented strategies and alliances for winning and holding political power in Rome.

GAIUS GRACCHUS   In 123 B.C.E., ten years after the death of Tiberius, his brother Gaius Gracchus became a tribune. Gaius kept himself in power by putting together packages of legislation that formed alliances among disparate groups of voters. He revived efforts to redistribute public land; when supplies of land proved insufficient, he proposed new colonies; and he put through a law stabilizing the price of grain in Rome. Gaius also weakened the rich by pitting the republic's two wealthiest classes (the senatorial and the equestrian) against each other. The equestrians—the men who could afford to equip themselves for the most expensive form of military service, the cavalry—were businessmen with interests in the provinces. In 129 B.C.E., Gaius allowed them, but not senators, to serve on the courts that tried provincial governors. This prevented senators from sitting in judgment on themselves, but it did not improve the administration of the provinces. No senator now dared interfere with the equestrian tax collectors in his province lest he find himself dragged before their court.

In 122 B.C.E., Gaius celebrated reelection to the tribunate—which was now legal—by proposing that Rome's Italian allies be given citizens' rights. The allies had not received a fair share of the profits from the empire they had helped Rome win, and their resentment was threatening Italy's stability. Ordinary Romans, however, did not want to dilute the power of their votes by creating more citizens. This issue cost Gaius support, and he lost the election of 121 B.C.E. The Senate then trumped up a charge against him and killed him—and some 3,000 of his followers. Once again, the senatorial oligarchy triumphed over the *populares,* but the struggle was by no means over. Gaius's death simply taught the *populares* that they would have to resort to violence to oppose the Senate's violence. Marius, an officer who rose to prominence in the Jugurthine War, showed them the way.

Marius and Sulla

In 111 B.C.E. a group of Italian businessmen who were working in Numidia, a client kingdom in Africa, were caught and killed in the crossfire of a dispute over succession to the throne. The Roman electorate promptly declared war against Jugurtha, the perpetrator of this insult to their nation's honor. When the war dragged on longer than expected, rumors circulated that Rome's generals were being bought off.

In 107 B.C.E. the assembly elected C. Marius (157–86 B.C.E.) to a consulship and (usurping the Senate's right to control foreign policy) commissioned him to end the Jugurthine War. Marius was a *novus homo,* a "new man" (i.e., the first of his family to hold a consulship), not a member of the old Roman aristocracy. Marius quickly defeated Jugurtha, and the grateful Romans elected him to a second consulship to deal with another problem. In 105 B.C.E., two barbaric tribes, the Cimbri and the Teutones, had crushed a Roman army in the Rhone Valley. The long struggle to contain them kept Marius in office for five consecutive terms.

Marius won battles because he persuaded Rome to make changes in recruitment that enabled him to put larger armies in the field. He convinced the assembly to drop the property qualification for military service. This was a popular idea for it opened the way to a career for impoverished citizens such as those whom the Gracchi had tried to help. Marius's reforms built a strong army, but they also altered the balance of power in Roman politics. Marius's soldiers were semiprofessional clients of their general. They were dependent on him for their pay and for the grants of land on which they retired as veterans. Since they thought of themselves as his men more than the state's, he was able to use them to frighten the Senate into giving him whatever he needed to keep them happy.

Marius's example inspired imitation, and competitors soon challenged him. The most successful was L. Cornelius Sulla (138–78 B.C.E.), an impoverished aristocrat who had served under Marius in the Jugurthine War. Sulla made his mark in a campaign that Gaius Gracchus had tried to prevent: a war between Rome and its Italian allies. In 90 B.C.E. the allies gave up hope of receiving fair treatment from Rome and established a separate confederation with its own capital and coinage. Rome tried to undercut this by offering citizenship to cities that remained loyal and to rebels who laid down their arms. Despite this, hard fighting was still needed to put down the uprising. By 88 B.C.E. the war was over, and all the Italians became Roman citizens.

Sulla's performance in the war brought him the consulship for 88 B.C.E. and command of a war against Mithridates, a native king who was leading an uprising in Asia Minor. Marius, at the age of seventy, suddenly emerged from obscurity to demand this assignment for himself. When the assembly acquiesced, Sulla loosed the army he had been recruiting against Rome. Marius had used the army as a kind of political party, but now a Roman general used it to directly threaten his fellow citizens. Sulla regained his command. But when he left for the east, Marius and the consul Cinna occupied Rome with their armies. Marius died soon after his election to a seventh consulship in 86 B.C.E., and Cinna became the leader of Marius's party. In 83 B.C.E. Sulla, who had forced Mithridates to retreat and agree to a truce, returned to Rome. He drove Marius's followers from Italy and assumed dictatorial powers.

His first step was to wipe out his opponents. He posted lists of names of men whom he proscribed as enemies of the state. Proscribed individuals could be executed by anyone who found them, and their executioners could claim rewards from the state. Sulla confiscated their property and gave it to his supporters. As many as 100,000 Romans may have died in Sulla's purge.

Sulla could have made himself the permanent ruler of Rome, but he saw himself as the Republic's savior, not its enemy. His intent was to restructure and restore traditional senatorial government. The Senate's political privileges were reaffirmed, and the powers of the office of tribune, which the Gracchi had used to attack senatorial rule, were severely curtailed. In 79 B.C.E. Sulla declared his work complete and retired from public life. The example of what he had done long outlived the political arrangements he had made. It led to a civil war that destroyed the republic.

The Fall of the Republic

Pompey, Crassus, Caesar, and Cicero

Within a year of Sulla's death in 78 B.C.E. the Senate had to begin making exceptions to the very rules Sulla had designed to safeguard its power. The Senate discovered that the only way to deal with emergencies was to create "special commands," which were special because they were free of the constitutional limitations within which ordinary magistrates had to work. The most important of these commands went to a young general named Pompey (106–48 B.C.E.) who had never been elected to any office.

Pompey spent several years subduing a Marian army that had occupied Spain. In 73 B.C.E. the Senate sent him and Marcus Licinius Crassus, a wealthy senator, to put down a slave rebellion led by a gladiator called Spartacus. Crassus and Pompey used their growing influence to repeal most of Sulla's constitution so that ambitious generals and demagogic tribunes could undercut the Senate by appealing directly to the people.

In 67 B.C.E. a special law aimed at the suppression of piracy gave Pompey *imperium* for three years over the entire Mediterranean and its coast inland for fifty miles. In three months Pompey cleared the seas of pirates. The assembly then authorized Pompey to deal with a new war that had broken out with Mithridates. Pompey defeated Mithridates, drove him to suicide, and pushed Rome's frontier to the Euphrates River.

When Pompey returned to Rome in 62 B.C.E., he had more power than any Roman in history. The Senate suspected that he would emulate Sulla and establish a dictatorship. Crassus had most to fear. Although rich and influential, he did not have the kind of military backing Pompey enjoyed. He, therefore, sought alliances with popular political leaders. The ablest of these was Gaius Julius Caesar (100–44 B.C.E.), a descendant of an old but obscure patrician family. Despite noble lineage, Caesar was connected to the popular party. His aunt had been Marius's wife, and he had married Cinna's daughter. Caesar's rhetorical skill made him a valuable ally for Crassus, for he could rally the people to the cause of the *populares*. Each man needed the help of the other to win the military commands they had to have to build armies to compete with Pompey's.

Cicero (106–43 B.C.E.), a "new man" from Marius's home town of Arpinum, marshaled the opposition to Crassus and Caesar. Although he was an outsider to the senatorial aristocracy, he was no fan of the *populares*. He hoped to create a "harmony of the orders" between the Senate and the equestrians that would consolidate the power of the propertied classes. The Senate supported him primarily to block a bid for office made by an extremist named Catiline.

Cicero defeated Catiline for the consulship in 63 B.C.E., but Catiline refused to accept the verdict and hatched a plot to take over the state. News of it leaked to Cicero who speedily suppressed the plot and thereby annoyed Pompey.

A bust of Julius Caesar. Alinari/Art Resource, NY

Formation of the First Triumvirate

Toward the end of 62 B.C.E. Pompey landed at Brundisium. He had delayed his return, hoping to find Italy facing some crisis that would justify his keeping his army. But Cicero's quick suppression of Catiline deprived him of a pretext, and Pompey had to disband his army to avoid the appearance of treason.

Pompey had achieved amazing things for Rome, and he expected the Senate to show its gratitude by deferring to him. He wanted the Senate to approve the treaties he had negotiated in the East and to give him land for his veterans. The Senate should have prudently granted his requests, which were reasonable, but it chose instead to try to curtail his power and influence. This forced him to ally with his natural enemies, Crassus and Caesar. They joined him in an informal political arrangement called the First Triumvirate. By working together they were able to control the republic.

Julius Caesar and His Government of Rome

With the aid of his colleagues, Caesar was elected to the consulship for 59 B.C.E., and he used the office to make sure that each of the triumvirs got what he wanted. Pompey obtained land for his veterans and confirmation of his treaties. Crassus won tax concessions for the equestrians who were his chief supporters. Caesar got a special military command that gave him a chance to rival Pompey. When Caesar's consulship ended, the triumvirs secured their gains by arranging for the election of friendly consuls and by forcing their enemies to leave Rome.

Caesar's special command gave him authority, for five years, over Cisalpine Gaul in the Po Valley and Narbonese Gaul on the other side of the Alps. From these provinces, he set about conquering the rest of Gaul. In 56 B.C.E. he bought himself additional time by persuading Crassus and Pompey to renew the triumvirate. By 50 B.C.E. Caesar had completed the conquest of Gaul and acquired the wealth, fame, and military power he needed to compete against Pompey.

The triumvirate dissolved in 53 B.C.E. when Crassus died leading an army into Parthia, the successor to the Persian Empire, and Pompey saw no reason to sit by while Caesar's star continued to rise. In the late 50s B.C.E. the Senate appointed Pompey sole consul, for it concluded that Pompey was less of a threat than Caesar—and it hoped to help Pompey bring Caesar down. Caesar searched for some way to retain an office that would allow him to keep his army, but the Senate refused to extend his term in Gaul. In January 49 B.C.E. it ordered him to lay down his command. Caesar knew that this meant exile or death. Preferring treason, he ordered his legions to cross the Rubicon River, the boundary of his province, and march on Rome. A civil war ensued that Caesar won in 45 B.C.E.

Caesar made few changes in Rome's government. In theory, the Senate continued to play its role. But Caesar increased its size and packed it with his supporters. His monopoly of military power made a sham of senatorial decrees. In 46 B.C.E. Caesar was appointed dictator for ten years, and a year later his term was extended for life. His enemies concluded that he was aiming at monarchy, and they began to plot his destruction. Gaius Cassius Longinus and Marcus Junius Brutus recruited some sixty senators who helped them assassinate Caesar at a meeting of the Senate on March 15, 44 B.C.E. The assassins expected that once Caesar was dead the republic would automatically flourish. Instead, civil war returned, and it raged for thirteen more years. The assassins had not saved the republic but doomed it.

The Second Triumvirate and the Emergence of Octavian

Caesar had designated his eighteen-year-old grandnephew Gaius Octavian (63 B.C.E.–14 C.E.) his heir. The Senate hoped to use the sickly, inexperienced young man to block Mark Antony, the second-in-command to whom Caesar's men had spontaneously turned for leadership. But Octavian broke with the Senate, marched on Rome, assumed the consulship for 43 B.C.E., and declared war on Caesar's assassins. Mark Antony and another of Caesar's officers, M. Aemilius Lepidus, joined him in the Second Triumvirate, a legally established shared dictatorship charged, ostensibly, with the restoration of the republic.

In 42 B.C.E. the triumvirs defeated Brutus and Cassius at Philippi in Macedonia. Each of the victors rewarded himself with a command. The weakest member, Lepidus, was given Africa.

Octavian took the West—and the troubles that went with it (i.e., a war with one of Pompey's sons, the settlement of some 100,000 veterans, and the restoration of order in Italy). Antony received the most promising assignment: command of the East. This gave him a chance to invade Parthia and build an army large enough to sweep his fellow triumvirs aside.

In 36 B.C.E. Antony attacked Parthia, and the result was disastrous. His soldiers' faith in him was further undercut by a propaganda campaign that Octavian mounted. It convinced them that Antony had fallen under the spell of Egypt's queen, Cleopatra. By 32 B.C.E. all pretense of cooperation came to an end. Lepidus had already been shoved aside, and at Actium in western Greece in 31 B.C.E. Octavian defeated Antony.

The suicides of Antony and Cleopatra ended the civil war and left Octavian, at the age of thirty-two, absolute master of the Mediterranean world. His power was enormous, but so was the task that faced him. To restore peace, prosperity, and stability to Rome he needed to create a form of government that could handle the empire without violating the republican traditions to which the Romans were passionately attached.

In Perspective

The Roman Republic, at its start, resembled the early Greek poleis, *but Rome long remained a nation of simple farmers and herdsmen. As Rome organized itself for war, the traditional distinctions between Rome's patrician and plebeian castes became less important than the wealth that determined how well a man could equip himself for battle. The republic needed a strong army, for it was engaged in virtually continuous warfare in defense of its lands and allies. Rome created something unique: an empire ruled not by a king or bureaucracy but by a republic. Rome acquired and managed its territory as a state guided by an aristocratic Senate and governed by magistrates elected annually by its citizens.*

The temptations and responsibilities of governing an empire proved too much for the republican constitution. As trade increased, a class of merchants and financiers (the equestrians) grew strong enough to inject their commercial interests into Roman politics. Masses of slaves captured in war undermined the small farmers who had been the backbone of the Roman state and its army. Many impoverished citizens moved to Rome and survived by selling their only asset, their vote. Rome's armies of self-supporting farmers were then replaced by volunteer armies of landless men who made careers of being soldiers. They expected to be paid for their service with gifts of land or money and gave the generals who rewarded them the power to ignore constitutional restraints. When their leaders began to jockey among themselves for the upper hand, a long civil war sent the republic down the path to destruction. Despite itself, Rome drifted toward a form of monarchical government similar to those of the ancient states of Egypt and Mesopotamia.

REVIEW QUESTIONS

1. How did the institutions of family and clientage and the establishment of patrician and plebeian classes contribute to the stability of the early Roman Republic? How important was education to the success of the republic? How essential was the institution of slavery?

2. What was "the struggle of the orders"? What methods did plebeians use to get what they wanted? How was Roman society different after the struggle ended?

3. Until 265 B.C.E., how and why did Rome expand its territory? How was Rome able to conquer and to control Italy? How did Rome's desires for security, wealth, power, and fame shape its relations with Greece and Asia Minor in the second century B.C.E.?

4. Why did Romans and Carthaginians clash in the First and Second Punic Wars? Could the wars have been avoided? How did Rome profit from its victory over Carthage? What problems did the victory create for Rome?

5. What social, economic, and political problems did Italy have in the second century B.C.E.? How did Tiberius and Gaius Gracchus propose to solve them? What were the political implications of the Gracchan reform program? Why did reform fail?

6. What were the problems that plagued the Roman Republic in the last century B.C.E.? What

caused these problems, and how did the Romans try to solve them? To what extent were ambitious, power-hungry generals responsible for the destruction of the republic?

SUGGESTED READINGS

R. A. BAUMAN, *Women and Politics in Ancient Rome* (1992). A useful study of women's role in Roman public life.

J. BOARDMAN, J. GRIFFIN, and O. MURRAY, *The Oxford History of the Roman World* (1990). An encyclopedic approach to the varieties of the Roman experience.

T. J. CORNELL, *The Beginnings of Rome: Italy and Rome from the Bronze Age to the Punic Wars* (1995). A fine new study of early Rome.

T. CORNELL and J. MATTHEWS, *Atlas of the Roman World* (1982). Much more than the title indicates, this book presents a comprehensive view of the Roman world in its physical and cultural setting.

E. S. GRUEN, *The Hellenistic World and the Coming of Rome* (1984). A new interpretation of Rome's conquest of the eastern Mediterranean.

S. LANCEL, *Carthage, a History* (1995). A good account of Rome's great competitor.

C. NICOLET, *The World of the Citizen in Republican Rome* (1980). A valuable study of the meaning of Roman citizenship.

J. RICH and G. SHIPLEY, *War and Society in the Roman World* (1993). A useful collection of essays on military topics.

E. T. SALMON, *The Making of Roman Italy* (1980). The story of Roman expansion on the Italian peninsula.

H. H. SCULLARD, *A History of the Roman World 753–146 B.C.E.*, 4th ed. (1980). An unusually fine narrative history with useful critical notes.

G. WILLIAMS, *The Nature of Roman Poetry* (1970). An unusually graceful and perceptive literary study.

Chapter 5

The Roman Empire

KEY TOPICS

- The Augustan constitution
- The organization and government of the Roman Empire
- Culture and civilization from the late republican through the imperial period
- The early history of Christianity
- The decline and fall of Rome

The victory of Octavian over Mark Antony at Actium ended a century of civil strife that had begun with the murder of Tiberius Gracchus. Octavian (subsequently known as Augustus) brought peace to Rome by establishing a monarchy hidden behind a republican facade. The unification of the Mediterranean world improved its government and facilitated economic expansion. The spread of Latin and Greek as the empire's official languages promoted growth of a common "classical" tradition, which had a great

This statue of Emperor Augustus (r. 27 B.C.E.–14 C.E.), now in the Vatican, stood in the villa of Augustus's wife Livia. The figures on the elaborate breastplate are all of symbolic significance. At the top, for example, Dawn in her chariot brings in a new day under the protective mantle of the sky god; in the center, Tiberius, Augustus's future successor, accepts the return of captured Roman army standards from a barbarian prince; and at the bottom, Mother Earth offers a horn of plenty. Charitable Foundation/Gemeinnutzige Stiftung Leonard von Matt

influence on the development of Christianity. Christianity appeared in the first century C.E. as one of the empire's many competing eastern cults.

In the third century C.E. Rome's institutions began to fail. Some emperors resorted to drastic measures to try to restore order. The result was growing centralization and militarization of an increasingly authoritarian government. A wave of barbarian attacks in the second half of the fifth century finally initiated the empire's collapse.

The Augustan Principate

The memory of Julius Caesar's fate was fresh in Octavian's mind in 31 B.C.E. as he pondered what to do with the empire he had won. Octavian had gained control of all of Rome's armies, and he had loyal, capable assistants. The confiscation of Egypt's treasury brought him ample capital. He had the means to be the strong ruler who could end the civil war and restore order, but he knew that it would be dangerous to appear to threaten the republican traditions to which the Romans were so passionately devoted.

Slowly Octavian pieced together a constitution that was acceptable to the Romans and capable of running an empire. It inaugurated a long era of stability and order called the *pax Romana* (i.e., "Roman peace"). Despite republican trappings and an apparent sharing of authority with the Senate, it was a monarchy. All real power, both civil and military, lay with the ruler. Octavian disguised this fact by referring to himself simply as *princeps* ("first citizen") or *imperator* ("commander-in-chief"), but these titles soon acquired connotations of royalty that accurately reflected the power of his office.

During the civil war Octavian's legal authority derived from the triumvirate, a temporary dictatorship set up to restore the republic. After his victory in the civil war terminated the triumvirate, Octavian governed by holding consecutive consulships. This was an unpopular violation of Roman tradition, and he sought an alternative to it. On January 13, 27 B.C.E., at a dramatic Senate meeting, he resigned most of his offices—except for the governorships of Spain, Gaul, and Syria—and returned command of the other provinces to the Senate. This was less risky than it seems, for Octavian's provinces were the border lands that contained twenty of Rome's twenty-six legions. The Senate, however, declared this to be the restoration of the republic and thanked Octavian by granting him the surname "Augustus" (i.e., "revered"). Historians use this title to indicate Octavian's role as founder of Rome's first truly imperial government, the "Principate." In 23 B.C.E. Octavian Augustus made another republican gesture. He resigned the consulship. Henceforth his authority rested on two special powers: proconsular *imperium maius* (supreme military command) and the political privileges of an honorary tribune.

Administration

The Romans were willing to go along with Augustus, for they benefitted from his administration. He weeded out inefficient and corrupt magistrates. He blocked ambitious politicians and generals who might otherwise have disturbed the peace. He eased tension among classes and between Romans and provincials. And he fostered rapid economic development.

The Senate took over most of the political functions of the assemblies, but it became a less parochial institution. Augustus manipulated elections to offices and saw to it that promising young men, whatever their origin, had opportunities to serve the state. Those who did well were rewarded with appointments to the Senate. This allowed equestrians and Italians who had no connection with the old Roman aristocracy to earn Senate membership, and it ensured a Senate composed of talented, experienced statesmen.

Augustus was careful to court the politically volatile residents of Rome. He founded the city's first public fire department and police force. He organized grain distribution for the poor and set up an office to oversee the municipal water supply. The empire's rapidly expanding economy enabled him to fund a vast, popular program of public works.

The provinces, too, benefitted from Augustus's union of political and military power. For the first time, Rome had a central government that was able to oversee the conduct of the men who administered its provinces. Good governors were appointed. Those who abused their power were disciplined, and the provincials themselves were granted a greater degree of political autonomy.

The Army and Defense

Augustus professionalized the military and reduced its numbers to about 300,000 men—a force barely adequate to hold the frontiers. The legions were recruited from Italians, but auxiliary companies admitted provincials. The term of enlistment was twenty years. Pay was good, with occasional bonuses and the promise of a pension on retirement. Armies were permanently based in the provinces where they were likely to be needed, and their presence helped acquaint native peoples with Roman culture. Soldiers married local women and settled new towns. Eventually, provincials qualified for Roman citizenship and developed a commitment to the empire that strengthened its defenses.

Augustus's chief military problem was the defense of the empire's northern frontier. Since very little Roman territory protected Italy from invasion by the barbarians who wandered about Germany, Augustus wanted to expand the empire eastward to a new shorter and more defensible border. But in 9 C.E., when a German tribal leader called Herrmann (or Arminius, in Latin) ambushed and destroyed three Roman legions, the aged Augustus was forced to abandon the campaign.

Religion and Morality

Augustus tried to repair the damage that a century of strife had done to Rome's fundamental institutions. He devised a program to restore traditional values of family and religion. He passed laws to curb adultery and divorce and encourage early marriage and large families. His own austere behavior set a personal example for his subjects, and he banished his only child (Julia) to punish her flagrant immorality.

Augustus restored the dignity of formal Roman religion. He built many temples, revived old cults, invigorated the priestly colleges, and banned the worship of some foreign gods. He did not accept divine honors during his lifetime, but, like his stepfather, Julius Caesar, he was deified after his death.

Civilization of the Ciceronian and Augustan Ages

Roman civilization reached its pinnacle in the last century of the republic and during the principate of Augustus. Hellenistic Greek influences were strong, but the spirit and sometimes the form of Roman art and literature were unique.

The Late Republic

CICERO Cicero (106–43 B.C.E.) was the most important literary figure of the late Republic. He wrote treatises on rhetoric, ethics, and politics, and developed Latin as an instrument for philosophical disputation. But it is the orations he delivered in the law courts and in the Senate and his private letters (which survive in large numbers) that are his most interesting works. They provide us with better insight into him than we have into any other figure from antiquity.

Ruins of the Roman Forum. From the earliest days of the city, the Forum was the center of Roman life. Augustus had it rebuilt, and it was frequently rebuilt and refurbished by his successors, so most of the surviving buildings date to the imperial period. Corbis

Cicero's thinking was pragmatic and conservative. He believed that the world was governed by a divine natural law that human reason could comprehend and use to guide the development of civilized institutions. His respect for law, custom, and tradition as guarantors of stability and liberty led him to champion the Senate against *populares* leaders such as Mark Antony. When the Second Triumvirate seized power and began its purges, it marked Cicero for execution.

HISTORY   Much of the work of the historians who wrote during the last century of the republic has been lost. A few pamphlets on the Jugurthine War and the Catilinarian conspiracy of 63 B.C.E. are all that survive from the pen of the man reputed to be the greatest historian of his generation, Sallust (86–35 B.C.E.). Julius Caesar wrote treatises on the Gallic and civil wars. They are military narratives that Caesar developed for use as political propaganda. Since their direct, simple, and vigorous style still makes them persuasive reading, they must have been most effective with their intended audience.

LAW   Before the generation of the Gracchi, Roman law evolved case by case from juridical decisions. However, contact with foreign peoples and the influence of Greek ideas forced a change. The edicts of praetors began to expand the Roman legal code, and the decisions of the magistrates who dealt with foreigners spawned the idea of the *jus gentium*—the law of all peoples as opposed to the law that reflected only Roman practice. In the first century B.C.E. Greek thought promoted the concept of the *jus naturale*, a natural law that lay behind the customary laws of different nations. This law reflected the principles of divine reason that Cicero and the Stoics believed to be at work in the world.

POETRY   Two of Rome's greatest poets, Lucretius (ca. 99–ca. 55 B.C.E.) and Catullus (ca. 84–ca. 54 B.C.E.), were Cicero's contemporaries. Each represented a different aspect of Rome's poetic tradition. Hellenistic literary theory maintained that poets ought to be both entertainers and educators, and that was what Lucretius attempted in his epic poem, *De Rerum Natura* (*On the Nature of Things*). Lucretius hoped to save his generation from fear and superstition by converting it to the materialistic philosophies of Epicurus and Democritus. They had claimed that if living beings accepted that they were nothing more than temporary agglomerations of lumps of matter, they would cease to be anxious about death.

Catullus's poems were personal, even autobiographical, descriptions of the joys and pains of love. He hurled invective at important contemporaries such as Julius Caesar, and he amused himself in witty poetic exchanges, but he offered no moral lessons. He celebrated himself—an affirmation of the importance of the individual that was one of the characteristics of Hellenistic art.

The Age of Augustus

The age of Augustus was the golden age of Roman literature. The great poets of the era relied on the patronage of the *princeps,* and their dependence on him limited their freedom of expression. But although their work served his political agenda, they were not mere propagandists. They were sincerely grateful for what he had done for Rome.

VERGIL   The early works (the *Eclogues* or *Bucolics*) of Vergil (70–19 B.C.E.), the most important of the Augustan poets, were somewhat artificial pastoral idylls. Maecenas, Augustus's chief cultural adviser, seems to have suggested the subject for Vergil's *Georgics,* a reworking of Hesiod's *Works and Days.* Vergil transformed the early Greek poet's praise of simple labor into a hymn to heroic human effort—the struggle to wrest civilization from the brutal world of nature. Vergil's celebration of the greatness of Italy's cults and institutions became the theme of his most important poem, the *Aeneid.*

During the civil war, Augustus rallied the Romans to his side by persuading them that Mark Antony had succumbed to alien Eastern influences. Augustus had won the war by depicting himself as the guardian of Italy's culture. He was committed, therefore, to granting Italy special status within his empire. The *Aeneid* helped justify this. It explained Rome's origin and greatness by grounding its history in the founding myth of Hellenic civilization, the *Iliad*'s account of the Trojan War. Vergil's hero, the Trojan prince Aeneas, is not motivated by Homeric lust for personal honor and excellence. He personifies Roman qualities: duty, responsibility, and patriotism—the civic virtues of men such as Augustus who maintain the peace and prosperity of the empire.

HORACE   Horace (65–8 B.C.E.), the son of a freedman, was a highly skillful lyric poet. His *Satires* are genial and humorous. His *Odes,* which ingeniously adapt Latin to the forms of Greek verse, glorify the new Augustan order.

PROPERTIUS   Sextus Propertius was, with Vergil and Horace, a member of the poetic circle favored by Augustus's friend Maecenas. He wrote elegies that were renowned for their grace and wit.

OVID   Ovid (43 B.C.E.–18 C.E.), who wrote light love elegies, was the only one of the great poets to run spectacularly afoul of Augustus's program. His celebration of the loose sexual mores of certain sophisticated Roman aristocrats was not consistent with the serious, family-centered life Augustus was advocating, and Ovid's poetic textbook on the art of seduction, *Ars Amatoria,* confirmed Augustus's decision to exile the poet in 8 C.E. Ovid tried, but failed, to recover favor by switching to less sensitive themes. His *Fasti* was a poetic essay on Roman religious festivals, and his most popular work, the *Metamorphoses,* was a charming survey of Greek mythology.

HISTORY   Augustus's emphasis on tradition and his desire to increase Rome's reverence for its unique cultural traditions encouraged the writing of history. The most important of the Roman historians was Livy (59 B.C.E.–17 C.E.), although only a quarter of his monumental *History of Rome* survives. It treats the period from the legendary origins of Rome until 9 B.C.E. Livy based his history on secondary accounts and did little original research, but he was a gifted narrator. His sketches of historical figures have become perennially popular illustrations of good and bad behavior and models of patriotism.

ARCHITECTURE AND SCULPTURE   Augustus embarked on a building program designed to make Rome worthy of its history. The Campus Martius and the Roman Forum were reconstructed. Augustus donated a new forum of his own to celebrate his victory in the civil war. A splendid temple to his patron god, Apollo, rose on Rome's Palatine Hill. Most of the new building conformed to the Greek classical style, which emphasized serenity and order. The same attributes are visible in the best surviving portrait sculpture of Augustus and his family: the reliefs carved for the Altar of Peace, which Augustus dedicated in 9 B.C.E.

Imperial Rome 14–180 c.e.

The Emperors

Because Augustus was ostensibly only the "first citizen" of a restored republic, he had no public office to which he could openly appoint an heir.

Tiberius (r. 14–37 C.E.), his stepson and immediate successor, at first tried to follow Augustus's example and hide the monarchical nature of his government. But as the Romans became accustomed to the new order, there was less reason to conceal its reality. The terms *imperator* and *Caesar* began to be used as titles for men whose connection with Julius Caesar's family brought them the military power that enabled them to run the Roman world.

Tiberius was followed by his nephew, Gaius Caligula (r. 37–41 C.E.). Caligula was succeeded by his uncle Claudius (r. 41–54 C.E.), and Claudius left the throne to his stepson Nero (r. 54–68 C.E.). Nero, who was not equal to the responsibility of his job, committed suicide when a rebellion in Gaul convinced him that he had lost control of the army. He was the last of the Julio-Claudians, the descendants of Augustus or of his wife Livia.

The year 69 C.E. saw four different emperors assume power in quick succession as different Roman armies marched on Rome. The victor, Vespasian (r. 69–79 C.E.), and his sons, Titus (r. 79–81 C.E.) and Domitian (r. 81–96 C.E.), composed the Flavian dynasty. Vespasian was the first emperor who had no connection with the old Roman nobility. He was a tough Italian soldier from the middle class. His sons inherited his excellent administrative talents, but Domitian may have succumbed to paranoia. His increasingly tyrannical behavior frightened his intimates into assassinating him.

Domitian had no close relative to succeed him, and those who killed him were not foolish enough to try to turn the clock back to the days of the republic. They appealed to the Senate to restore order by choosing a new emperor. The Senate elected one of its own, Nerva (r. 96–98 C.E.), the first of the "good emperors:" Trajan (r. 98–117 C.E.), Hadrian (r. 117–138 C.E.), Antoninus Pius (r. 138–161 C.E.), and Marcus Aurelius (r. 161–180 C.E.). None of the first four men had a son to succeed him, so each followed an example set by Nerva—each adopted an heir. This system of succession was a fortunate historical accident, for it guaranteed that worthy men were promoted to power. It produced a century of peaceful, competent government that ended when Marcus Aurelius allowed his unworthy son, Commodus (r. 180–192 C.E.), to follow him to the throne.

The Administration of the Empire

Although some of the emperors tried to enlist the cooperation of the senatorial class—as counselors, judges, and department heads—in running the empire, the imperial government was largely staffed by professionals. These career bureaucrats were in many ways an improvement over the amateurs who had annually exchanged offices in the republic.

The provinces especially benefitted from imperial government. Once exploitation by governors was curbed, they discovered the economic advantages of being part of a huge empire. Rome strove to both unify the empire and respect local customs and differences. By 212 C.E. citizenship had been extended to almost every inhabitant of the empire. The spread of *Romanitas* ("Romanness") was more than nominal, for senators and even emperors began to be chosen from provincial families.

LOCAL MUNICIPALITIES Administratively, the empire was structured as a federation of cities and towns. The typical city had about 20,000 inhabitants. Only three or four had a population of more than 75,000. Rome, however, certainly had more than 500,000 residents—perhaps more than a million. The central government dealt with city governments and had little contact with people who lived in the countryside. A municipal charter left much responsibility in the hands of local councils and magistrates. The holding of a magistracy or, at a later period, a seat on a municipal council earned a man Roman citizenship. In this way the Romans brought the upper classes of the provinces into their own government, spread Roman law and culture, and won the loyalty of influential people. Rome's policy of assimilation did not succeed everywhere. Jews, who on religious grounds refused to compromise with Rome, rebelled in 66–70, 115–117, and 132–135 C.E. and were savagely suppressed. Egypt's peasants were exploited with exceptional ruthlessness and not offered the opportunity to integrate.

The emperors took a broad view of their responsibility for the welfare of their subjects. Nerva conceived and Trajan introduced the *alimenta*, a program of public assistance for children of indigent parents. More and more the emperors intervened when municipalities got into

Map 5-1 Provinces of the Roman Empire to 117 c.e. *The empire's growth is shown here in three stages: to Augustus's death in 14 c.e., to Nerva's death in 98 c.e., and to Trajan's death in 117 c.e.*

MAJOR ROADS
OF THE
ROMAN EMPIRE

500 MILES
500 KILOMETERS

PARTHIAN
EMPIRE

Persian Gulf

Caspian
Sea

ARMENIA

ASSYRIA

MESOPOTAMIA

Tigris R.

Euphrates R.

CAPPADOCIA

ARABIA

PONTUS

BITHYNIA

GALATIA

CILICIA

PISIDIA

LYCIA

ARABIA PETRAEA

CYPRUS

PALESTINE

Jerusalem

Red Sea

EGYPT

Byzantium

THRACE

Black Sea

LOWER
MOESIA

SARMATIA

UPPER
MOESIA

MACEDONIA

GREECE

ILLYRIA

ACHAEA

CRETE

LIBYA

CYRENAICA

DACIA

DALMATIA

PANNONIA
(INF.)

(SUP.)

NORICUM

RHAETIA

Danube R.

Mediterranean Sea

ITALY

Rome

SICILY

SARDINIA

CORSICA

Carthage

AFRICA

NUMIDIA

GERMANIA

ALPS Mts.
CISALPINE
GAUL

GERMANIA
(SUP.)

NARBONENSIS

BALEARIC
ISLANDS

MAURETANIA

AFRICA

Cologne

GERMANIA
(INF.)

LUGDUNENSIS

GAUL

AQUITANIA

North
Sea

BRITAIN

Wall of
Antoninus

Wall of
Hadrian

TARRACONENSIS

LUSITANIA

BAETICA

ATLANTIC
OCEAN

HIBERNIA

500 MILES
500 KILOMETERS

14 c.e. – Death of Augustus

14-98 c.e. – Acquisitions,
Augustus to Trajan

98-117 c.e. – Acquisitions During
the Reign of Trajan

difficulties—sending imperial troubleshooters to deal with problems that were usually financial. As a result, the autonomy of the municipalities declined, and the central administration took on more and more functions. This caused the provincial aristocracy to lose interest in public service and to regard it as a burden rather than an opportunity. The price paid for increased efficiency was a loss of vitality by the empire's local governments.

FOREIGN POLICY   Augustus's successors, for the most part, continued his conservative, defensive foreign policy. Trajan was the first to take the offensive. He crossed the Danube and mounted a campaign (101–106 C.E.) that added a new province (Dacia) to the empire. His intent was probably to secure the empire by driving wedges into territory occupied by threatening barbarians. The same reasoning justified an invasion of the Parthian Empire in the East (113–117 C.E.) and the establishment of three more eastern provinces: Armenia, Assyria, and Mesopotamia. Trajan's lines, however, were overextended, and rebellions forced him to retreat. He died on his way back to Rome.

Hadrian, Trajan's successor, developed a new policy for the defense of Rome's frontiers. Heretofore, the Romans had taken the initiative against the barbarians. Although they rarely sought new territory, they conducted frequent military maneuvers to chastise and pacify troublesome tribes. Hadrian hardened Rome's defenses, building a stone wall in the south of Scotland and a wooden one across the Rhine-Danube triangle. As Rome's defensive strategy grew rigid, initiative passed to the barbarians. Marcus Aurelius had to spend most of his reign fending off dangerous attacks in the East and on the Danube frontier.

AGRICULTURE: THE DECLINE OF SLAVE LABOR AND THE RISE OF *COLONI*   The defense of the empire's frontiers made enormous demands on its resources, but the effect was not immediately felt. Economic growth continued well into the reigns of the "good emperors." Internal peace and efficient administration benefitted agriculture, as well as trade and industry, by making it easier to market products at a distance.

Small farms continued to exist, but more and more large estates, managed by absentee owners

Significant Dates from the Imperial Period

The Julio-Claudian Dynasty

27 B.C.E.–14 C.E.	Augustus
(ca. 4 B.C.E.–30 C.E.)	(Jesus of Nazareth)
14–37 C.E.	Tiberius
37–41 C.E.	Gaius "Caligula"
41–54 C.E.	Claudius
54–68 C.E.	Nero
69 C.E.	(Year of the Four Emperors)

The Flavian Dynasty

69–79 C.E.	Vespasian
79–81 C.E.	Titus
81–96 C.E.	Domitian
(ca. 70–100 C.E.)	(Composition of the Gospels)

The Antonine Dynasty (the "Good Emperors")

96–98 C.E.	Nerva
98–117 C.E.	Trajan
117–138 C.E.	Hadrian
138–161 C.E.	Antoninus Pius
161–180 C.E.	Marcus Aurelius

and growing cash crops, dominated agriculture. At first, these estates were worked by slaves, but in the first century C.E. this began to change. Economic pressures forced many members of the lower classes to become *coloni* (i.e., tenant farmers), and *coloni* steadily replaced slaves as the mainstay of agricultural labor. *Coloni* were sharecroppers who paid rent in cash, in labor, or in kind. Ultimately, their movements were restricted, and they were tied to the land they worked. Thanks to the *coloni*, the economic importance of slavery declined in the second century, but slavery survived the fall of Rome's empire.

Women of the Upper Classes

By the time the republic was drawing to its end, upper-class women in Rome were acquiring wealth, education, and political influence. The form of marriage that left a wife free of a husband's *manus* became popular, divorce was common, and some women conducted their sexual lives as freely as men. Privileged women were reluctant to have children and increasingly em-

Portrait of a Young Woman
from Pompeii

In 79 C.E. a volcanic eruption buried the Roman city of Pompeii (near Naples) and preserved its homes and their contents for excavation by modern archaeologists. This painting of a young woman comes from a modest two-story house whose residents were evidently educated and moderately well off. The woman holds a stylus and wax-coated tablets, common writing materials, and her husband (in a companion portrait) holds a volume of Plato. Her gold hair net and earrings (examples of which have been found at Pompeii) suggest that she was a fashionable lady of some means.

The paintings illustrate contemporary social values. The dual portraits suggest that women were thought of as worthy partners in marriage. Beauty is obviously an important female characteristic, but so, in this case, is pride in literacy. Pompeii was home to many competent women who owned property, conducted businesses, held religious offices, and received public honors for their various services and benefactions. There is no reason to assume that the town was unique in this regard.

Young Woman Writing, detail of a wall painting from Pompeii. Late 1st century C.E. Diameter 14 5/8″ Museo Archeologico Nazionale, Naples, Italy/Art Resource. © Photograph by Erich Lessing.

Sources: Marilyn Stokstad, *Art History*, revised edition, Harry N. Abrams and Prentice Hall, New York, 1999, pp. 258–259; E. Fantham, H. P. Foley, N. B. Kampen, S. B. Pomeroy and H. A. Shapiro, *Women in the Classical World*, Oxford University Press, Oxford and New York, 1994, pages 340–341 ployed contraception and abortion to avoid offspring. Augustus was concerned about falling birthrates and issued decrees that were intended to encourage procreation, restore moral standards, and protect the integrity of the family. His laws seem to have had little effect. Women defended their freedoms, and in the fourth century C.E., the emperor Diocletian liberated them from the need for male guardians and allowed them to conduct their own legal affairs.

Several of the women who belonged to the imperial family exercised great political influence, if only unofficially. Augustus's wife and adviser Livia was honored with the title "Augusta" and survived him to be a force to be reckoned with in the reign of his heir, Tiberius. Claudius's wife, Messalina, attempted to overthrow him, and Nero may have owed his ascension to the throne to his mother, Agrippina.

Life in Imperial Rome: The Apartment House

The typical Roman city had about 20,000 inhabitants. Only three or four had more than 75,000, although Rome itself may have approached a million. Crowding, noise, and bustle were inescapable features of city life. In Rome the rich lived in large, elegantly decorated single-storyed homes built around courtyards. These occupied about a third of the city's space. Since public buildings (e.g., temples, markets, baths, theaters, and forums) took up another quarter, this forced the vast majority of Romans to squeeze into less than half the city's territory. Ordinary folks found housing in *insulae,* apartment houses that soared to five, six, or more stories. Shortage of space kept rents high even though these buildings were as uncomfortable as they were dangerous. They had neither central heating nor plumbing. Water had to be carried up from public fountains and sewage toted down (or dumped out a window). Heating and cooking relied on smokey stoves, and light was provided by torches, candles, and oil lamps. All these open fires created a great risk of conflagration, for *insulae* were constructed, in part, of flammable materials. They were also cheaply built and kept in poor repair, which meant that collapse was not uncommon. Little wonder that the people of Rome spent most of their time out of doors.

The Culture of the Early Empire

LITERATURE The years between the death of Augustus and the reign of Marcus Aurelius (14–180 C.E.) are known as the silver age of Latin literature. In contrast to the hopeful, optimistic

This is a reconstruction of a typical Roman apartment house found at Ostia, Rome's port. The ground floor contained shops, and the stories above it held many apartments. Museo della Civitá Romana, Rome, Italy. Scala/Art Resource, NY

outlook of the Augustan authors, the writers of the silver age were gloomy and pessimistic. Their works are freighted with complaints and satires that reflect hostility to the growing power and personal excesses of the emperors. Writers also avoided commenting on contemporary affairs and events in recent history that might irritate their emperors. Historical writing about remote periods was safe, as were scholarly studies, but little poetry was produced. In the third century C.E., Greek romances became popular. They suggest that the readers of the age sought entertainment and escape from contemporary realities.

ARCHITECTURE Advances in engineering enabled Rome's architects to design new kinds of buildings—great public baths (e.g., those of Diocletian and Caracalla), and huge free-standing amphitheaters (e.g., the Flavian Colosseum). Romans continued the tradition of post-and-lintel construction pioneered by the Greeks but supplemented it with the semicircular arch developed by the Etruscans. Romans were also the first to exploit fully a Hellenistic invention: concrete. The Pantheon, the only major Roman temple to survive intact, combines all these elements. They are also visible in multitudes of mundane but useful structures, such as bridges and aqueducts.

SOCIETY The Roman Empire was at its peak during the first two centuries C.E., but by the second century C.E. it was clear that difficult times lay ahead. The literature of the era expresses a desire to flee the present—to retreat from reality and public life to the remote past, to romance, and to private concerns.

The age's declining interest in public affairs correlates with a loss of vitality in the government of the empire's cities. In the first century C.E., members of the upper classes vied with one another for election to municipal office and for the honor of serving their communities. By the second century C.E., the emperors had to intervene to force unwilling citizens to accept public office. Reluctance to serve was understandable, for the central government had begun to hold local magistrates personally responsible for the revenues due from their towns. Men sometimes fled to avoid an office that might lead to their property being confiscated to make up for arrears in the collection of a community's taxes.

The central government's extreme fiscal measures were a response to a declining economy. Initially, Rome had prospered from the end of civil war and the influx of wealth looted from the East, but the impact of these developments diminished in the first half of the second century C.E. For reasons that are unknown, population also seems to have declined. The cost of government, however, kept rising. An ever-increasing need for money compelled the emperors to raise taxes and to ignite inflation by debasing the coinage. These policies precipitated crises that finally overwhelmed the empire.

The Rise of Christianity

The triumph of Christianity in the West was most improbable. The faith originated among poor people in an unimportant, remote province of the empire, where it faced opposition from native religious institutions. It had to compete with numerous cults and philosophies throughout the Roman Empire, and it had to survive persecution by the imperial government.

Jesus of Nazareth

Christianity was one of the most important developments of the imperial era. It appeared in Judaea, a remote eastern province of the empire, in response to the life of an obscure Jew, Jesus of Nazareth. The Gospels tell us all we know about him. The Gospel of Mark, which is the earliest, is dated about 70 C.E. (perhaps forty years after Jesus' death), and the latest, the Gospel of John, is dated about 100 C.E. The Gospels were never intended to be read as objective historical narratives of a man's life. They were written to proclaim the faith that Jesus was the Son of God who had come into the world to redeem humanity and to bring immortality to those who believed in him.

Jesus was born during Augustus's reign. He was an effective teacher in the tradition of the early Hebrew prophets. Some of the prophets had predicted the coming of the Messiah, a redeemer who would help Israel triumph over its enemies and who would establish the kingdom of God on earth. Jesus modified this message by claiming that the Messiah would not establish an earthly kingdom but would end the world as human beings knew it at the Day of Judgment. God would then reward the righteous with immortality and happiness in heaven and condemn the wicked to eternal suffering in hell. While the faithful awaited the apocalyptic event, which they believed was imminent, Jesus advised them to forget worldly concerns, to trust in him, and to practice love, charity, and humility.

Jesus won a considerable following, but his criticism of the cultic practices associated with the temple in Jerusalem provoked the hostility of the Jewish religious authorities. The Roman governor of Judaea concluded that Jesus was a threat to peace and ordered his crucifixion (probably in 30 C.E.). Jesus' followers believed that he was resurrected on the third day after his death and that resurrection proved him to have been the Christ (*christos*, the Greek term for "Messiah," the "anointed").

Paul of Tarsus

The most important missionary at work in the generation that founded the Christian church was a Jew named Paul (born Saul), a Roman citizen and native of the city of Tarsus in Asia Minor. Paul was originally a Pharisee, a member of a Jewish sect known for strict adherence to the Jewish law. He began his career as an ardent opponent of Christianity, but about 35 C.E. he experienced a mysterious, precipitous conversion while traveling from Jerusalem to Damascus.

To define themselves the early Christians had to define their relationship to Judaism. James, the brother of Jesus, led those Christians who believed that the new faith was a version of Judaism and that its members had to adhere to the Jewish law. The less conservative Hellenized Jews, like Paul, saw Christianity as a new universal religion. They feared that the imposition of the Jewish law—with its many technicalities, dietary prohibitions, and painful rite of circumcision—would be a tremendous and unnecessary deterrent to conversion. Paul had great success making converts among the gentiles, and the triumph of his point of view in the church greatly facilitated the work of its missionaries.

Paul inaugurated Christian theology. He believed that the followers of Jesus had to spread the gospel, the "good news" of God's gift of the Messiah. But he warned that faith in Jesus as the Christ was a necessary but not sufficient agent of salvation. Salvation was a gift of God's grace that could not be earned by an act of will or by good deeds.

Organization

Christianity had a unique appeal that enabled it to spread throughout the Roman Empire and beyond Rome's borders. Christ's declaration of the spiritual importance of love and charity focused the Christian community's attention on the needs of the weak, the sick, and the unprotected. Consequently, early churches were characterized by a warmth and a human appeal that stood in marked contrast to the coldness and impersonality of the pagan cults. The Christian promise of salvation, which confirmed the importance of each individual human soul to God, also implied the spiritual equality of all believers, no matter what their social class or gender.

At first, Christianity appealed most to the uneducated urban poor, and its early rites were simple ceremonies congruent with the poverty of its people. Baptism by water brought converts into the community by cleansing them of original sin (i.e., the state of alienation from God into which they had been born). The central ritual of the church was a common meal, the *agape* or "love feast," followed by a *eucharist* (Greek for "thanksgiving"), a celebration of the Lord's Supper in which bread and wine were blessed and consumed. Prayers, hymns, and readings from the Gospels were also part of worship.

The church owed its success in part to the unique organization it evolved. At first, Christian groups had little formal structure, and Christianity was in danger of dissolving into a gaggle of tiny sects. But the need to support missionary preachers and to administer charities prompted churches to elect officers: presbyters (i.e., "elders") and deacons (i.e., "servers"). By the second century C.E., when converts had increased to the point where a city was likely to have many churches, a bishop (from the Greek word *episkopos*, "overseer") was chosen to coordinate their activities. Bishops then extended their authority over the Christian communities in outlying towns and the countryside. Bishops acting together in councils could resolve disputes and preserve the unity of the church, and it was soon accepted that the powers that Jesus had given his original disciples were passed on in the church from one generation of bishops to another. (This is called the doctrine of apostolic succession.) It is unlikely that Christianity could have survived the travails of its early years without the strong government provided by its bishops.

The Persecution of Christians

The Roman authorities could not at first distinguish Christians from Jews and, therefore, gave Christians the same protection under the law as Jews. It soon became clear, however, that Christians were different in potentially dangerous ways. Christians and Jews both incurred suspicion by their hostility to aspects of Roman tradition. (Both, for instance, denied the existence of the pagan gods and refused to take part in the state cult of the emperor.) But although the Jews were not eager to spread their ancient faith, Christians were ardent missionaries, proclaiming an imminent end to the Roman world. They had a network of local associations spreading across the empire, and they were oddly secretive about the rituals they practiced.

Romans were traditionally suspicious of secret organizations, particularly those of a religious nature. Claudius expelled Christians from the city of Rome, and Nero made them scapegoats for the great fire that struck the city in 64 C.E. But for the most part the Roman government did not take the initiative in attacking Christians in the first two centuries. Most of the persecutions in this period were the work of mobs, not governmental officials. Christians alarmed their pagan neighbors by ridiculing the ancient cults on which the state had always depended for its security. When misfortunes befell communities, Christians were blamed for having angered the gods. Persecution was not all bad for the church. It weeded out weaklings, united the faithful, and created the martyrs who became the heroes of Christian legend.

The Emergence of Catholicism

The survival of the church was threatened as much by internal disputes as by external persecution. The simple beliefs held by the great majority of Christians were open to a wide range of interpretations and left many questions unanswered. As a result, differences of opinion about the content of orthodox (i.e., "correct") faith developed. Minorities who disagreed with the catholic (i.e., "universal") majority were branded heretics (i.e., "takers" of unique positions) and driven out of the church.

The need to combat heretics compelled the orthodox to formulate their own views more clearly. By the end of the second century C.E., the church had agreed upon the core of a canon (i.e., a "standard," a collection of holy writings): the Old Testament, the Gospels, and the Epistles of Paul. It took at least two more centuries before consensus was reached on the rest of the Scriptures. The church also drew up creeds, brief statements of faith to which true Christians were expected to adhere, and empowered its bishops to enforce conformity of opinion. Whatever the shortcomings of this development, it ensured the clarity of doctrine, unity of purpose, and discipline needed for the church's survival.

Rome as a Center of the Early Church

During this period, when the church's administrative structures were evolving, the bishop of the city of Rome began to lay claim to "primacy" (highest rank among bishops). Rome was, after all, the capital of the empire, and it had the largest number of Christians of any city. Rome also claimed to be the place where Peter and Paul, the two most important missionaries of the early church, were martyred. Peter, who was said to have been the first bishop of Rome, was an especially important figure. The Gospel of Matthew (16:18) claims that Peter was the first of the apostles to recognize Jesus as the Messiah and that Jesus acknowledged Peter's faith by saying: "Thou art Peter [*Petros*, in Greek] and upon this rock [*petra*] I will build my church." Eventually the bishops of Rome would come to interpret this passage as granting Peter—and his episcopal successors in Rome—supremacy over the church.

The Crisis of the Third Century

Signs of serious trouble for the Roman Empire began during the reign of Commodus, the son and heir of Marcus Aurelius. Unlike his predecessors, the "good emperors" of the Antonine Dynasty, he was incompetent and autocratic.

Barbarian Invasions

The pressure on Rome's frontiers, already serious in the time of Marcus Aurelius (d. 180 C.E.), reached massive proportions in the third century C.E. The eastern frontiers were threatened by a new power arising in the lands that had belonged to the Persians and their successors, the Parthians. In 224 C.E. a new Iranian dynasty, the Sassanians, replaced the Parthians and began to make raids deep into Roman provinces. In 260 C.E. they captured and imprisoned a Roman emperor named Valerian.

On the western and northern frontiers the pressure came from an ever-increasing number of seminomadic German tribes. Though they had been in contact with the Romans since the second century B.C.E., they had not been much affected by civilization. German males were hunters, fighters, and carousers. The limited farming Germans engaged in was done by women and slaves. Tribes were led by chiefs, usually elected from the princes of a royal family by an assembly of fighting men. A chief headed a *comitatus* ("fraternity," in Latin) of warriors pledged by oath to his personal service. Eager for plunder, these career raiders were attracted by the delights they knew to exist in the civilized lands across the Rhine and Danube Rivers.

The most aggressive of the Germans were the Goths. By the third century C.E., they had wandered from the coast of the Baltic Sea, their original home, into southern Russia. From there they launched attacks on Rome's Danube frontier, and, about 250 C.E., they overran the Balkan provinces. To meet the threats posed by the Goths and the Persian Sassanids, the Romans transferred soldiers from their western to their eastern armies. This weakened the defenses of the West and made it easier for the tribes of the Franks and the Alemanni to cross the Rhine frontier.

Rome's internal weakness invited an unprecedented number of simultaneous attacks. A manpower shortage, brought on by a plague, had forced Marcus Aurelius to resort to the conscription of slaves, gladiators, barbarians, and brigands. By the second century C.E., the Roman army was made up mostly of Romanized provincials, and the training, discipline, and professionalism of Rome's forces had begun to decline.

Septimius Severus, who followed Marcus Aurelius's son Commodus to the throne (r. 193–211 C.E.), played a crucial role in the transformation of the character of the Roman army. Septimius was a military usurper who owed everything to the support of his soldiers, many of whom were peasants from the less civilized provinces. He was prepared to make Rome into an undisguised military dictatorship.

Economic Difficulties

The financial crisis exacerbated by the barbarian attacks also forced changes in Rome's military. Inflation had forced Commodus to raise the soldiers' pay, and the Severan emperors had to double it to keep up with prices. This increased the imperial budget by as much as 25 percent. To raise money, emperors resorted to new taxes, debased the coinage, and even sold the palace furniture. To attract men into the army, Septimius relaxed its discipline and made military service the path to social advancement.

The same developments that caused problems for the army did damage to other parts of society. As emperors devoted their attention to the defense of the empire's frontiers, they were less able to preserve internal order. Piracy, brigandage, and the neglect of roads and harbors all hampered trade—as did the debasement of the coinage and inflation. Taxation confiscated property that was badly needed as capital for commercial enterprises, and a shortage of workers reduced agricultural production.

More and more the government had to compel people to provide the food, supplies, money, and labor needed to sustain the armies. As the state began to demand that urban magistrates meet deficits in tax revenue out of their own pockets, the upper classes fled the cities. In the countryside, peasants abandoned farms made unprofitable by excessive taxation.

The Social Order

The new political and economic conditions led to changes in the social order. The senatorial and ruling classes were decimated by attacks from hostile emperors and by economic losses, and their ranks were filled by men coming up through the army. As a result, the state was increasingly militarized. Classes had been distinguished by dress since the days of the republic, but in the third and fourth centuries C.E. the people's everyday clothing became a kind of uniform that precisely declared their status. Titles were assigned to ranks in society just as in the army. Septimius Severus drew a sharp line between the *honestiores* (i.e., the senators, equestrians, municipal aristocrats, and all soldiers) and the lower classes, the *humiliores*. The *honestiores* enjoyed legal privileges: lighter punishments for crimes, immunity from torture, and a right of appeal to the emperor. As time passed, it became more difficult to move from the lower order to the higher. Peasants were tied to their lands, artisans to their crafts, soldiers to the army, and merchants and shipowners to the service of the state. Freedom and private initiative declined as the state strengthened control over its citizens.

Civil Disorder

In 235 C.E. the death of Alexander Severus, the last member of the dynasty founded by Septimius Severus, brought on a half-century of internal anarchy that invited foreign invasion. The empire teetered on the brink of collapse as conspirators overthrew and replaced emperors in rapid succession. A few able men appeared. Claudius II Gothicus (r. 268–270 C.E.) and Aurelian (r. 270–275 C.E.) drove back the barbarians and restored some discipline. But the soldiers who followed Aurelian on the throne employed strategies for defending the empire that acknowledged that it was losing ground. They built walls around Rome, Athens, and other cities and drew back their best troops from the frontiers. Their armies were mobile infantry and heavy cavalry that functioned as a kind of expanded imperial bodyguard. They recruited their soldiers from the least civilized provinces and even from the German tribes. Military power made these men the empire's new aristocrats. They dominated its government and monopolized its throne. In effect, the Roman people succumbed to an army of foreign mercenaries they had hired to protect them.

The Late Empire

As Roman emperors sought to mobilize resources to meet the mounting problems of the empire, they instituted policies that smothered individuality, freedom, and initiative. The state became ever more autocratic, centralized, and intrusive.

The Fourth Century and Imperial Reorganization

At the start of the fourth century C.E. an effort was made to save the empire by extensively reorganizing it. Emperor Diocletian (r. 284–305 C.E.), a native of the Balkan province of Illyria, was a man of undistinguished birth who rose through the ranks of the army. Recent history convinced him that the job of defending and governing the empire was too great for one man. Therefore, he set up a tetrarchy—a committee of four rulers, each of whom had responsibility for a different part of the empire. Diocletian administered the provinces of Thrace, Asia, and Egypt. He assigned Italy, Africa, and Spain to his friend, Maximian. Those two men were the senior members of the tetrarchy and shared the title "Augustus." Their subordinates, the "Caesars" Galerius and Constantius, were given responsibilities, respectively, for the provinces of the Danube-Balkan region and Britain with Gaul.

The tetrarchy stabilized the empire by giving four powerful men a stake in the status quo and by providing for an orderly process of succession to the throne. The Augusti recognized the Caesars whom they appointed as their successors and enhanced their loyalty by dynastic marriages. The system was a return, in a way, to the precedent set by the "good emperors" of 96–180 C.E., who adopted their successors from the pool of ablest men.

Each tetrarch established a residence at a place convenient for frontier defense. No one chose Rome, for it was too remote from the centers of military activity. Maximian's base at Milan commanded the Alpine passes and functioned as the effective capital of Italy. Diocletian donated monumental baths to Rome, but he visited the city only once and resided at Nicomedia in Bithynia.

In 305 C.E. Diocletian retired and compelled Maximian to do the same, but the hope for a smooth succession faded when Constantius died prematurely and his son, Constantine, claimed his father's throne. Other pretenders followed his example, and by 310 C.E. there were five Augusti and no Caesars. Constantine (r. 306–337 C.E.), who began the confusion, was responsible for ending it. In 324 C.E., he defeated his last opponent and made himself sole emperor. He continued Diocletian's policies—with one exception. Where Diocletian had tried to stamp out Christianity, Constantine became the patron of the church.

DEVELOPMENT OF AUTOCRACY The mounting crises facing the government encouraged a drift toward total military mobilization. In the name of efficiency, the government stifled the individuality, freedom, and initiative of its citizens. Traditions of popular government were forgotten. More and more emperors ruled by decree, consulting only a few high officials whom they themselves appointed. They protected themselves from assassination by distancing themselves from their people and becoming unapproachable, remote figures surrounded by elaborate courts. Their subjects prostrated themselves before them and kissed the hems of their purple robes. The emperor's new title, *dominus* ("lord"), asserted a claim to an authority that derived not from the Roman people but from the gods.

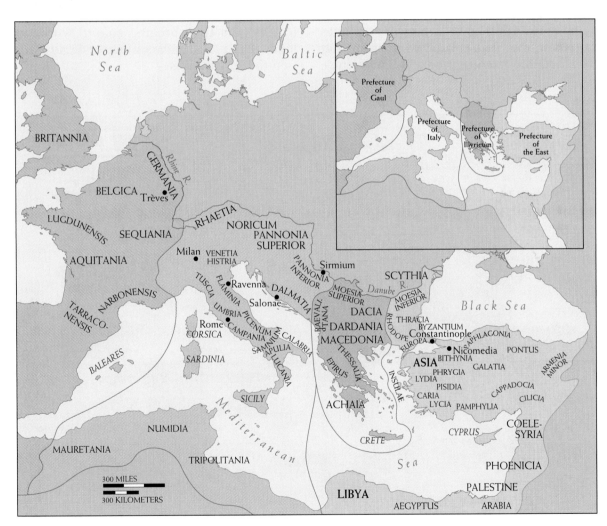

MAP 5–2 DIVISIONS OF THE ROMAN EMPIRE UNDER DIOCLETIAN *Diocletian divided the empire into four prefectures. The inset map shows their boundaries, and the larger map details regions and provinces.*

Constantine gave the empire a new capital. He chose the district of Byzantium on the Bosporus as the location for "Constantinople" (modern Istanbul) because it was midway between the eastern and Danubian frontiers. The site was also easy to defend, for it was surrounded on three sides by water. The dedication of the city of Constantinople in 330 C.E. marked the start of a new empire that repudiated Rome's pagan and republican traditions and embraced Christian autocracy.

The Byzantine emperors of Constantinople secured their position by keeping the civilian and military bureaucracies separate. This reduced the chance that someone might combine both kinds of power and mount a coup. An elaborate administrative hierarchy was set up to divide responsibility and prevent anyone from having very much power, and the entire system was kept under surveillance by a network of spies and secret police. This created a situation that was an invitation to corruption and inefficiency.

The cost of a 400,000-man army, a vast civilian bureaucracy, an imperial court, and the splendid buildings the government erected was more than the empire's already weak economy could sustain. The fiscal experiments that Diocletian began and Constantine continued only made things worse. In 301 C.E., Diocletian had instituted price controls to deal with inflation, but his Edict of Maximum Prices, which set legal limits for the costs of goods and services, simply drove commerce underground. When the peasants who could not pay their taxes and the officials who could not collect them tried to escape, Diocletian had used force to keep them in their places. Peasants, faced with enslavement by their government, often sought protection on a villa, the country estate of a powerful landowner. He protected them from the tax collectors, and they became *coloni*, working his land. Their descendants increasingly became tied to these estates.

MAP 5–3 THE EMPIRE'S NEIGHBORS *The map identifies the location of the various peoples who began to put pressure on the frontiers of the Roman Empire in the fourth century* C.E.

DIVISION OF THE EMPIRE Constantine's death was followed by a struggle for succession among his sons. Constantius II (r. 337–361 C.E.), the victor, reunited the empire and bequeathed it to his cousin Julian (r. 361–363 C.E.). The new emperor, whom Christian historians dubbed "the Apostate," concluded that Constantine's pro-Christian policy had caused more strife within the empire than it had resolved, and he set about reviving Rome's traditional cults. His reign, however, was too short to permit his ideas to take root. When he died in battle against Persia, the pagan renaissance died with him.

By the time that Emperor Valentinian (r. 364–375 C.E.) came to the throne, there were so many trouble spots that he concluded that he could not defend the empire alone. He appointed his brother Valens (r. 364–378 C.E.) as co-ruler. Valentinian resided at Milan and spent his reign defending the West against the German tribes of the Franks and Alemanni.

Valens was posted to the East, where he was confronted by a different kind of threat from another group of Germans. In 376 C.E., the Visigoths asked permission to enter the empire to escape the Huns, a fierce tribe migrating out of central Asia. Valens acquiesced but was unable to provide for the huge number of refugees who fled into the empire. In desperation the Goths began to plunder the Balkan provinces. Valens confronted the Goths at Adrianople in Thrace in 378 C.E., and he and his army were destroyed.

Theodosius (r. 379–395 C.E.), an able general, was then named co-ruler for the East. He pacified the Goths, enrolling many of them in his army. After the death of his colleague in the West, Theodosius united the empire for the last time.

THE RURAL WEST The disintegration of the empire was encouraged not just by wars and politics, but by the divergence of the cultures of its eastern and western halves. The West, which had fewer and younger cities, was increasingly rural. The institution of the villa, a fortified country estate, reorganized its society. The *coloni* who lived on a villa served its owner in return for economic assistance and protection from both barbarian invaders and imperial officials. As the upper classes moved to the country and slipped from the control of the imperial authorities, the central government lost its ability to provide fundamental services such as the

maintenance and policing of roads. This hastened the decline of trade and communications, depressed the standard of living, and forced regions to become self-sufficient. By the fifth century C.E., the western empire had dissolved into isolated estates belonging to rural aristocrats who dominated a large class of dependent laborers. Only the Christian church kept alive a memory of imperial unity.

THE BYZANTINE EAST In the East the situation was quite different. The loss of the West enabled Constantinople to concentrate on its own affairs. A vital and flourishing hybrid of Christian and classical culture emerged, and the East entered the "Byzantine" phase in its civilization. Because of its defensible location and the relative health of its economy, Constantinople was able to divert most of the barbarians into the West. Eastern cities continued to prosper, and the East's central government retained its power. Christian emperors reigned in Constantinople until the Turks conquered the city in 1453. For a thousand years Constantinople saw itself as chief heir to the cultural legacy of ancient Greece and Rome.

The Triumph of Christianity

Christianity's rise to dominance over the empire was connected with the political and cultural developments that were causing it to be transformed in other ways. Pagan religions lost much of their appeal as the old Roman cities declined. People still took some comfort in traditional rites, but the deities worshiped in these cults seemed less and less effective as the problems of the fourth and fifth centuries C.E. mounted. Worshipers sought more powerful, personal gods who could offer them safety and prosperity in this world and immortality in the next. Consequently, new religions appeared and old ones were combined and interpreted in new ways.

Manichaeism, named for Mani, a Persian prophet who lived in the third century C.E., was an especially potent rival for early Christianity. The Manichaeans saw human history as a war between forces of light and darkness, good and evil. The human body was a material prison for the element of light that was the human soul. To achieve salvation, humans had to free the light by mastering the desires of the flesh. Manichaeans led ascetic lives, worshiped simply, and sustained a sophisticated religious organization. Their faith persisted into the Middle Ages. Christianity drew much from the cults with which it competed for converts. But none had its universal appeal, and none was as great a threat as the ancient philosophies and the state religion.

IMPERIAL PERSECUTION   Until the middle of the third century C.E., Rome's emperors generally ignored Christianity. But as the empire's problems increased and Christians became more numerous and visible, government policy changed. A growing sense of insecurity made rulers less willing to tolerate dissent.

Serious trouble erupted in 250, when Emperor Decius (r. 249–251 C.E.) invoked the aid of the gods in his war against the Goths. He ordered all citizens to sacrifice to the state gods. True Christians could not obey, and Decius launched a major persecution to uphold his law. Valerian (r. 253– 260 C.E.) continued the policy, partly in order to confiscate the wealth of rich Christians. His successors, however, were preoccupied by other more pressing matters, and persecution lapsed until the end of the century.

By Diocletian's day the number of Christians had grown still greater—as had hostility to Christians. Diocletian, who was struggling to hold the empire together, was not tolerant of unorthodox movements. In 303, he launched the most serious persecution Rome ever inflicted on the church. The policy was self-defeating. Christians were, by then, too familiar to seem threatening to most people, and the government's extreme actions horrified many pagans. The courageous demeanor of Christian martyrs also aroused sympathy and made new converts.

In 311 C.E. the Eastern emperor Galerius, who had been one of the most vigorous persecutors, was persuaded, perhaps by his Christian wife, to issue an edict of toleration permitting Christian worship. Constantine concurred, and his support began Christianity's rise to the status of the empire's sole legal religion.

EMERGENCE OF CHRISTIANITY AS THE STATE RELIGION   Constantine's son supported the new religion, but the succession of Julian the Apostate posed a brief threat. Julian was a student of Neoplatonism, a religious philosophy devised by Plotinus (205–270 C.E.). It combined rational speculation and mysticism and was harshly crit-

ical of the church's lack of intellectual sophistication. Julian refrained from persecuting the church, but he withdrew its privileges, removed Christians from high offices, and introduced new forms of pagan worship. His reform lasted only as long as his brief reign.

In 394 C.E. Theodosius forbade the celebration of pagan cults, and Christianity became the official religion of the empire. Its victory ended some of the church's problems but created others. As the church acquired prestige and influence, it began to attract converts for the wrong reasons and to lose its spiritual fervor. It also had to work out a relationship with the state. In the East the state was strong enough to subordinate the church. But in the West imperial power faded, and church leaders exercised remarkable independence.

ARIANISM AND THE COUNCIL OF NICAEA   As Christianity matured, doctrinal disputes arose among Christians. These created factions that struggled for control of the state church, and the threat they posed to the social order forced governments to intervene to preserve the peace. Christians, as it turned out, could persecute Christians with as much zeal as pagan fanatics.

The most disruptive of the doctrinal controversies was the fight over Arianism, an explanation of Christ's role advanced by a priest named Arius of Alexandria (ca. 280–336 C.E.). Arius argued that Jesus was a unique being created by God the Father through whom the Father created all other beings. For Arius, Jesus was neither fully man nor fully God but something in between. In Arius's opinion, proponents of the doctrine of the Trinity, which asserts that God is a unity of three persons (Father, Son, and Holy Spirit), were indistinguishable from polytheists. Arian theology had the advantage of seeming simple and rational, but Athanasius (ca. 293–373 C.E.), bishop of Alexandria, objected that the Arian view of Christ destroyed Christ's effectiveness as an agent of human salvation. Athanasius believed that only a fully human and fully divine Christ could have the power to turn humanity into divinity and, thus, bestow eternal life on his followers.

In 325 C.E., Constantine tried to resolve the issue by inviting all the Christian bishops to a meeting at Nicaea, not far from Constantinople. Athanasius's arguments prevailed and were enshrined in the council's Nicene Creed. Arianism, however, continued to spread. Some later emperors were Arians, and some of the most successful missionaries to the barbarians were Arians. Many of the German tribes that overran the empire were Arian Christians. Christianity was a unifying force for the late Roman Empire, but it was also a source of new conflicts.

Arts and Letters in the Late Empire

The art and literature of the late empire reflect the confluence of pagan and Christian ideas and the changing tastes of the aristocracy. Much of the literature of the period is polemical, and much of its art is propagandist. The men who came to power as the empire declined were soldiers from the provinces whose roots were in the lower classes. By restoring and absorbing classical culture they hoped to stabilize their world and confirm their credentials as aristocrats.

The Preservation of Classical Culture

Acquisition of classical culture by the newly arrived ruling class was facilitated in several ways. Works by great authors were reproduced in many copies and were transferred from inconvenient papyrus rolls to sturdier codices (with separate pages stitched together like modern books). Scholars also condensed long works into shorter versions and wrote commentaries to make them more intelligible. Grammars for the classical languages also had to be compiled, for various native tongues were replacing Latin and Greek in many of the provinces.

This late-Roman ivory plaque shows a scene from Christ's Passion. The art of the late empire was transitional between the classical past and the medieval future. Crucifixion, carving, c. 420 A.D. (ivory). British Museum, London, UK/Bridgeman Art Library, London/New York

Christian Writers

Original works by pagan writers of the late empire were neither numerous nor especially distinguished. But the late empire saw a great outpouring of Christian writings. Christian "apologists" (authors who explained Christian practices to pagans) produced much poetry and prose. There were also sermons, hymns, and biblical commentaries designed for use by Christians.

The church was served by several important scholars in this period of its history. Jerome (348–420 C.E.), who was thoroughly trained in classical Latin literature and rhetoric as well as Hebrew, produced a Latin translation of the Bible—the Vulgate (i.e., "common use"). It became the standard text for the Roman Catholic Church. Eusebius of Caesarea (ca. 260–ca. 340 C.E.) wrote an idealized biography of Constantine and an *Ecclesiastical History* that set forth a Christian view of history as a process whereby God's will is revealed. But it is the work of Augustine (354–430 C.E.), bishop of Hippo in North Africa, that best illustrates the complexity of the relationship between classical culture and Christian faith.

Augustine was born at Carthage and trained as a teacher of rhetoric. His father was a pagan, but his mother was a Christian and hers was ultimately the stronger influence. He had a difficult intellectual journey that carried him through Manichaeism, skepticism, and Neoplatonism before he was converted to Christianity. His skill in pagan rhetoric and his gifts as a philosopher made him peerless among his contemporaries as a defender of Christianity. Augustine reconciled Christianity and classical culture by arguing that reason prepares people to receive what is revealed by faith.

Augustine's greatest works are his *Confessions*, an autobiography describing his path to faith, and *The City of God*, a response to the pagan charge that a sack of Rome by the Goths in 410 C.E. took place because Rome had abandoned its old gods. Augustine separated the destiny of the church from that of the Roman Empire. He contrasted the evil secular world, the "City of Man," with the spiritual realm represented by the church, the "City of God." The former was fated to be destroyed on the Day of Judgment, and there was no reason to expect that its conditions would improve before that. The fall of Rome was, therefore, neither surprising nor important. All states, even a Christian Rome, were part of the City of Man and were, therefore, corrupt and mortal. Only the City of God was immortal, and it, home to all the saints on earth and in heaven, was untouched by earthly calamities.

The Problem of the Decline and Fall of the Empire in the West

Whether important to Augustine or not, the massive barbarian invasions of the fifth century C.E. terminated imperial government in the West. Since that time, people have speculated about the causes of the collapse of the ancient world. Theories have been advanced that cite soil exhaustion, plague, climatic change, and even poisoning caused by lead water pipes. Some scholars blame the institution of slavery for Rome's failure to make the advances in science and technology that might have solved its economic problems. Others target excessive governmental interference in the economic life of the empire, and still others point out the significance of the destruction of the urban middle class—the carrier of classical culture.

Although all these things may have been contributing factors, a simpler explanation for Rome's failure can be found. The growth of Rome's empire was fueled by conquests that provided the Romans with the means to continue to expand. Ultimately, there were not enough Romans to conquer and govern any more territory. When pressure from outsiders grew, the overextended Romans could not expand their territory to acquire the additional resources they needed to defeat yet another enemy. Still, their tenacity and success in holding out for so long were remarkable. To blame the ancients for their failure to end slavery and bring on industrial and economic revolutions is no help, for no one has yet satisfactorily explained why those revolutions took place in the modern era. The real question may not be why Rome fell but how it managed to last so long.

In Perspective

Augustus ended the civil wars that plagued the republic and created an era of unity, peace, order, and prosperity. As a result, he was regarded with almost religious awe and was, at his death, able to pass his power down through his family, the Julio-Claudians. For almost 200 years, with a few brief interruptions, the empire was prosperous, peaceful, and well run.

Problems developed when the government assumed numerous responsibilities that promoted the growth of a large, expensive bureaucracy. The costs of government also grew as pressure on the frontiers from barbarian tribes forced Rome to maintain a great standing army. Higher taxes and bureaucratic control combined to stifle civic spirit and private enterprise.

Rome's rulers developed numerous schemes for dealing with the empire's difficulties. More and more, their power and their safety came to depend on the loyalty of the army. To win that, they courted the soldiers with gifts that increased the burden of taxes. The rich and powerful succeeded in avoiding many of their obligations, but this forced the government to bear down ever more heavily on vulnerable ordinary people. Ultimately, even extreme measures failed, and the Roman Empire fell. Something of its culture survived, however, to lay a foundation for the modern West.

REVIEW QUESTIONS

1. How did Augustus alter Rome's constitution and government? How did his innovations solve the problems that had plagued the republic? Why were the Romans willing to accept him?
2. How was the Roman Empire organized, and what enabled it to function smoothly? What role did the emperor play in maintaining its stability?
3. How did the literature of the "golden age" differ from that of the "silver age"? What did poets contribute to the success of Augustus's reforms?
4. Why were Christians persecuted by the Roman authorities? What enabled them to acquire such an enormous following by the fourth century C.E.?
5. What were the political, social, and economic problems that beset Rome in the third and fourth centuries C.E.? How did Diocletian and Constantine deal with them? Were these men able to halt Rome's decline? Were there problems they could not solve?
6. What are the difficulties involved in explaining the fall of the Roman Empire? What sorts of theories have scholars advanced to explain Rome's decline? Which explanations do you find most convincing? Why?

SUGGESTED READINGS

T. BARNES, *The New Empire of Diocletian and Constantine* (1982). A study of the character of the late empire.

A. R. BIRLEY, *Hadrian the Restless Emperor* (1997). A biography of an important emperor.

P. BROWN, *The World of Late Antiquity, C.E. 150–750* (1971). A brilliant and readable essay.

A. FERRILL, *The Fall of the Roman Empire, The Military Explanation* (1986). An interpretation that emphasizes the decline in the quality of the Roman army.

M. GRANT, *The Fall of the Roman Empire* (1990). A lively, well-written account.

A. H. M. JONES, *The Later Roman Empire*, 3 vols. (1964). A comprehensive study of the period.

J. LEBRETON and J. ZEILLER, *History of the Primitive Church*, 3 vols. (1962) The Catholic viewpoint.

H. LIETZMANN, *History of the Early Church*, 2 vols. (1961). From the Protestant viewpoint.

F. G. B. MILLAR, *The Roman Near East, 31 B.C.–A.D. 337* (1993). A valuable study of Rome's relations with an important part of its empire.

H. M. D. PARKER, *A History of the Roman World from A.D. 138 to 337* (1969). A good survey.

G. E. M. DE STE. CROIX, *The Class Struggle in the Ancient World* (1981). A Marxist perspective on classical civilization.

R. SYME, *The Roman Revolution* (1960). A brilliant study of Augustus, his supporters, and their rise to power.

Ancient Warfare

The Causes of War

War has an extremely ancient and enduring lineage. There may be evidence of organized warfare as early as the late Paleolithic era, and war was clearly a preoccupation of the first civilizations of Egypt, Mesopotamia, India, and China. In 1968, Will and Ariel Durant calculated that of the previous 3,421 years, only 268 had been free of war. None has since.

Various explanations have been offered for the persistence of the human species' inclination to make war. Ancient philosophers, such as Plato and Aristotle, simply took it for granted that men were naturally aggressive and acquisitive and that governments had been invented to curb humanity's disruptive inclinations. Thucydides, an ancient Greek historian who described his people's experiences during a catastrophic civil war, concluded that men were driven to fight for three reasons: fear of an enemy, greed for personal gain, and the need to defend honor (i.e., one's sense of duty and of personal integrity). At most times in history, there has been general agreement that some things are worth fighting for—namely, freedom, religious allegiance, and the pursuit of wealth.

Wars are not launched by blind instinct. They are the results of choices that people make. Those who start wars always believe that they have good reasons for doing so and usually make rational cases for their decision. Fundamentally, however, all the arguments for war may boil down to one concern: access to power—the source of security, reputation, and privilege.

War and Technology

From the earliest times war and technology have had a mutually stimulating effect. Warriors' needs inspire the invention of new weapons, and changes in weapons alter the characteristics of war.

Fortress Walls

About 7000 B.C.E. (several millennia before the appearance of the earliest Western civilizations), the Neolithic people who settled at Jericho felt so threatened by war that they surrounded their homes with a thirteen-foot-high stone wall and a ten-foot-deep moat. Their example was followed by the Sumerians who pioneered civilization in Mesopotamia about 3000 B.C.E. By 2000 B.C.E. Egypt's southern border was guarded by a string of forts. A paucity of stone and wood prevented early Chinese communities from being fortified, but by the era of the Shang dynasty (ca. 1766–1050 B.C.E.) walls of hard-packed earth were being erected around settlements in China.

The history of warfare is the story of an interplay between defense and offense. The development of fortified stongholds encouraged the invention of new devices and techniques for besieging them. The ancient Mesopotamians and Egyptians employed scaling ladders, battering rams, and mobile siege towers, and they burrowed beneath walls to undermine them. By the fourth century B.C.E., Greeks were using catapults to hurl stones at enemy fortresses. Until the invention of gunpowder and cannons, however, the most effective means for taking a walled city was to blockade it and starve it into submission.

Army Against Army

Combat did not always involve an assault on a defended position. As early as the Stone Age, groups of men had begun to engage each other in the open field with clubs, spears, axes, and bows and arrows. The Bronze Age saw the appearance of sharper, sturdier weapons and metal body armor. These weapons, when combined with techniques of fortification and large supplies of manpower, enabled the rulers of ancient Mesopotamia and Egypt to extend their authority over vast areas.

This mound marks the ancient city of Jericho. Thought by some to be the earliest Neolithic site in the Middle East, it sprang up around an oasis about 7000 B.C.E. The thick stone walls and moat that surround it show that it was meant to be a fortress that could resist sieges, showing that warfare was common at least as early as the construction of this city. © Zev Radovan, Jerusalem, Israel

The Chariot and the Bow

The next great revolution in warfare came about 1800 B.C.E. with the invention of the chariot and the composite bow. The chariot was a light, two-wheeled, horse-drawn vehicle capable of carrying two men—a driver and a warrior. By gluing together strips of wood and horn, a bow could be made that was small enough to wield from a chariot but powerful enough to fell an enemy at long range. From a rapidly wheeling chariot, an archer could devastate a company of foot soldiers, hitting as many as six a minute.

Beginning about 1800 B.C.E., peoples who spoke Indo-European languages began to descend on the Middle East with chariot-equipped armies. One group of them, the Aryans, destroyed the indigenous Indus civilization. China's Shang dynasty used the new fighting techniques in its rise to power. The nation that brought this form of ancient military technology to its peak was Assyria. By the eighth century B.C.E, the Assyrian kings had discovered how to exploit the full potentials of the new weapons by training companies of men to use them cooperatively and strategically.

Mounted Cavalry

By 612 B.C.E., when the Assyrian empire fell, something new was appearing on ancient battlefields: mounted cavalry. A cavalryman had to learn to control a horse with his knees so as to leave both his hands free to shoot his bow. The first people to become proficient at this were the nomads from the steppes of northern Eurasia. About 690 B.C.E., they began to prey on the civilized lands to the south. They invaded Asia Minor and contributed to Assyria's fall. There is

This carving in low relief from the seventh century B.C.E. shows an Assyrian war-chariot and its charioteer. It comes from the palace of King Ashurbanipal at Nineveh, the capital of the mighty Assyrian Empire that dominated the Middle East in his time. Erich Lessing/Art Resource, NY

no clear evidence of their attacks on China before the fourth century B.C.E., but they may have brought down the western Chou dynasty in 771 B.C.E. Persian and Chinese rulers usually protected their frontiers by paying one group of nomads to fend off another. The Ch'in dynasty (256–206 B.C.E.) constructed China's Great Wall as a defense against the horse warriors from the steppes, but it was not very effective. Mobility and inexpensive weapons gave the men of the grasslands an enduring advantage over the men of the plowlands and produced a pattern of recurrent nomad conquests of civilized regions.

Iron-Wielding Warriors
Since horses were expensive to maintain and the tin needed to make bronze was rare, armies that relied on horses and bronze weapons tended to be small. They were recruited from the members of wealthy warrior aristocracies whose monopoly of weapons made them the ruling classes of their societies. About 1400 B.C.E., however, techniques for manufacturing iron tools and weapons were invented in Asia Minor. Iron is an abundant metal, and its availability made weapons affordable by common people. This enabled them to challenge the power of older aristocratic govern-

ments and progress toward a more democratic order.

The Shield and the Phalanx
Hellenic, or classical, Greek civilization was the product of the *polis,* a city-state defended by an army of yeoman farmers. These were common men who could afford to equip themselves with iron weapons. The methods they developed to employ these weapons restored infantry as the dominant fighting force. Greek infantrymen were equipped with helmets, body armor, round shields, short swords, and iron-tipped pikes, but the chief source of their power was the formation in which they fought—a compact company called a *phalanx.* These disciplined units of highly motivated freemen remained supreme on the battlefield until they were confronted by the more flexible Roman legion in the second century B.C.E.

Trireme Warfare
The Greeks achieved supremacy at sea as well as on land. Oared galleys had appeared about 1000 B.C.E., and the Phoenicians had improved them by adding up to three banks of rowers. The Greeks adapted these *triremes* and employed them in new ways. The earliest form of naval combat entailed coming aside an enemy's ship and boarding it. The Greeks, however, attached rams to the prows of their warships and charged into the hulls of enemy vessels.

Roman Legions
After the development of the phalanx and the trireme, the great success enjoyed by the Greek armies of the Hellenistic era owed more to the discipline of their men and the skill of their generals than to further innovation. In the third and second centuries, military dominance of the Mediterranean world passed to the Roman infantry. The Romans abandoned the phalanx for a more open order of battle. Rome's legions were composed of small, self-sufficient units that could be utilized in a variety of ways. The army attacked by first hurling heavy iron javelins into

The Great Wall of China was originally built during the Ch'in dynasty (256–206 B.C.E.), but what we see today is the wall as it was completely rebuilt during the Ming dynasty (1368–1644 C.E.). Paolo Koch/Photo Researchers, Inc.

the enemy's ranks and then engaging at close quarters with short, double-edged swords. As the ancient world neared its end, the Romans developed a horse soldier called the *cataphract.* He was a heavily armored man on horseback who charged his opponents with a lance. His appearance marked the start of another revolution in the history of warfare, a revolution that passed military supremacy to the medieval knight.

❖ *How early is the evidence for warfare among human beings? Why did Thucydides think that people went to war? Can you think of any good reasons for fighting a war? How did war and technology affect one another in the ancient world?*

Chapter 6
The Early Middle Ages (476–1000): The Birth of Europe

KEY TOPICS

- How the fusion of Germanic and Roman cultures laid the foundation for a distinctively European society following the collapse of the Roman Empire
- The Byzantine and Islamic empires and their impact on the West
- The role of the church in Western society during the early Middle Ages
- The political and economic features of Europe under the Franks
- The characteristics of feudal society

The collapse of Roman civilization forced the peoples of the Mediterranean world to experiment with new ideas and institutions. In what had been the northern and western provinces of the Roman Empire, aspects of Greco-Roman and German cultures combined with Christianity to create a uniquely European way of life. In the East, two other medieval civilizations appeared: Byzantium and Islam.

On the Eve of the Frankish Ascendancy

The attempts made to save the Roman Empire in the late third century influenced how it fell. Diocletian (r. 284–305) dealt with simultaneous threats to the empire in the East and the West by sharing leadership with a colleague, Maximian. His division of the central government set the stage for the halves of the empire to evolve separately. Imperial rule gradually faded from the West, but in the East it grew increasingly autocratic.

Constantine the Great (r. 306–337) reunited the empire and, in 324, relocated its capital to Constantinople, a new city he built in Byzantium on the border between Europe and Asia Minor. The "new Rome" flourished as the old one declined. The city of Milan, which had direct communications with the Rhine and Danube fron-

tiers, assumed Rome's place as the seat of government for the western empire. In 402 Milan itself was judged too exposed to barbarian invasions, and the western court relocated to Ravenna on the Adriatic coast. By the late fourth century, the West was in political disarray, the city of Rome was no longer of much political significance, and imperial power and prestige had shifted decisively to Constantinople.

Germanic Migrations

The German tribes did not burst on the West all of a sudden. Roman and Germanic cultures had commingled peacefully for centuries, thanks to trade and Roman "imports" of barbarian domestics, slaves, and soldiers. Some Germans even rose to command posts in Roman legions. The arrival of the Visigoths (i.e., the "West Goths") in 376, however, signaled the start of an accelerated

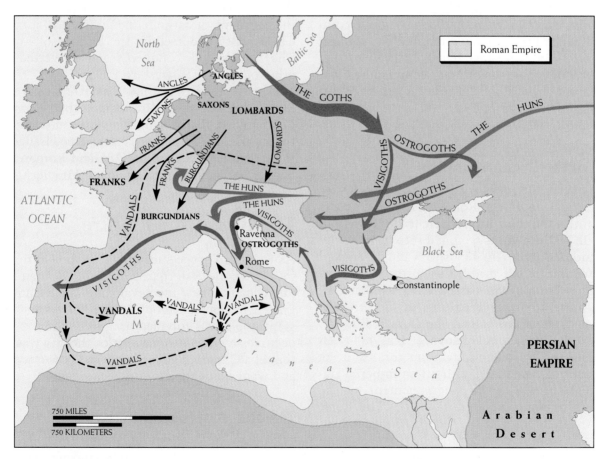

MAP 6–1 BARBARIAN MIGRATIONS INTO THE WEST IN THE FOURTH AND FIFTH CENTURIES *The intrusion of barbarians into the empire created a constantly shifting pattern of migration. The map shows the routes taken by the newcomers and the areas most affected.*

rate of barbarian migration that would overwhelm the western half of the empire. The Visigoths were pushed into the empire by the notoriously violent Huns of Mongolia. The eastern emperor Valens (r. 364–378) admitted the Visigoths to the empire in exchange for their promise to help defend its eastern frontier. They became the first *foederati*—the first allied alien nation resident within the empire.

The Visigoths entered the empire as impoverished refugees. Exploitation of their misery by Roman profiteers caused them to rebel, and in 378, at the battle of Adrianople, they destroyed Valens and his army. Constantinople defended itself by persuading the Visigoths to move west. The western government responded by withdrawing troops from the frontiers to guard Italy, and this cleared the way for other German tribes to cross those frontiers unopposed.

It may seem surprising that there was so little resistance in the West to the migration of the Germanic tribes. The largest tribe probably numbered no more than 100,000 people, a small group compared to the Roman population. But the western empire was badly overextended, divided by struggles among ambitious military commanders, and weakened physically by decades of famine, pestilence, and overtaxation.

Fall of the Roman Empire

In the early fifth century, Italy suffered a series of devastating blows. Rome was sacked by the Visigoths and their king Alaric (ca. 370–410) in 410. In 452 the Huns were led into Italy by the infamous Attila. In 455 the Vandals sacked Rome, and by the mid-fifth century, power in western Europe had passed from Roman emperors to barbarian chieftains. In 476, a traditional date for the fall of the Roman Empire, the barbarian general Odovacer (ca. 434–493) deposed the West's nominal emperor, Romulus Augustulus, and ruled without an imperial figurehead. In 493, with encouragement by the eastern emperor Zeno (r. 474–491), Theodoric (ca. 454–526), king of the Ostrogoths (the "East Goths"), took Odovacer's place. By that time barbarians had thoroughly overrun the West. The Ostrogoths settled in Italy, the Franks in northern Gaul, the Burgundians in Provence, the Visigoths in southern Gaul and Spain, the

Vandals in Africa and the western Mediterranean, and the Angles and Saxons in England.

Despite the rise of barbarian leaders, western Europe did not become a savage land. The Germans respected Roman culture and were willing to learn from the people they had conquered. Except in Britain and northern Gaul, Roman language, law, and government coexisted with Germanic institutions. Only the Vandals and the Anglo-Saxons—and, after 466, the Visigoths—refused to profess at least titular obedience to the emperor in Constantinople.

Religion was a potential link between the Romans and their new rulers. The Visigoths, the Ostrogoths, and the Vandals had converted to Christianity before entering the West. Unfortunately, western Christians considered them heretics. Many of the missionaries to the Germans were followers of Arius, the heretical theologian who argued that Christ was a creature subordinate to God the Father. This problem was resolved about 500 when the Franks converted to the orthodox or catholic (i.e., universal) form of Christianity endorsed by the bishops of Rome. The Franks then conquered and converted the other barbarians in western Europe.

Despite Rome's military defeat, Goths and Franks became more Romanized than Romans Germanized. Latin language, orthodox Christianity (i.e., the kind based on the creed issued by the Council of Nicaea in 325), and Roman law triumphed in the West during the Middle Ages.

The Byzantine Empire

As western Europe succumbed to the Germanic invasions, the eastern part of the old Roman Empire became a new medieval state, the Byzantine Empire of Constantinople. From 324, when Constantinople was founded, to 1453, when it was occupied by the Ottoman Turks, the city was the seat of a Christian government. Its power waxed and waned, but the city itself endured.

The Reign of Justinian

The Byzantine Empire reached a territorial and cultural peak during the reign of the emperor Justinian (r. 527–565). Although urban institutions were disappearing in the West, Justinian's domain boasted more than 1,500 cities. The largest (with perhaps

Empress Theodora and her attendants. The union of political and spiritual authority in the person of the empress is shown by the depiction on Theodora's mantle of three magi carrying gifts to the Virgin and Jesus.
Scala/Art Resource, NY

350,000 inhabitants) was Constantinople—the center of Western commerce and communications. The greater provincial cities of the empire had populations of about 50,000 and sustained thriving economies.

Justinian's most important counselor was his brilliant wife Theodora (d. 548). If the controversial *Secret History* by Procopius, Justinian's court historian, is to be believed, Theodora, the daughter of a bear trainer in the circus, began her career as a prostitute. Her background may have given her a toughness that was useful to her husband, for she guided him through crises that might have overwhelmed his government. She was particularly useful in dealing with the religious quarrels that troubled the peace of the empire. Whereas Justinian was a strictly orthodox Christian, Theodora's patronage pacified a powerful faction of Christian heretics, the Monophysites. The Monophysites believed that Jesus had a single nature that was partially human and divine, whereas the orthodox church claimed that he had two distinct natures: one fully human and the other fully divine. The Monophysites were strong enough to form a separate church in the eastern provinces of the empire. After Theodora's death, the imperial government made the mistake of trying to stamp them out. As a result, a few years later when Persian and Arab armies invaded, the resentful Monophysites offered little resistance.

LAW   Byzantine policy was to centralize government and enforce legal and doctrinal conformity throughout the empire: "one God, one empire, one religion." One of Justinian's major achievements was the codification of Roman law, the *Corpus Juris Civilis (Body of Civil Law)*. It contained four parts. The *Code,* which appeared in 533, revised imperial edicts issued since the reign of Hadrian (117–138). The *Novellae (New Things)* consisted of Justinian's decrees—which were added to by his successors. The *Digest* was a summary of the opinions of famous legal experts. The *Institutes* was a textbook for young lawyers. It spelled out the principles of law implied by the *Code* and the *Digest*. These works had little immediate effect on medieval common law, but from the Renaissance on they greatly influenced the development of law in Europe.

RELIGION   Like law, religion was used to promote the centralization of the Byzantine Empire. Christianity was proclaimed the official religion of the eastern empire in 380. The coronation of emperors became a Christian religious ceremony presided over by the "patriarch" (i.e., the chief bishop) of Constantinople. And as the great churches of Constantinople, Alexandria, Antioch, and Jerusalem acquired enormous wealth, they took on the functions of state welfare agencies.

Paganism was curtailed by persecution and the absorption of some of its practices into popular

Hagia Sophia: A Temple Surpassing That of Solomon

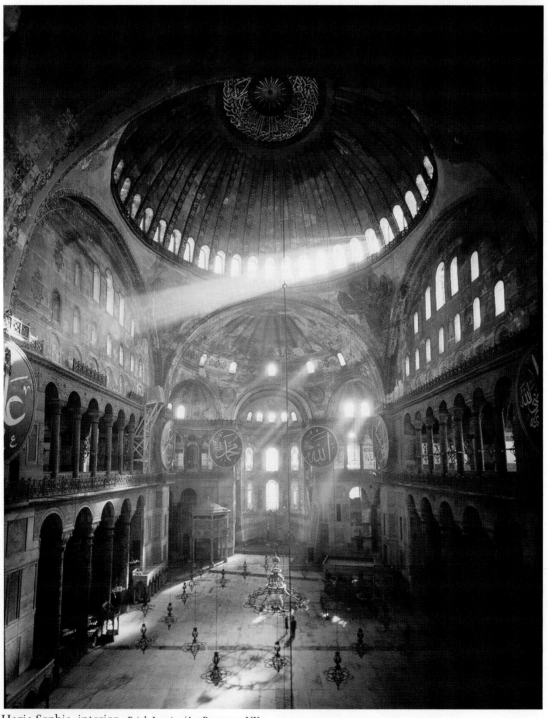

Hagia Sophia, interior. Erich Lessing/Art Resource, NY

The greatest extant monument to the reign of the emperor Justinian is also one of the greatest achievements of all Byzantine art and architecture, the Church of the Holy Wisdom (i.e., *Hagia Sophia*). In 532 Justinian was nearly driven from the throne by rioting mobs, and in the confusion the church that served his court was destroyed. When order was restored, Justinian commissioned two architects (Anthemius of Tralles and Isidore of Miletus) to build a splendid new imperial chapel. With the help of a team of engineers and master masons and 10,000 laborers, they completed the project in about five years.

The new church employed a novel system of domes and pendentives to roof a huge rectangular space. Its most awe-inspiring feature was a central dome 112 feet in diameter that soared to a height of 184 feet. A row of windows circled the base of the crowning cupola to flood the room with light and illuminate the acres of brilliantly colored mosaics that covered the sanctuary's walls. The result was a monumental open, airy, luminous hall that proclaimed the majesty of God and God's illustrious servant, the emperor.

Two decades after the church was completed, Justinian's court historian, Procopius, published an account of its construction. He claimed that Justinian conceived the church in a divine vision and helped to solve the engineering challenges its construction posed. Justinian's chief contribution to the project was, however, probably financial, for the building allegedly cost 320,000 pounds of gold. Justinian doubtless concluded that the money was well spent. A ninth-century source claims that the emperor's intent was to build a church that would surpass the legendary splendor of the temple King Solomon had built for the ancient Jews in Jerusalem. Although the story is fictional, it describes the effect the building still has on its visitors.

When the Turks conquered Constantinople in 1453, *Hagia Sophia* was transformed into a Muslim mosque. Four minarets were added to the building and its mosaics were covered with paint. Muslim faith regarded the efforts of Byzantine artists to depict God as blasphemy.

Sources: H. W. Janson and A. F. Janson, *History of Art*, 5th ed. (Upper Saddle River, NJ: Prentice Hall, 1997), pp. 252–254; Cyril Mango, "Byzantine Writers on the Fabric of Hagia Sophia," in *Hagia Sophia from the Age of Justinian to the Present*, ed. R. Mark and A. S. Cakmak (Cambridge, U.K.: Cambridge University Press, 1992). pp. 41–50.

Christianity, but orthodox Christianity never succeeded in stamping out all the heresies that proliferated throughout the empire. Large numbers of Jews had also to be accommodated. Under Roman law Jews had legal protection so long as they did not proselytize Christians, build new synagogues, or attempt to enter sensitive public offices or professions. Justinian pressured Jews to convert, and later emperors both ordered Jews to be baptized and granted tax breaks to those who voluntarily complied. Neither policy was very successful.

Eastern Influences

Justinian tried but failed to conquer Italy and reestablish the old Roman Empire. His successors were much too preoccupied by developments in the East to devote any thought to the West. Under the emperor Heraclius (610–641), the Byzantine Empire took a decidedly Eastern turn. Heraclius spoke Greek, not Latin, and spent his entire reign struggling with Persians and Muslims. He fought the Persians to a draw, but after 632 Islamic armies advanced relentlessly into his territory. They overran Asia Minor, and in 677 they besieged Constantinople for the first, but not the last, time. Not until the reign of Leo III (717–740), founder of the Isaurian dynasty, were they driven back and Asia Minor recovered.

Leo's relations with western Christians worsened when he outlawed the use of images in Christian worship. Islam equated image veneration with idolatry, and this may have had some influence on Leo and his successors. Be that as it may, western Christians were deeply affronted by the East's iconoclasm, for they had great affection for holy images of Jesus, Mary, and the saints. Leo's assumption that secular rulers have the right to legislate religious practices—a doctrine called Caesaro-papism—was also rejected by the Western church. The ban on images in the East was ultimately lifted in the late eighth century, but in the interim it worsened the divisions in Christendom and destroyed much religious art.

In 1071 the Byzantines were defeated in a battle at Manzikert, and the Muslim Seljuk Turks overran the eastern provinces of the empire. This was the beginning of a long, slow decline for the eastern empire. In 1092 the Byzantine emperor Alexius I Comnenus (r. 1081–1118) appealed to the West for help, and three years later the West responded with the first of the great Crusades. The First Crusade enabled Constantinople to recover some territory, but a century later (in 1204) the Fourth Crusade overwhelmed Constantinople itself and did more damage to the city than all previous Muslim attacks.

Despite its vicissitudes, the Byzantine Empire maintained a protective barrier between Europe and its non-Christian enemies in the East until 1453. Byzantine civilization was also, for much of this time, more advanced than European civilization and the source of much of the classical learning that filtered through to the West.

Islam and the Islamic World

A new religion called Islam arose in Arabia in the sixth century in response to the work of the Prophet Muhammad. It sparked the creation of a third medieval civilization and a rapidly expanding empire that quickly became a threat to Byzantium's Greek emperors and Europe's German kings.

Muhammad's Religion

Muhammad (570–632) was orphaned at a young age and raised by relatives in modest circumstances. As a youth, Muhammad worked on caravans as a merchant's assistant. At the age of twenty-five, he married a wealthy Meccan widow and with her support became a kind of social activist. He opposed the materialism of Meccan society and some of his people's pagan practices. When he was about forty, he had a deep religious experience in which he received visitations from the angel Gabriel. Muhammad then began (and continued for the rest of his life) to recite what his followers believe literally to be God's words. Between 650 and 651, the revealed texts that God had chosen him to convey were collected in a sacred book, the Qur'an ("reciting"). At the heart of Muhammad's message was a call for all Arabs to submit to God's will as revealed through "the Prophet." The terms *Islam* and *Muslim* both imply "submission" or "surrender."

Muhammad did not claim that his message was new—only that it was final and definitive. What he taught was consistent with what a long line of Jewish prophets, from Noah to Jesus Christ, had taught. His special role was to be the last of the prophets that God would send. Islam, like Judaism, was a strictly monotheistic and theocentric religion, and it concurred with Judaism in rejecting Christianity's trinitarian view of God and concept of God's incarnation in the person of Jesus.

Muhammad's birthplace, the community of Mecca, was the location of the Ka'ba, one of Arabia's most holy shrines. The Ka'ba was a simple, rectangular building containing a sacred black stone and various other holy objects. Muhammad's attack on the idols of the Ka'ba was not only an offense to traditional Arab religion. It threatened to diminish Mecca's appeal as a center for trade. In 622 the Meccan authorities forced Muhammad and his followers to flee to Medina, 240 miles to the north. This event, the *Hegira*, has been chosen as the pivotal date for the Islamic calendar, for it marks the moment when Muhammad founded the first Muslim community.

Muhammad and his followers prospered in Medina by raiding the caravans that went to and from Mecca. Success brought him throngs of converts, and by 624 he was powerful enough to persuade Mecca to submit to his authority. He returned in triumph, cleansed the Ka'ba of its idols, and designated it the chief shrine for his new religion. Islam, like Christianity, eased life for its converts by making some compromises with their cherished pagan customs.

Muhammad stressed practice more than doctrine, and, as Islam matured, it evolved characteristic customs and values: (1) to be honest and modest in all dealings and behavior, (2) to be absolutely loyal to the Islamic community, (3) to abstain from pork and alcohol, (4) to pray facing Mecca five times a day, (5) to contribute to the support of the poor and needy, (6) to fast during daylight hours for one month each year, and (7) to make a pilgrimage to the Ka'ba at least once in a lifetime. Muslim men were allowed as many as four wives—provided they were able to treat them all justly and equally. A man could divorce a wife with a simple declaration of his intent. A wife could also initiate divorce, although the procedure was more complicated for her. She was expected to be totally loyal and devoted to her husband, and only her husband was to be allowed to see her face.

Islam made no rigid distinction between clergy and laity. It had no priesthood, but looked for leadership to a scholarly elite of laymen, the *ulema* ("persons with correct knowledge"). The authority of these men derived from their reputations for great piety and learning, and their opinions had the force of law in Muslim society. They also kept a critical eye on Muslim rulers to ensure that they adhered to the letter of the Qur'an.

Islamic Diversity

Islam was very successful in unifying the Arab tribes and various pagan peoples, for it appealed to the pride of groups that had been marginalized in a world dominated by Judaism and Christianity. Islam proclaimed Muhammad to be history's most important religious figure and his followers to be the people God chose to receive his most significant revelation.

Passionate faith in Muhammad did not prevent divisions from emerging within Islam. Factions contested who had the best right to the caliphate, the office held by the men who succeeded to Muhammad's leadership of the Muslim community. Doctrinal differences were debated, as was the issue of the extent to which Islam was meant to be a religion only for Arabs.

The most radical positions were taken by the Kharijites. Their leaders seceded from the camp of the fourth caliph, Ali (r. 656–661). In their opinion, he sacrificed important principles for political advantage, and in 661 one of their members assassinated him. The Kharijites were "Puritans" who excluded from Islam all but rigorously virtuous Muslims.

More influential were the Shi'a, or "partisans" of Ali. The Shi'a regarded Ali and his descendants as the only rightful successors to Muhammad—not only by virtue of their kinship with the Prophet but also by his expressed will. To the Shi'a, Ali's assassination represented a basic truth of devout Muslim life: a true imam ("ruler") and his followers should expect to suffer unjustly even unto death. A theology of martyrdom is the mark of Shi'a teaching, and the Shi'a are still an embattled minority within Islam.

A third group, which has been dominant for most of Islamic history, is the majority centrist party, the Sunnis (i.e., the followers of *sunna*, "tradition"). Sunnis emphasize loyalty to the

Muslims are enjoined to live by the divine law, or Shari'a, *and have a right to have disputes settled by an arbiter of the* Shari'a. *Here we see a husband complaining about his wife before the state-appointed judge, or* qadi. *The wife, backed up by two other women, points an accusing finger at the husband. In such cases, the first duty of the* qadi, *who should be a learned person of faith, is to try to effect a reconciliation before the husband divorces his wife, or the wife herself seeks a divorce.* Cliche Bibliothèque Nationale de France, Paris

fundamental principles of Islam more than to the particular issues that cause the Kharijites and the Shi'a to exclude various people from the Muslim community.

Islamic Empires

Muhammad's first three successors, the caliphs Abu Bakr (r. 632–634), Umar (r. 634–644), and Uthman (r. 644–656), won control of the southern and eastern rim of the Mediterranean. Islam's capital shifted from Mecca to the more centrally located Damascus, and by the eighth century the caliphs ruled an empire that stretched from Spain to India. In 750 the Abbasid family overthrew the Umayyad caliphs of Damascus and moved the

seat of their government to Baghdad. Shortly thereafter, their huge domain began to break up into separate states, and rival caliphs contested their authority.

The Muslim conquests proceeded rapidly because the Arabs' opponents, the Byzantines and Persians, had exhausted themselves in a long war. The Arabs struck just as the Byzantine emperor Heraclius drove the Persians out of Egypt, Palestine, Syria, and Asia Minor. Before Heraclius died in 641, Arab armies had taken all these conquests, except for Asia Minor, from him. By 643 they had overrun what remained of the Persian Empire, and by the end of the century the last Byzantine outpost in North Africa had fallen to them.

Most of the inhabitants of the Byzantine lands the Muslims occupied were Christians, but many were also Semitic peoples with links to the Arabs. Heraclius's efforts to stamp out heresy and impose Greek orthodoxy on the Monophysite communities of Egypt and Syria led many of them to welcome the Islamic invaders as liberators from Byzantine oppression.

Islam won control of Christian territories in North Africa and Spain, but its thrust into the European heart of Christendom was rebuffed in 732 by Charles Martel, ruler of the Franks. His defeat of an Arab raiding party at Poitiers (in central France) marked the point at which the Muslim advance in the West began to be reversed. The Isaurian dynasty, which Leo III (r. 717–740) established in Constantinople, defended Asia Minor from Islamic aggression and blocked Muslim access to Europe from the east.

The Western Debt to Islamic Culture

The Christian West was very hostile to Islam, but it profited a great deal from contact with the Muslims. Arab cultures of the early medieval period were far superior to those of Christian Europe. Europe learned important technologies from the Muslims, and Muslim scholars made major works of Greek science and philosophy available to the West in Latin translation. As late as the sixteenth century, in addition to the works of the ancient world's physicians, Hippocrates and Galen, the basic gynecological and child care manuals in use in the West were those of a Baghdad physician, Al-Razi, and the philosophers Avicenna (980–1037) and Averröes (1126–1198), Islam's great authorities on Aristotle. The works

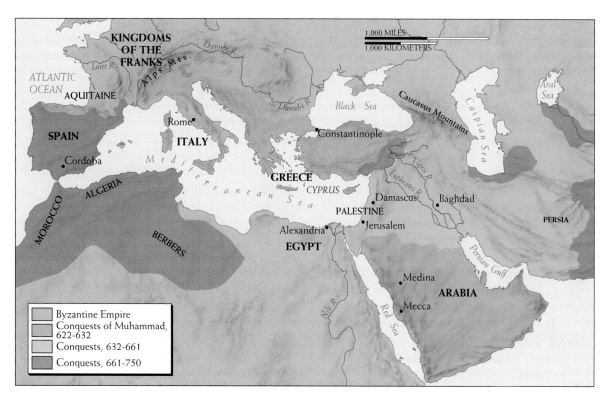

MAP 6–2   MUSLIM CONQUESTS AND DOMINATION OF THE MEDITERRANEAN TO ABOUT 750 C.E. *Within 125 years of Muhammad's rise, Muslims came to dominate Spain and all areas south and east of the Mediterranean.*

of multilingual Jewish scholars also helped create bridges between the Muslim and Christian worlds.

Western Society and the Developing Christian Church

Europe, overrun by barbarians from the north and east and threatened in the south by a vigorous and expansive Islam, declined during the fifth and sixth centuries. As trade waned in the increasing chaos, the West lost the urban centers where exchanges of goods and ideas promoted cultural growth. The beleaguered westerners had no help from the East, for the Byzantine emperors of the seventh century were preoccupied with the Islamic threat to their domains. As the Muslims conquered Mediterranean islands and ports and strangled Christian shipping, Europe's communications with the East declined even further. Forced by these developments to rely on their own resources, westerners drew on their Germanic and Greco-Roman heritages to create distinctive new cultures.

As western cities and governments declined, people sought employment and protection on the self-sufficient estates of the great landholders. Peasants made up 90 percent of the population of medieval Europe. Some were free and owned their own land. Some surrendered their land to a more powerful man in exchange for assistance and became serfs. Serfs were bound to the land they worked. They were not free to leave it, but, on the other hand, custom protected them from being separated from it and sold as slaves.

As trade declined, agricultural districts became insular and self-contained. Barter sufficed for exchanging goods among the great estates that were the basic political and economic units of medieval society. Producers adjusted their output to local need. And since there was no way to turn excess goods into profit, there was little incentive to experiment with more efficient techniques or expand production. This was the background for the evolution of the characteristic medieval institutions: an economic system called manorialism and a political system called feudalism.

The Christian church kept some of medieval Europe's fading urban centers alive. During the period of the late empire the church had modeled itself on Rome's imperial government and had located its administrative offices in cities, the empire's centers of power. As the western empire crumbled and secular magistrates disappeared, many of their functions were transferred to bishops, the only Roman officials still available. The local cathedral (a church served by a bishop) became the center of urban life and its bishop the effective governor of his city. The church thus preserved some of the skills and procedures of Roman government.

The church was forced by Rome's decline and the loss of the state's protection to involve itself in politics. The struggle to survive the period of the German and Islamic invasions cost the church some of its spiritual integrity but did not diminish its effectiveness as a civilizing and unifying force. Its rituals and creeds united people across barriers of social class, education, and gender, and its clergy—the best-educated minds in Europe—had knowledge that was invaluable to the German kings who were trying to reestablish order.

Monastic Culture

The early medieval church drew much of its strength from religious institutions called monasteries. The first monks were hermits who protested the relaxation of standards of Christian discipline that followed Constantine's popularization of Christianity in the fourth century. They fled to remote areas to find the freedom to practice the extreme ascetic disciplines that they believed were the mark of true Christian commitment. They became the new Christian heroes—the successors to the martyrs that the Roman government no longer persecuted.

Medieval Christians viewed monastic life—governed, as it was, by the biblical "counsels of perfection" (chastity, poverty, and obedience)—as humanity's highest calling. Monks and the secular (i.e., parish) clergy (whom popular opinion forced to adopt some monastic disciplines) were expected to meet a more demanding spiritual standard than ordinary believers. Consequently, clergy appeared superior to laity, a belief that served the papacy well in struggles with secular rulers.

Although early monasticism was modeled on the lives of hermits such as Anthony of Egypt (ca. 251–356), it soon evolved communal institutions. In the first quarter of the fourth century, Pachomius (ca. 286–346), another Egyptian recluse, set up a highly regimented community in which hundreds of monks lived in accordance with a strict penal code. Such monastic communities tried to become "cities of God," isolating themselves from the collapsing Roman Empire and its nominally Christian society. The form of monasticism that spread throughout the East, however, was that championed by Basil the Great (329–379). It put less stress on personal asceticism and urged monks to care for the needy outside their communities.

Athanasius (ca. 293–373) and Martin of Tours (ca. 315–ca. 399) introduced the West to the monastic practices that were evolving in the East. But in 529 Benedict of Nursia (ca. 480–547) wrote a rule (i.e., a constitution) for a monastery he established at Monte Cassino near Naples, Italy, which defined a uniquely Western style of monasticism and became standard throughout Europe. Benedict's Rule governed a monk's every activity, including sleep. It discouraged the kind of flamboyant asceticism that was popular in the East. Benedict insisted that monks have adequate food, some wine, serviceable clothing, and proper amounts of sleep and relaxation. Periods of time were set aside each day for prayer, communal worship, and study—and for the manual labor by which monks supported themselves. The program was designed to create autonomous religious communities that were economically, spiritually, and intellectually self-sufficient. Benedictine monks did not turn their backs on the world. They were chiefly responsible for the missionary work that converted England and Germany to Christianity, and their discipline and devotion to hard work made them both an economic and a spiritual force wherever they went.

The Doctrine of Papal Primacy

Constantine and the eastern emperors treated the church like a department of state. They intervened in its theological debates and legislated its doctrine. The bishops of Rome, however, acquired independence as imperial power faded in the West. The doctrine of "papal primacy" that they proclaimed asserted their right to undisputed leadership of a church that was totally independent of the state.

Papal primacy was a response to the decline of imperial Rome and the increasing pretensions of Constantinople. In 381 when the ecumenical Council of Constantinople declared the patriarch of Constantinople to be first in rank after the bishop of Rome, Pope Damasus I (366–384) objected. He claimed that Rome had a unique "apostolic" primacy, for its bishops were heirs to the Apostle Peter and his personal legacy as the "rock" on which Jesus had said (Matthew 16:18) that the church was to be built. After the Council of Chalcedon (451) accorded the Byzantine patriarch the same primacy over the East that Rome traditionally had in the West, Pope Leo I (440–461) assumed the title *pontifex maximus* ("supreme priest") to assert his claim to supremacy over all bishops everywhere. At the end of the fifth century, Pope Gelasius I (492–496) further clarified the nature of papal authority by declaring it to be "more weighty" than that of the state—his reason being that the church was responsible for the means of salvation, the most serious human concern.

The Germanic and Islamic invasions prevented Constantinople from exercising much control over the popes and the Western church. When the Lombard tribes invaded Italy late in the sixth century, Pope Gregory I, "the Great" (590–604), ignored the imperial authorities and assumed the right to negotiate with the barbarians as the chief representative of the Italian people.

The Division of Christendom

By the time Gregory became pope, the patriarch of Constantinople was using the title "universal" patriarch to imply a claim to supremacy over Rome. Since he had no authority in the West, this was really an admission that separate churches were functioning in the East and West. The division of the church was apparent in language, doctrine, disciplinary codes, and liturgies. The Greek Byzantine church had a mystical, other-worldly orientation that contrasted with the more practical Christianity of the West's Latin church. Ecclesiastical organization in the East more closely paralleled the hierarchy of imperial government than did the structure of the Western church. But the power of the Byzantine patriarch over the clergy was limited by the

power the emperor had over him. Where the Western church tried to impose monastic celibacy on all clergy, parish priests in the Eastern church (except for bishops) were allowed to marry. The Eastern church used leavened bread in the Eucharist; Rome mandated unleavened bread. The Byzantines rejected the Catholic doctrine of purgatory. They also permitted divorce and, unlike the Catholics, performed their liturgies in the vernacular of the laity.

From time to time, Eastern and Western Christians differed markedly on doctrine. Where the Latin church looked to the Roman pope to define doctrine, the Greek church relied on the authority of the Bible and ecumenical councils. Disputes over the right to define doctrine became acute when the East endorsed iconoclasm (i.e., repudiating the veneration of holy images) and when the West added the word *filioque* ("and from the Son") to the Nicene Creed. The latter was the West's attempt to subvert compromises the East had made with Arianism. It was meant to make it clear that the Holy Spirit proceeded from the Father and the Son as equal partners in the Godhead and not from the Father alone. The claims of Roman popes to a primacy of authority over the whole church were dismissed in the East, for eastern Christianity evolved not as a single organization but as a communion of independent national churches. In the ninth century, when the crucial issue of authority over the universal church came to a head, Pope Nicholas I and Patriarch Photius excommunicated each other. In 1054 Pope Leo IX and Patriarch Michael Cerularius again officially divided the church by repeating the mutual condemnation.

Rome took a risk in quarreling with Constantinople, for popes looked to the eastern empire to defend them from barbarian invaders. But as help declined from that quarter and Christianity spread to the invaders, the popes sought new allies among the Germans. They correctly intuited that the Franks of northern Gaul were Europe's ascendant power and the church's most promising potential protectors. In 754, Pope Stephen II (752–757) took the dramatic step of throwing in his lot with the Germans. He persuaded Pepin III, ruler of the Franks, to defend Rome from the Lombards. This acknowledged the end of the old empire and the transfer of the West to new hands.

The Kingdom of the Franks

Merovingians and Carolingians: From Clovis to Charlemagne

A warrior chieftain named Clovis (ca. 466?–511) founded the first Frankish dynasty. It is called Merovingian after Merovich, an early tribal leader. Clovis and his successors united the Salian and Ripuarian Franks, subdued the Burgundians and Visigoths, won the support of the Gallo-Romans by converting to orthodox Christianity, and turned the Roman province of Gaul into France (i.e., "land of the Franks").

GOVERNING THE FRANKS The Merovingians struggled with the perennial problem of medieval politics: the competing claims of the "one" and the "many." As kings worked to centralize governments, powerful local magnates fought to preserve their regional autonomy. The result was a battle between forces that tried to unify society and those that promoted fragmentation.

The Merovingian kings hoped to pull their nation together by making pacts with the landed nobility and by relying for help in running their domain on a new kind of royal official, the count. Counts were sent out to manage districts in which they had no hereditary estates. Kings hoped that counts would be easier to control than landed aristocrats, for the people the counts governed would have no tradition of loyalty to the counts' families. But as time passed, kings found it impossible to prevent counts from establishing hereditary claims to their offices and becoming as independent as the older nobility. The unification of the Frankish state was also impeded by Frankish inheritance customs, which gave all a king's legitimate male heirs a right to a share in his kingdom.

By the seventh century the Merovingian king was king in title only. Real executive authority had devolved on one of his officials, the "mayor of the palace." The family of Pepin I of Austrasia (d. 639) monopolized this post until 751, when, with the connivance of the pope, one of its members shoved the Merovingians aside, expropriated the Frankish crown, and founded the Carolingian dynasty.

Pepin I's descendent, Pepin II (d. 714), who had ruled the Frankish kingdom in fact but not in title, bequeathed that anomalous situation to his illegitimate son, Charles "Martel" (Charles "the Hammer"). Martel (d. 741) created a great cavalry by bestowing lands as fiefs or benefices ("provisional" grants) on powerful noblemen on condition that they use the income to equip themselves to fight for him. His army proved its worth at Poitiers in 732, when it broke the momentum of the Muslim advance and secured the Pyrenees as the border of western Europe.

Much of the land that Martel distributed as fiefs to create his army came from the church. The church was dependent on the protection of the Franks, and it could do little to prevent the confiscation of property that was used to fund its own defense. Eventually, however, the church was partially compensated for its losses.

Where the Merovingians had tried to weaken the aristocrats by raising landless men to power, the Carolingians forged an alliance with the landed aristocracy and staffed their government almost entirely from its ranks. By playing to strength rather than challenging it, the Carolingians secured their position in the short run.

THE FRANKISH CHURCH The church played a major role in the Frankish government, for its monasteries were the intellectual centers of Carolingian society. In Merovingian times the higher clergy were employed in tandem with counts as royal agents, and the Carolingians—particularly Charles Martel and his successors, Pepin III, "the Short" (d. 768), and Charlemagne (r. 768–814)—relied on Christian missionaries to pacify the barbarian lands that they conquered. Conversion to Nicene Christianity was an essential part of the process of assimilating new subjects. The cavalry broke their bodies, and the clergy reworked their hearts and minds.

The missions of the church and state tended to be confused when the king appointed Christian bishops to govern the lands they were converting. An event from the career of Boniface (born Wynfrith, 680?–754), an Anglo-Saxon monk who was the most famous of the Carolingian missionaries, illustrates how deeply involved in politics the church became. In 751 Pope Zacharias (741–752) sanctioned Pepin the Short's bid for the Frankish throne. Pepin was proclaimed king by the nobility in council, and the last of the Merovingians, the puppet king Childeric III, was hustled off to a monastery where enforced celibacy guaranteed the extermination of his line. Boniface may have anointed Pepin at his coronation. Since anointing was part of the ritual of priestly ordination, the rite was apparently intended to give the Carolingian monarchy a sacral character.

In 753 Pope Stephen II (752–757), Zacharias's successor, asked for a favor in return. He came to Pepin's court to ask the Franks to defend Rome from the Lombards and confirm papal claims to central Italy. In 755 the Franks defeated the Lombards and turned over to the pope the lands surrounding Rome, including some to which the eastern emperor had title. This confirmed the pope's secular authority over a region known as the Papal States.

About this time (750–800) a document called the *Donation of Constantine* began to be circulated to support the church in its dealings with the Franks. It said that Constantine had given the papacy title to the western half of his empire. If so, this implied that the papacy had the right to pass judgment on the legitimacy of western governments. The *Donation* was exposed as a forgery in the fifteenth century, but initially it gave the popes some leverage in dealing with their potentially overwhelming protectors. The Franks drew almost as slight a boundary between state and church as did the eastern emperors, and the church had to fight hard to avoid being subordinated to the Frankish monarchy.

The Reign of Charlemagne (768–814)

In 774 Charlemagne, the son of Pepin the Short, completed his father's work by conquering Italy's Lombards and assuming their crown. He devoted the rest of his reign to expanding the size of the kingdom he had inherited. The Saxons of northern Germany were brutally subdued and pacified by being evicted from their homes for resettlement elsewhere. The Muslims were chased beyond the Pyrenees, and the Avars (a tribe related to the Huns) were practically annihilated—bringing the Danubian plains into the Frankish orbit. By the time of Charlemagne's death on January 28, 814, his kingdom embraced modern France, Belgium, Holland, Switzerland, almost the whole of western Germany, much of Italy, a portion of Spain, and the island of Corsica—an area about equal to the nations of the European Economic Community (EEC).

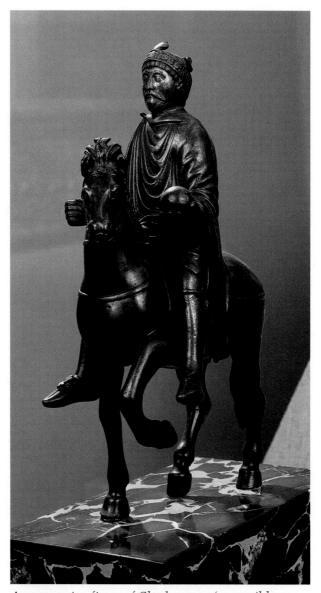

An equestrian figure of Charlemagne (or possibly one of his sons) from the early ninth century. Giraudon/Art Resource, NY

THE NEW EMPIRE Charlemagne believed that his huge domain entitled him to an imperial title, and to win support for assuming it he tried to look as imperial as possible. Since eastern emperors ruled from a fixed capital, he constructed a palace city for himself at Aachen (or Aix-la-Chapelle), and he turned to the church for help.

Charlemagne's imperial pretensions were confirmed on Christmas Day, 800, when Pope Leo III (795–816) crowned him emperor. The ceremony, which established a fateful link between German kings and Roman Italy, was in part an effort by

Map 6–3 THE EMPIRE OF CHARLEMAGNE TO 814 *Building on the successes of his predecessors, Charlemagne greatly increased the Frankish domains.*

the pope to gain some leverage over a powerful king. By arranging for the emperor to receive the crown from the hands of the pope, a precedent was set that was useful for the church in its future dealings with the state. At the time, however, the coronation in no way diminished Charlemagne's power over the church, and it strengthened him abroad by confronting the eastern emperors with a *fait accompli.* They reluctantly acknowledged his title once he disclaimed any ambition to move into their lands.

THE NEW EMPEROR Charlemagne stood a majestic six feet three and one-half inches tall. (His tomb was opened in 1861, and exact measurements of his remains were made.) He was restless, informal, and gregarious—ever ready for a hunt or for a swim with his friends in Aachen's hot springs. He was widely known for his practical jokes, lusty good humor, and warm hospitality. Aachen was a festive court to which visitors and gifts came from all over the world. In 802 the caliph of Baghdad, Harun-al-Rashid, even sent

Charlemagne a white elephant, the transport of which was as great a wonder as the creature itself.

Charlemagne had five official wives (in succession), many mistresses and concubines, and numerous children. This connubial variety caused some political upheavals when Pepin, his oldest son by his first marriage, grew jealous of the attention the emperor showed the sons of his second wife. Pepin joined some nobles in an ill-fated conspiracy against Charlemagne and spent the rest of his life confined to a monastery.

PROBLEMS OF GOVERNMENT   Charlemagne relied on counts for help in governing his empire. There may have been as many as 250 deployed to strategic locations. A Carolingian count was usually a local magnate who had soldiers and who was persuaded by royal generosity to put them at the service of his king. He maintained a local army, collected tribute and dues, and administered justice—all in the name of the king.

A count presided over a district law court called the *mallus.* Its job was to hear testimony and to pass judgment based less on evidence than on the character or believability of each party to a quarrel. In situations in which such testimony was insufficient, recourse was had to duels or to various tests or ordeals. A defendant's hand might be immersed in boiling water and his innocence determined by the way his wounds healed. Or a suspect might be bound with ropes and thrown into a river or pond that had been blessed by a priest. If the sacred water rejected him and he floated, he was assumed to be guilty. God was believed to render the verdict in an ordeal. Once guilt was determined, the *mallus* ordered monetary compensation to be paid to injured parties. This settled grievances that otherwise might have caused bloody vendettas.

Charlemagne never solved the problem of creating a loyal bureaucracy to govern his kingdom. The counts he appointed, like their Merovingian predecessors, tended to become little despots within their districts. Charlemagne issued "capitularies" (i.e., royal decrees) to establish policies he wanted his administrators to implement. He tried to exercise some oversight by sending envoys called *missi dominici* to check up on the counts and report back on their behavior. When the *missi*'s infrequent inspections had little impact, Charlemagne created provincial governors (e.g., prefects, dukes, and margraves) to keep permanent watch over the counts. They, however, proved no more trustworthy than the counts.

Charlemagne often appointed churchmen to government offices, for bishops, like counts, were considered royal servants. This, however, did little to improve the situation. The higher clergy shared the secular lifestyles and aspirations of the counts and were generally indistinguishable from the lay nobility. To be a Christian at this difficult period in the history of Europe was largely a matter of submitting to rituals such as baptism and assenting to creeds. Both clergy and laity were too preoccupied with the struggle to survive to worry much about elevated ethical issues.

ALCUIN AND THE CAROLINGIAN RENAISSANCE   Charlemagne tried to improve the government of his empire by making an intensive effort to advance the education of the aristocratic boys who were destined for offices in the church and state. His conquests brought him a great deal of wealth, and he used some of it to attract Europe's best scholars to Aachen—men such as Theodulf of Orleans, Angilbert, Einhard (Charlemagne's biographer), and Alcuin of York (735–804), a famous Anglo-Saxon educator who became director of the king's palace school. The school provided basic instruction in the seven liberal arts with special concentration on grammar, logic, rhetoric, and simple mathematics.

The curriculum was designed to give bureaucrats the simple tools of their trade, but it accomplished more than that. It improved the accuracy of the Latin used in official documents, and it spread a new and much more legible style of handwriting throughout the empire. This Carolingian "minuscule" made reading far easier and more pleasurable than the Merovingian scripts. A modest renaissance or rebirth of interest in antiquity also took place at the palace school as its scholars collected and copied ancient manuscripts. Alcuin worked on the text of the Bible and made editions of the works of Gregory the Great and the Rule of Saint Benedict. Most scholarly projects aimed at concrete reforms. They helped to establish uniformity in church law and liturgy, to educate the clergy, and to raise personal and professional standards for monks and priests.

THE CAROLINGIAN MANOR Early medieval Europe's chief economic institution was a kind of communal farm called a manor. Medieval farmers often preferred to cluster in villages rather than to live on individual farms. This increased security and enabled them to share labor and expensive agricultural implements such as plows and oxen. But instead of dividing harvests equally among all a manor's workers, each family on the manor had its own strips of land and lived from what they produced.

The status of peasants was determined by the nature of their holdings. A freeman had allodial property (i.e., land free from the claims of an overlord). If he surrendered this to an overlord in exchange for protection, he became a serf and received his land back from his lord with a new set of rights and obligations. Although the land was no longer his property, he had full use of it and could not be separated from it. His chief duty to his lord was to work his lord's *demesne,* the fields on the manor that produced the crops meant for the lord's table. Peasants who entered the service of a lord with little real property (e.g., only a few farm implements and animals) became unfree serfs. Such serfs were much more vulnerable to a lord's demands, often spending up to three days a week working their lord's fields. Truly impoverished peasants, those who had nothing to offer except their hands, had the lowest status and were the least protected from excessive demands.

By Charlemagne's day, a new type of plow was coming into use. It was heavy enough to break up the dense, waterlogged soils of northern Europe and open to cultivation lands that had defeated Roman farmers. Unlike the ancient "scratch" plow (a pointed stick), it cut deeply into the soil and had a moldboard that turned earth over to utilize more of its fertility. Ancient farmers had maintained the fertility of their fields by using a two-field system of crop rotation. That is, they simply alternated fallow and planted fields annually. A fallow field was plowed to keep down weeds but was not planted. The medieval three-field system left only one-third of a farm fallow in a given year. This decreased the amount of unproductive land that had to be plowed and used crop rotation to help maintain fertility. In the fall, one field was planted with winter crops of wheat or rye, which were harvested in early summer. In late spring, a second field was planted

with summer crops of oats, barley, lentils, and legumes, which were harvested in August or September. The third field was left fallow.

RELIGION AND THE CLERGY Religion had an intrinsic appeal for the masses of ordinary men and women who were burdened, fearful, and had little hope of improving their lots this side of eternity. The privileged upper classes were, however, no less pious. Charlemagne frequented the Church of Saint Mary in Aachen several times a day and decreed on his deathbed that all but a fraction of his great treasure be spent to endow masses and prayers for his soul.

The priests who served the people (the lower clergy as opposed to the ecclesiastical administrators) were poorly prepared to provide spiritual leadership. They were recruited from the ranks of the serfs and fared no better than other peasants. Lords owned the churches on their lands and often staffed them with their own serfs. The church expected a lord to liberate a serf who entered the clergy, but many "serf priests" said mass on Sunday and toiled as peasants during the rest of the week.

Because priests on most manors were no better educated than their congregations, religious instruction barely existed. For most people religion was more a matter of practice than doctrine. They baptized their children, attended mass, tried to learn the Lord's Prayer and the Apostles' Creed, and received the last rites when death approached. They were in awe of sacred relics and devoted to an army of saints who they hoped would intercede for them with their divine overlord in the court of heaven. Simple faith had little need for understanding.

Breakup of the Carolingian Kingdom

As Charlemagne aged, his empire became progressively ungovernable, for there was no way to prevent his nobles from doing what they wanted with the lands they held. In feudal society the intensity of one's loyalty to one's lord diminished as one's distance from that lord increased, and local people obeyed local leaders more readily than distant kings. Charlemagne had to appoint powerful men if he hoped to keep the far-flung regions of his empire under control, but their power always diminished his. In the Carolingian as in the Merovingian kingdom, the noble tail increasingly wagged the royal dog.

LOUIS THE PIOUS The Carolingians did not give up easily. Charlemagne's successor was his only surviving son, Louis the Pious (r. 814–840). During Charlemagne's last years the emperor shared the imperial title with Louis, for it symbolized the Carolingian hope of consolidating the kingdom by persuading its subjects to transcend regional and tribal loyalties. Unfortunately, in the next generation Louis's fertility undercut this objective. Louis had three sons by his first wife, and, according to Salic (i.e., Salian Frankish) law, each was entitled to a share of his kingdom. Louis tried to break with tradition by making his eldest son, Lothar (d. 855), co-regent and sole imperial heir (817). In 823, however, Louis's second wife bore him a fourth son, Charles "the Bald" (d. 877). In the interest of securing an inheritance for her boy, the queen incited her stepsons, Pepin and Louis the German, to rebel. Supported by the pope, they joined forces and defeated their father in a battle near Colmar in 833.

THE TREATY OF VERDUN AND ITS AFTERMATH Pepin's death in 838 and his father's in 840 helped clear the field of contenders. In 843 the Treaty of Verdun divided the empire among the three remaining Carolingian princes. Lothar retained the meaningless imperial title and authority over a region called Lotharingia (equivalent to modern Holland, Belgium, Switzerland, Alsace-Lorraine, and Italy). Charles the Bald reigned over much of what was to become France, and Louis the German over Germany.

The Treaty of Verdun was only the start of the division of the Carolingian lands. When Lothar died in 855, his "middle kingdom" was split up among his three sons. This upset the balance of power and tempted the larger eastern and western Frankish kingdoms of France and Germany to stake claims to portions of Lothar's diminished legacy. The decline of the Carolingian Empire in Italy created a political vacuum the popes tried to fill. But both popes and kings became pawns in the hands of the landed nobility. It is at this juncture in European history (i.e., the last quarter of the ninth and the first half of the tenth centuries) that one may speak accurately of a "dark age." Historical record keeping declined not only because the empire and papacy deterio-

The tenth-century crown of the Holy Roman Emperor (the title applied to rulers who succeeded to the remains of Charlemagne's empire) reveals the close alliance between church and throne. The crown is surmounted by a cross, and it includes panels depicting the great kings of the Bible, David and Solomon. Kunsthistorisches Museum, Vienna

rated politically but because barbarian attacks on Europe were renewed. Successive waves of Vikings (i.e., "North-men" or Normans) from Scandinavia, Magyars (i.e., Hungarians from the plains of Russia), and Muslims (from Sicily and Africa) simultaneously invaded Europe from different directions.

The Vikings were the most serious threat. Thanks to their unique skills as seamen, they were able to raid Europe's coasts and use its rivers to reach targets deep inland. Since they moved rapidly and randomly, there was little defense against them. The Franks built fortified towns and castles to serve as refuges. Sometimes they bought off the invaders with silver or grants of land. France even created a duchy of "Normandy" for the newcomers. Since there was little that the central governments of kings could do against myriad bands of raiders descending from multiple directions, communities looked to resident local strongmen for protection.

Feudal Society

In the absence of effective central governments that were able to protect them, medieval people resorted to feudal arrangements. The weaker submitted to the stronger, and those who could guarantee security from rapine and starvation ruled. Medieval feudalism emerged from a world dominated by warlords.

Feudal society was held together by the oaths that individuals made—that is, by promises to provide subordinates with protection or maintenance in exchange for their pledge of service. Men who were equipped as soldiers became vassals and formed a professional military class with its own code of knightly conduct. Networks of personal relationships among members of this class created regional military organizations. The leaders of these organizations, whether or not they had a legal right, assumed responsibility for governing the people who lived under their protection.

Origins

The roots of feudal government go back to the sixth and seventh centuries, when the weakness of the West's governments made it necessary for freemen who were unable to fend for themselves to seek alliances with more powerful neighbors. Freemen who entered into various kinds of contractual relations of dependence on superiors were known as *vassi* or vassals (i.e., "those who serve"). Owners of large estates tried to acquire as many vassals as they could afford to equip as soldiers for their private armies. Originally, such men were maintained as part of their lord's household. But as their numbers grew, this became impractical. Since the collapsing economy was taking money out of circulation, there was no way to pay vassals salaries. Hence, the custom developed of granting them benefices or fiefs (i.e., the right to use a piece of their lord's land to maintain themselves for his service). Vassals lived on their fiefs and were responsible for the peasants who farmed them.

Vassalage and the Fief

A vassal swore fealty to his lord. That meant that he promised to serve his lord and to refrain from actions contrary to his lord's interests. His chief obligation was military. He served as a mounted knight. Bargaining might take place over terms of service, but custom limited the number of days a lord could keep a vassal in the field. (In France in the eleventh century, forty days was standard.) In addition to military duty a vassal was expected to attend his lord's court when summoned and to render his lord financial assistance at times of special need, especially (1) to ransom him from his enemies, (2) to outfit him for a major military campaign, or (3) to defray the costs of the festivities at the marriage of a daughter or the knighting of a son.

Louis the Pious extended vassalage beyond the lay nobility to the higher clergy by requiring bishops and abbots to swear fealty and to accept their appointments on the same terms as royal benefices. He formally "invested" clerics with the rings and staffs that were the symbols of their spiritual offices. This practice was offensive to the church, for it implied the subservience of the church to the state. In the late tenth and eleventh centuries, reform-minded clergy rebelled against the ceremonies of vassalage and "lay investiture," but the reformers never suggested surrendering the grants of land that were the rewards for oaths of homage.

A lord's obligations to his vassals were very specific. He had to protect the vassal from physical harm, to stand as his advocate in court, and to provide for his maintenance by giving him a fief. In Carolingian times a fief varied in size from one or more small villas to several *mansi* (a unit of twenty-five to forty-eight acres). Royal vassals might receive fiefs ranging from 30 to 200 *mansi*. With prizes like this in the offing, vassalage was acceptable to the highest classes of Carolingian society. In the short run the policy marshaled the nobility behind the king, but in the long run the granting of fiefs undercut royal power. Kings found it difficult or impossible to reclaim land once it was granted to vassals. A vassal whom a king enriched sufficiently could then create vassals of his own.

Fragmentation and Divided Loyalty

Since it was possible for a vassal to accept fiefs from more than one lord, all kinds of conflicts of interest might arise. The ninth century developed the concept of the "liege lord," the master to whom a vassal owed primary duty, but this did not halt progressive fragmentation of land and loyalty.

Kings were further weakened by the fact that the fiefs they granted tended to become the real property of their vassals. Although title to a fief remained with the lord who granted it, it was hard for him to prevent his vassal from passing the fief on to an heir. In the ninth century, hereditary possession became a legally recognized principle and laid the basis for claims to outright ownership. In this way, the nobility gradually appropriated much of the royal domain.

Lay society was illiterate. Consequently, the feudal era used symbols and ceremonies to seal the contracts involved in vassalage. A freeman became a vassal by a secular act of "commendation." In the mid-eighth century, a religious oath of fealty was added to increase the solemnity of the act. A vassal reinforced his promise of fidelity to a lord by swearing an oath with his hand on a sacred relic or a Bible. In the tenth and eleventh centuries, paying homage to the lord involved not only the swearing of such an oath but also the placement of the vassal's hands between his lord's hands and the sealing of the ritual with a kiss.

Despite feudalism's obvious vulnerability to abuse and confusion, it created social stability in early medieval Europe and helped restore political centralization during the High Middle Ages. The genius of feudal government lay in its adaptability. Contracts of different kinds could be made with almost anybody to serve almost any purpose. The foundations of the modern nation-state were laid in France and England as kings compromised with vassals and fine-tuned feudal arrangements to reconstruct centralized government.

In Perspective

Between 476 and 1000 the eastern and western halves of the old Roman Empire lost contact with each other and developed in different directions. Classical civilization faded, and three new medieval civilizations took its place. In the East the Byzantine Empire, with its capital at Constantinople, preserved classical literature but used it to nourish a passion-
ately Christian culture. Religion also provided the means for uniting the Arabs and sending them forth to conquer an empire that soon stretched from Spain to China. Islamic culture, as well as the Islamic state, reached its creative peak during the earlier medieval centuries while the West was still recovering from the barbarian invasions and the collapse of the ancient economy. In the West, cities diminished, and society became largely agrarian. Although the Latin church preserved some classical literature and some shreds of Roman institutions, the West was slow to reclaim its classical heritage.

The West's "renaissances" began with the reign of the Frankish emperor Charlemagne and continued through the sixteenth century. They produced a uniquely European way of life that was a mixture of barbarian customs, Christian faith, and remnants of classical culture. But early medieval Europe made slow progress in that direction, for its society was primitive and fragmented. Its people were preoccupied with the pursuit of basic needs—food, which was supplied by manorialism, and public order, which was maintained by feudalism. Europe could not yet aspire to a civilization as elaborate as those of Byzantium and Islam.

REVIEW QUESTIONS

1. What changes took place in Christianity between its founding and the coronation of the Emperor Charlemagne in 800? What were the distinctive features of the early church? What role did the church play in the Western world after the fall of the Roman Empire?
2. What changes took place in the Frankish kingdom between its foundation and the end of Charlemagne's reign? What were the characteristics of Charlemagne's government? Why did Charlemagne encourage learning at his court? Could the Carolingian renaissance have endangered his authority? Why did his empire break apart?
3. How and why was the history of the eastern half of the former Roman Empire so different from that of its western half? Did Justinian strengthen or weaken the Byzantine Empire? How does his reign compare to Charlemagne's?

4. What were the tenets of Islam? How were the Muslims able to build an empire so quickly? What contributions did the Muslims make to the development of Western Europe?

5. How and why did feudal society begin? What were the essential features of feudalism? Do you think that modern society could "slip back" into a feudal pattern?

SUGGESTED READINGS

G. BARRACLOUGH, *The Crucible of Europe: The Ninth and Tenth Centuries* (1976). Sweeping survey of political history.

H. CHADWICK, *The Early Church* (1967). Among the best treatments of early Christianity.

F. L. GANSHOF, *Feudalism,* trans. by Philip Grierson (1964). The most profound brief analysis of the subject.

R. HODGES and D. WHITEHOUSE, *Mohammed, Charlemagne and the Origins of Europe* (1982). For the social and economic history of early medieval Europe.

A. HOURANI, *A History of the Arab Peoples* (1991). A comprehensive text that includes an excellent overview of the origins and early history of Islam.

B. LEWIS, *The Muslim Discovery of Europe* (1982). Authoritative account from the Muslim perspective.

C. MANGO, *Byzantium: The Empire of New Rome* (1980). Perhaps the most readable account.

R. McKITTERICK, *The Frankish Kingdoms under the Carolingians, 751–987* (1983). The fate of Carolingian government.

R. W. SOUTHERN, *The Making of the Middle Ages* (1973). Originally published in 1953 but still a fresh account by an imaginative historian.

W. WALTHER, *Woman in Islam* (1981). One hour spent with this book teaches more about the social import of Islam than days spent with others.

S. WEMPLE, *Women in Frankish Society: Marriage and the Cloister, 500–900* (1981). What marriage and the cloister meant to women in these early centuries.

L. WHITE, JR., *Medieval Technology and Social Change* (1962). Often fascinating account of the way primitive technology changed life.

Chapter 7
The High Middle Ages: The Rise of European Empires and States (1000–1300)

KEY TOPICS

- Germany's Saxon dynasty and the Holy Roman Empire
- A movement to reform the church and free it from political domination by kings and emperors
- The emergence of strong national monarchies in England and France
- The fragmentation of Germany, the conclusion of a struggle for supremacy between the Hohenstaufen dynasty and the papacy

The High Middle Ages (1000–1300) was a period of political expansion and consolidation and of intellectual flowering and synthesis. With respect to the development of Western institutions, this may have been a more creative era than the Italian Renaissance or the German Reformation.

The borders of western Europe were secured against foreign invaders, and Europeans, who had long been the prey of foreign powers, mounted a military and economic offensive against the East. The rulers of England and France established nuclei for nation-states by *adapting feudal principles of government to the creation of centralized political realms. Parliaments and popular assemblies emerged in some places to enable the propertied classes to influence the development of the new monarchies. Germany and Italy (i.e., the Holy Roman Empire) were the great exceptions to the trend toward political consolidation. They remained fragmented until the nineteenth century.*

The High Middle Ages also saw the establishment of the distinctive Western custom of separating church and state. By asserting monarchical authority over the church, the popes prevented it from being split up by and absorbed into Europe's emerging states. The cost to the papacy was the charge that it was diverting the church from its spiritual mission into the murky world of politics.

Otto I and the Revival of the Empire

The fortunes of both the empire and the papacy began to revive in the early tenth century, bringing an end to the medieval "dark ages."

Unifying Germany

In 918 the duke of Saxony, Henry I "the Fowler" (d. 936), founded the Saxon dynasty, Germany's first non-Frankish monarchy. Henry reversed the process of political fragmentation that had set in with the decline of the Carolingian Empire. He consolidated the duchies of Swabia, Bavaria, Saxony, Franconia, and Lotharingia and checked the invasions of the Hungarians and the Danes.

The German state that Henry bequeathed to his son Otto I "the Great" (r. 936–973) was the strongest kingdom in Europe. In 951 Otto invaded Italy and proclaimed himself its king. In 955 he defeated the Hungarians at Lechfeld. This secured German borders against barbarian attack and established the frontiers of western Europe.

Embracing the Church

Otto secured the power of the throne by refusing to allow Germany's dukes to turn their duchies into hereditary properties. He also diminished the role powerful lay lords played in his government by appointing bishops and abbots of monasteries to administer his lands and be his agents. Clergy were more likely than laymen to be sympathetic to his plans to restore imperial authority, and, unlike laymen, they could not marry and pass on to their sons the lands they held from the king. The church sensed no conflict between its spiritual and political duties and eagerly embraced the wealth and power Otto pressed on it.

In 961 Otto rescued Pope John XII (955–964) from a scuffle with the Italian nobility, and on February 2, 962, the pope bestowed the lapsed imperial title on Germany's king. Otto's intervention in Italian politics increased his power over the church. Otto appointed the higher clergy and declared himself special "protector" of the Papal States. When Pope John belatedly recognized the royal web in which he had become entangled, he joined a plot against the new emperor. Otto promptly ordered an ecclesiastical synod to depose John and to decree that no pope take office without first swearing allegiance to the emperor. Otto's popes ruled at his pleasure.

The Italian interests that Otto bequeathed to his successors, Otto II (r. 973–983) and Otto III (r. 983–1002), distracted them from events in Germany, and they allowed their German base to disintegrate. It had been unwise to dream of empire before monarchy was firmly in place. As the fledgling empire began to crumble in the first quarter of the eleventh century, the papacy seized the opportunity to reassert its independence.

The Reviving Catholic Church

The papacy was fortunate in that the weakening of Germany's overextended empire corresponded with the rise within the church of a reform movement that restored respect for the authority of the clergy.

The Cluny Reform Movement

In the tenth century a campaign designed to reform the church by liberating the clergy from the control of the feudal nobility was launched from a monastery in east central France. Since the last days of the Roman Empire, monks, who were the least worldly of the clergy, had been the church's most popular representatives. Their educations were the best available, the relics and rituals they

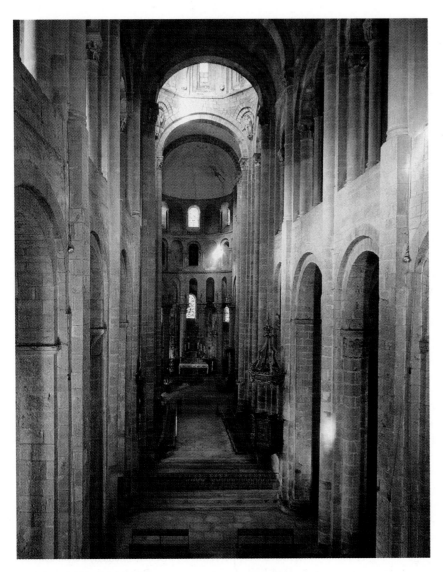

The central nave of the Romanesque abbey of St. Faith (Foy) in Conques, France, where the female saint's relics lie. Roasted alive and beheaded in third-century Gaul, she became widely revered in France, England, Italy, and Spain, and was later a popular South American saint. The interior of the abbey reveals bulky and tightly built pillars, uniform rounded arches, and the restricted lighting that are characteristic of classic Romanesque architecture. Compare and contrast the abbey of St. Faith with the Gothic cathedral of Salisbury, England, on page 138.
Scala/Art Resource, NY

maintained were believed to have magical potency, and the religious ideals embodied in their way of life set the standard for Christian society.

In 910 William the Pious, duke of Aquitaine, founded a new monastery at Cluny that was pledged to maintaining the strictest observance of the Benedictine Rule and to restoring the purest liturgical practices. The Cluniac reformers claimed that the church could not reach its full spiritual potential so long as laymen had the power to appoint and dominate clerics. The lords who endowed the Cluniac houses gave them complete independence, and the abbots who ran them were sincere churchmen who enforced the strictest religious discipline.

Cluniac ideals spread from the monastery to the parish, for the reformers argued that the "sec-ular clergy" (i.e., those serving the *saeculum*, the "world") ought to adopt the ascetic lifestyle of the "regular" clergy (i.e., those living by a *regula*, a monastic "rule"). They also insisted that bishops be freed from the authority of feudal governments and made accountable only to an independent papacy.

Men trained at Cluny were dispatched to reform monasteries throughout France and Italy. Thanks to aggressive abbots, such as Saint Odo (926–946), Cluny acquired nearly 1,500 dependent cloisters and took the lead in various social reform movements. In the late ninth and early tenth centuries, Cluny inspired the "Peace of God" movement. This was an attempt to ease the suffering caused by the endemic warfare that plagued medieval society. It threatened excommunication for all soldiers who attacked members of noncombatant groups (e.g., women, peasants, merchants, and clergy). A "Truce of God" was subsequently proclaimed. It prohibited combat during part of each week (Wednesday night to Monday morning) and in all holy seasons.

During the reign of Emperor Henry III (r. 1039–1056), Cluniac reformers won high offices in the church. Pope Leo IX (1049–1054) appointed them to key administrative posts in Rome, and they encouraged him to suppress simony (i.e., the selling of church offices) and to enforce celibacy among parish priests. The papacy itself, however, continued to be dominated by powerful laymen. Leo IX was himself appointed by Henry III. In the course of his reign, Henry deposed three popes who were pawns of the Roman aristocracy.

When Henry died, he left the empire to an underage son, Henry IV (r. 1056–1106). Reform-minded popes took advantage of the weakness of the boy-king's regents to assert their independence. Pope Stephen IX (1057–1058) reigned without seeking imperial confirmation of his title, and in 1059 Pope Nicholas II (1059–1061) decreed that a body of high church officials (the College of Cardinals) would henceforth choose the popes. The procedures that were developed (and which are still followed) were designed to prevent the Italian nobles and the German kings from interfering in papal elections. The reformers made the papacy an independent, self-perpetuating ecclesiastical monarchy.

The Investiture Struggle: Gregory VII and Henry IV

The German monarchy did not react to the church's new policies until the reign of Pope Gregory VII (1073–1085), a fierce advocate of Cluny's reforms. In 1075 Gregory condemned "lay investiture," the appointment of a clergyman to a church office by a layman. The pope's decree attacked the foundations of imperial government. Since the days of Otto I, German kings had preferred to use bishops rather than lay nobles to administer state lands. If the king lost the right to appoint men to ecclesiastical office, he lost the power to choose some of the most important agents of his government. By prohibiting lay investiture the pope proclaimed the spiritual nature of the episcopacy, but he failed to recognize

that the church's religious offices had long since become entwined with the secular offices of the state.

Henry opposed Gregory's action on the grounds that it violated a well-founded tradition on which imperial authority rested. But the pope had important allies. The German nobles were eager for opportunities to undercut their king, for his strength threatened their independence. When German bishops loyal to Henry assembled at Worms in January 1076 to repudiate Gregory, Gregory excommunicated Henry and absolved his subjects from their oaths of allegiance to him. This gave the German magnates an excuse to rebel against Henry and forced Henry to come to terms with Gregory. Henry crossed the Alps in midwinter to reach Gregory's castle at Canossa. There he reportedly stood barefoot in the snow for three days until the pope agreed to absolve him. The pope only appeared to win, for Henry's absolution deprived his nobles of their excuse for continuing their rebellion. The king regrouped his forces and regained much of his power. In March 1080, Gregory excommunicated Henry once again, but this time the German nobles refused to rise to the bait. Four years later Henry drove Gregory into exile and placed his own man, Clement III, on the papal throne.

The investiture controversy ended in 1122 with a compromise spelled out by the Concordat of Worms. Emperor Henry V (r. 1106–1125) agreed to cease investing bishops with the ring and staff that symbolized spiritual office. In return, Pope Calixtus II (1119–1124) recognized the emperor's right to be present at episcopal consecrations and to preside at the ceremonies that bestowed fiefs on bishops. The old church-state "back scratching" continued, but now on a basis that made the church at least look like an independent organization. The pope's attempts to weaken the emperor did little to promote freedom for the church. As the power of emperors declined, Germany's feudal nobles grew stronger and better able to impose their wills on the clergy.

The First Crusades

What the Cluny reform was to the clergy the Crusades to the Holy Land were to the laity—that is, an outlet for the religious zeal and self-confidence that invigorated Europe in the High Middle Ages.

Late in the eleventh century, Alexius I Comnenus, emperor of Constantinople, appealed to the Christian West for help against the Seljuk Turks. At the council of Clermont in 1095, Pope Urban II answered this appeal by proclaiming the First Crusade. The Crusade was popular with different people for different reasons. By calling the Crusade, the pope was able to show that he truly was the West's spiritual leader and to gain leverage in dealing with the Eastern church. The departure of large numbers of warring nobles eased the task of maintaining the peace in Europe, and hordes of restless young knights were enthralled by the opportunity to enrich themselves from foreign conquests. Many were the younger sons of noblemen who, in an age of growing population and limited land, had few prospects of obtaining fiefs at home.

Although motives were mixed, the First Crusade owed more to genuine piety than the mercenary ventures organized by the later Crusaders. Popes recruited Crusaders by promising those who died in battle a plenary indulgence—a complete remission of punishment for their unrepented mortal sins and from all suffering in purgatory. The Crusaders were driven by the passions of a Holy War, a struggle against a hated infidel who had seized control of the most sacred Christian shrines. The Crusade was also the ultimate pilgrimage to the Holy Land. The desire to be part of it even affected those who did not go East. They crusaded at home by launching the first massacres of Europe's Jews.

THE FIRST VICTORY Three great armies, which mustered perhaps 100,000 men, gathered in France, Germany, and Italy. In 1097 they converged on Constantinople by different routes. They were not the disciplined, professional force the East had hoped to enlist. The Eastern

MAP 7–1 THE EARLY CRUSADES *Routes taken by some of the major leaders of the early Crusades are shown, as is the pattern Christian reconquest took in Spain.*

emperor was suspicious of their motives, and the common people whom they pillaged along the route of their march hardly considered them Christian brothers. Nonetheless, these fanatical Crusaders accomplished what no Eastern army had ever done. They defeated one Seljuk army after another and, on July 15, 1099, captured Jerusalem. The Crusaders' success was due to the superior military technology the West had evolved and to the inability of the Muslim states to cooperate in mounting an effective resistance.

The Crusaders set up governments in Jerusalem, Edessa, and Antioch. Godfrey of Bouillon (and after him his brother Baldwin) was chosen to rule a new kingdom of Jerusalem. The pretentious claims of the "Crusader States" ignored the fact that they were little more than precarious European outposts in a Muslim world. This became clear as the Muslims rallied and took the offensive against the "savages" who had invaded their lands. The Crusaders erected castles and hunkered down in a state of perpetual siege. The once fierce warriors became international businessmen promoting trade between East and West. Some, such as the Knights Templars, built huge fortunes. The Templars were an order of soldier-monks devoted to protecting pilgrims to the Holy Land. Their services to travelers led them into the profitable fields of banking and money-lending and made their monastic order one of Europe's greatest commercial institutions.

THE ULTIMATE DEFEAT   After forty years the Latin hold on the East began to weaken. When Edessa fell to Islamic armies in 1144, Bernard of Clairvaux (1091–1153), Christendom's most influential monastic leader, called for a Second Crusade. It was a dismal failure.

In October 1187 Saladin (r. 1138–1193), king of Egypt and Syria, conquered Jerusalem, and Europe responded with a Third Crusade (1189–1192). It enlisted the most powerful western rulers: Emperor Frederick Barbarossa; Richard "the Lion-Hearted," king of England; and Philip Augustus, king of France. Despite its resources, the Third Crusade degenerated into a tragicomedy. Frederick Barbarossa accidentally drowned while fording a stream in Asia Minor. Richard and Philip Augustus reached the outskirts of Jerusalem, but their intense personal rivalry

The crusaders capture the city of Antioch in 1098 during the First Crusade. From Le Miroir Historial *(fifteenth century) by Vincent de Beauvais.* Musée Conde Chantilly. E. T. Archive, London.

doomed their campaign. Philip Augustus quickly returned to France to prey on Richard's continental possessions. When this forced Richard finally to head home, he was captured and held for ransom by the Emperor Henry VI. England's bill for its king's Eastern adventure was greatly increased by the sum Germany demanded for his release.

The Crusades failed to achieve their political and religious objectives, and the Holy Land remained under Muslim control into the modern era. Economically and culturally, however, the Crusades were more constructive. They stimulated trade between the East and the West, and the merchants of Venice, Pisa, and Genoa, who followed the Crusaders, succeeded at sea where the Crusades failed on land at challenging Islamic domination. Wherever trading centers sprang up, cultural as well as economic exchanges were made.

The Pontificate of Innocent III (1198–1216)

The pope who inaugurated the Crusades hoped that they would unite Europe behind the leader of its church. The papal dream of establishing some kind of supremacy over the nations that were emerging in Europe during the High Middle Ages reached its apogee during the reign of Pope Innocent III.

THE NEW PAPAL MONARCHY Under Innocent, the papacy became a great secular power with a treasury and a bureaucracy equal to that of any king. Innocent increased ecclesiastical taxation—both in amount and in effectiveness of collection. A tax known as Peter's pence was imposed on all but the poorest laymen. The clergy paid the pope an income tax of 2.5 percent—as well as annates (i.e., the forfeiture to the papacy by an appointee of the first year's income from his benefice) and fees for the bestowal of things such as the pallium, the stole that was the archbishop's symbol of office. Innocent also reserved to the pope the right to grant absolution for many kinds of sins and religious crimes. The penalties imposed were frequently monetary payments to the papacy.

CRUSADES IN FRANCE AND THE EAST Innocent did not shrink from using the Crusade, the church's weapon against Islam, to suppress dissent in Europe. Protests were raised against the church as it became increasingly secular and materialistic, and the papacy accused some of its critics of heresy. Heresy was often the laity's response to clerical greed and negligence.

In 1209 Innocent launched a Crusade to exterminate heretics called either the Albigensians (from the French town of Albi) or the Cathars ("pure ones"). These people advocated a simple, pious way of life modeled on the New Testament's description of Jesus and his apostles. But they rejected important Christian doctrines. They were dualists. They denied that the wrathful deity of the Old Testament who created the sinful material world was the same god as the heavenly Father to whom Jesus prayed. Their belief that the flesh was the source of sin and a threat to the spirit led them to reject the Christian claim that God was incarnate in Jesus and to

Significant Dates from the Period of the High Middle Ages	
910	Cluniac reform begins
955	Otto I defeats Magyars
1059	College of Cardinals empowered to elect popes
1066	Norman conquest of England
1075–1122	Investiture Controversy
1095–1099	First Crusade
1144	Edessa falls; Second Crusade
1152	Hohenstaufen dynasty founded
1154	Plantagenet dynasty founded
1187	Jerusalem falls to Saladin
1189–1192	Third Crusade
1202	Fourth Crusade sacks Constantinople
1209	Albigensian Crusade
1210	Franciscan Order founded
1215	Fourth Lateran Council; Magna Carta
1250	Death of Frederick II

assert that the true church was an invisible, spiritual entity and not the worldly institution headed by the pope. The more radical Cathars recommended celibacy, contraception, or abortion to prevent more immortal souls from being captured and imprisoned in sinful matter. (The Catholic Church's current positions on social issues such as contraception and abortion were shaped in this environment.) Paradoxically, the Cathars' dualism might also be used to justify moral laxity. If the flesh and the spirit are fundamentally different and separate realities, it matters little what the former does.

Since the Albigensian lands were wealthy, knights from northern France were eager to enlist in the pope's Crusade. The church gave them an excuse to seize their neighbors' lands. After a succession of massacres and a special campaign that King Louis VIII of France headed in 1226 utterly devastated the prosperous Albigensian districts, Pope Gregory IX (1227–1241) sent in the Inquisition to root out any heretics who remained. An inquisition was a formal ecclesiastical tribunal set up to detect and punish heresy. Bishops had used inquisitions in their dioceses since the mid-twelfth century, but Innocent III created a centralized court of inquisition that dispatched papal legates to preside at trials and executions throughout Europe.

Innocent also called the fourth of the Crusades intended for the Holy Land. In 1202 some 30,000 Crusaders gathered in Venice, planning to sail for Egypt. Many were poor soldiers of fortune who were unable to pay the price the Venetians demanded for their transport. Venice persuaded them to work off their passage by conquering Zara, a Christian city that was one of Venice's commercial rivals. To the shock of Pope Innocent III, the Crusaders obliged and then allowed Venice to seduce them into storming the most important Christian city in the East, Constantinople.

Although the assault on Constantinople in 1204 was an embarrassment to the pope, the papacy came to terms with the Venetians and shared the spoils. One of Innocent's confidants was appointed patriarch of Constantinople and ordered to win the Greeks and the Slavs to the Roman church. Westerners retained control of Constantinople until 1261 when the Genoese, who envied Venice's coup, helped the exiled Eastern emperor, Michael Paleologus, recapture the city. The half-century of occupation did nothing to reunite the church or improve relations between East and West.

THE FOURTH LATERAN COUNCIL   At the Fourth Lateran Council, which met in 1215, Innocent defined crucial disciplines and doctrines that the church was to enforce throughout Europe. Most significant for the development of Catholicism was the council's endorsement of the doctrine of transubstantiation as the church's explanation of the miracle of the Eucharist. Transubstantiation is the belief that at the moment of priestly consecration the bread and wine of the Lord's Supper become the body and blood of Christ. This idea was consistent with the popular piety of the twelfth century. But since the power to perform this miracle was reserved to priests, it also helped Innocent achieve his goal of enhancing the power of the clergy over the laity. This was also the effect of the council's formalization of the sacrament of penance and its order to every adult Christian to confess and take communion at least once a year (usually at Easter).

FRANCISCANS AND DOMINICANS   The laity's interest in religious devotion surged at the turn of the twelfth century and won recruits for new movements that preached a life of poverty in imitation of Christ. Idealization of poverty was not necessarily heretical, but it could promote criticism of the church that caused groups such as the Waldensians, Beguines, and Beghards to fall under suspicion of heresy.

By licensing two new religious orders (the Franciscans and the Dominicans) Innocent fought fire with fire. Unlike the regular monks, these orders of friars (i.e., "brothers") were mendicants (i.e., "beggars"). Refusing to accept land and endowments, they devoted themselves to preaching and caring for the poor and supported themselves by begging and working. Their saintly behavior did much to refute the heretics who argued that Christian unworldliness was incompatible with obedience to the orthodox church. The tertiaries, or "Third Orders," created by the friars provided refuges for pious laypersons whose desire to live according to high religious ideals might otherwise have led them into heresies.

The Franciscan Order was founded in 1210 by Saint Francis of Assisi (1182–1226), the son of a rich cloth merchant. The Dominican Order (the Order of Preachers) was founded in 1216 by Saint Dominic (1170–1221), a well-educated Spanish cleric. Since both orders reported directly to the pope and not to any local bishops, they provided the central government of the church with an army of dedicated servants who could be dispatched on special missions.

Pope Gregory IX (1227–1241) canonized Saint Francis only two years after Francis's death. But the pope also turned the Franciscans from the path their founder had charted for them. The pope declared that a nomadic life of strict poverty and extreme asceticism was both impractical and unbiblical. Most Franciscans accepted the pope's modification of their order's rule, but a radical branch, the Spiritual Franciscans, resisted and drifted into heresy.

The Dominicans were dedicated to combating heresy. They preached, staffed the offices of the Inquisition, and taught at universities. The man who most furthered their mission was the great theologian, Thomas Aquinas (d. 1274). His synthesis of faith and reason has been embraced by the Catholic Church as the definitive statement of its beliefs.

William the Conqueror on horseback urging his troops into combat with the English at the Battle of Hastings (October 14, 1066). Detail from the Bayeux Tapestry, scene 51, about 1073–1083. Musée de la Tapisserie, Bayeux, France. Giraudon/Art Resource, NY

England and France: Hastings (1066) to Bouvines (1214)

While Germany and Italy were engaged in struggles between popes and emperors, new dynasties were establishing themselves in England and France. They laid the foundations for medieval Europe's strongest nations.

The old Roman province of Britain became England (i.e., "Anglo-land") as Germans from the tribes of the Angles and Saxons took it over at the start of the Middle Ages. When the last of their kings, Edward the Confessor, died childless in 1066, the English throne was claimed by his distant relative, Duke William of Normandy (d. 1087). The Anglo-Saxon assembly—which, in accordance with the ancient traditions of the German tribes, had the right to enthrone kings—preferred a native son, Harold Godwinsson. William invaded England, and at Hastings on October 14, 1066, he destroyed Harold and decimated the Anglo-Saxon nobility.

William the Conqueror

By judiciously combining continental feudalism and Anglo-Saxon custom, William constructed the most effective monarchy in Europe. To discover what the country he had conquered was worth, he carried out a county-by-county survey of its people, animals, and implements. The results, which were compiled as the *Domesday Book* (1080–1086), offer a uniquely detailed description of a medieval kingdom. William com-pelled every man of property to become his vassal and to hold all land in fief from the king. The Norman nobles who replaced the Anglo-Saxon magnates had no following among their new subjects. They realized, therefore, that they needed the help of a strong leader, and they rarely challenged their king. William's government was further strengthened by unique Anglo-Saxon tax and court systems, and the king honored the Anglo-Saxon tradition of "parleying"—that is, of holding conferences with people who had vested interests in royal policies. By consulting with his nobles on affairs of state, William kept England on track toward the creation of the parliamentary traditions that have shaped the constitutions of so many modern states.

Henry II

The English monarchy continued strong under William's sons and heirs, William Rufus (r. 1087–1100) and Henry I (r. 1100–1135). When Henry died without a male heir, a civil war erupted that threatened to undo the Conqueror's work. But a compromise between the factions resulted in the accession of Henry II (r. 1154–1189), son of the duke of Anjou and Matilda, daughter of Henry I. Henry II established the Plantagenet dynasty, the family name of the Angevin (or Anjouan) kings who ruled England until the death of Richard III in 1485. Henry, by his own rights of inheritance and those of his wife, Eleanor of Aquitaine (ca. 1122–1204), controlled much more of France than did the king of France. Henry also conquered a part of Ireland and made the king of Scotland take an oath of homage to him. The French king, Louis VII, who had good reason to fear these developments, tried to contain the English. French efforts to drive them from the continent were ultimately successful but not until the mid-fifteenth century and the end of the Hundred Years' War.

Eleanor of Aquitaine and Court Culture

Eleanor of Aquitaine had been married to King Louis VII of France before she wed King Henry II of England in 1152, and she was a powerful influence on the politics and culture of both nations. Women of Eleanor's generation were beginning to venture into the masculine fields of politics and business, and she blazed the way. She insisted on accompanying her first husband on the Second Crusade, and she stirred up so much trouble for her second husband that from 1179 until his death in 1189 he kept her under house arrest.

After marrying Henry, Eleanor established a court in Angers, the chief town of Anjou, that became a center of patronage for musicians and poets. The troubadour Bernart de Ventadorn composed many of the popular love songs of the period in her honor. From 1154 to 1170, the queen resided in England, but then she separated from Henry and moved to Poitiers to live with her daughter Marie, the countess of Champagne. Poitiers popularized a new fad among the aristocracy. It was called "courtly love." The troubadours who elaborated the rules of game composed erotic stories to satirize physical passion. They contrasted carnal love with "courteous" love, a spiritual passion for a lady that ennobled her lover. Chrétien de Troyes's stories of King Arthur and the Knights of the Round Table—and of Sir Lancelot's tragic, illicit love for Arthur's wife, Guinevere—are the most famous products of the movement.

Popular Rebellion and Magna Carta

Henry II was a strong king who believed in autocratic monarchy. He insisted that the church operate within parameters set by the state, and he spelled these out in 1164 in the Constitutions of

Clarendon. The Constitutions limited the right to appeal cases from England to the papal court, subjected clergy to the king's courts, and gave the king control over the election of bishops. The archbishop of Canterbury, Thomas à Becket (1118?–1170), who was once Henry's compliant chancellor, fled England rather than accept the Constitutions. He was induced to return in 1170, but his continued opposition to the king prompted some of Henry's men to assassinate him. The church leapt at the opportunity to canonize Becket (1172) and to use his martyrdom to bolster its case for freedom from state control.

Henry was followed on the throne by two of his sons: Richard the Lion-Hearted (r. 1189–1199) and John (r. 1199–1216). Neither was a success. Richard imposed ruinous taxation to fund the disastrous Third Crusade and died fighting to recover lands the French had taken from him while he was in the East. In 1209 Pope Innocent III excommunicated Richard's successor, John, in a dispute over the appointment of an archbishop for Canterbury. To extricate himself from a mess of his own making and to win support for a war with France, John surrendered to the pope and declared his kingdom a papal fief. John's efforts to restore his father's Angevin empire foundered, however, when the French defeated him at Bouvines in 1214. England's disillusioned barons then rebelled and forced their king to accept limitations on royal authority.

A document known simply as the Magna Carta (i.e., "Great Charter") spelled out the terms that John and his subjects agreed to in 1215. Among other things, the king promised not to arrest and hold people without giving his reasons, and he acknowledged the necessity of consulting with representatives of the propertied classes before imposing new taxes. Magna Carta was designed to put some constraints on monarchy without fatally weakening it. In the short run, it had little effect, for John's successors largely ignored it. But Magna Carta helped keep alive the traditions that undergird modern English law.

Philip II Augustus

In England during the High Middle Ages, the propertied classes had to fight a strong monarchy to secure their rights. In France the shoe was on the other foot. There, weak kings were confronted by powerful subjects who opposed the growth of monarchy.

In 987 when the Carolingian line came to an end in France, the French nobles chose Hugh Capet, count of Paris, to be king. Although his descendants managed to hang on to the title and to create a Capetian dynasty, for the next two centuries the great feudal princes were France's real rulers. The early Capetian kings even had a struggle to control their own royal domain, the area around Paris and the Île-de-France to the northeast. By the time Philip II (1180–1223) came to the throne, the Capetians had secured hereditary rights to the crown. Only then was it possible for them to begin to impose their will on their vassals and made Paris the center of French government and culture.

In a way the Norman conquest of England in 1066 helped the Capetian kings to unify France and build a true national monarchy. As the Plantagenet dynasty extended its control over French territory, the Capetians were able to enlist support from powerful nobles who considered the English king the greater threat to their independence. The Capetians also won the help of the wealthy merchant class that was beginning to appear in France's reviving cities.

The king of England was at a disadvantage in dealing with the king of France, for, as duke of Normandy, he was a vassal of the French king. A skillful politician such as Philip II Augustus was able to exploit the ambiguity of this relationship. By accusing his English rival of violating the duties of vassalage, Philip could enlist his other vassals in campaigns to repossess the English king's French fiefs. During the reigns of Richard the Lion-Hearted and John, France's armies seized all the territories the English had occupied in France (with the exception of part of Aquitaine).

King John of England enlisted the help of the German emperor Otto IV (r. 1198–1215) against France in what became Europe's first multinational war. France won decisively at the battle at Bouvines in Flanders on July 27, 1214. The victory helped the French king to unite his people, and it greatly weakened his opponents. Otto IV fell from power, and John's subjects welcomed him home with the rebellion that culminated in Magna Carta.

France in the Thirteenth Century: The Reign of Louis IX

The growth of Capetian royal power under Philip Augustus seemed to receive divine confirmation during the reign of his grandson Louis IX (r. 1226–1270). Louis embodied the medieval view of the perfect ruler, and he was canonized shortly after his death. The saintly king was an ascetic whose ethics were far superior to those of his royal and papal contemporaries. But he was also what his generation expected a king to be, a decisive leader and an enthusiastic soldier.

Generosity Abroad

Some of Louis's decisions suggest naiveté or an overly scrupulous conscience. Although he could have driven the English off the continent, he refused to take advantage of King Henry III's weakness. In 1259 he negotiated a generous compromise, the Treaty of Paris, to end the long-simmering dispute between England and France. Had he been more ruthless and confiscated English territories in France, he might have prevented the resumption of hostilities between the two nations and spared Europe the bloodshed of the Hundred Years' War.

King Louis IX (1226–1270) giving justice. Louis, who was canonized in 1297, was the medieval ideal of a perfect ruler. From "Justiniani in Fortiatum," fol. 34. France, 14th C. Biblioteca Real, El Escorial, Madrid, Spain. Giraudon/Art Resource, NY

Salisbury Cathedral: A Church Filled with Light

Salisbury Cathedral, England. © Christopher Cormack/Corbis

$\mathcal{B}$etween 1050 and 1150 the fortress-like Romanesque style dominated European architecture. Thick walls were needed to support the weight of the round Roman arches that composed its stone vaulting. The small windows that could be cut through these walls admitted little light and made the interiors of Romanesque churches dim. About 1140, a new style called Gothic began to evolve in France. It turned the next century into the "Age of Great Cathedrals" as magnificent churches were raised throughout Europe.

Gothic designs sought a mathematical harmony that builders hoped would illustrate the divine laws fundamental to the universe and philosophers' theories about the nature of beauty. Architects strove hard to find ways to flood sanctuaries with light to symbolize the divine presence. The use of broken or pointed arches allowed them to erect vaults of unprecedented height. The development of flying buttresses (i.e., buttresses set away from the walls and linked to them by arches) enabled masons to cut away large portions of walls to make space for great windows. These were filled with pictures executed in a colored glass that filled churches with a mysterious light.

Salisbury Cathedral is a prime example of English Gothic. Built between 1220 and 1226, its construction required 60,000 tons of stone. Soaring arches and rib vaulting, however, impart lightness to its interior, and flying buttresses and intricate carving give its exterior an airy, lacy grace.

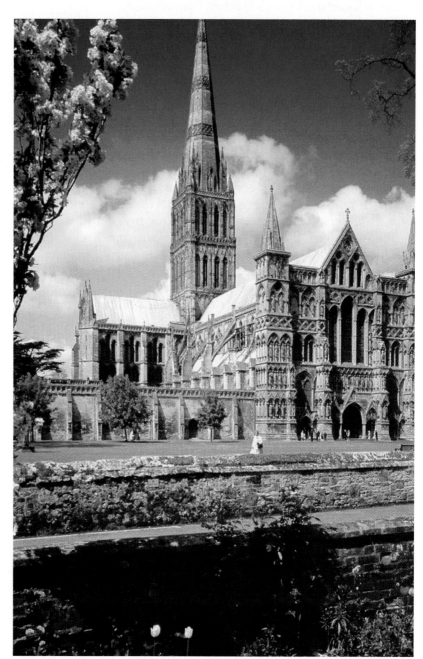

Salisbury Cathedral, England. The Image Works.

Louis remained officially aloof while the papacy fought with Frederick II, an emperor from Germany's Hohenstaufen dynasty. But after Frederick's death, Louis's brother, Charles of Anjou, entered the fray on the pope's side, exterminated Frederick's dynasty, and seized its lands in Italy and Sicily. The pope rewarded him by crowning him king of Sicily.

Order and Excellence at Home

Louis's greatest achievement was to improve the government of France. He used the efficient bureaucracy that his predecessors had developed to exploit their subjects to provide his people with more secure order and justice. He sent out *enquêteurs* (i.e., auditors) to monitor royal officials—especially the *baillis* and *prévôts* whom Philip Augustus had appointed to run the government's grass-roots offices. He abolished private warfare among the nobles and serfdom on the lands of the royal domain. He gave his subjects the judicial right of appeal from local to higher courts, and he made the tax system more equitable. The services the French people received from their king generated enthusiasm for the monarchy and for the nationhood it symbolized.

Developments of other kinds helped to shape a French national identity during Louis's reign. His was the golden age of Scholasticism, a time when thinkers such as Thomas Aquinas and the Franciscan scholar Bonaventure made the University of Paris Europe's intellectual center. France became the showcase for monastic reform, chivalry, and the new Gothic style in art and architecture that had been pioneered by Suger, abbot of St. Denis and adviser to Louis IX's great-grandfather, Louis VII. France began to set the cultural standard for Europe, a pattern that continued into the modern era.

Louis's virtues reflected medieval ideals of kingship. He was something of a religious fanatic. He supported the work of the Inquisition, and he personally led the last two of the great Crusades for the Holy Land. Both were failures, but Louis's death of a fever during the second of his holy wars only enhanced his reputation as a saintly king. His successors pointed to him to confirm their claim that God had bestowed a divine right to rule on the Capetians.

The Hohenstaufen Empire (1152–1272)

During the twelfth and thirteenth centuries, while stable governments were developing in both England and France, something quite different happened within the Holy Roman Empire (Germany, Burgundy, and northern Italy). There disunity and feuding created a legacy of political fragmentation that endured into modern times.

Frederick I Barbarossa

The Investiture Controversy, in which the popes had challenged the right of emperors to appoint the higher clergy, had weakened Germany's kings and strengthened its barons. The church was unable to prevent the German princes from dominating episcopal appointments and appropriating their rich endowments.

Imperial authority revived with the accession to the throne of Frederick I Barbarossa (r. 1152–1190), founder of the Hohenstaufen dynasty. Frederick had some help in laying a strong foundation for a new empire. Disaffection with the incessant squabbling of the feudal princes was widespread, and there was growing resentment of the theocratic pretensions of the papacy. At the University of Bologna a scholar named Irnerius (d. 1125) was also reviving the study of Roman law (i.e., Justinian's Code). Frederick found this useful, for Roman law promoted the centralization of states and provided a secular foundation for imperial power that minimized the significance of papal coronation.

From Frederick's base of operation in Switzerland, the bridge between Germany and Italy, he conducted a relatively successful campaign to regain control over the German nobility. In 1180 his strongest rival, Henry the Lion (d. 1195), duke of Saxony, fell from power and was exiled to Normandy. Although Frederick was not strong enough to intervene in the internal affairs of Germany's great duchies, he was vigilant in enforcing his rights as their feudal overlord. This kept memories of royal authority alive until the king was strong enough to risk a showdown with his greater vassals.

Italy proved to be the major obstacle to the realization of Frederick's imperial dreams. In

1155 Frederick restored Rome to Pope Adrian IV (1154–1159) after a religious revolutionary, Arnold of Brescia (d. 1155), had wrested control of the city from the papacy. Frederick's reward was a papal coronation, which he believed gave him title to Italy. Although the imperial Diet of Roncaglia in 1158 officially sanctioned Frederick's claim to Italy, the Italian people, particularly those of Lombardy, refused to accept the governors he appointed.

Just as this challenge to royal authority was being mounted, one of Europe's most skilled lawyers, Cardinal Roland, was elected Pope Alexander III (1159–1181). Frederick soon found himself at war with the pope, the city of Milan, and the kingdom of Sicily. In 1167, the combined forces of the northern Italian cities drove him back into Germany, and a decade later (1176) an Italian army soundly defeated him at Legnano. In the Peace of Constance in 1183 Frederick recognized the claims of the Lombard cities to rights of self-rule.

Henry VI and the Sicilian Connection

Frederick's reign ended with stalemate in Germany and defeat in Italy. But in the last years of his life, he discovered a new opportunity for his dynasty. The Norman ruler of the kingdom of Sicily, William II (r. 1166–1189), asked Frederick for help in launching a campaign for the conquest of Constantinople. In 1186 an alliance was sealed by a marriage between Frederick's son, the future Henry VI (r. 1190–1197), and Constance, heiress to Sicily.

Sicily was a fatal acquisition for the Hohenstaufen kings, for it tempted them to sacrifice their territorial base in northern Europe for projects in Italy. It also stirred up greater resistance to them in Italy. By encircling Rome the Hohenstaufens convinced the papacy that the church's survival hinged on the empire's destruction.

When Henry VI came to the throne in 1190, he faced a multitude of enemies: a hostile papacy; independent German princes; and an England whose adventurous king, Richard the Lion-Hearted, was encouraged to plot against Henry by the exiled duke of Saxony, Henry the Lion. In 1194, Constance bore her husband a son, the future Frederick II. To strengthen his dynasty, Henry cam-

paigned vigorously for recognition of the boy's hereditary right to the imperial throne. The German princes were reluctant to abandon the custom of electing emperors, and the encircled papacy was determined to prevent anything that might secure Hohenstaufen power.

Otto IV and the Welf Interregnum

After Henry's premature death in September 1197, his widow tried to save her young son's Sicilian legacy by arranging for him to become a ward of the papacy. The boy's uncle, Philip of Swabia, claimed the title of German king, but the Welf family, which opposed the Hohenstaufens, backed a rival—Otto of Brunswick, the son of the troublesome Henry the Lion. Richard of England supported Otto; the French supported the Hohenstaufens; and the papacy switched its allegiance back and forth to prevent anyone from surrounding Rome. The result was anarchy and civil war.

Otto outlasted Philip and won general recognition in Germany and coronation as emperor by Pope Innocent III (1198–1215). Within four months of his coronation (October 1209), the wind suddenly changed. Otto attacked Sicily, and this convinced Innocent that he was a threat to Rome. The pope excommunicated him and raised up a rival for his throne.

Frederick II

Pope Innocent's ward, the Hohenstaufen prince Frederick, was now of age, and unlike Otto he had a hereditary claim to the throne. In December 1212 the pope, Philip Augustus of France, and Otto's German enemies arranged for Frederick to be crowned king of the Romans in Mainz. When Philip Augustus defeated the armies of Otto and John of England at the battle of Bouvines in 1214, the way was cleared for Frederick II to mount the imperial throne in Charlemagne's city of Aachen (1215). The young ruler's allies probably expected him to be their puppet, but he quickly demonstrated an independent streak.

Frederick, who had grown up in Sicily, disliked Germany. He spent only nine of the thirty-eight years of his reign in Germany, and he wanted only one thing from the German princes: the imperial title for himself and his sons. To secure it,

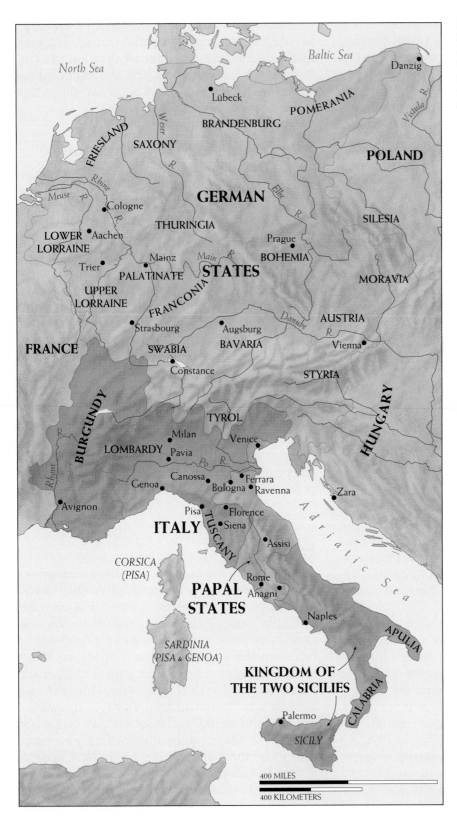

MAP 7–2 GERMANY AND ITALY IN THE MIDDLE AGES   *The Holy Roman Empire embraced lands under direct imperial administration and hundreds of independent territories that the emperor ruled only in name.*

he was willing to grant Germany's feudal nobility absolute authority over their domains. Frederick's lack of interest in building a centralized monarchy for Germany halted the development of the nation and condemned it to six centuries of chaotic disunity.

Frederick's policy with respect to the papacy was equally disastrous. The popes excommunicated Frederick four times and came to view him as the Antichrist, the biblical beast of the Apocalypse whose persecution of the faithful signaled the end of the world. Although Frederick abandoned Germany, he was determined to win control over Lombardy, unite it with his Sicilian kingdom, and surround Rome. This the popes were determined to prevent.

The popes won the fight with the Hohenstaufens, but their victory was Pyrrhic. The contest led Pope Innocent IV (1243–1254) to immerse the church more deeply in European politics than ever before. Wholesale secularization increased criticism of the church by religious reformers and by the patriotic champions of national monarchies. Innocent organized and led the German princes against Frederick, and German and Italian resistance kept Frederick on the defensive throughout his last years.

When Frederick died in 1250, the German monarchy died with him. The German nobility repudiated the idea of hereditary succession to the throne, and in 1257 the barons formed an electoral college that claimed the right to bestow the title "king of the Romans." This ensured that the kings they created would be their puppets.

Manfred, Frederick's illegitimate son, fought hard to save something of the Hohenstaufen legacy, but he was defeated in 1266. In 1286 Charles of Anjou, the adventurous brother of the saintly Louis IX, destroyed the last of the Hohenstaufens (Frederick's grandson Conradin). Germany temporarily ceased to meddle in Italy's affairs, but this did not free Italy from the threat of outside interference. France and, to a lesser extent, England aspired to the role Germany had tried to play in Italy.

In Perspective

With borders that were finally secured at the start of the High Middle Ages, western Europe *began to develop its characteristic cultural and political institutions. The map of Europe as it appears today began to take shape. England and France built centralized monarchies that unified them as modern nation-states. Germany and Italy, however, failed to overcome the forces of feudal fragmentation.*

The dream of creating a Holy Roman Empire tempted German rulers into Italy, where they made enemies of the popes and the rising commercial cities. The result was an unprecedented contest between church and state that promoted the growth of a powerful papal monarchy. The church's involvement with politics alienated kings, secularized the papacy, and increased the church's vulnerability to attack on the grounds that it was failing in its spiritual mission.

REVIEW QUESTIONS

1. How did the Saxon king Otto I rebuild the German Empire? How did he establish control over the various German duchies? How did he use the church to achieve his political goals? Does he deserve to be called "the Great"?

2. What were the main reasons for the Cluny reform movement? How do you account for its success? What was the impact of the reform on the subsequent history of the medieval church and state?

3. In the dispute between Pope Gregory VII and King Henry IV over the issue of lay investiture, what were the causes of the controversy, the actions of the contending parties, and the outcome of the struggle? What was at stake for each of the disputants, and what were the ramifications of the conflict?

4. What did Voltaire, the eighteenth-century French intellectual, mean when he said that the Holy Roman Empire was neither holy nor Roman? Do you agree with him?

5. What developments in western and eastern Europe promoted the crusading movement? Why did the Crusaders fail to establish lasting political and religious control over the Holy Land? What impact did the Crusaders have on the West's politics, religion, and economies? Which of its outcomes do you consider most important? Why?

6. Why does Hohenstaufen rule deserve to be remembered as a disaster for Germany? What

factors prevented German consolidation during the Hohenstaufen era? If France and England could coalesce into reasonably strong states, why was Germany not able to do the same?

SUGGESTED READINGS

J. W. BALDWIN, *The Government of Philip Augustus* (1986). An important scholarly work.

G. BARRACLOUGH, *The Origins of Modern Germany* (1946). Dated but penetrating political narrative setting modern Germany in the perspective of the Middle Ages.

G. BARRACLOUGH, *The Medieval Papacy* (1968). Brief survey with pictures.

H. E. J. COWDREY, *Popes, Monks, and Crusaders* (1984). Re-creation of the atmosphere that gave birth to the Crusades.

E. M. HALLAM, *Capetian France, 987–1328* (1980). Very good on politics and heretics.

J. C. HOLT, *Magna Carta,* 2nd ed. (1992). The famous document and its interpretation by succeeding generations.

H. E. MAYER, *The Crusades,* trans. by John Gilligham (1972). Extremely detailed; the best one-volume account.

J. B. MORRALL, *Political Thought in Medieval Times* (1962). Readable and illuminating account.

C. PETIT-DUTAILLIS, *The Feudal Monarchy in France and England from the Tenth to the Thirteenth Century,* trans. by E. D. Hunt (1964). Political narrative in great detail.

S. REYNOLDS, *Kingdoms and Communities in Western Europe, 900–1300* (1984). For the medieval origins of Western political and cultural traditions.

J. RILEY-SMITH, *The Crusades: A Short History* (1987). Up-to-date, lucid, and readable.

W. ROESENER, *Peasants in the Middle Ages* (1992). Up-to-date overview.

Chapter 8
Medieval Society: Hierarchies, Towns, Universities, and Families (1000–1300)

KEY TOPICS

- The major groups composing medieval society
- The rise of towns and a new merchant class
- The founding of universities and educational curriculum
- How women and children fared in the Middle Ages

From the tenth to the twelfth centuries, the effects of increasing political stability were felt in Europe. Agricultural production increased, population exploded, and trade and urban life revived. Crusades promoted contacts with foreign lands that stimulated both economic and cultural development. A new merchant class, the ancestors of modern capitalists, appeared to serve the West's growing markets, and an urban proletariat developed.

Guided by Muslim intellectuals, Western scholars began again to study classical literature. Schools and universities opened. Literacy increased among the laity, and the twelfth century witnessed a true renaissance. The creative vigor of the new European civilization was proclaimed by the awesome Gothic churches that were the supreme products of its art and science.

The Traditional Order of Life

Medieval political theorists identified three activities that were essential for society's functioning and assigned each to a separate class: protection by knights and landed nobility, prayer by clergy, and production of supplies by peasants and village artisans. The revival of towns in the eleventh century created a fourth class: traders and merchants. They were thought of as a "middle" class, for their lifestyle combined aspects of the roles of the peasantry and aristocracy. They were economically productive like peasants, but they did not work the land. They had wealth like nobles and clergy, but they were not integrated into the institutions of feudal government. Their appearance unbalanced the old social order and ultimately caused it to collapse.

Nobles

As medieval society evolved, a landed aristocracy with special social and legal status emerged from the ranks of the feudal vassals and warrior knights. In the late Middle Ages the aristocratic class was composed of a higher and lower nobility. The higher were the great landowners and territorial magnates; the lower were petty knights with fiefs, newly rich merchants who bought country estates, and wealthy farmers whose prosperity raised them from serfdom. Land ownership was important, for it was the special mark of the nobility that they lived off the labor of others. Nobles were lords of manors. They neither tilled the soil nor engaged in commerce—activities considered beneath the dignity of aristocrats.

WARRIORS   In the eighth century, European warfare changed dramatically. The appearance of the stirrup enabled cavalry to rout the infantry that had dominated ancient battlefields. The stirrup gave a rider a firm mount so that he could charge an enemy and strike a blow without lofting himself off his horse. Cavalry equipment and training were expensive, so lords divided their lands up to create fiefs to support the vassals who staffed their armies. Thus, arms became the nobleman's profession and war the justification for his way of life.

The code by which the nobility lived exalted strength, honor, and aggression. Nobles welcomed war as an opportunity to increase their fortunes by plunder and their reputations by acts of courage. Peace threatened them with economic stagnation and boredom. Peasants and townspeople, on the other hand, needed peace in order to prosper. Consequently, the interests of the classes conflicted, and the nobility looked down on the commoners as cowards.

The quasi-sacramental dubbing ceremony that bestowed knighthood marked a man's entrance into the noble class. A candidate for knighthood took a bath of ritual purification, confessed, communed, and maintained a nightlong prayer vigil. A priest then blessed his standard, lance, and sword and girded him with the weapons he was to use in the defense of the church and the service of his lord. Dubbing (i.e., striking) on the shoulders with a sword by a senior knight raised the candidate to a state as sacred in his sphere as clerical ordination made the priest in his.

In the twelfth century, knighthood was legally restricted to men of high birth. The closing of the ranks of the nobility was a reaction to the growing wealth and power of the social-climbing commercial classes. Kings, however, maintained some social mobility by reserving the right to bestow knighthood on anyone. The sale of titles to wealthy merchants was an important source of royal revenue.

WAY OF LIFE   When not warring, noblemen honed their military skills at hunts and tournaments. Their passion for hunting was so great that they forbade commoners to take game from the forests. Peasants greatly resented being deprived of this source of free food, and anger at the nobility's hunting monopoly contributed to peasant uprisings in the late medieval period.

Tournaments sowed seeds of social disruption of a different kind. Mock battles provided military training, but they tended to get out of hand—leading to serious bloodshed and animosity among the combatants. The church opposed tournaments as occasions for pagan revelry and senseless violence, and kings and princes finally agreed that they were a danger to public order. Henry II of England proscribed tournaments in the twelfth century, but they continued in France until the mid-sixteenth century.

During the twelfth century, distinctive standards for courtesy (i.e., "conduct at court") began

A lady and her knight going hunting. Bildarchiv Preussischer Kulturbesitz

to be imposed on vassals when they attended their lords. Thanks to the influence of powerful women such as Henry II's queen, Eleanor of Aquitaine, knowledge of court etiquette became almost as important for a nobleman as battlefield expertise.

Knights were expected to be literate gentlemen, capable of praising ladies in lyric poetry. The poetry of courtly love was sprinkled with frank eroticism, and courtly poets wrote rapturously of women married to other men. But the love that ennobled a knight was usually not assumed to be the kind consummated by sexual intercourse. Court poets warned that illicit carnal love led to suffering, and the courtly love movement may actually have been an attempt to curtail the notorious philandering of the noble classes.

SOCIAL DIVISIONS The noble class was composed of many different kinds of noblemen, and some were superior to others. Status within the nobility was a function of how much authority one had over others; a chief with many vassals obviously far outranked the small country nobleman who was lord over none but himself.

In the late Middle Ages there were shifts in wealth and power that sent the landed nobility into a decline from which it never recovered. Climatic changes depressed the agricultural economy that was the source of its wealth, and famines and plagues caused massive demographic dislocations. Changing military tactics rendered noble cavalry nearly obsolete. And wealthy towns helped kings curtail the power of the nobles in local government. After the fourteenth century, possession of land and wealth counted far more than family tree as a qualification for entrance into the highest social class.

Clergy

Unlike the nobility and the peasantry, the rank of clergy was acquired by training and ordination, not by birth. Consequently, people of talent could climb the clerical hierarchy, and the church provided a ladder of social mobility for gifted individuals.

SECULAR AND REGULAR CLERICS There were two clerical vocations: secular and regular. The secular clergy lived and worked among the laity in the *saeculum* (i.e., the world). The most prestigious among them were the wealthy cardinals, archbishops, and bishops who were recruited almost exclusively from noble families. Below them in rank were the urban priests, the cathedral canons, and the court clerks. At the bottom of the clerical hierarchy was the great mass of poor parish priests, who were neither financially nor intellectually superior to the laypeople they served. Until the eleventh century, parish priests routinely lived with women in a relationship akin to marriage, and they stretched their meager incomes by "moonlighting" as teachers, artisans, and farmers. This practice was accepted and even admired by their parishioners.

Regular clergy were monks and nuns—although women were not, strictly speaking, entitled to clerical status—who lived under the *regula* (i.e., rule) of a cloister. By retreating from the world and adopting rigorous ascetic disciplines, monks and nuns emulated the suffering of Christ and practiced what their contemporaries believed to be the ideal Christian way of life. This

Illuminated Manuscripts:
The Luttrell Psalter

Sir Geoffrey Luttrell on Horseback. From *The Luttrell Psalter,* by permission of the British Library.

$\mathcal{M}$edieval people combined religious and secular interests much more than most modern people tend to. The illustrations reproduced here ornament a Psalter (i.e., a collection of Psalms used in personal devotions), but the events they depict have little to do with the practice of religion. They celebrate the noble lifestyle of a late thirteenth-century English knight, Sir Geoffrey Luttrell. They show him feasting and receiving a token from his lady as he prepares for a tournament.

An illuminated manuscript supplemented a written text with pictures and ornamentation. (When gold leaf was combined with brilliant paints, a manuscript was literally "illuminated," i.e., "filled with light.") It was prized not only for

[Top] *The Lord of the Manor Dining.* From *The Luttrell Psalter*, by permission of The British Library. *[Bottom] Kitchen Scene; Chopping Meat.* From The Luttrell Psalter, by permission of the British Library.

its literary content, but for its materials and workmanship. Its pages were made from parchment—a thin, bleached leather that was labor-intensive to produce. Early medieval manuscripts were usually made by monks for clergy. But in the thirteenth century the market for such items changed. Laypeople began to commission them, and secular workshops were established to produce them. In addition to religious themes, lay readers also wanted stories, romances, legal and medical texts, and genealogical records. Each manuscript was specially made for an individual customer. Expensive editions, such as *The Luttrell Psalter,* might be designed to commemorate events in the lives of their owners, but there were also shops that produced cheap copies that university students could afford. The development of the printing press in the 1480s brought this industry and its arts to an end.

Sources: Alexander, J. J. G. *Medieval Illuminators and Their Methods of Work.* New Haven: Yale University Press, 1992. Backhouse, Janet. *The Luttrell Psalter.* London: British Library, 1989. Camille, M. *Mirror in Parchment: The Luttrell Psalter and the Making of Medieval England.* Chicago: University of Chicago Press, 1998. De Hamel, C. *A History of Illuminated Manuscripts.* (7th–16th centuries) London: Phaidon, 1986. Sandler, L. F. *Gothic Manuscripts, 1285–1385* (A Survey of Manuscripts Illuminated in the British Isles, General editor J. J. G. Alexander, Vol. 6), 2 vols. (London: University of Toronto Press, 1996).

earned them respect and influence. The regular clergy were never completely cut off from the secular world. They maintained contact with the laity through charitable activities (such as feeding the destitute and tending the sick), as instructors in monastic schools, and as supplemental preachers and confessors in parish churches. Some monks of great learning and rhetorical skill rose to prominence as secretaries and private confessors to kings and queens. Nunneries produced famous female scholars, and monasticism inspired many of the religious and social reform movements of the medieval era.

The Benedictine rule had been adopted by most Western monasteries by the end of the Carolingian era, but during the High Middle Ages numerous new orders appeared. Saint Benedict had designed a monastic lifestyle that pursued economic self-sufficiency through hard physical labor more than rigorous ascetic discipline. Thanks, however, to generations of bequests and careful husbandry of resources, many Benedictine houses, like the famous Cluny, grew wealthy and self-preoccupied. They devoted much of their time to creating ever more elaborate liturgies for their elegantly appointed sanctuaries. The new orders rejected Benedictine "luxury." They modeled their rules on the example of poverty and self-sacrifice set by Christ and the apostles in the New Testament.

The Carthusians, who were founded in 1084, were the strictest of the new orders. Carthusian monks lived in isolation, fasted three days a week, observed long periods of silence, and disciplined their flesh by acts of self-flagellation.

The Cistercians, who were established in 1098 at Cîteaux in Burgundy, claimed to restore what they believed was the original intent of the Benedictine rule. They condemned materialism and stressed cultivation of the inner life and the spiritual goals of monasticism. To avoid contamination by the secular world and the temptations of wealth, they located their houses in remote areas where there were few worldly comforts.

The monastic ideal was so popular in the eleventh century that many secular clergy (and some laypersons) chose to live as Canons Regular. These people stayed in the world to serve the laity but lived according to a rule that was credited to Saint Augustine. They merged the spiritual disciplines of the cloister with traditional pastoral duties. Early in the thirteenth century,

the desire to combine the virtues of the secular and regular clerical professions inspired another innovation: the mendicant friars—the Dominicans and Franciscans. And during the late thirteenth and fourteenth centuries, laymen and laywomen set up satellite convents known as Begard (male) and Beguine (female) houses. These were religious communes formed by people who worked in the world but lived together under a quasi-monastic rule. The church was uncomfortable with them, for their religious enthusiasm sometimes blossomed into heresy. The Franciscans and Dominicans often assumed responsibility for directing spiritual practices in these establishments.

PROMINENCE OF THE CLERGY   The clergy were far more numerous in medieval than in modern society. Estimates suggest that 1.5 percent of fourteenth-century Europe was in clerical garb. The clergy as a whole, like the nobility, lived on the labor of others. Their income came from tithes, church taxes, and endowments. The church was a major landowner that collected huge sums in rents and fees, and monastic communities and high prelates acquired great fortunes and immense secular power.

Respect for clergy as members of society's "first estate" derived in large part from their role as mediators between God and humankind. When the priest celebrated the Eucharist, he brought the very Son of God down to earth in tangible form. The priest alone had the power to extend God's forgiveness to sinners or to block their access to it by imposing excommunication—a decree that cut a sinner off from the sacraments that were the only avenue to salvation.

Since the priest was the agent of an authority far superior to any earthly magistrate, it was considered inappropriate for him to be subservient to the laymen who ran the state. Clergy, therefore, had special privileges and immunities. They were not to be taxed by secular governments without approval from the church. Clerical crimes were under the jurisdiction of special ecclesiastical tribunals, not the secular courts. The churches and monasteries where clergy worked were also deemed to be outside the legal jurisdiction of the state. People who took refuge in them received asylum and could not be apprehended by officials of secular governments.

By the late Middle Ages laypeople came increasingly to resent the special privileges of the clergy. The anticlerical sentiments that developed during the medieval era contributed to the success of the Reformation of the sixteenth century. The Protestant theologians insisted that clergy and laity had equal spiritual standing before God.

Peasants

The largest and lowest class in medieval society was the one on whose labor the welfare of all the others depended: the agrarian peasantry. Many peasants lived and worked on manors, the primitive cells of rural social life. When the Frankish tribes moved into Europe at the start of the Middle Ages, individuals divided up the lands belonging to farming villages. They became the lords of these estates or "manors," and those who lived on them became their property. A manor was a kind of rural plantation supporting a lord. It was not necessarily equated with a village, for a single village could be home to serfs who belonged to different manors.

THE DUTIES OF TENANCY   A lord was given a manor to support him as a soldier, not a farmer. The peasants who lived on his land worked it for him. They were free to divide the labor as they wished, and any products they raised above and beyond what they owed their lord they could keep for themselves. No set rules governed the size of manors, nor the number a lord could hold.

There were both servile and free manors. The tenants of free manors were descendants of Roman *coloni*, free persons who had traded their land and freedom for a guarantee of protection by their lord. Tenancy obligations on free manors were limited because their residents had some leverage in negotiating terms. Tenants of servile manors were, by comparison, far more vulnerable to the whims of their landlords. Time, however, tended to obscure differences between the two types of manors. Free, self-governing peasant communities that acknowledged no lords also survived in many regions.

The lord was the supreme authority on his manor. Cultivation of his *demesne*, the plots of land producing his income, took precedence over those of his tenants. He could impress his tenants into labor gangs for special projects or lead them

The livelihood of towns and castles depended on the labor of peasants. Here a peasant family collects the September grape harvest outside a fortified castle in France, most likely for the making of wine. Limbourg Brothers. The Month of September Grape Harvest. From Les Tres Riches Heures du Duc de Berry, Chateau de Saumur, Musée Condé, Chantilly, France. Giraudon/Art Resource, NY

out as foot soldiers when he went to war. He owned and leased to his peasants some of the instruments and facilities they used to raise and process food. His income was fattened by petty taxes and monopolies called banalities (e.g., the requirement that all his tenants grind their grain in his mill or bake their bread in his oven). The lord also collected an inheritance tax—usually the best animal from a deceased serf's estate. A serf who wished to travel or to marry outside his manor also had to obtain (i.e., buy) his lord's permission.

THE LIFE OF A SERF   Burdened as a serf's life was, it was superior to chattel slavery. Serfs had their own dwellings and modest strips of land. They managed their own labor. They were permitted to market surpluses for their own profit. They were free to choose spouses from the local village community. Their marriages were protected by the church. They could pass on property to their children. And they could not be sold away from their land.

Serfs seldom ventured far from the villages where they were born. Since the church was the only show in town, life on the manor was organized around religion. But poverty of religious instruction meant that beliefs and practices were by no means unambiguously Christian. Although there were social and economic distinctions among the peasants, common dependence on the soil forced them to work together to survive. The ratio of seed to grain yield was poor; about two bushels of seed were required to produce six to ten bushels of grain in good times. There was rarely an abundance of bread and ale, the staple peasant foods. Two crops on which the modern West depends, potatoes and corn (maize), were unknown in Europe until the sixteenth century. Pork was the major source of animal protein, for pigs, unlike cattle, could forage for themselves in the forests. Excess plow teams were also slaughtered when winter set in. Survival hinged on the grain crops. When they failed or fell short, famine threatened.

CHANGES IN THE MANOR   As the medieval era waned, the manor and serfdom gave way to the free single-family farm. Many things contributed to the change. Technological advances such as the collar harness (ca. 800), the horseshoe (ca. 900), and the three-field system of crop rotation improved agricultural productivity. To meet the demand of the new markets created by the towns that sprang up during the High Middle Ages, peasants brought more fields into production. They used the surplus income they produced to buy their freedom from the obligation of labor services. As the towns revived trade and brought back a money-based economy, lords found it more profitable to lease their holdings to tenant farmers than to work them with serfs. Although tenants thereby gained greater personal freedom, they were not necessarily better off materially. In hard times serfs might expect assistance from their lords, for their lords viewed them as valuable personal resources. But independent, rent-paying workers were expected to take care of themselves.

As the medieval economy expanded and costs of living rose, the landed aristocracy found it hard to make ends meet. The incomes they drew from their manors were fixed by tradition. In the mid-fourteenth century the nobles in England and France tried to increase taxes on the peasants and limit their freedom of movement. The result was often a mass revolt. Although such uprisings were brutally crushed, they revealed that traditional medieval society was breaking up.

Towns and Townspeople

In the eleventh and twelfth centuries, only about 5 percent of western Europe's population lived in towns. Most urban communities were small. Of Germany's 3,000 towns, 2,800 had populations under 1,000. Only 15 exceeded 10,000, and the largest (Cologne) had a mere 30,000. London was the only English city greater than 10,000. Paris was bigger than London, but not by much. Europe's most populous towns were in Italy. Florence and Milan approached 100,000.

The Chartering of Towns

Despite their comparatively small size, towns were where the action was. In the beginning, they tended to be dominated by the feudal lords who granted the land on which they were built, but most acquired political independence. The charter that a lord issued to the residents of a town gave them much greater freedom than rural workers enjoyed. Freedom was a requirement of life for men and women who lived by invention and audacious commercial enterprise, and lords and bishops were willing to grant it to them in exchange for the products that they made available in their markets.

The oases of freedom from lordship that developed in towns hastened the disintegration of feudal society by providing serfs with options. A serf who fled a manor could find refuge in a town. It offered a chance for a better life, for skill and industry could lift a craftsperson into a higher social class. The mere threat of migration of serfs to towns also forced lords to offer them more favorable terms of tenure to keep them on the land. The growth of towns, therefore, improved the lot of all peasants—both those who stayed in the countryside and those who left.

The Rise of Merchants

The first merchants were probably enterprising serfs or outcasts who found no place in the feudal system. Only men who had nothing to lose and everything to gain would have been tempted by the enormous risks and dangers of foreign trade. Merchants traveled together in armed caravans and convoys, buying goods and products as cheaply as possible at the source, and selling them elsewhere for all they could get. The greed and daring of these rough-hewn men, more than anything else, created our modern urban lifestyle.

Merchants were considered an oddity, for they did not fit into the three classes that theoretically constituted feudal society (i.e., the nobility, the clergy, and the peasantry). As late as the fifteenth century, nobles were still snubbing the urban "patriciate" (the hereditary ruling class that arose in some cities). Over time, however, the politically powerful grew to respect the merchants as much as the weak aspired to imitate them, for wherever merchants went, they left a trail of wealth behind.

Challenging the Old Lords

As the traders established themselves in towns and grew in wealth and numbers, they organized to challenge the feudal authorities. They wanted to end the tolls and tariffs demanded by the myriad of nobles through whose domains their caravans traveled. Wherever merchants settled, they opposed all the tolls, tariffs, and petty restrictions that hampered the flow of goods. Merchant guilds (i.e., unions or protective associations) sprang up in the eleventh century, and they were followed in the twelfth century by guilds of craftsmen. These groups worked together to change what the feudal classes had assumed to be a natural and static social order.

Townspeople wanted simple, uniform laws that were valid over large areas. They objected to the fortress mentality that led feudal lords to split up the countryside into tiny jurisdictions. City-dwellers set up independent communes to wrest control of their towns from the nobles, and they began to try to overcome the political fragmentation created by feudalism. Both the church and the king were eager, for reasons of their own, to join the townspeople in a fight to weaken local magnates.

The Rue du Matelas, a French street in Rouen, Normandy, was preserved intact from the Middle Ages to World War II. Note the narrowness of the street and the open sewer running down its center. The houses were built of rough cast stone, mud, and timber.
H. Roger Viollet/Liaison Agency, Inc.

New Models of Government

By 1100 the old urban nobility and the new burgher upper class had merged in many cities. The wealthiest citizens cooperated to create town councils that became the chief organs of municipal government. Small artisans and craftsmen formed their own associations and won political representation for them on town councils. Townspeople thought of themselves as citizens with basic rights, not as subjects liable to a master's whim. The urban poor certainly knew economic hardship and political exploitation, but so long as there was some social mobility, they had a stake in a system and a reason to support it.

SOCIAL TENSIONS   Despite democratic tendencies, class distinctions were prominent in towns.

The wealthiest urban groups aped the lifestyle of the old landed nobility. They acquired coats of arms, castles, and country estates. Once businesses had set up lines of communication and worked out banking procedures for moving funds around, their managers left most traveling to underlings. Investors could settle down on country manors and still run companies. The departure from town of social-climbing entrepreneurs was an economic loss for the communities that had given these people their starts.

A need to be socially distinguished and distinct was not confined to the rich. Towns tried to restrain competition by defining grades of luxury in dress and residence for each social group and vocation. Overly conspicuous consumption was a kind of indecent exposure punishable by "sumptuary" laws—regulations that restricted the type of clothing one might wear or the decoration of one's home. These rules were meant to maintain order by keeping everyone clearly and peacefully in place.

The need for laws to limit competition among classes suggests that medieval towns were not internally harmonious. They were collections of self-centered groups, each seeking to advance its own interests. Conflict between haves and have-nots was inevitable. The poorest workers in the export trades (usually the weavers and woolcombers) were distinct from the economically better off and socially ascending independent artisans and small shopkeepers. The interests of these latter also differed from those of the merchants who brought foreign goods into the city to compete with domestic products. Theoretically, poor men could work their way up this hierarchy, and some lucky ones succeeded. But until they did, they were excluded from the city council. Only property-owning families of long standing had full rights of citizenship. Urban self-government, therefore, tended to become inbred and aristocratic.

Artisans formed guilds to gain the clout needed to win a direct voice in government. Guilds empowered the more successful among them but curtailed the social mobility of poor laborers. The guilds' representatives on city councils worked to monopolize the local market for their members by discouraging imports. They protected the health of that market by ensuring that those who served it produced ac-

ceptable products at fair prices. On the other hand, guilds discouraged improvements in techniques of production for fear that this might give some persons advantages over others. They were also often reluctant to license new producers. This infuriated the journeymen who trained in guild shops, for it prevented them from setting up in business for themselves. It condemned them to the status of politically disenfranchised workers who had no hope of advancement, a true urban proletariat. The protectionism practiced by guild-dominated urban governments ultimately depressed the economy for everyone.

Towns and Kings

A natural alliance developed between the governments of towns and the centralized nation-states that medieval kings labored to build. Towns supplied royal governments with experienced bureaucrats and lawyers who knew Roman law, the tool for designing kingdoms and empires. Towns provided the money that kings needed to hire professional armies and free themselves from dependence on the feudal nobility. Towns, in short, had the human, financial, and technological resources to empower kings.

Towns wanted strong monarchs because national governments provided the best support for commerce. A powerful king could control the local despots whose tolls and petty wars disrupted trade. Unlike a local magnate, kings also tended to keep their distance and allow towns to exercise autonomy. Kings could provide security for large areas, create standardized currencies to ease buying and selling, and simplify the payment of dues and taxes.

The relationship between kings and towns fluctuated with the fate of monarchy in various nations. In France, where the Capetian dynasty flourished, towns were integrated into royal government. In England, towns supported the barons against unpopular kings like John but cooperated with more effective monarchs in subduing the nobility. In Germany, where the feudal magnates triumphed over their kings, towns came under the control of territorial princes. Italy offered towns unique opportunities. Italy had no native royal family for towns to support against the nobility, and a shared opposition to the political ambitions of German kings and Roman popes encouraged Italy's town-dwellers and nobles to work together. As the two classes fused, town governments extended their authority into the countryside and revived the ancient institution of the city-state.

Between the eleventh and fourteenth centuries, towns enjoyed considerable autonomy and once again became the centers of Western civilization. But when true nations began to appear in the fourteenth century, both towns and the church tended to come under the control of kings. By the seventeenth century, few had escaped integration into the larger purposes of the "state."

Jews in Christian Society

The Jews who survived in medieval Europe tended to congregate in towns. Since they could not take Christian oaths of homage, they were excluded from feudal land tenure and forced to earn their livings from trade. For reasons of protection and the practice of their religion, they gathered together in tight communities. The church forbade them to employ Christians, and efforts to keep the two peoples apart promoted mutual suspicion. Ignorance of Jewish practices, resentment of the wealth acquired by some Jews, and a popular tendency to hold the Jews responsible for Christ's crucifixion, fueled baseless rumors of Jewish plots against Christian society. These sparked periodic mob violence against Jews and decisions by church and state authorities to exile them or penalize them in some way.

Schools and Universities

In the twelfth century, European scholars discovered Aristotle's treatises on logic, the writings of Euclid and Ptolemy, Roman law, and the basic works of Greek physicians and Arab mathematicians. Islamic scholars living in Spain were chiefly responsible for the translations and commentaries that made these ancient texts accessible to Westerners. The result was a cultural renaissance and the invention of a new center of intellectual activity, the university.

University of Bologna

When the term *university* was first used, all it implied was a corporation of individuals who "united" for mutual protection. Schools attracted students and teachers from great distances, and many were foreigners who had no civil rights in the towns where they worked. Unless they organized to protect themselves—like the members of an urban trade guild—they could be exploited by the townspeople on whom they were dependent for food and lodging.

The first of the great medieval universities was chartered in Bologna, Italy, by Emperor Frederick Barbarossa in 1158. Bologna, which became a model for schools in Italy, Spain, and southern France, was organized by its students. They "unionized" to guarantee fair rents and prices and high-quality teaching from their masters. They hired their teachers, set pay scales, and assigned lecture topics. Masters who did not live up to student expectations were boycotted, and price-gouging by townspeople was countered by threats to take the university and its profitable business to another town.

Bologna was most famous for the courses in law it offered advanced students. In the late eleventh century, Western scholars discovered the *Corpus Juris Civilis,* the collection of ancient Roman law made by the Byzantine emperor Justinian in the sixth century. In the early twelfth century, Irnerius of Bologna began to use the Roman law to create "glosses" (i.e., commentaries) on current laws. Around 1140, another resident of Bologna, a monk named Gratian, wrote the standard legal text in church (i.e., canon) law, the *Concordance of Discordant Canons* (known simply as the *Decretum*).

Masters, as well as students, formed protective associations, and their guilds dominated the universities of northern Europe, among which Paris was preeminent. Masters' guilds had a monopoly on teaching, and their tests for admission set standards for certification of teachers. The licenses to teach that medieval guilds awarded were the predecessors of modern academic degrees.

Cathedral Schools

The basic course of study at all medieval universities was the liberal arts program. It consisted of the *trivium* (grammar, rhetoric, and logic) and the *quadrivium* (arithmetic, geometry, astronomy, and music). This amounted to instruction in reading, writing, and computation. Students usually entered the university between the ages of twelve and fifteen. Since all books and all instruction were in Latin, they were expected to arrive knowing how to read and speak that language. The first four years of their course of study were devoted to the *trivium*, which polished their Latin and earned them a bachelor of arts degree. A master's degree entailed an additional three or four years of work on the *quadrivium*, the study of classical texts dealing with mathematics, natural science, and philosophy. Doctoral degrees were available in a few fields such as law, medicine, and theology. It could take twenty or more years to earn a degree in theology at the University of Paris.

The liberal arts curriculum evolved in the cathedral and monastery schools that trained clergy. In the early Middle Ages these were the only schools that existed, and the clergy were the only literate class. But by the late eleventh century, students who had no interest in clerical vocations, but who needed Latin and related intellectual disciplines for careers as notaries or merchants, began to frequent the church's schools. In 1179 a papal decree ordered cathedrals to provide teachers gratis for laity who wanted to learn. By the thirteenth century, the demand for literate men to staff the growing urban and territorial governments and expanding merchant firms gave rise to schools offering secular vocational education.

University of Paris

The University of Paris, which provided the model for the schools of northern Europe, evolved, in part, from the cathedral school of Notre Dame. King Philip Augustus and Pope Innocent III chartered Paris in 1200 and gave its students protections and privileges denied ordinary citizens. Only in self-defense, for instance, might a citizen strike a student, and all citizens were obligated to testify against anyone seen abusing a student. University regulations required teachers to be carefully examined before being licensed to teach. French law, in short, recognized students as a valuable and a vulnerable resource.

Paris originated the college or house system. The first colleges were charitable hospices providing room and board for poor students who would not otherwise be able to afford to study. The university soon discovered that these insti-

tutions were useful for overseeing students, and it encouraged all students to enroll in them. The most famous of the Parisian colleges was the Sorbonne, which was founded around 1257 by a royal chaplain named Robert de Sorbon. Early universities had been highly mobile institutions that used rented or borrowed space. But the buildings provided by endowed colleges rooted a university to a particular spot. This reduced the university's leverage in negotiating with townspeople, for it could no longer threaten to move to another place.

The Curriculum

The education provided by cathedral and monastery schools was limited to grammar, rhetoric, and some elementary geometry and astronomy. The standard texts were the Latin grammars of Donatus and Priscian, Saint Augustine's *On Christian Doctrine*, Cassiodorus's *On Divine and Secular Learning*, Boethius's treatises on arithmetic and music, and a few of Aristotle's logical works. The books that entered Europe from Muslim lands in the early twelfth century vastly expanded libraries and made possible the more elaborate curricula of universities. The most revolutionary of the new texts were works by Aristotle, which had previously been unknown in Europe. They were in general circulation by the mid-thirteenth century, and they shaped the dominant intellectual movement of the day: Scholasticism.

In the High Middle Ages scholars assumed that truth was not something one had to go out and find for oneself. It was already enshrined in the works of the great authorities of the past—men such as Aristotle and the fathers of the church. It had only to be apprehended and absorbed. Teachers did not encourage students to strive independently for undiscovered truth. They taught them rather to use logic and dialectic to organize and harmonize the accepted truths of tradition. Dialectic, the art of discovering a truth by finding the contradictions in arguments against it, reigned supreme in all disciplines. Instead of observing phenomena for themselves, students read the traditional authorities in their fields, made short summaries of their teaching, disputed interpretations by elaborating arguments pro and con, and then took positions based on logical cogency.

Because printing with movable type did not yet exist, only a few expensive, hand-copied books were available. Few students could afford texts for quiet, private study. Most had to learn from discussions, lectures, and debates. They memorized the information with which they worked, and they were required to think on their feet. Rhetorical skill, the ability to make an eloquent defense of the points one had clarified by logic and dialectic, was the goal of an education. To win debates, students had to become walking encyclopedias filled with information they could regurgitate as needed.

THE SUMMA   The *summa*, a summary of all that was known about a particular subject, was the characteristic intellectual product of the High Middle Ages. The *summa*'s chief purpose was to clarify all that was known about a subject by reconciling apparent contradictions among authorities.

Medieval scholars labored to produce universal summaries for all disciplines, but the most influential were those that appeared in theology, the "queen of the sciences." About 1122 Peter Abelard (1079–1142) published *Sic et Non*, a book that facilitated scholastic debate by juxtaposing seemingly contradictory statements from the works of sacred authorities. A few years later (1155–1157), Peter Lombard (1100–1169) worked this material into his *Four Books of Sentences*, which became the standard theological textbook of the Middle Ages. About 1265 Thomas Aquinas entered the field with the *Summa Theologiae*. It was, in the opinion of Catholic theologians, the epitome of what the *summa* aspired to be: the last word.

CRITICS OF SCHOLASTICISM   Even in its heyday Scholasticism had opponents. Some complained that the regimen of the schools was heartless and potentially damaging to Christian faith. The *dictatores*, the professional grammarians and rhetoricians who taught good writing and speaking rather than the highly abstract dialectic of Scholasticism, urged students to go directly to sources (in their original languages) and draw their own conclusions. Their point of view was championed by the humanists of the sixteenth-century Renaissance, and it still informs modern liberal arts curricula.

The church, too, was not completely at ease with Scholasticism. Scholastic thinkers relied heavily on Aristotelian logic to develop their arguments, and there were obvious conflicts between Christian doctrine and ideas that Aristotle defended. For example, since logic cannot account for why there is something rather than nothing or deal with an infinite regression of causes, Aristotle claimed that the world was not created but was eternal. Christianity, however, affirmed the Jewish concept of creation found in the book of Genesis. Aristotle also taught that since logic was the same in all minds, intellect or mind was ultimately the same in all people. This obliterated individuality and threatened Christian ideas about personal responsibility and immortality.

Some of the early Scholastics were inclined to question Christian doctrines that could not be reconciled with Aristotle's teachings. Berengar of Tours (d. 1088), for example, concluded that the church's claim that the bread and wine of the Eucharist became the body and blood of Christ was logically indefensible. Peter Abelard attempted a reinterpretation of the Trinity that preserved a premise of Aristotle's logic, namely, that three could not be one and one could not be three. The boldness of the new logicians shocked conservatives, who concluded that the love of learning at the universities had clearly got in the way of the love of God.

A century of suspicion that Aristotle was undermining Christian theology culminated in 1277, when the bishop of Paris condemned 219 philosophical propositions. The condemnation was a warning to scholars who were more interested in secular philosophy than in Christian truth, and it chilled the relationship between learning and religion. Thinkers ceased to look for ways to reconcile reason and revelation. William of Ockham (d. 1349), for instance, denied that theological truths could be dealt with as if they were of the same order as the truths that came from empirical experience of natural phenomena. Knowledge of God, he insisted, was available only through biblical revelation.

Women in Medieval Society

The concept of femininity developed by medieval scholars was at odds with the lives of the real women of the era. Christian theologians concluded from the evidence contained in Greco-Roman medical, philosophical, and legal

A fifteenth-century rendering of an eleventh- or twelfth-century marketplace. Medieval women were active in all trades, but especially in the food and clothing industries.
Scala/Art Resource, NY

texts—and the Bible—that women were physically, mentally, and morally inferior to men. The Bible clearly taught that a female was a "weaker vessel" who required protection and guidance from a male. Wives were to submit to their husbands and accept corrective beatings from them. The celibate Christian clergy felt that women were debased by marriage and that virgins and chaste widows were more to be honored than wives.

Contrary forces shaped the roles women played in medieval society. The church reinforced many traditional negative assumptions about women, but it condemned bawdy literature that denigrated women and it insisted on the female's spiritual equality with the male. The learned churchman Peter Lombard argued, for instance, that God took Eve from Adam's side because he wanted woman neither to rule over nor to be enslaved by man. She was to stand beside him as his partner in a marriage characterized by mutual aid and trust. In chivalric romances, in courtly love literature, and in the cult of the Virgin Mary that swept Europe in the twelfth and thirteenth centuries, female traits of gentleness, compassion, and grace were exalted over the rougher male virtues. In these traditions, women were put on pedestals and praised as superior to men in the delicate arts of self-control and civilized life.

Germanic traditions tended to moderate Roman customs. They gave medieval women basic rights that prevented their being treated as mere chattel. Roman women in their teens married men much older than themselves, but German women married later in life and took husbands who were their own age. In German lands a groom provided a dowry for his bride to hold as her own property, and all the Germanic law codes granted women economic freedom. They could inherit, administer, dispose of, and confer on their children family property and personal possessions. They could also prosecute men in court for bodily injury and rape.

In the ninth century, the Carolingians, who had tolerated polygyny, concubinage, and divorce, were influenced by Christianity to make monogamous marriage official policy. The result was both a gain and a loss for women. On the one hand, the choice of a wife became a very serious matter, and wives gained greater dignity and legal security. But on the other hand, a woman's burden as household manager and bearer of children greatly increased. Where previously several women may have shared the tasks of running a nobleman's estate and providing heirs to continue his line, now all these duties rested on the shoulders of one woman. After the ninth century, mortality rates for Frankish women rose and their longevity decreased.

LIFE CHOICES   The demands placed on wives explain the cloister's appeal as a refuge for women, but few women were able to choose the celibate life. (There may, for instance, have been no more than 3,500 nuns in all of England at the end of the Middle Ages.) Entrance into a nunnery was contingent on a woman's ability to bring the house a sizable donation as a dowry. Only a few upper-class women could afford the price of admission. Those who did could acquire educations, rise to positions of leadership, and enjoy economic and political power beyond the reach of their sisters in secular life.

Most medieval women were neither aristocratic housewives nor nuns. They were laboring family women who were as prominent and as creative a part of a community's work force as its men. They could not attend the universities and were excluded from the learned professions of scholarship, medicine, and law. They were, however, admitted to the blue-collar trades. Between the ages of ten and fifteen, girls, like boys, held apprenticeships, and many learned to be skilled workers. When they married, they might continue their trades, operating bake shops or dress shops next to a husband's business, or they might become assistants and partners in a husband's line of work. Women held virtually every job from butcher to goldsmith, and they were especially prominent in the food and clothing industries and in domestic service. Women, as well as men, earned membership in guilds and were accorded the rank of master, but they often found that their opportunities were more restricted than a man's. Women's wages for comparable work averaged 25 percent less than men's. Townswomen had opportunities to go to school and acquire literacy in the vernacular, but peasant women, who tilled the fields, had no such chance for self-improvement.

The Lives of Children

With children, as with women in the Middle Ages, image diverged from life's realities. In medieval art children are rarely portrayed as different from adults, and some historians have questioned whether people in the Middle Ages thought of childhood as a distinct period of life requiring special treatment. The same historians have also noted that infant and child mortality was extremely high, and they have speculated that a parent could not have risked becoming emotionally attached to a child who had a 30 to 50 percent chance of dying before the age of five.

The practice of infanticide, which continued despite its condemnation by the church, suggests that children were held in low esteem in ancient and early medieval society. The Romans regulated family size by exposing unwanted children, but showered attention and affection on the offspring they chose to raise. The Germans, on the other hand, had large families but tended to neglect their children. Among the German tribes one paid a much lower *wergild*, or compensatory fine, for injury to a child than for injury to an adult.

It is possible that instead of distancing parents from children, high rates of infant and child mortality increased attachment to offspring. Evidence of special attention being paid to children is found in the great variety of children's toys and child-rearing equipment (e.g., walkers and potty chairs) that existed in the Middle Ages. Medieval medical authorities also offered advice on postnatal care and childhood diseases—cautioning against abuse and recommending moderation in discipline. The church urged parents to love children as Mary loved Jesus. And evidence from medieval art and literature suggests that when infants and children died in the Middle Ages, parents grieved as pitiably then as now.

Childhood was brief in the Middle Ages, for very young children shared adult responsibilities. Peasant children joined their parents in the fields as soon as they could physically manage the labor. The urban working class sent children as young as eight away from home to begin apprenticeships. The church allowed boys to marry at fourteen and girls at twelve. The pressure put on children to mature and learn may have been a sign of concern for them, for no parental responsibility was deemed greater than that of equipping a child for useful employment.

In Perspective

The economic expansion of the High Middle Ages revived urban life in Europe. As cities grew, new social groups—most notably the merchant-artisan classes—rose to prominence. They successfully challenged the old feudal nobility and brought European communities the blessings and problems of nascent capitalism. The seeds of social conflict and class struggle were sown, but a potentially significant alliance was also struck between the urban classes and the kings who were struggling to reverse the fragmenting influences of feudalism. Together they defeated feudalism and began to consolidate Europe's nations.

The new wealth of towns provided patronage for education and culture. The first universities appeared in the eleventh century and, with them, a new way of thinking (Scholasticism) and a revival of art and science. The creativity of the era testifies to the vitality of the rising "middle" class and its determination to reshape the social and political institutions of the Western world.

REVIEW QUESTIONS

1. How did the responsibilities of the nobility differ from those of the clergy and peasantry during the High Middle Ages? In what ways did each social class contribute to the stability of society?
2. What led to the revival of trade and the growth of towns in the twelfth century? What political and social conditions were essential for a revival of trade? How did towns change medieval society?
3. What were the strengths and weaknesses of the educations provided by medieval universities? How would you evaluate the standard curriculum?
4. How would you define Scholasticism? What was the Scholastic program and method of study? Who were the main critics of Scholasticism and what were their complaints?
5. Do Germanic law and Roman law reflect different understandings of the position of women in society? How did options and responsibilities differ for women in each of the social classes? What are the theories concerning the concept of childhood in the Middle Ages?

SUGGESTED READINGS

P. Ariès, *Centuries of Childhood: A Social History of Family Life* (1962). Pioneer effort on the subject.

J. W. Baldwin, *The Scholastic Culture of the Middle Ages: 1000–1300* (1971). Best brief synthesis available.

M. Bloch, *French Rural History*, trans. by J. Sondheimer (1966). A classic by a great modern historian.

J. Goody, *The Development of the Family and Marriage in Europe* (1983). Interesting effort to explain the church's stake in regulating family and marriage.

B. A. Hanawalt, *The Ties That Bound: Peasant Families in Medieval England* (1986). Elucidating demographic and economic study of rural life.

B. A. Hanawalt, *Growing Up in Medieval London* (1993). Positive portrayal of parental and societal treatment of children.

C. H. Haskins, *The Renaissance of the Twelfth Century* (1927). Still the standard account.

C. H. Haskins, *The Rise of Universities* (1972). A short, minor classic.

D. Herlihy, *Medieval Households* (1985). Bread-and-butter account of household structure in antiquity and the Middle Ages.

G. Künstler, *Romanesque Art in Europe* (1973). Standard survey.

E. Mâle, *The Gothic Image: Religious Art in France in the Thirteenth Century* (1913). An enduring classic.

A. MURRAY, *Reason and Society in the Middle Ages* (1978). A view of the Middle Ages as an age of reason as well as of faith.

E. PANOFSKY, *Gothic Architecture and Scholasticism* (1951). A controversial classic.

H. PIRENNE, *Medieval Cities: Their Origins and the Revival of Trade*, trans. by Frank D. Halsey (1970). A minor classic.

I. S. ROBINSON, *The Papacy, 1073–1198: Continuity and Innovation* (1990). A fresh look at the papacy in a period of reform and independence.

S. SHAHAR, *The Fourth Estate: A History of Women in the Middle Ages* (1983). A comprehensive survey, making clear the great variety of women's work.

B. STOCK, *The Implications of Literacy* (1983). How the ability to read changed medieval society.

L. THORNDIKE, *University Records and Life in the Middle Ages* (1975). Rich primary sources for curricular and extracurricular life.

The Invention of Printing in China and Europe

It was the desire of rulers to govern more effectively—that is, to shape and control the course of events—that brought the printing press into existence both in China and in Europe. Before there was a printing technology there were governors, religious leaders, and merchants who were eager for ways to disperse their laws, scriptures, and goods more widely and more effectively. To train the skilled help they needed, they promoted education. This spread literacy through the middle and upper urban classes and created a broad market for reading materials. Literacy came more slowly to the lower classes, for authorities feared that it might promote their discontent with the status quo. Even after the invention of printing, many people remained illiterate and acquired their information orally.

Resources and Technology: Paper and Ink

The invention of printing would have been impossible without other inventions that supplied sizable quantities of inexpensive, durable paper and a reliable ink. A water-based soot and gum ink was in use across Asia as early as the Shang period (1776–1122 B.C.E.). Europe did not have anything comparable until the early Middle Ages. Shang officials used their ink to authenticate documents by stamping them with images carved on seals. Similar seals were made in ancient Mesopotamia and Egypt, where they were reserved for religious uses.

The chief print medium in the East was silk. In the West it was parchment. Both were expensive. In the second century B.C.E., the Chinese began to manufacture a crude paper from hemp fibers. It was used as wrapping material. In 105 C.E., a man named Ts'ia Lun developed a blend of ingredients that produced a paper on which one could write. By the Tang period (618–907), paper manufacturing had become a major industry in China, and knowledge of its techniques began to make its way to the West. By the ninth century, Samarkand (in Turkestan) had become the East's leading supplier of paper, and a century later fine paper was being shipped to Europe from Baghdad and Damascus. Italy became the major western center of manufacture in the thirteenth century and Germany in the fourteenth century.

Early Printing Techniques

By the seventh century C.E., copies of Confucian scriptures were being made by taking rubbings from stone and metal engravings. At the same time, the West was inching toward the invention of moveable type thanks to improvements in the arts of engraving and in techniques for striking coins. The Chinese were printing with blocks of carved wood as early as the eighth century, and they outpaced the West in inventing moveable type (i.e., printing with individual characters that could be arranged by hand to compose a page of text). Pi Scheng developed this in the 1040s, four hundred years before Johann Gutenberg set up the first press in Europe.

The earliest moveable type was composed of ceramic characters that were bound together by wax or resin to form a printing plate. When a print job was finished, the plate could be heated to melt the wax and free the characters for reuse. Ceramic was, however, fragile, and it and later metal characters did not hold water-based Chinese inks very well. Wooden blocks created clearer imprints, but carving an adequate supply of them to print Chinese texts was difficult. The Chinese script numbered 10,000 individual characters.

Printing Comes of Age

In 952, a quarter century of preparation was crowned by a large-scale printing of a standardized edition of the Confucian Classics. These

The Diamond Sutra. This Chinese translation of a Sanskrit Buddhist work was printed in 868 and found at Tunhuang. It is the earliest dated piece of block printing yet discovered. The Granger Collection

scrolls were the chief reading material of the elite and the basis for the examinations that qualified candidates for government offices. Their appearance was an epochal event. The Sung period (960–1278) witnessed the first sustained output of block printing. It completed three monumental projects: the histories of the earlier Chinese dynasties and both the Buddhist and the Taoist scriptures. Numerous manuals on medicine and agriculture also became available, and paper money made its first appearance (in Szechwan).

Europeans acquired the knowledge of papermaking from the East, but there is no certain evidence that they learned printing from the same source. Europe seems to have invented its inks, types, and presses independently. This may reflect the fact that the different writing systems in use in the East and the West encouraged different approaches to printing. Carved wood blocks suited the Chinese ideographic script in which a single character expressed a complete concept. European writing systems utilized a brief phonetic alphabet, the characters of which had to be combined to make intelligible words and sentences. This was most efficiently done with moveable type. China's complex script was best reproduced by the simpler machinery of block printing whereas the West's far simpler script required the more complicated machinery of moveable type.

Society and Printing

Cultural and emotional factors help to explain the advent of printing. In the East Buddhists believed that salvation could be earned by copying and disseminating sacred writings. Taoists wanted sacred texts that could be worn as charms.

163

A European Printshop. This 1568 woodcut by Hans Sachs shows typesetting (rear) and printing (front) underway in an early printshop. Printing made it possible to reproduce exactly and in quantity both text and illustrations, leading to the distribution of scientific and technical information on a scale unimaginable in the preprint world. Houghton Library, Harvard University

Confucianists were concerned to find methods to preserve their sacred writing from the mistakes that crept in when they were copied by hand. In the West the religious orders of monks and friars promoted the printing of standardized, orthodox editions of the Bible and other religious materials. The spread of literacy among the laity created a demand for such things as calendars, newssheets, and how-to pamphlets, but the large-print runs in Europe, as in China, tended to be texts dealing with religious and moral topics.

By 1500 (fifty years after Gutenberg made his invention) there were two hundred presses operating in Europe, and with them came concerns about intellectual property, copyright, and censorship. The increasing availability of books increased the anxiety of governmental and church leaders about the circulation of materials that they considered dangerous. In 1527, the first publisher was executed for printing a book that the church had banned, and in 1559 the pope established an Index of Forbidden Books. For society's authorities, the growing numbers of literate citizens made changes and reforms both easier and more difficult. As a tool of propaganda, the press could work both for and against the state and its favored institutions.

❖ *Why did the invention of printing occur earlier in the East than in the West? Did the West inherit all its knowledge of printing from the East? How do Chinese and European writing systems differ, and what problems do their differences pose for printers? What was the impact of printing on societies?*

Sources: Thomas F. Carter, *The Invention of Printing in China and Its Spread Westward* (1925). Elisabeth L. Eisensrein, *The Printing Press as an Agent of Change*, I–II (1979). Rudolf Hirsch, *Printing, Selling and Reading 1450–1550* (1967). Constance R. Miller, *Technical and Cultural Prerequisites for the Invention of Printing in China and the West* (1983). Denis Twitchett, *Printing and Publishing in Medieval China* (1983).

Chapter 9
The Late Middle Ages: Social and Political Breakdown (1300–1527)

**The Hundred Years'
and the Rise
of National Sentiment**
The Causes of the War
Progress of the War

**Ecclesiastical Breakdown and
Revival: The Late Medieval Church**
The Thirteenth-Century Papacy
Boniface VIII and Philip the Fair
The Avignon Papacy (1309–1377)
The Great Schism (1378–1417)
    and the Conciliar Movement to 1449

The Black Death
Preconditions and Causes
Social and Economic Consequences

Medieval Russia
Politics and Society
Mongol Rule (1243–1480)
Liberation

KEY TOPICS

- The Hundred Years' War between England and France
- The effects of the bubonic plague on population and society
- The growing power of secular rulers over the papacy
- Schism, heresy, and reform of the church

During the late Middle Ages, the West endured so many calamities that European civilization seemed in imminent danger of collapse. From 1337 to 1453, France and England waged an increasingly bloody conflict known as the Hundred Years' War. Between 1348 and 1350, the first wave of the bubonic plague (the Black Death) swept over Europe, carrying off a third of its population. In 1378 a quarrel between competing candidates for the papacy tore the church apart and inaugurated a schism that endured for thirty-seven years. And in 1453, the Turks overran Constantinople and charged up the Danube valley toward the heart of Europe.

These crises were accompanied by intellectual developments that undercut assumptions (e.g., about God, mankind, and the social order) that had given comfort to earlier generations. Some philosophers came to the conclusion that human reason was much more limited in scope than the Scholastics had imagined. Feudal institutions, which had been assumed to be divinely ordained, were assaulted by kings who aspired to absolute monarchy. Claims to absolute authority were made by both kings and popes—and challenged by political theorists who argued that subjects could hold rulers accountable for their actions.

The Hundred Years' War and the Rise of National Sentiment

Late medieval rulers practiced the art of feudal government but on a grander scale and with greater sophistication than their predecessors. The Norman kings of England and the Capetian kings of France centralized royal power by fine-tuning feudal relationships by stressing the duties of lesser magnates to greater ones and the unquestioning loyalty of all vassals to the king. They also carefully negotiated alliances with powerful factions within their domains: the feudal nobility, the church, and the towns. These strategies fostered a sense of "national" consciousness that equipped both kingdoms for war on an unprecedented scale.

The Causes of the War

The Hundred Years' War began in May 1337 as a fight over the right of succession to the French throne. In 1328 Charles IV of France died without male issue. This extinguished the senior branch of the Capetian royal house. Edward III (r. 1327–1377), king of England, claimed France's throne by right of his mother, Charles IV's sister. But the French barons had no intention of turning themselves over to England's king. They pledged their allegiance to a cadet branch of the Capetian house, to Charles IV's cousin, Philip VI, duke of Valois (1328–1350). Philip inaugurated the Valois dynasty that ruled France into the sixteenth century.

England and France had long been on a collision course, and the English king's assertion of a claim to the French throne was more a justification than a cause for war. Since the days of the Norman conquest, the king of England had held fiefs on the continent as a vassal of the king of France. English possession of French land hampered attempts by the French kings to centralize the government of their nation. England and France also had competing economic interests in Flanders and on the high seas. The Hundred Years' War was, in light of its many causes, a struggle for national identity as much as for territory.

FRENCH WEAKNESS   France should have had no difficulty in winning the war. It had three times the population of England, far greater resources, and the advantage of fighting on its own soil. Yet, until 1415, the major battles were stunning victories for the English.

Internal disunity prevented France from marshaling all its forces against the English, and powerful feudal traditions slowed France's adaptation to new military strategies employed by the English. England's infantry was more disciplined than France's, and English archers wielded a formidable weapon, the longbow. It was capable of firing six arrows a minute and could pierce the armor of a knight at 200 yards.

Progress of the War

The war unfolded in three stages.

THE CONFLICT DURING THE REIGN OF EDWARD III The war began when Edward stirred up rebellions against France in the cities of Flanders by placing an embargo on the English wool that fed Flemish mills. In 1340 the Flemish cities decided that their economic interests lay with England and acknowledged Edward's claim to be king of France and, therefore, overlord of Flanders. On June 23 of that same year, Edward defeated the French fleet in the Bay of Sluys, the first great battle of the war.

In 1346 Edward attacked Normandy. After a series of easy victories that culminated at the battle of Crécy, he seized the port of Calais. Exhaustion and the onset of the Black Death forced a truce in late 1347. There was no further action until 1356, when the English won their greatest victory. Near Poitiers, they routed France's feudal nobles and captured the French king, John II, "the Good" (1350–1364). The loss of king and vassals led to a breakdown of government in France.

Power in France shifted momentarily to the Estates General, a body (resembling England's Parliament) that represented the propertied classes. The powerful merchants of Paris, led by Étienne Marcel, demanded rights similar to those granted the English privileged classes by Magna Carta. But unlike the English Parliament, which expressed the will of a comparatively unified island people, the French Estates General was too divided to be an instrument for effective government. It took time for the leaders of the far-flung regions of a large nation such as France to come to know and trust each other.

MAP 9–1 THE HUNDRED YEARS'
WAR *These maps show English
territorial gains up to the point
when Joan of Arc turned the tide
of battle in favor of the French in
1429.*

The French privileged classes were able to avoid taxation by foisting the costs of the war onto the backs of the peasants. Beginning in 1358, the desperate peasants launched a series of bloody rebellions called the Jacquerie (from "Jacques Bonhomme," a peasant caricature). The nobility restored order by matching the rebels atrocity for atrocity.

On May 9, 1360, England compelled France to accept terms spelled out in the Peace of Brétigny. Edward renounced his claim to the French throne, but he demanded an end to his vassalage to the king of France and confirmation of his sovereignty over the lands he held in France (including Gascony, Guyenne, Poitou, and Calais). France was also required to pay a ransom of 3 million gold crowns for the return of King John. The treaty was completely unrealistic, and sober observers on both sides knew that the peace it brought could not last long. Within a few years France had reopened hostilities, and by the time of Edward's death in 1377, the English possessed only a few coastal enclaves and the territory around Bordeaux.

FRENCH DEFEAT AND THE TREATY OF TROYES After Edward's death, domestic problems caused England to lose interest in war with France. During the reign of Edward's grandson and successor, Richard II (r. 1377–1399), England experienced its own version of the Jacquerie. In June 1381, John Ball, a secular priest, and Wat Tyler, a journeyman, led a mob of peasants and artisans in an assault on London. The revolt was quickly put down, but it left scars that took decades to heal.

Richard's autocratic behavior turned his nobles against him, and he was replaced on the throne by his cousin, Henry IV. Henry spent his reign confirming his hold on England. His son and heir, Henry V (r. 1413–1422), revived the war with France as a strategy for uniting his people behind their king.

Henry's moment was well chosen, for antagonistic factions had split the French nobility. When Henry V invaded Normandy, the duke of Burgundy's party refused to assist its opponents, the Armagnacs, in defending France. After Henry routed the Armagnacs at Agincourt on October 25, 1415, the Burgundians came to terms with the Armagnacs. But their fragile alliance was shattered in September 1419, when the duke of Burgundy was assassinated by an Armagnac.

Burgundy's son and heir decided to avenge his father's death by helping the English invade Armagnac territory.

With Burgundian assistance Henry V took Paris, captured the French king (Charles VI), and married his daughter. In 1420 the Treaty of Troyes disinherited the French king's son and proclaimed Henry V heir to the French throne. When Henry and Charles died within months of one another in 1422, Henry's infant son, Henry VI, was declared king of both France and England.

JOAN OF ARC AND THE WAR'S CONCLUSION Charles VI's son, the future Charles VII, escaped the English and asserted his right to his father's throne. But the success of the campaign that won him that prize owed less to him than to a remarkable young woman called Joan of Arc (1412–1431). Joan was a peasant from Domrémy who informed Charles VII, in March 1429, that God had commissioned her to deliver Orléans from the English armies that besieged it. The king was skeptical, but he was willing to try anything to reverse French fortunes.

A contemporary portrait of Joan of Arc (1412–1431) in the National Archives in Paris. 15th c. Franco-Flemish miniature. Archives Nationales, Paris, France. Giraudon/Art Resource, NY

Circumstances worked to Joan's advantage. The siege of Orléans had gone on for six months, and the exhausted English troops were at the point of withdrawal when Joan arrived with a fresh French army. The English retreat from Orléans was followed by a succession of victories popularly attributed to Joan. She deserved credit but not for military leadership. Joan's talent lay in inspiring her men with self-confidence and a sense of commitment to a nation. Within a few months of the liberation of Orléans, Charles VII had recovered the city of Rheims and been anointed king in its cathedral—the traditional place for French coronations.

Charles showed little gratitude to his unconventional female ally. When the Burgundians captured Joan in May 1430, Charles abandoned her. The Burgundians and the English, hoping to demoralize their opponents by discrediting Joan, accused her of heresy and turned her over to the Inquisition. After ten weeks of interrogation, the "Maid of Orléans" was executed as a relapsed heretic (May 30, 1431). Twenty-five years later (1456), Charles reopened her trial and had her cleared of all charges, but it was not until 1920 that she was canonized and became Saint Joan.

Once France was united behind its king, the English had no hope of clinging to their continental possessions. In 1435 the duke of Burgundy recognized the inevitable and came to terms with Charles. By the time the war ended in 1453, the English held only a little territory around the port of Calais.

Once separated, England and France had to adjust to their new situation. The war had awakened French nationalism and hastened France's transition from a feudal monarchy to a powerfully centralized state. The loss of England's continental empire, on the other hand, disillusioned the English people with their government and set them on the path to civil war. It ended the medieval phase in the history of their monarchy.

The Black Death

Preconditions and Causes

European society in the late Middle Ages was still thoroughly agrarian. Nine-tenths of the population worked the land. The three-field system of seasonal planting and crop rotation had increased food production, but population growth

Significant Dates from the Period of the Late Middle Ages	
1309–1377	Avignon papacy
1340	Sluys: first major battle of Hundred Years' War
1346	Battle of Crécy and seizure of Calais
1347	Black Death strikes
1356	Battle of Poitiers
1358	Jacquerie disrupts France
1360	Peace of Brétigny
1378–1417	Great Schism
1381	English Peasants' Revolt
1414–1417	Council of Constance
1415	Battle of Agincourt
1422	Treaty of Troyes
1431	Joan of Arc executed as a heretic
1431–1449	Council of Basel
1453	End of Hundred Years' War

kept pace with the food supply. The number of people living in Europe doubled between 1000 and 1300—until there were more mouths than could be fed. The average European probably faced extreme hunger at least once during a life span that averaged only thirty-five years.

Between 1315 and 1317, crop failures contributed to the worst famines of the Middle Ages. Starvation undermined health and increased vulnerability to a virulent bubonic plague that struck in 1348. This "Black Death" (so called because of the way it discolored the bodies of its victims) followed the trade routes from Asia into Europe. Appearing first in Sicily, it entered Europe through the ports of Venice, Genoa, and Pisa. Some places such as Bohemia, which lay outside the major trade routes, were virtually unaffected, but by the early fifteenth century the plague may have reduced the population of western Europe by two-fifths.

The plague bacilli were injected into an individual's bloodstream by flea bites. Pneumonic infection—from a victim's sneezing—was also possible. Medieval physicians had no understanding of these processes and could offer no explanation, defense, or cure. Consequently, the plague inspired deep pessimism, panicky superstition, and an obsession with death and dying.

Images of Death in the Late Middle Ages

The he medieval church taught that life is doomed to end in death but that death is a transition to new life. To make this point, the church's artists represented death from both realistic and religious perspectives. The sculpture shown here, *The Prince of the World*, depicts a healthy young man—when viewed from the front. From the rear, however, the youth's earthly vigor is seen to be impermanent. His body is eaten by worms and frogs, and a serpent (a biblical symbol for sin) spirals up his left leg and enters his back. The church used art and sermons to give the laity graphic lessons in the "art of dying" and urged people to meditate on death, expose themselves to dying people, and often visit graves. In 1424, in the Church of the Holy Innocents in Paris, a new theme appeared that was to become very common in late medieval art: the "dance of death." It represented death as a living skeleton in the

The Prince of the World in the Church of St. Sebald, Nürnberg, 1320–1330. Germnisches Nationalmuseum, Nürnberg.

company of everyone from popes and kings to humble workers. Its point was that no one, no matter how exalted, escaped death.

The point of meditating on death was to strengthen resolves to resist the temptations of sin and, thus, become eligible for rewards rather than punishments in the afterlife. The church promised its obedient sons and daughters that they could share the resplendent glory of the Christ who triumphed over the grave. The *Isenheim Altarpiece* (1509/10–1515) depicted death from the positive perspective of resurrection to an eternal life of blessedness.

Sources: Alberto Tenenti, "Death in History," in *Life and Death in Fifteenth Century Florence*, ed. M. Tetel et al. (Durham, NC: Duke University Press, 1989); Donald Wenstein, "The Art of Dying Well and Popular Piety in the Preaching and Thought of Girolamo Savonarola," in *ibid.*, 88–104; and James M. Clark, *The Dance of Death in the Middle Ages and the Renaissance* (Glasgow: Jackson, Son, and Col, 1950), pp. 1–4, 22–24, 106–110. Joseph L. Koerner, *The Moment of Self-Portraiture in German Renaissance Art* (Chicago, University of Chicago Press, 1993), pp. 199–200. H. W. Janson et al., *History of Art* (Upper Saddle River, NJ: Prentice Hall, 1997), p. 528.

Gruenwald, Mathias (1460–1528), *The Resurrection*. A panel from the Isenheim Altar. Limewood (around 1515), 250 × 650 cm. Musée d'Unterlinden, Colmar, France.

The Apparition of the Knight of Death, an allegory of the plague approaching a city, whose defenses against it are all too unsure. From the *Tres Riches Heures du Duc de Berry* (1284), Limbourg Brothers. Ms. 65/1284, fol. 90v. Musée Conde, Chantilly, France. Giraudon/Art Resource, NY

Amulets and folk remedies abounded. Some people recommended a temperate, disciplined regimen. Others hastened to enjoy as many of life's pleasures as possible before it was too late. Troops of flagellants, religious fanatics who whipped themselves in ritual penance, paraded through the countryside stirring up mass panic. Sometimes unpopular minorities, such as the Jews, were accused of spreading the disease and were murdered.

Social and Economic Consequences

FARMS DECLINE   The plague was most virulent in places where people lived close together. Whole villages and urban districts were some-times wiped out. As the number of laborers decreased, the wages of those who survived increased. This tempted serfs to abandon farming and seek more rewarding jobs in towns. Agricultural prices fell because of lowered demand, and the price of luxury and manufactured goods—the work of scarce, skilled artisans—rose. These economic developments hurt the nobility. Without workers, the value of their estates declined. To keep workers on their manors, landowners had to offer them better deals. As a result, incomes from rents declined steadily after the plague.

The church was insulated from some of the problems that afflicted the nobility. As a great landholder, it suffered economic losses. But these were offset by an increased demand for masses for the dead and by a flood of gifts and bequests.

To recoup their losses, some landowners converted arable land to sheep pasture. Herding required far fewer expensive laborers than the cultivation of grain. The nobility also used their monopoly of political power to reverse their declining fortunes. They passed laws ordering peasants to stay on the land and freezing wages at low levels. Resentment of such legislation helped fuel the Jacquerie in France and in England a similar rebellion known as the Peasants' Revolt.

CITIES REBOUND   Although the plague hit urban populations especially hard, cities ultimately prospered from its effects. Cities carefully controlled immigration and limited competition in their markets. The omnipresence of death whetted the appetite for pleasure and for the luxuries produced by cities. Initially the demand for manufactured goods could not be met, for craft guilds purposely kept the numbers of masters and apprentices low. The first wave of plague drastically reduced the already restricted supply of artisans, and this caused the prices of manufactured and luxury items to rise to new heights. As high prices for manufactured goods caused wealth to pour into cities, reduced demand for agricultural products (caused by the fall in the numbers of consumers) lowered the cost of living for urban dwellers and the value of investments in farm land. The forces that enriched townspeople impoverished the landed nobility. This enabled cities to extend their influence into the countryside, and the rural gentry began to be absorbed into the ranks of the urban patriciate.

The rapidly changing economic conditions created by the plague were not an unmixed blessing for towns. They increased some of the tensions that had long seethed within urban communities. The merchant classes found it difficult to maintain their traditional dominance over the prospering artisans' guilds. The guilds used their growing political clout to enact restrictive legislation designed to protect local industries. Master artisans kept demand for their products high by limiting the number of shops licensed to share their market. This frustrated many journeymen who were eager to set up in business for themselves, and it created strife within the guilds.

Ecclesiastical Breakdown and Revival: The Late Medieval Church

Kings took full advantage of the rising power of the towns and the declining status of the feudal nobility to centralize governments and economies. The church, which might have resisted the royal drift toward nationalism, faltered just as the new monarchies began to flex their muscles. The plague had weakened the church by killing large numbers of clergy, but the church owed its most serious problems to its own leaders.

The Thirteenth-Century Papacy

In the latter half of the thirteenth century the papacy appeared to be in a strong position. Frederick II had been vanquished. Imperial pressure on Rome had been removed. The saintly French king, Louis IX, was an enthusiastic supporter of the church. The Eastern orthodox clergy even accepted reunion with Rome in 1274 in an attempt to persuade the West to send Constantinople help against the Turks.

But as early as the reign of Pope Innocent III (1198–1216), when papal power reached its height, there were signs of trouble. By creating a centralized papal monarchy with a clearly political mission, Innocent had increased the church's secular power but diminished its spiritual authority. The thirteenth-century papacy became a powerful political institution. It legislated its own laws and enforced them in its own courts. It presided over an efficient international bureaucracy and was preoccupied with finances and the pursuit of secular influence. The papacy thought more in terms of its own needs than those of the church at large.

Many observers noted how far the papacy had departed from the simplicity and other-worldliness of the New Testament apostolic community. In the minds of some, a crucial distinction began to be made between the papal monarchy and the "true" church of faithful Christians.

POLITICAL FRAGMENTATION The papacy was undermined by its own success. The demise of imperial power meant that popes could no longer appeal for support as leaders of Italian resistance to German kings. As external threats from Germany retreated, political intrigues swept the Italian states, and the papacy became just another prize up for grabs.

Pope Gregory X (1271–1276) tried to guarantee the freedom of papal elections by ordering the cardinals to be sequestered when choosing successors to the papal throne. He hoped that physical isolation would prevent outsiders from promoting candidates simply for political reasons, but the College of Cardinals was already too politicized for this to have much effect. Infighting was so great that from 1292 to 1294 the college was unable to elect a pope. In frustration, the cardinals finally chose a compromise candidate—a saintly but inept Calabrian hermit, Celestine V. Celestine shocked Europe by abdicating under suspicious circumstances after only a few weeks in office. His death, which soon followed, led to rumors that he had been murdered to guarantee that his successor had a clear title to office. The new pope, Boniface VIII (1294–1303), was as worldly wise as Celestine had been naively innocent.

Boniface VIII and Philip the Fair

Boniface won the papacy just as England and France were forming nation-states. France's Philip IV, "the Fair" (r. 1285–1314), was a ruthless politician who taught Boniface that the pope's inheritance from Innocent III was not the reality, but only the illusion, of power. Papal monarchy was no match for a king at the helm of one of Europe's new nations.

THE ROYAL CHALLENGE TO PAPAL AUTHORITY If Edward I (r. 1272–1307) of England had been able to resolve problems with Scotland, the Hundred Years' War might have been underway by the time Boniface became pope. France and England were both mobilizing resources for a war they considered inevitable, and their preparations created a problem for Boniface. Both states were levying extraordinary taxes on their clergy. Since Pope Innocent III had decreed in 1215 that rulers had no right to tax the clergy without papal approval, Boniface had to take a strong stand in defense of papal prerogatives. On February 5, 1296, he issued a bull (*Clericis Laicos*) forbidding lay taxation of the clergy.

Edward I retaliated by denying the clergy the protection of the state's laws and courts, and Philip the Fair cunningly deprived the papacy of the bulk of its income by forbidding the exportation of money from France to Rome. Boniface, who had no choice but to come to terms, issued a second bull that conceded the right of a king to tax clergy "during an emergency." To smooth things over, he also agreed to canonize Philip's grandfather, Louis IX.

For much of his reign Boniface was besieged by powerful enemies in Italy. The Colonnas—rivals of Boniface's family, the Gaetani—joined the Spiritual Franciscans in a campaign to invalidate Boniface's election. They alleged that Boniface had forced his predecessor (Celestine V) from office, murdered him, and won the papacy by bribing the cardinals. Boniface fought back, and his fortunes slowly improved. In 1300 Rome celebrated a jubilee, an occasion on which pilgrims to the city received an especially generous indulgence (remission of sin). Tens of thousands flocked to Rome in what the papacy took to be a show of support.

This emboldened Boniface to reassert the papacy's claim to leadership in international politics. He infuriated Edward by supporting the Scots against the English. But his most serious confrontation was with Philip. Philip had arrested Boniface's Parisian legate, Bishop Bernard Saisset of Pamiers, and convicted him in the royal courts of heresy and treason. Philip demanded that Boniface recognize the legitimacy of the proceedings, but to do so would have been to relinquish the pope's jurisdiction over the French clergy. Boniface demanded Saisset's unconditional release and revoked his previous concessions on the matter of clerical taxation. In December 1301, Boniface sent Philip another

bull: *Ausculta Fili (Listen, My Son)*. It pointedly informed the king that "God has set popes over kings and kingdoms."

Philip responded with a ruthless antipapal campaign that forced Boniface to justify the papacy's claim that it and not the state should control the churches within a nation's boundaries. On November 18, 1302, the bull *Unam Sanctam* declared that the temporal authority of kings was "subject" to the spiritual power of the church. Philip viewed the pope's letter as a declaration of war.

Guillaume de Nogaret, Philip's chief minister, denounced Boniface to the French clergy and led an army into Italy to take the pope prisoner. In mid-August 1303, Nogaret surprised Boniface in his retreat at Anagni. The pope was badly beaten and

A book illustration of the Palace of the Popes in Avignon in 1409, the year in which Christendom found itself confronted by three duly elected popes. The "keys" to the kingdom of God, which the pope held on Earth as the vicar of Christ, decorate the three turret flags of the palace. In the foreground, the French poet Pierre Salmon, then journeying via Avignon to Rome, commiserates with a monk over the sad state of the church and France, then at war with England. Book illustration, French, 1409. Paris, Bibliotheque Nationale. AKG Photo.

nearly killed before the people of Anagni rescued him. He returned to Rome, but the ordeal was too much for an aged man. He died in October 1303.

Boniface's successor, Benedict XI (1303–1304), excommunicated Nogaret, but he was in no position to retaliate against the French government. His successor, Clement V (1305–1314), a Frenchman and former archbishop of Bordeaux, utterly capitulated. He lifted Nogaret's excommunication and explained that *Unam Sanctam* was not intended to diminish royal authority in any way. He also gave in to Philip's demand that the Crusading order, the Knights Templars, be condemned for heresy and dissolved—so that Philip could confiscate its wealth. France's victory seemed complete in 1309, when Clement, pleading safety and convenience, moved the papal court to Avignon. Avignon was an independent city situated on land that belonged to the pope, but it was in the southeast corner of territory that was culturally French. The papacy was to remain in Avignon for almost seventy years (until 1377), and no pope was ever again seriously to threaten a king.

The Avignon Papacy (1309–1377)

The Avignon popes were in appearance, although not always in fact, dominated by the French king, and during Clement V's pontificate Frenchmen flooded into the College of Cardinals. Cut off from their Roman estates, the popes at Avignon had to find new sources of income. Their ingenuity and success quickly earned them unfortunate reputations as greedy materialists. Clement V expanded papal taxes on the clergy. Clement VI (1342–1352) began selling indulgences (releases from penance for sin). The doctrine of purgatory—a place of punishment where souls ultimately destined for heaven atoned for venial sins—developed as part of this campaign. By the fifteenth century, the church was urging the living to buy reduced sentences in purgatory for deceased loved ones.

POPE JOHN XXII By the time Pope John XXII (1316–1334) ascended the throne, the popes were well enough established in Avignon to reenter the field of international politics. The result was a quarrel with the German emperor, Louis IV, that inspired an important debate about the nature of legitimate authority.

John backed a candidate who lost the imperial election of 1314 to Louis, and he obstinately—and without legal justification—refused to confirm Louis's title. Louis retaliated by accusing John of heresy and declaring him deposed in favor of an antipope. Two outstanding pamphleteers made the case for the king: William of Ockham, whom John excommunicated in 1328, and Marsilius of Padua (ca. 1290–1342), whose teaching John declared heretical in 1327.

William of Ockham (d. 1349) was a brilliant logician and critic of the "realist" philosophers who claimed that general terms, such as *church*, corresponded to transcendent realities that actually existed. Ockham, a nominalist, insisted that such words were only names the human mind gave to abstract ideas it invented. This position led Ockham to conclude that the real church was the historical human community, not some supernatural entity. The pope was only one of its members and, as such, had no special powers that made him infallible. The church was best guided not by popes, he believed, but by scripture and by councils representing all Christians.

In *Defender of Peace* (1324), Marsilius of Padua argued that clergy were limited to purely spiritual functions and had no right to coerce laity. The spiritual crimes over which the pope had jurisdiction would be punished in the next life, not in this one. An exception might be made if a secular ruler declared a divine law also a law of the state, for God had given the state exclusive authority to maintain secular order by force. A true pope lived according to the strictest apostolic ideals and presumed to lead only by spiritual example.

NATIONAL OPPOSITION TO THE AVIGNON PAPACY John's successor, Benedict XII (1334–1342), began construction of a great palace at Avignon, and his high-living French successor, Clement VI (1342–1352), presided over a splendid, worldly court. The cardinals became lobbyists for various secular patrons, and Avignon's fiscal tentacles spread farther and farther afield.

Secular governments responded by passing legislation restricting papal jurisdiction and taxation. The English had no intention of supporting a papacy that they believed was the puppet of their French enemy. The French monarchy insisted upon its "Gallican liberties," a well-founded tradition that granted the king control of ecclesiastical appointments and taxation. German and Swiss cities also took the initiative to limit and even to overturn traditional clerical privileges and immunities.

JOHN WYCLIFFE AND JOHN HUSS   Discontent with the worldly clergy and politicized papacy was expressed not only in government legislation, but in popular lay religious movements. The most significant were the Lollards in England and the Hussites in Bohemia. The Lollards drew their ideas from the writings of John Wycliffe (d. 1384)—as did John Huss (d. 1415), the martyr of the Hussite movement. Neither man would have approved, however, of all that his alleged followers did in his name.

Wycliffe was an Oxford theologian and a major intellectual spokesman for the rights of royalty against the secular pretensions of popes. Wycliffe strongly supported the actions English kings took from 1350 on to reduce the power of the Avignon papacy over the church in England. Like the Franciscans, he believed that clergy "ought to be content with food and clothing," and his arguments for clerical poverty provided justification for confiscations of ecclesiastical property by the state.

Wycliffe maintained that since all authority came from God, only leaders who lived pious lives could lay claim to legitimacy. He believed that faithful laypeople had the right to pass judgment on corrupt ecclesiastics and undertake the reform of the church. This argument could also be used to justify resistance to secular rulers whose immoral lives proved that they held no mandate from God. Wycliffe anticipated some positions that Protestants would eventually take—challenging papal infallibility, the dogma of transubstantiation that gave the priesthood power over the laity, and policies that restricted the laity's access to the Scriptures.

The Lollards, English advocates of Wycliffe's teaching, preached in the vernacular, disseminated translations of Holy Scripture, and championed clerical poverty. So long as they restricted their attention to religious matters, the English government tolerated them. But after the Peasants' Revolt of 1381 popularized egalitarian notions that were linked to Wycliffe's works, the state decided that Lollardy was subversive. In 1401 it was declared a capital offense.

Heresy was not so easily dealt with in Bohemia where government was weak. The University of Prague, founded in 1348, became the center for a Czech nationalistic movement opposing German encroachments on Bohemia. John Huss, the leader of the movement, became rector of the university in 1403. He believed that a reformed religion would help the Czechs develop a national identity.

The Czech reformers advocated vernacular translations of the Bible and rejected practices they labeled superstitions (particularly some customs associated with the Eucharist). Like the Lollards, they doubted that a priest guilty of mortal sin could perform a valid sacrament. They repudiated the Catholic rubric that reserved the cup at communion to the priest. By offering both the wine and the bread to the laity, they removed any suggestion that the clergy were spiritually superior to the people. Hussites also rejected the doctrine of transubstantiation and asserted that bread and wine remained bread and wine after priestly consecration.

Wycliffe's teaching was partly responsible for the Hussite movement. After Anne of Bohemia married King Richard II of England in 1381, Czech students enrolled at Oxford and sent copies of Wycliffe's works home. Huss was the leader of the Wycliffe faction at the University of Prague.

Huss was excommunicated in 1410, and in 1414 he successfully petitioned for a hearing before an international church council that was assembling at Constance, Switzerland. Although he was guaranteed safe conduct by Emperor Sigismund, he was imprisoned and executed for heresy on July 6, 1415. The reaction in Bohemia to his execution and that of his colleague, Jerome of Prague, a few months later was fierce. The Taborites, a militant branch of the Hussites, took up arms under John Ziska and declared their intention to transform Bohemia into a religious and social paradise. Within a decade, they had won control of the Bohemian church.

The Great Schism (1378–1417) and the Conciliar Movement to 1449

In January 1377, Pope Gregory XI (1370–1378) yielded to international pressure and announced that the papacy would leave Avignon and return to Rome. Europe rejoiced—prematurely, as it turned out—at the end of the church's "Babylonian Captivity" (a reference to the exile of the ancient Israelites from their homeland).

URBAN VI AND CLEMENT VII Gregory died soon after returning to Rome, and the cardinals elected an Italian archbishop, Pope Urban VI (1378–1389). When Urban announced his intention to reform the Curia (the church's central administration), the cardinals, most of whom were French, sensed a challenge to their power and insisted on returning the papacy to their base of operation in Avignon. Five months after Urban's enthronement, a group of thirteen cardinals announced that Urban's election was invalid because it had been forced on them by the Roman mob. They then proceeded to elect a "true" pope, Clement VII (1378–1397), a cousin of the French king. Urban denied their allegations and appointed new cardinals to replace them in his college.

Europe, confronted with two papal courts, distributed its support along political lines: England and its allies (the Holy Roman Empire, Hungary, Bohemia, and Poland) acknowledged Urban VI, whereas France and those in its orbit (Naples, Scotland, Castile, and Aragon) supported Clement VII. (The Roman Catholic Church has subsequently decided that the Roman line of popes was the legitimate one.)

Since the schism threatened the survival of the church in its traditional form, responsible leaders hoped to end it quickly. The easiest solution would have been for one or both of the popes to resign for the good of all, but neither was willing to sacrifice himself.

CONCILIAR THEORY OF CHURCH GOVERNMENT Europe's leaders, seeing no other option, began to listen to scholars who argued that an ecumenical church council was needed to end the schism. There were problems: Only a pope could call a legitimate council, and none of the popes wanted to summon a council that might depose him. Also, since a pope's authority derived directly from God and not from his people, it was not at all certain that a council could depose a pope.

To make their argument for a council, the conciliarists had to examine medieval assumptions about the nature of authority. This led them to develop a rationale for popular government. The conciliarists defined the church as the whole body of the faithful and argued that, therefore, ultimate authority rested with all the people. Since popes were chosen to care for the people's church, they were accountable to the people and served at the people's pleasure.

THE COUNCIL OF PISA (1409–1410) In 1409, thirty-one years after the schism began, cardinals from both sides who embraced the conciliarists' position attempted to resolve the problem. They met in Pisa, deposed their respective popes, and agreed on a single new one. To their consternation, neither of the two competing popes accepted their action, and the result was the establishment of a third pope.

THE COUNCIL OF CONSTANCE (1414–1417) Emperor Sigismund finally prevailed on John XXIII, the Pisan pope, to summon a council to meet in the Swiss city of Constance in 1414. Deprived of all support, the competing popes either came to terms or were abandoned. The cardinals at the council then chose a new pope whom everyone agreed to acknowledge, Martin V (1417–1431). Before the council disbanded, it passed a resolution (*Sacrosancta*) that stated that the council was the true government of the church and supreme over popes. Provisions were also made for councils to meet at regular intervals.

THE COUNCIL OF BASEL (R. 1431–1449) Conciliar power peaked when a council meeting at Basel presumed to negotiate church doctrine with the heretic Hussites of Bohemia. In November 1433, it granted the Bohemians jurisdiction over their church (similar to that held by the French and the English), a unique liturgy, and an exalted role for the laity.

The pope believed that these actions trespassed on his jurisdiction, and in 1438 he upstaged the council by negotiating reunion with the Eastern church. The agreement signed in Florence in 1439 was short-lived, but at the time it enhanced papal prestige. When Basel responded by threatening the pope with deposition, the kings of Europe, fearing a return to schism, withdrew their support for the conciliar movement. A decade later the papal bull *Execrabilis* (1460) condemned conciliarism. The movement had, however, achieved something. It had planted the thought that the role of the leader of an institution was to care for the well-being of its members. This idea had wide-ranging ramifications for the state as well as the church.

Medieval Russia

According to legend, Vladimir (972–1015), prince of Kiev (early Russia's greatest city), decided to modernize his people by converting them to one of the world's great religions. He invited delegations from Muslims, Roman Catholics, Jews, and Greek Orthodox Christians to come to his court to make cases for their faiths. After viewing what each had to offer, Vladimir chose the Greek option. Given Kiev's proximity to Constantinople and Russia's commercial ties with the Byzantine Empire, his decision must have been a foregone conclusion.

Politics and Society

Vladimir's successor, Yaroslav the Wise (1016–1054), turned Kiev into a magnificent political and cultural center that rivaled Constantinople. After his death, however, rivalry among the Russian princes split their people into three groups: the Great Russians, the White Russians, and the Little Russians (Ukrainians). Kiev was reduced to being simply one principality among many.

The governments of the Russian states combined monarchy (a prince), aristocracy (a council of noblemen), and democracy (a popular assembly of all adult males). The broadest social division was between freemen and slaves. Freemen included clergy, army officers, boyars (wealthy landowners), townsmen, and peasants. Slaves were mostly prisoners of war. There was also a large semifree group composed of debtors who were working off their obligations.

Mongol Rule (1243–1480)

In the thirteenth century, Mongol (or Tatar) armies swept over China, much of the Islamic world, and Russia. Ghengis Khan's forces (1155–1227) invaded Russia in 1223, and Kiev fell to the Mongol general Batu Khan in 1240. When the Mongols divided their empire, a group called the Golden Horde (a name derived from the Tatar words for the color of Batu Khan's tent) exacted tribute from the Russian cities. The Golden Horde established its seat at Sarai on the lower Volga and ruled the steppe region of what

Genghis Khan holding an audience. This Persian miniature shows the great conqueror and founder of the Mongol empire with members of his army and entourage as well as an apparent supplicant (lower right). E. T. Archive

is now southern Russia. Its agents were stationed in all the principal Russian towns to oversee taxation and the conscription of soldiers.

Mongol rule distanced the Russians from Western culture. Russian women who married Mongols were influenced by Islam, the religion adopted by the Golden Horde. They began to wear veils and to lead secluded lives. But the Mongols interfered little with the political institutions and religion of their Russian subjects, and the peace they maintained brought Russia economic benefits.

Liberation

The princes of Moscow assisted the Mongols with the collection of tribute and grew wealthy in the service of their masters. When Mongol rule began to weaken, the princes added to the territory Moscow controlled. In pursuit of a policy called "the gathering of the Russian Land," they expanded the principality of Moscow by purchase, colonization, and conquest.

In 1380 Grand Duke Dimitri of Moscow (1350–1389) defeated Tatar forces at Kulikov Meadow. His victory precipitated the decline of Mongol hegemony. Another century passed before Ivan III, "the Great," (d. 1505) brought all of northern Russia under Moscow's control and ended Mongol rule (1480). By the last quarter of the fourteenth century, Moscow had become the political and religious center of Russia. In 1453, when Constantinople fell to the Turks, Moscow took on a new role. It proclaimed itself the "third Rome" and the guardian of Orthodox civilization.

In Perspective

War, plague, and schism convulsed Europe in the late Middle Ages. Even God's house became a shambles as competing popes fought over it. William of Ockham, the leading intellectual of the day, embraced philosophical skepticism and acknowledged the limits of human reason. As the leadership of traditional institutions failed, ordinary men and women endeavored to take things into their own hands. But there was more to the age than loss, doubt, and desperation. The fourteenth century saw the birth of humanism, *an explosion of lay education, and artistic and cultural movements that heralded Italy's great Renaissance.*

REVIEW QUESTIONS

1. What were the causes of the Hundred Years' War? What advantages did each side have? Why were the French ultimately victorious?

2. What were the causes of the Black Death? Why did it spread so quickly? What were its effects on European society? How important do you think disease is in changing the course of history?

3. What was at issue in the struggle between Pope Boniface VIII and King Philip the Fair? Why was Boniface unable to put up a stronger fight? How had political conditions changed since the reign of Pope Innocent III? What did the changes mean for the future of the papacy?

4. What changes took place in the church and in its relationship to secular society between 1200 and 1450? How did it respond to political threats from increasingly powerful monarchs? How great an influence did the church have on secular events?

5. What is meant by the term *Avignon Papacy?* How did this period in the church's history shape the development of the papacy? What caused the Great Schism? How was it resolved? Why was the conciliar movement a threat to the papacy?

6. Why did kings in the late thirteenth and early fourteenth centuries have more power over the church than it had over them? What had changed to make this era different from earlier ones in which popes dominated rulers? What did kings hope to achieve through their struggles with the church?

SUGGESTED READINGS

C. ALLMAND, *The Hundred Years' War: England and France at War, c. 1300–ca. 1450* (1988). Good overview of the war's development and consequences.

P. ARIÈS, *The Hour of Our Death* (1983). People's familiarity with and philosophy of death in the Middle Ages.

J. Huizinga, *The Waning of the Middle Ages: A Study of the Forms of Life, Thought, and Art in France and the Netherlands in the Dawn of the Renaissance* (1924). A classic study of "mentality" at the end of the Middle Ages. Exaggerated but engrossing.

W. H. McNeill, *Plagues and Peoples* (1976). The Black Death in a broader context.

F. Oakley, *The Western Church in the Later Middle Ages* (1979). Eloquent, sympathetic survey.

E. Perroy, *The Hundred Years' War*, trans. by W. B. Wells (1965). Still the most comprehensive one-volume account.

Y. Renovard, *The Avignon Papacy 1305–1403*, trans. by D. Bethell (1970). The standard narrative account.

B. Tierney, *Foundations of the Conciliar Theory* (1955). Important study showing the origins of conciliar theory in canon law.

P. Ziegler, *The Black Death* (1969). Highly readable account.

Chapter 10

Renaissance and Discovery

KEY TOPICS

- The politics, culture, and art of the Italian Renaissance
- Political struggle and foreign intervention in Italy
- The powerful new monarchies of northern Europe
- The thought and culture of the northern Renaissance

T*he late medieval period was an era of creative disruption. The social order that had persisted in Europe for a thousand years failed, but Europe did not decline. It merely changed direction. By the late fifteenth century, Europe's population was recovering from the losses inflicted by the plagues, famines, and wars of the fourteenth century. In many places, able rulers were establishing stable, centralized governments. The city-states of Italy were doing especially well. Italy's strategic location permitted it to dominate world trade, which still centered on the Mediterranean. The great wealth that trade brought Italy's rulers and merchants allowed them to become patrons of government, education,* *and the arts. The result was a cultural Renaissance led by Italians.*

Renaissance humanists revived the study of Greek and Latin and recovered the classical literary heritage. They reformed education and, thanks to the invention of the printing press, became the first scholars able to reach out to the general public. In their eagerness to educate ordinary men and women, they championed the development of vernacular languages as vehicles for art and serious thought.

During the late fifteenth and sixteenth centuries, powerful nations arose in western Europe and inaugurated an era of unprecedented territorial expansion. The colonies they planted around the world yielded a flood of gold and exotic new products that transformed the Western way of life.

The Renaissance in Italy (1375–1527)

The Renaissance was a time of transition from the medieval to the modern world. Medieval Europe, especially before the twelfth century, was a fragmented feudal society with a marginal agrarian economy. Intellectually, it was dominated by the church. Renaissance Europe, especially after the fourteenth century, was characterized by growing national consciousness and political centralization, an urban economy based on commerce and capitalism, and an increasingly secular culture. These changes appeared first in Italy.

The Italian City-State

Italy had always had a cultural advantage over the rest of Europe, for its location made it the link between East and West. Trade with the Middle East, which continued uninterrupted throughout the Middle Ages, supported a vibrant urban culture in Italy. During the thirteenth and fourteenth centuries, Italy's cities extended their influence into the countryside and became great city-states.

GROWTH OF CITY-STATES The growth of Italy's cities and urban culture was promoted by the endemic warfare between Guelf (pro-papal) and Ghibelline (pro-imperial) political factions. Either the pope or the emperor might have brought

MAP 10–1 RENAISSANCE ITALY *The city-states of Renaissance Italy were self-contained principalities characterized by internal strife and external aggression.*

the cities under control if either had been free to concentrate on the task. Instead, each tried to weaken the other, and the merchant oligarchies that governed the cities were the winners. Free from dominance by kings or territorial princes, the Italian cities expanded into the surrounding countryside and assimilated the rural nobility. The five greatest were the duchy of Milan, the republics of Florence and Venice, the Papal States, and the kingdom of Naples.

SOCIAL CLASS AND CONFLICT Social strife and competition for power were intense within Italy's city-states. By the fifteenth century, most had concluded that they could preserve order only by turning themselves over to despots. Venice was a notable exception; it remained an oligarchic republic controlled by a small group of merchant families. Florence, on the other hand, was fairly typical of the forces that contended within Italian urban governments.

There were four politically active groups in Florence: the old rich (the *grandi,* the nobles and merchants who were traditional leaders), an emergent newly rich merchant class (capitalists and bankers known as the *popolo grosso* or "fat people"), the middle-burgher ranks (guildmasters, shop owners, and professionals), and the *popolo minuto* (the "little people" of the lower middle classes). In 1457 about 30,000 Florentines, one-third of the population, were listed as paupers.

DESPOTISM AND DIPLOMACY In 1378 the economic dislocation of the Black Death prompted the Ciompi Revolt, a great uprising of the poor in Florence. Stability was not restored until Cosimo dé Medici (1389–1464) took over in 1434. Cosimo dé Medici, in addition to being the richest man in Florence, was an astute statesman. He controlled the city from behind the scenes, skillfully manipulating the constitution and influencing elections. Florence was governed by a council of six (later, eight) men, the *Signoria,* elected from the most powerful guilds. Through informal, cordial relations with the electoral committee, Cosimo saw to it that the members of the *Signoria* were his men. His grandson, Lorenzo the Magnificent (1449–1492), had absolute control of Florence. After 1478, when the pope and a rival Florentine family (the Pazzi) assassinated Lorenzo's brother, Lorenzo ruled with a firm hand. But he was careful to court popular support.

Despotism was less subtle elsewhere. When internal fighting and foreign intrigue got so bad that city governments were paralyzed, warring factions agreed to the appointment of a *podestà.* He was a neutral outsider, a hired strongman who was empowered to do whatever was necessary to maintain law and order and foster a good climate for business. Because a despot could not depend on everyone's cooperation, he policed and protected his town with a mercenary army hired from military brokers called *condottieri.*

The *podestà's* job was hazardous. He could be dismissed by the oligarchy that hired him or assassinated by those whom he offended. The potential spoils of such a career were, however, tempting, for a *podestà* might establish a dynasty. The Visconti family that came to power in Milan in 1278 and the Sforza family that followed them in 1450 both had such roots.

No matter what kind of government it had, a disciplined Italian city provided a congenial climate for intellectual and artistic pursuits. Despots promoted Renaissance culture as enthusiastically as republicans, and spiritually minded popes were no less generous than worldly vicars of Christ.

Humanism

The Florentine Leonardo Bruni (1374–1444) was the first to describe the scholarship of the Renaissance as the study of *humanitas* (i.e., "humanity"). Modern authorities do not agree on how to define the term. For some, humanism is an un-Christian philosophy that exalts human dignity, individualism, and secular values. There were, however, Christian humanists who defended faith from attack by extreme rationalists. Humanism, for many, may have been less a philosophical position than an educational program emphasizing rhetoric and sound scholarship. It championed the study of Latin and Greek classics and Christian church fathers as an end in itself and as a guide to reforming society. The first humanists were orators and poets. Some taught at universities, but many worked as secretaries, speech writers, and diplomats at princely and papal courts.

The humanists were not the first Europeans to take an interest in the study of classical and Christian antiquities. There had been a Carolingian renaissance in the ninth century. Another was led by the cathedral school of Chartres in the twelfth century. The University of Paris in the thirteenth century was transformed by the study of Aristotle, and the works of Saint Augustine reinvigorated intellectual life in the fourteenth century. These earlier scholarly revivals pale, however, in comparison with Italy's late medieval Renaissance.

Humanists did not use the same techniques of debate as those on which the medieval Scholastics relied. Instead of summarizing and reconciling the views of respected commentators on a topic, they went directly to original sources. Avidly searching out neglected manuscripts, Italian humanists recovered all that remained of Greek and Latin literature and made it generally

Dante Alighieri (1265–1321) portrayed with scenes of hell, purgatory, and paradise from the Divine Comedy, *his classic epic poem.* Scala/Art Resource, NY

available to all scholars. They so assimilated the classics and so identified with the ancients that they came to think of the previous centuries as a hiatus, a dark "middle age" separating ancient civilization from its rebirth in their day.

PETRARCH, DANTE, AND BOCCACCIO Francesco Petrarch (1304–1374), "the father of humanism," tried to write like one of the giants of Roman literature. His *Letters to the Ancient Dead* was an imagined correspondence with Cicero, Livy, Vergil, and Horace. His epic poem *Africa* (a tribute to the Roman general Scipio Africanus) continued Vergil's *Aeneid.* His biographies of famous Romans, *Lives of Illustrious Men,* were modeled on those of Plutarch, but his most popular work was more original and not in a classical language. It was a collection of highly introspective Italian love sonnets, which he addressed to a married woman named Laura. He admired her as a courtly lover—from a safe distance.

Classical and Christian values coexist in Petrarch's work. He rejected scholastic learning as sterile and useless, but published tracts refuting Aristotelian arguments that undercut faith in personal immortality. His imagined dialogues with Saint Augustine bear witness to his acceptance of many traditional medieval Christian beliefs.

Petrarch's point of view was more secular than that of his famous near-contemporary, Dante Alighieri (1265–1321). Dante's *Vita Nuova* and *Divine Comedy* rank with Petrarch's sonnets as cornerstones of Italian vernacular literature. They are also moving testimonies to medieval piety. Petrarch's student, Giovanni Boccaccio (1313–1375) created bridges of another kind between medieval literature and humanism. His *Decameron* consists of 100 (often bawdy) tales—many of which are retold from medieval sources.

EDUCATIONAL REFORMS AND GOALS Humanists were activists who treated the magnificent manuscript collections they assembled as if books were potent medicines for the ills of society. The goal of their studies was to discover the good and to practice virtue. Humanist learning was intended to ennoble people by fitting them for the free use of their gifts of mind and body.

Traditional methods of education had to be reformed to nurture the kind of well-rounded people the humanists wanted to produce. The rediscovery in 1416 of the complete text of Quintilian's *Education of the Orator* provided humanists with a classical guide for the revision of curricula. Mentors, such as Vittorino da Feltre (d. 1446), articulated the goals and methods of the reform. Vittorino required his students to master difficult works by Pliny, Ptolemy, Terence, Plautus, Livy, and Plutarch, and to undergo vigorous physical training.

Humanist learning was not confined to the classroom. Baldassare Castiglione's (1478–1529) influential *Book of the Courtier* was written as a practical guide for the nobility at the court of Urbino. It urged them to combine the study of ancient languages and history with the practice of athletic, military, and musical skills. In addition to these accomplishments, a courtier was to have good manners and an exemplary moral character.

Women, most notably Christine de Pisan (1363?–1434), helped shape and profit from educational reform. Christine's father was physician and astrologer to the court of King Charles V of France. At the French court she received as fine an education as any man and became an expert in classical, French, and Italian languages and literature. Married at fifteen and widowed with three children at twenty-seven, she turned to writing lyric poetry to support herself. Her works were soon being read at all the European courts. Her most famous book, *The City of Ladies,* chronicles the accomplishments of the great women of history.

THE FLORENTINE "ACADEMY" AND THE REVIVAL OF PLATONISM

The revival of the study of ancient Greek literature, particularly the works of Plato, was the most important of the Renaissance's renewed contacts with the past. Interest in the Greek language led Florence, in 1397, to invite a Byzantine scholar, Manuel Chrysoloras, to immigrate and open a school. The Council of Ferrara-Florence, which met in 1439 to negotiate the reunion of the Eastern and Western churches, brought more Greek scholars and manuscripts to Italy. Their numbers increased greatly when Turks overwhelmed the city of Constantinople in 1453.

Medieval Scholastics were preoccupied with Aristotle's logic and science, but Renaissance thinkers were enthralled by Plato's poetry and mysticism. Platonism's appeal lay in its flattering view of human nature and its apparent congruence with Christianity. Platonism posited the existence of a realm of eternal ideas that were the prototypes for the imperfect, perishable things of the world in which humans lived. Plato argued that the presence in the human mind of an innate knowledge of mathematical truths and moral standards proved that a part of a human being was rooted in the eternal.

To encourage the study of Plato and the Neoplatonic philosophers, Cosimo dé Medici (1389–1464) funded a Platonic Academy, a gathering of influential Florentine humanists headed first by Marsilio Ficino (1433–1499) and later by Pico della Mirandola (1463–1494). From Florence Plato's work circulated throughout the West to promote a new, more optimistic view of human nature. Pico's *Oration on the Dignity of Man* succinctly articulated the Renaissance's faith in human potential. Published in Rome in December 1486, the *Oration* was a preface to a collection of 900 theses proposed for a public debate on all of life's important issues. It lauded human beings as the only creatures in the world possessed of the freedom to become whatever they wanted—angels or pigs.

CRITICAL WORK OF THE HUMANISTS: LORENZO VALLA

The careful study of classical languages conducted by humanist scholars sometimes led to conclusions that had wide-ranging ramifications. The leader in this field was Lorenzo Valla (1406–1457), a papal secretary who wrote the era's standard text for the study of Latin philology, *Elegances of the Latin Language.* Valla's linguistic skills enabled him to carry out a devastating critique of *The Donation of Constantine,* a document that popes had used since the eighth century to bolster their claims to power. By pointing out the use of anachronistic terms in the *Donation,* Valla proved that it was a forgery and not an authentic charter from the period of the Emperor Constantine (i.e., the fourth century). Valla also pointed out errors in the Vulgate, the church's authorized Latin Bible. Such historical-critical work helped pave the way for the Protestant Reformation.

CIVIC HUMANISM

Although some humanists were clubbish snobs—an intellectual elite with narrow, antiquarian interests—others preached a "civil humanism," an education that promoted virtue and equipped one for public service. They entered politics, produced art and literature to celebrate the cities where they lived, promoted the use of vernacular languages so that ordinary people could profit from their work, and wrote histories of contemporary events.

Renaissance Art

In Renaissance Italy—and in Reformation Europe—the interests of the laity triumphed over those of the clergy. As people began to value the secular world, secular learning, and purely human pursuits as ends in themselves, medieval Christian attitudes adjusted to accommodate a more this-worldly spirit. This development owed something to the crises within the papacy that cost the late medieval church much of its power and prestige. It was also encouraged by the rise of patriotic nationalism, the creation of governmental bureaucracies staffed by laypersons rather than clerics, and the rapid growth of lay education during the fourteenth and fifteenth centuries.

The new perspective on life can be perceived in the painting and sculpture of the "High" or mature Renaissance (the late fifteenth and early sixteenth centuries). Whereas medieval art was abstract and formulaic, Renaissance art focused on describing the natural world and communicating human emotions. It displayed a rational (chiefly mathematical) order, a symmetry and proportionality that reflected a humanistic faith in the harmony and intelligibility of the universe.

During the fifteenth century, artists developed new technical skills. Slow-drying oil-based paints were invented, and new methods of drafting were devised. *Chiaroscuro*, the use of shading, and linear perspective, the adjustment of the size of figures to create the illusion of depth, permitted artists to paint a more natural world. Whereas flat Byzantine and Gothic paintings were intended to be read like pages in a book, Renaissance paintings were windows on a three-dimensional world filled with life.

Giotto (1266–1336), the father of Renaissance painting, was the first to intuit what could be done with the new techniques. Though still filled with religious seriousness, his work was less abstract and more naturalistic than that of a medieval painter. The Black Death of 1340 slowed the development of art, but ideas such as Giotto's emerged again in the fifteenth century in the work of the painter Masaccio (1401–1428) and the sculptor Donatello (1386–1466). The heights were reached by the great masters of the High Renaissance: Leonardo da Vinci (1452–1519), Raphael (1483–1520), and Michelangelo Buonarroti (1475–1564).

LEONARDO DA VINCI Leonardo came closer than anyone to achieving the Renaissance ideal of universal competence. He was one of the greatest painters of all time—as is demonstrated by his famous portrait of Mona Lisa. Kings and dukes employed him as a military engineer. As an early advocate of scientific experimentation, he defied the church by dissecting corpses to study human anatomy. He also did significant descriptive work in botany. Leonardo's sketch books were filled with designs for such modern machines as airplanes and submarines. He had so many ideas that it was difficult for him to concentrate long on any one of them.

RAPHAEL Raphael, an unusually sensitive man, was loved for both his work and his kindly personality. He is best known for his tender depictions of madonnas. Art historians consider his fresco *The School of Athens*, a group portrait of the great Western philosophers, a perfect example of Renaissance technique.

MICHELANGELO Michelangelo was a more melancholy genius, but he also excelled in several fields. His David, an eighteen-foot-high sculpture of a biblical hero in the guise of a Greek god, splendidly illustrates the Renaissance artist's devotion to harmony, symmetry, and proportion—and to the glorification of the human form. Four different popes commissioned works from Michelangelo. The most famous are the frescoes that Pope Julius II (1503–1513) ordered for the Vatican's Sistine Chapel. They originally covered 10,000 square feet and featured 343 figures—most of which Michelangelo executed himself with minimal help from his assistants. It took him four years to complete the extraordinarily original images that have become the best-known icons of the Christian faith.

Michelangelo lived to be nearly ninety, and his later works illustrate the passing of the High Renaissance and the advent of a new style known as mannerism. Mannerism was a reaction against the simplicity and symmetry of High Renaissance art. It made room for the strange, even the abnormal, and gave free reign to the subjectivity of the artist. The name reflects a tendency by artists to employ "mannered" or "affected" techniques—distortions that expressed individual perceptions and feelings. The Venetian Tintoretto (d. 1594) and the Spanish El Greco (d. 1614) represent mannerism at its best.

The frescoes of Michelangelo on the west wall ceiling of the Sistine Chapel in the Vatican Palace. Above the altar is his Last Judgment. Brett Froomer/The Image Bank

Slavery in the Renaissance

The vision of innate human nobility that inspired the Renaissance was marred by what modern observers would consider a major blind spot. Slavery flourished in Italy as extravagantly as art and culture. The slave market developed as early as the twelfth century when Spaniards began to sell Muslim war captives to wealthy Italians. Many of these slaves were employed as domestic servants, but collective plantation slavery also appeared in the eastern Mediterranean during the High Middle Ages. Venetian sugar cane plantations were models for later west Mediterranean and New World slavery.

The demand for slaves soared after the Black Death (1348–1350) reduced the supply of laborers throughout western Europe. A strong, young slave cost the equivalent of the wages paid a free servant over several years. But given the prospect of a lifetime of free service, slaves were considered good bargains. Owners could also dispose of them like any other pieces of property. Slaves of all races were imported from Africa, the Balkans, Constantinople, Cyprus, Crete, and the lands surrounding the Black Sea. Most well-to-do Italian households had slaves, and even clergy kept them.

As in ancient Greece and Rome, slaves of the Renaissance era were often integrated into households like family members. Some female slaves became mothers of their masters' children, and quite a few of these children were adopted and raised as legitimate heirs. It was clearly in the self-interest of owners to protect their investments by keeping slaves healthy and happy, but slaves remained an uprooted and resentful people—a threat to social stability.

Italy's Political Decline: The French Invasions (1494–1527)

The Treaty of Lodi

The protection of Italy from foreign invasion depended on the ability of its independent city-states

Art & the West

An Unprecedented Self-Portrait

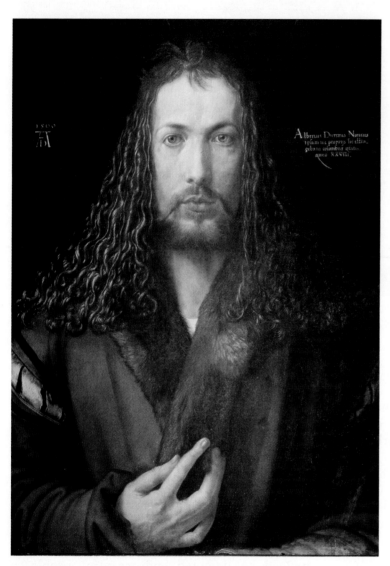

Dürer, Albrecht (1471–1528). *Self-portrait at Age 28 with Fur Coat.* 1500. Oil on wood, 67 × 49 cm. Alte Pinakothek, Munich, Germany. Scala/Art Resource, NY

The greatest German painter of the Renaissance was Albrecht Dürer (1471–1528), son of a Nuremberg goldsmith. Dürer studied in Venice where he honed his skills as a painter of extraordinarily realistic scenes. He claimed that one of his self-portraits was so realistic that his dog mistook it for the man himself and gave it an affectionate lick.

The self-portrait depicted here dates from 1500 and is one of about thirty that Dürer painted. His interest in minutely and frequently describing himself witnesses to the new spirit of the age in which he lived. Instead of divine or regal images, the artist turned his attention to exploring and celebrating his own individuality. Here he represented himself in a pose that utilized conventions traditionally reserved for pictures of Christ, and he signed his work with a bold assertion of his own importance: "I, Albrecht Dürer, divinely inspired artist." The power of the picture derives from its strict geometric proportionality and its painstaking attention to detail. It asserts and validates the artist's claim to be a divinely inspired individual who is capable of great deeds.

Sources: Jane Campbell Hutchison, *Albrecht Dürer: A Biography* (Princeton: Princeton University Press, 1990); Joseph Leo Koerner, *The Moment of Self-Portraiture in German Renaissance Art* (Chicago, 1993), esp. pp. xviii, 8–9, 40–42.

to cooperate. During the last half of the fifteenth century, the Treaty of Lodi (1454–1455) brought Milan and Naples, traditional enemies, into alliance with Florence against Venice and the Papal States. This created a balance of power within Italy and a united front against external enemies.

The peace established by the Treaty of Lodi ended in 1494 when Naples, Florence, and Pope Alexander VI prepared to attack Milan. Ludovico il Moro, the despot of Milan, asked France for help. He urged the French to revive their claim to Naples, which they had ruled from 1266 to 1435. He did not pause to consider that France also had a claim on Milan.

Charles VIII's March Through Italy

Charles VIII (r. 1483–1498) was an eager youth in his twenties, and he responded to Ludovico's call with lightning speed. It took him only five months to cross the Alps (August 1495) and march through Florentine territory and the Papal States to Naples. Piero dé Medici, ruler of Florence, tried to placate him by handing over Pisa and other Florentine possessions. This angered his people, and the radical preacher Girolamo Savonarola (1452–1498) persuaded them to rebel and drive him into exile. Savonarola told the Florentines that France's invasion was God's punishment for their sins, and they paid Charles a large ransom to spare the city. Savonarola remained in power for four years. The Florentines then tired of his puritanical tyranny and pro-French policy and executed him (May 1498).

Charles's lightning march through Italy alarmed Ferdinand of Aragon, who believed that a French-Italian axis constituted a threat to his homeland. Ferdinand proposed an alliance (the League of Venice) to unite Aragon, Venice, the Papal States, and the Emperor Maximilian I against the French. When Milan, which regretted inviting the French into Italy, joined the league, Charles was forced to retreat.

Pope Alexander VI and the Borgia Family

Louis XII (r. 1498–1515), Charles's successor, was able to return to Italy, for he made an ally of Pope Alexander VI (1492–1503). Alexander was a member of the infamous Borgia family and probably the church's most corrupt pope.

Alexander's goal was to use the power of the papacy to recover Romagna, a district on the Adriatic coast northeast of Rome that had broken free from the Papal States during the Avignon papacy. His intent was to turn it over to his children, Cesare and Lucrezia, as a hereditary duchy. Venice's opposition to this plan led the pope to break with the League of Venice and ally with France. The dissolution of the league allowed the French to reconquer Milan, and the pope claimed as his reward the hand of the sister of the king of Navarre for his son and the promise of French military aid in Romagna. In 1500 Louis and Ferdinand of Aragon divided up Naples while the pope and Cesare completed the conquest of Romagna.

Pope Julius II

When Cardinal Giuliano della Rovere became Pope Julius II (1503–1513), he suppressed the Borgias and restored Romagna to Rome's control. Julius, the "warrior pope," brought the Renaissance papacy to a peak of military prowess and diplomatic intrigue. Once he had driven the Venetians out of Romagna (1509) and fully secured the Papal States, he set about ridding Italy of his former allies, the French. Julius, Ferdinand of Aragon, and Venice formed a second Holy League in October 1511. Emperor Maximilian I and the Swiss joined them, and by 1512 the French were in full retreat.

The French were nothing if not persistent. Louis's successor, Francis I (r. 1515–1547), led yet another assault on Italy. The Holy League weakened after French armies massacred its Swiss allies at Marignano in September 1515, but the Habsburg emperor then took up the cause. Four Habsburg-Valois wars finally ended in defeat for France.

Francis was more successful in dealing with the pope. The Concordat of Bologna (August 1516) gave the French king control over the French clergy in exchange for France's recognition of the pope's supremacy over church councils and his right to collect certain fees from clergy in France. This virtually nationalized the French Catholic church, thereby undercutting any appeal the Reformation might have had for France's kings.

Significant Dates from the Italian Renaissance (1375–1527)	
1434	Medici rule established in Florence
1454–1455	Treaty of Lodi
1494	Charles VIII of France invades Italy
1495	League of Venice
1499	Louis XII invades Italy
1500	The Borgias conquer Romagna
1512–1513	The Holy League defeats the French
1515	Francis I invades Italy
1527	Sack of Rome by imperial soldiers

Niccolò Machiavelli

As the armies of France, Spain, and Germany made a shambles of Italy, Niccolò Machiavelli (1469–1527), a Florentine scholar, struggled to make sense of the tragedy befalling his homeland. The lesson it taught him was that political ends—the maintenance of peace and order—are justified by any means.

Machiavelli's humanist education had included a close, if somewhat romanticized, study of the history of ancient Rome. He was impressed by the apparent ability of the Romans to act decisively and heroically for the good of their country, and he lamented the absence of such traits among his compatriots. He believed that if the Italians could cease their internal feuding and unite in defense of their nation, they could drive out the invaders. Machiavelli was devoted to republican ideals, but the realities of political life in Italy convinced him that only a strongman could rescue the Italians from the consequences of their own short-sightedness. The salvation of Italy required a cunning dictator who was willing to use "Machiavellian" techniques to manipulate his people.

Machiavelli may have intended *The Prince*, which he wrote in 1513, to be a satire on politics, not a serious justification for despotism. But he seems to have been in earnest when he advised rulers to consider fraud and brutality necessary means to the higher end of unifying Italy.

Machiavelli hoped that the Medici family might produce the leader Italy needed. In 1513

its members controlled both the papacy—Leo X (1513–1521)—and the powerful territorial state of Florence. *The Prince* was dedicated to Lorenzo dé Medici, duke of Urbino and grandson of Lorenzo the Magnificent. The Medicis, however, failed to rise to the challenge Machiavelli set them. In the year he died (1527), a second Medici pope, Clement VII (1523–1534), watched helplessly as Rome was sacked by the army of Emperor Charles V.

Revival of Monarchy in Northern Europe

The feudal monarchies of the High Middle Ages divided the powers of government between kings and their vassals. The nobility and the towns—through representative assemblies such as the English Parliament, the French Estates General, and the Spanish *Cortes*—tried to thwart the growth of royal authority. But by 1450, territorial magnates in many parts of Europe were being brought under the control of centralized national monarchies.

Towns were the crucial factor in this political transition. With the help of townspeople, kings could escape the limitations feudalism imposed on them. Townspeople made the nobility anachronistic by taking their place as royal officials. They helped kings reclaim the powers of taxation, war making, and law enforcement that under the feudal system were the prerogatives of semiautonomous vassals. As the vassals ceded these functions to centralized governments, the regions they had ruled combined to form true nations. Unlike the nobility who were identified with certain districts, the careers of professional civil servants—the Spanish *corregidores*, the English justices of the peace, and the French bailiffs—depended on advancing national, not regional, issues.

As kings acquired the bureaucratic machinery needed to enforce their decrees, they were able to bypass feudal councils and representative assemblies. Ferdinand and Isabella of Spain rarely called the *Cortes* into session. The French Estates General did not meet from 1484 to 1560. And after 1485, when England's Parliament granted Henry VII (r. 1485–1509) the right to collect the customs revenues he needed to cover the costs of government, the king summoned no more parliaments.

By the fifteenth century, monarchies had also begun to create standing national armies that ended the nobles' traditional military monopoly. Changing technologies—such as artillery—enhanced the importance of the common man's infantry and diminished the significance of the noble cavalry. Professional soldiers—even foreign mercenaries—who fought for pay and booty were far more efficient than feudal vassals who fought for honor's sake.

Since the strength of infantry is dependent upon numbers, monarchs wanted large armies. Professional soldiers tend to mutiny, however, if payrolls are not met. Fifteenth- and sixteenth-century governments had, therefore, to find new sources of income to meet the rising costs of warfare. Efforts to expand royal revenues were hampered by the upper classes' determined resistance to taxation. The nobles believed that their king should live as they did—from the income of personal estates. They considered taxation demeaning. In light of their opposition, kings usually found it easier to levy taxes on those who were least able to resist and least able to pay.

Monarchs had several sources of income. As feudal lords, they collected rents from the royal domain. They could levy national taxes on basic food and clothing. (France, for instance, had a tax on salt, and Spain had a 10 percent sales tax.) Rulers could also, with the approval of parliamentary bodies that did not represent the lower classes, levy direct taxes on the peasantry. (France's king relied heavily on such a tax: the *taille*.) Some governments sold public offices and issued high-interest bonds. But instead of taxing the nobility, they turned to them and to bankers for loans. A king's most powerful subjects were often also his creditors.

France

Charles VII (r. 1422–1461) was a king made great by those who served him. His ministers created a permanent professional army, which—thanks to the inspiration of Joan of Arc—drove the English out of France. An enterprising merchant banker, Jacques Coeur, devised policies to strengthen France's economy, diplomatic corps, and national administration. These tools helped the ruthless Louis XI (r. 1461–1483), Charles's son, make France a great power.

The rise of France in the fifteenth century depended on the defeat of two opponents: the king of England, and the duke of Burgundy. The Hundred Years' War cost England its continental possessions. But Burgundy, England's sometime ally in that war, emerged in the mid-fifteenth century as Europe's strongest state. Burgundy's duke, Charles the Bold, hoped to pull together his scattered family domains to create a new "middle" kingdom between France and Germany. It required a coalition of continental powers to stop him.

When Charles the Bold died in battle in 1477, the dream of a Burgundian empire died with him. Louis XI and the Habsburg emperor, Maximilian I, divided up Burgundy's lands. The Habsburgs got the better parts, but the dissolution of Burgundy freed Louis XI to concentrate on France's internal affairs. Louis harnessed France's nobility, fostered its trade and industry, and ended his reign with a kingdom almost twice the size of that with which he had started.

Louis's successors failed to build on the excellent foundation he laid. Their invasions of Italy in the 1490s and the long series of losing wars with the Habsburgs that resulted left France, by the mid-sixteenth century, almost as divided internally as it had been during the Hundred Years' War.

Spain

In 1469 the marriage of Isabella of Castile (r. 1474–1504) and Ferdinand of Aragon (r. 1479–1516) greatly accelerated the process of creating a unified Spanish monarchy. Castile was the richer and more populous of the two states, having about 5 million inhabitants to Aragon's 1 million. Castile also had a lucrative, centrally managed sheep-farming industry managed by a state-backed agency called the *Mesta*. Although both kingdoms shared a dynasty (Ferdinand and Isabella's family), each retained its own government agencies, laws, armies, coinage, taxation, and cultural traditions.

Together, Ferdinand and Isabella were able to do what neither could do alone: that is, bring the nobility under control, secure the borders of their realms, launch wars of conquest, and enforce a common Christian faith among all their subjects. In 1492 they conquered the last Muslim state on the Iberian peninsula, Granada. Naples became a Spanish possession in 1504, and by

1512 Ferdinand had acquired the kingdom of Navarre.

Ferdinand and Isabella relied on the *Hermandad,* a league of cities and towns, for help in subduing the powerful landowners who dominated the countryside. Townspeople replaced the nobility within the royal administration, and the monarchy circumscribed the power of the nobility by extending its authority over wealthy chivalric orders.

Spain had long been remarkable among European lands as a place where three religions—Islam, Judaism, and Christianity—coexisted with a certain degree of toleration. Ferdinand and Isabella ended this by imposing a state-controlled Christianity on all their subjects. They ran the church and used it to promote national unity. Of particular utility was the Inquisition, the ecclesiastical court that tried cases of heresy. In 1479 the Inquisition, run by Isabella's confessor Tomás de Torquemada (d. 1498), was assigned the task of monitoring the activities of the converted Spanish Jews (*conversos*) and Muslims (*Moriscos*). In 1492 the Jews who refused to convert were exiled and their properties were confiscated. In 1502 the same fate befell the Moors of Granada. The state's rigorous enforcement of orthodoxy kept Spain a loyal Catholic country and made it a base of operation for the Counter-Reformation, the Catholic response to the Protestant Reformation of the sixteenth century.

The marriages arranged for Ferdinand and Isabella's children were part of a grand plan to contain France, and they set the stage for Europe's politics in the sixteenth century. In 1496 their eldest daughter and heir, Joanna (later known as "the Mad") wed Archduke Philip, the son of Emperor Maximilian I. Charles, the child of this union, inherited a united Spain from his grandparents. This, augmented by his Habsburg patrimony and election as emperor in 1519, created a European kingdom almost as large as Charlemagne's. Ferdinand and Isabella's second daughter, Catherine of Aragon, wed Arthur, heir to England's King Henry VII. After Arthur's premature death, Catherine was betrothed to his brother, the future King Henry VIII. Henry's desire to end this marriage forced him to break with the papacy and declare England a Protestant nation.

Spain's power was also enhanced by the overseas explorations that Ferdinand and Isabella sponsored. The discoveries made in their names by the Genoese adventurer Christopher Columbus (1451–1506) founded Spain's empire in Mexico and Peru. Gold and silver from this "new world" enabled Spain to dominate Europe during the sixteenth century.

England

The last half of the fifteenth century was an especially difficult period for the English. While they were adjusting to their loss of the Hundred Years' War, a fight broke out between branches of their royal family, the House of York and the House of Lancaster. For thirty years (1455–1485) a dynastic struggle—the Wars of the Roses (York's heraldic emblem was a white rose and Lancaster's a red one)—kept England in a state of turmoil.

Henry VI (r. 1422–1461), a weak king from the Lancastrian house, was challenged by his cousin, the duke of York, who had supporters in England's prosperous southern towns. In 1461 the duke of York's son seized power as Edward IV (r. 1461–1483). Although his reign was interrupted in 1470–1471, by a short-lived restoration of Henry VI, Edward retained the upper hand and greatly increased the power and wealth of the monarchy.

Edward's brother, Richard III (r. 1483–1485), usurped the throne from Edward's young son. He was, in turn, overthrown by Henry Tudor, a distant royal relation who had inherited the leadership of the Lancastrian faction. Henry established England's Tudor dynasty. Shakespeare's powerful play *Richard III* reflects the influence of Tudor propaganda in its portrayal of Richard as an unprincipled villain.

Henry Tudor, Henry VII (r. 1485–1509), married Edward IV's daughter (Elizabeth of York) to unite the rival branches of the royal family and create an uncontestable claim to the throne for their offspring. Henry also devised something called the Court of Star Chamber to bring the English nobility under tighter royal control. Created with the sanction of Parliament in 1487, the court was granted jurisdiction over cases involving the nobility. Since it was staffed by the king's chief councillors, the nobles could not use the tactics of intimidation and bribery that had enabled them to make a mockery of courts staffed by more vulnerable men. Henry construed legal precedents to the advantage of the crown, and he confiscated so much property from the nobility that he did not have to convene Parliament to raise the money he needed to govern. Henry shaped a monarchy that, during the reign of his granddaughter (Elizabeth I), became one of the most effective in early modern Europe.

The Holy Roman Empire

Germany and Italy were exceptions to the general trend toward political centralization seen in the histories of other European nations during the last half of the fifteenth century. Germany's rulers maintained the ancient practice of partitioning lands among all their sons. As a result, by the end of the Middle Ages Germany was divided into some 300 autonomous entities, and its fragmented authorities were powerless to halt the development of revolutionary movements such as the Reformation.

German princes and cities worked together to maintain law and order, if not unity, within the Holy Roman Empire. In 1356 the emperor and the major German territorial rulers issued the *Golden Bull* and created a system that encouraged cooperation among regions of the empire. It allotted choice of an emperor to a seven-member electoral college: the archbishops of Mainz, Trier, and Cologne; the duke of Saxony; the margrave of Brandenburg; the count Palatine; and the king of Bohemia.

The emperor reigned more than ruled, for the extent of his powers, especially over the seven electors, was renegotiated with every imperial election. In the fifteenth century an effort was made to create some unity of purpose among the principalities. A regular national meeting—the imperial diet or *Reichstag* (composed of the seven electors, the nonelectoral princes, and the sixty-five imperial free cities)—began to be held.

In 1495 the diet won concessions from Maximilian I (r. 1493–1519) that were intended to promote order in the nation. Private warfare was banned. A court (the *Reichskammergericht*) was established to enforce internal peace, and an imperial Council of Regency (the *Reichsregiment*) was appointed to coordinate the development of policy. Although these reforms were important, they fell far short of the creation of a centralized state. During the sixteenth and seventeenth centuries, the territorial princes were virtually sovereign rulers in their domains.

The Northern Renaissance

The humanist scholars of the Renaissance were responsible for the development of a climate in Europe favorable to religious and educational reform. Humanism spread to northern Europe from Italy through such intermediaries as students who studied in Italy and merchants who traded there. Reform was also promoted by the Brothers of the Common Life, an influential lay religious movement that began in the Netherlands and permitted men and women to live a shared religious life without making formal vows of poverty, chastity, and obedience.

The northern humanists developed a distinctive culture. They tended to come from more diverse social backgrounds and to be more interested in religious reform than their Italian counterparts. They were also more willing to write for lay audiences. This latter was a crucial factor, for the invention of printing with movable type was about to create a world in which intellectual elites could argue their cases before the public and spark mass movements.

The Printing Press

Since the days of Charlemagne, kings and princes had encouraged literacy. Without people who could read, think critically, and write reliable reports, no kingdom, large or small, could be properly governed. During the late Middle Ages new schools spread literacy far beyond the ranks of the clergy, and the number of universities in Europe tripled from twenty to sixty.

Medieval scribes had written books on expensive sheets of leather called vellum. Since it required 170 calfskins or 300 sheepskins to make a single vellum Bible, few people could afford the complete text. Whole pages were sometimes carved on wooden blocks for printing, but the production of such blocks was difficult and did not much reduce cost.

In the mid-fifteenth century Johann Gutenberg (d. 1468) of Mainz was stimulated by the growing market for books to invent printing with movable type. The development of a process of cheap paper manufacture also helped

This portrait of Katharina, by Albrecht Dürer, provides evidence of African slavery in Europe during the sixteenth century. Katharina was in the service of one João Bradao, a Portuguese economic minister living in Antwerp, then the financial center of Europe. Dürer became friends with Bradao during his stay in the Low Countries in the winter of 1520–1521. Albrecht Dürer, "Portrait of the Moorish Woman Katharina". Uffizi Florence, Italy. Foto Marburg/Art Resource, NY

to bring down the costs of production and make books on subjects ranging from theology to farming and child-rearing available in all price ranges. The new technology generated a great demand, and the number of presses exploded. By 1500, about fifty years after Gutenberg opened his shop, printers were operating in over 200 European cities.

Literacy deeply affected people everywhere, nurturing self-esteem and a critical frame of mind. By standardizing texts and prompting discussions, the print revolution made anyone who could read an authority. As a result, ordinary men and women became less credulous and docile than their ancestors. But print also gave their rulers a powerful tool for manipulating their beliefs.

Erasmus

The career of Desiderius Erasmus (1466?–1536), the most famous of the northern humanists, illustrates the impact of the printing press. Erasmus was both an educational and a religious reformer—a man whose career proves that many loyal Catholics advocated religious reform long before the Reformation erupted.

Erasmus published short Latin dialogues that were intended to teach students how to live as well as how to speak. In their later editions, these pieces (entitled *Colloquies*) included anticlerical dialogues and satires of religious superstitions that were designed to prompt reforms. Erasmus also published a collection of proverbs, the *Adages*. It grew from a first edition containing 800 examples to a final edition composed of over 5,000. It popularized common expressions that are still in use (e.g., "to leave no stone unturned," and "where there is smoke, there is fire").

Erasmus wanted to unite the classical ideals of humanity and civic virtue with the Christian virtues of love and piety. He believed that disciplined study of the classics and the Bible offered the best hope for reforming individuals and society. He taught the *philosophia Christi*—the philosophy of Christ: a simple, ethical piety modeled on Christ's life. Erasmus opposed anyone, Catholic or Protestant, who let doctrine and disputation overshadow humble piety and Christian practice.

Erasmus used his knowledge of classical languages to produce an improved version of the Bible based on the best manuscript sources available at the time. He believed that true reform was possible only if people were guided by a pure, unadulterated source. His Greek edition of the New Testament in 1516 made possible a more accurate Latin translation in 1519.

The church authorities were unhappy with Erasmus's "improvements" on their traditional Bible, the Latin Vulgate, and his popular anticlerical satires. At one point in the mid-sixteenth century all of Erasmus's works were placed on the Catholic church's *Index of Forbidden Books*. Luther, the Protestant leader, also condemned some of Erasmus's views. But friends and foes in both camps used the scholarly tools that Erasmus had created to promote reform.

Humanism and Reform

The work of the humanists encouraged educational and religious reform.

GERMANY Rudolf Agricola (1443–1485) introduced Italian learning to Germany. Conrad Celtis (d. 1508), the first German poet laureate, and Ulrich von Hutten (1488–1523), a knight, promoted a nationalistic version of humanism that was hostile to non-German cultures and especially antagonistic to papal Rome. Hutten, who attacked indulgences and published an edition of Valla's exposé of the *Donation of Constantine*, died in 1523 fighting in a hopeless revolt of the German knights against their princes.

A *cause célèbre* helped to unite reform-minded German humanists. About 1506 a converted Jew named Pfefferkorn, assisted by the Dominican friars of Cologne, launched a campaign to suppress Jewish literature. Johann Reuchlin (1455–1522) was, at the time, Europe's foremost Christian authority on Hebrew and Jewish learning. He was the first Christian scholar to compile a reliable Hebrew grammar, and he was personally attracted to Jewish mysticism. When Pfefferkorn attacked Reuchlin, many German humanists (motivated by a love of academic freedom rather than Judaism) rushed to Reuchlin's defense. The controversy produced one of the great books of the period, the *Letters of Obscure Men* (1515), a merciless satire of monks and Scholastics. It also predisposed the humanists to rally around Martin Luther, for in 1517 some of the same people who attacked Reuchlin attacked Luther for publishing arguments challenging the validity of indulgences.

ENGLAND English scholars and merchants and touring Italian prelates brought Italy's learning to England. Erasmus lectured at Cambridge, and his close friend, Thomas More (1478–1535), became the most famous of the English humanists. More's *Utopia* (1516), a critique of contemporary values, rivals the plays of Shakespeare as the most-read English work from the sixteenth century. Utopia described an imaginary society that overcame social and political injustice by holding all property and goods in common and requiring all persons to earn their bread by their own labor.

Humanism in England, as in Germany, paved the way for the Reformation, but some humanists, such as More and Erasmus, remained steadfastly loyal to the Roman Catholic Church. When More, one of Henry VIII's chief councillors, refused to accept the king's divorce of Catherine of Aragon and England's break with the papacy, Henry ordered his execution (July 1535).

FRANCE When France invaded Italy, Italian learning invaded France. Guillaume Budé (1468–1540), an accomplished Greek scholar, and Jacques Lefèvre d'Étaples (1454–1536), a biblical authority, were the leaders of French humanism. Lefèvre's scholarly works exemplified the new critical scholarship that was to stimulate Martin Luther's thinking and bring on the Reformation. Marguerite d'Angoulême (1492–1549), sister of King Francis I and queen of Navarre, was a noted spiritual writer. She also provided patronage for a generation of young reform-minded humanists that numbered among its members the Protestant reformer John Calvin.

SPAIN In Spain humanism was enlisted to defend the Catholic faith, not promote reform. Francisco Jiménez de Cisneros (1437–1517), confessor to Queen Isabella and (after 1508) the Grand Inquisitor and chief defender of orthodoxy, was the country's leading humanist. In 1509 he founded the University of Alcalá near Madrid. He printed a Greek edition of the New Testament, and he translated many religious tracts that were used to reform clerical life and improve the clergy's direction of the piety of the laity. His greatest achievement was the *Complutensian Polyglot Bible*, a six-volume edition of the Hebrew, Greek, and Latin texts of the Bible in parallel columns.

Voyages of Discovery and the New Empire in the West

The intellectual restlessness that marked the Renaissance and the Reformation was accompanied by a literal restlessness. In the fifteenth century, the Atlantic ceased to be regarded as a wall closing Europe in and began to be explored as a highway to global adventure.

Gold and Spices

Henry the Navigator (r. 1394–1460), prince of Portugal, took the lead by sponsoring exploration of the African coast. By the last decades of the fifteenth century, the Portuguese were importing gold from Guinea by sea and competing with the land routes controlled by Arab traders.

The rush for Africa's gold became a search for India's spices. Spices, especially pepper and cloves, were in great demand in Europe. They were used to preserve food as well as to enhance its taste. In 1487 Bartholomew Dias (d. 1500) rounded the Cape of Good Hope at the tip of Africa. In 1498, Vasco da Gama (d. 1524) reached India, and the cargo he brought back to Portugal was worth sixty times the cost of his voyage. The Portuguese quickly built an empire in the East that gave them control of the European spice trade.

While Portugal explored the Indian Ocean, Spain attacked the Atlantic. Christopher Columbus (1451–1506) dreamed of finding a short route to the spice islands of the East Indies, but he blundered onto something much greater. On October 12, 1492, after a thirty-three-day voyage from the Canary Islands, he landed in San Salvador (Watlings Island) in the eastern Bahamas. He thought he was near Japan. Not until his third voyage to the Caribbean did Columbus realize that the island of Cuba was not Japan and that the South American continent beyond it was not China. Amerigo Vespucci (1451–1512) and Ferdinand Magellan (1480–1521) proved that the lands Columbus found were not, as he died believing, the edge of the Orient. They were a new continent separated from the East by an ocean even greater than the Atlantic. Magellan ventured onto this Pacific Ocean and died in the Philippines.

The Spanish Empire in the New World

Columbus's voyage in 1492 began more than three centuries of Spanish exploitation of a vast American empire. That empire transformed cultures on both sides of the Atlantic. As Europeans and their technologies entered the Americas, American goods and bullion flooded Europe's markets. In neither place was life ever again the same. In parts of both South and North America, Spain established a Roman Catholic faith, a system of economic dependence, and a hierarchical social structure that has endured to the present day.

A Conquered World

Since Columbus was convinced that he had landed in the East Indies, he called the peoples he encountered "Indians." The name persisted even after it was clear that America was not the Indies. The ancestors of the Native Americans had migrated across the Bering Strait from Asia many thousands of years before the European voyages of discovery. As early as the first millennium B.C.E., those who lived in Mesoamerica (i.e., central Mexico to the Yucatan and Guatemala) and the Andean region (Peru and Bolivia) were pioneering advanced civilizations.

The earliest of the Mesoamerican civilizations was the Olmec, which dates from about 1200 B.C.E. By the first millennium C.E., its city of Teotihuacán was one of the largest urban centers in the world. The first millennium C.E. also saw the flowering of the civilization of the Mayas in the Yucatan region. The Mayans acquired considerable knowledge of mathematics and astronomy and built great cities centered on huge pyramids.

The first great interregional civilization in Andean South America, the Chavín, emerged during the first millennium B.C.E. Between 100 C.E. to 600 C.E., regional cultures, the Nazca on the southern coast of Peru and the Moche on the northern coast, appeared. The Huari-Tiahuanco culture again imposed interregional conformity from 600 to 1000, and the Chimu Empire flourished on Peru's northern coast from 800 to 1400. These early Andean societies built great ceremonial centers throughout the Andes; constructed elaborate irrigation systems, canals, and highways; and created exquisite pottery, textiles, and metalwork.

THE AZTECS When the Spanish explorers arrived, Mesoamerica was dominated by the Aztecs and Andean America by the Incas. The forebears of the Aztecs entered the Valley of Mexico early in the twelfth century. In 1428 a chief named Itzcoatl inaugurated an era of Aztec conquest that reached its climax just after 1500. The Aztec state, which centered on Tenochtitlán (modern-day Mexico City), was a collection of enslaved and terrorized tribes. Aztec religion involved the sacrifice of thousands of people a year to the gods of the sun and the soil. By extorting this grim tribute, the Aztecs nourished resentment among their subjects and caused them to dream of liberation.

Armored Spanish soldiers, under the command of Pedro de Alvarado (d. 1541) and bearing crossbows, engage unprotected and crudely armed Aztecs, who are nonetheless portrayed as larger than life by Spanish artist Diego Duran (16th century). Codex Duran: Pedro de Alvarado (c. 1485–1541), companion-at-arms of Hernando Cortés (1485–1547) besieged by Aztec warriors. Biblioteca Nacional, Madrid, Spain. The Bridgeman Art Library International Ltd.

In 1519 Hernán Cortés landed on the coast of Mexico with a mere 600 men. Montezuma, the Aztec ruler, initially believed Cortés to be a god, for an Aztec legend claimed that a priest named Quetzalcoatl, who had been driven into exile four centuries earlier, would return about the time that Cortés appeared. Montezuma tried to appease Cortés with gold, for the Aztecs, who had recently been ravaged by epidemics of European origin (principally smallpox), were in no condition to fight. Gold only stimulated the Spaniards' appetites. Cortés's forces marched on Tenochtitlán and captured Montezuma, who died under unexplained circumstances. The Aztecs rose up to defend themselves. But by 1521 they were defeated, and Cortés was proclaiming the former Aztec Empire "New Spain."

THE INCAS   The Incas of the highlands of Peru, like the Aztecs, had conquered many tribes. By the early sixteenth century they ruled harshly over several million subjects—using impressed labor to build roads and cities, to farm, and to fight. In 1531 Francisco Pizarro, who was inspired by Cortés's example, invaded the Inca Empire. His army of 200 men was equipped with guns, swords, and horses—the military potential of which escaped the Incas. Pizarro lured the Inca chief Atahualpa to a conference where he captured him and killed several thousand Indians. Atahualpa raised a huge ransom in gold, but in 1533 Pizarro executed him. Division within the ranks of the Spaniards prevented them from establishing control of the sprawling Inca territories until the late 1560s.

The conquests of Mexico and Peru are among the most brutal episodes in modern Western history. In addition to loss of life, they prevented the Indian civilizations from having significant impact on Western civilization. The Spaniards and the Indians made some accommodations to each other, but in the end European values, religion, economic goals, and language dominated. South America became Latin America.

The Economy of Exploitation

The native peoples of America and their homelands were immediately drawn into the Atlantic economy and the world of competitive European commercialism. For the Indians of Latin America—and later the blacks of Africa—that meant various forms of forced labor. The colonial economy of Latin America had three components: mining, agriculture, and shipping.

MINING   The early *conquistadores* ("conquerors") were primarily interested in gold, but by the middle of the sixteenth century, silver mining had become more profitable. The chief mining centers were Potosí in Peru and various smaller sites in northern Mexico. The Spanish crown received one-fifth (the *quinto*) of all mining revenues and monopolized the production and sale of the mercury that was required in the silver-mining process. Mining by native forced labor for the benefit of Spaniards epitomized the extractive economy that was fundamental to colonial life.

AGRICULTURE   The West Indies (i.e., Cuba, Hispaniola, Puerto Rico, and other islands) evolved a plantation system that used the labor of black slaves from Africa to produce sugar for the European market. But the agricultural institution that characterized most of the Spanish colonies was the *hacienda*, a large landed estate owned by persons born in Spain (*peninsulares*) or persons of Spanish descent born in America (*creoles*). The *hacienda* economy was subordinate to the mining economy, for its major products (food and leather) were consumed by American mining communities. Laborers on the *hacienda* were usually bound to the land and prevented from moving from the service of one landowner to another.

LABOR SERVITUDE   The Spaniards initially developed a number of ways to use the Indian population to supply the labor needed for mining and agriculture in the New World. The earliest was the *encomienda*, a grant of the right to the labor of a specific number of Indians for a particular period of time. Spain's monarchs were suspicious of this arrangement, for they feared that the holders of *encomienda* might become a powerful independent nobility in the New World. The *encomienda* was phased out in favor of the *repartimiento*, a kind of tax paid in labor. All adult male Indians were required to devote a certain number of working days annually to Spanish economic enterprises. Although this sounded more humane than the servitude of the *encomienda*, *repartimiento* service was often extremely harsh. The term limitation for laborers led some Spanish managers to work them to death on the assumption that new men were always scheduled to replace those currently employed. Eventually a shortage of workers and the crown's opposition to extreme kinds of forced labor promoted the use of free labor. But the freedom of Indian workers was more apparent than real. They had to purchase the goods they needed from the landowners or mine owners for whom they worked. This created debts that bound them to their employers, a form of exploitation known as debt peonage.

The enslavement of Africans was introduced to the New World on the sugar plantations of the West Indies. It was an extension of a system of forced labor that the Spanish and the Portuguese had previously used in Europe.

Deaths in combat, by forced labor, and from European diseases had devastating demographic consequences for the Indian population. Europeans lived in a far more complex human and animal environment than did Native Americans. Their interaction, over a long period, with different ethnic groups and animal species helped them develop strong immune systems that enabled them to survive the ravages of measles, smallpox, and typhoid. Native Americans evolved in a simpler, more sterile environment, and they were defenseless against Europe's diseases. Within a generation of the conquest, the Indian population of New Spain (Mexico) was reduced by 92 percent—from 25 million to 2 million.

The Impact on Europe

The loss of life and destruction of cultures in the New World was a mixed blessing for the Old World. The bullion that flowed into Europe through Spain vastly increased the amount of money in circulation and created an inflation rate of 2 percent a year. Prices doubled in Spain by 1550 and quadrupled by 1600. In Luther's Wittenberg, the cost of basic food and clothing increased almost 100 percent between 1519 and 1540. Wages and rents, on the other hand, lagged well behind the rise in prices.

The new money enabled governments and private entrepreneurs to sponsor basic research and industrial expansion and to promote the growth of capitalism. The economic thinking of the age favored the creation of monopolies, the charging of high interest for loans, and the free and efficient accumulation of wealth. The late fifteenth and the sixteenth centuries saw the maturation of this type of capitalism and its attendant social problems. Those who owned the means of production were ever more clearly separated from the workers who operated them. The new wealth raised the expectations of the poor and encouraged reactionary behavior by the rich. Social distinctions became ever more visible in the new economic system, and this prepared the way for the upheaval of the Reformation. Columbus's discoveries also encouraged rebels by increasing scepticism about the wisdom of the ancients and the obvious rightness of traditional modes of thought. Europe's explorers proved that there was much more to the world than their ancestors had imagined. This encouraged criticism of traditional institutions and sparked and appetite for new ideas—especially innovations that promised freedom and a chance at a better life.

In Perspective

During the late Middle Ages, previously divided lands came together as nations, and the foundations of modern France, Spain, England, Germany, and Italy were laid. Byzantine and Islamic scholars made ancient Greek science and scholarship available to the West, and Europeans reclaimed a classical cultural heritage from which they had been separated for almost eight centuries. This prompted renaissances of intellectual and artistic activity in both southern and northern Europe.

The new political unity spurred national ambition, and by the late fifteenth century Europeans were venturing far afield—to the shores of Africa, to the southern and eastern coasts of Asia, and to the New World of the Americas. For the first time, they confronted truly non-European civilizations. The savage exploitation of the peoples and lands of the New World revealed the dark side of Europe's culture, and the influx of New World gold and silver exacerbated Europe's economic and social problems. Some Europeans were driven by what they saw to question their traditional values.

REVIEW QUESTIONS

1. In what senses was what happened in Italy in the fifteenth and sixteenth centuries a "renaissance"?
2. How would you define Renaissance humanism? In what ways was the Renaissance a break with the Middle Ages? In what ways was it indebted to medieval civilization?
3. Who were the leading, or most characteristic, literary and artistic figures of the Italian Renaissance? What was "the spirit of the Renaissance" that they all shared?
4. Why did the French invade Italy in 1494? How did this event trigger Italy's political decline?

In what ways do the actions of Pope Julius II and the ideas of Niccolò Machiavelli signify the start of a new era for Italy?
5. Does the history of Renaissance Italy support or refute the common assumption that creative work proceeds best in periods of calm and peace?
6. How did the northern Renaissance differ from the Italian Renaissance? In what ways was Erasmus the embodiment of the northern Renaissance?
7. What prompted the voyages of discovery? How did the Spanish establish their empire in the Americas? What did native peoples experience during and after the conquest?

SUGGESTED READINGS

H. BARON, *The Crisis of the Early Italian Renaissance*, vols. 1 and 2 (1966). A major work, setting forth the civic dimension of Italian humanism.

B. BERENSON, *Italian Painters of the Renaissance* (1957). Eloquent and authoritative.

G. A. BRUCKER, *Renaissance Florence* (1969). Comprehensive survey of all facets of Florentine life.

J. BURCKHARDT, *The Civilization of the Renaissance in Italy* (1867). The old classic that still has as many defenders as detractors.

R. E. CONRAD, *Children of God's Fire: A Documentary History of Black Slavery in Brazil* (1983). Not for the squeamish.

A. W. CROSBY, *The Columbian Exchange: Biological and Cultural Consequences of 1492* (1973). A study of the epidemiological disaster that Columbus visited upon Native Americans.

E. L. EISENSTEIN, *The Printing Press as an Agent of Change: Communications and Cultural Transformations in Early Modern Europe*, 2 vols. (1979). Bold, stimulating account of the centrality of printing to all progress in the period.

W. K. FERGUSON, *Europe in Transition, 1300–1520* (1962). A major survey that deals with the transition from medieval society to Renaissance society.

D. HERLIHY and C. KLAPISCH-ZUBER, *Tuscans and Their Families* (1985). Important work based on quantitative data; excellent specimen of quantitative history.

D. L. JENSEN, *Renaissance Europe: Age of Recovery and Reconciliation* (1981). Comprehensive survey.

F. KATZ, *The Ancient American Civilizations* (1972). An excellent introduction.

P. O. KRISTELLER, *Renaissance Thought: The Classic, Scholastic, and Humanist Strains* (1961). A master shows the many sides of Renaissance thought.

I. MACLEAN, *The Renaissance Notion of Women* (1980). An account of the views of Renaissance intellectuals and their sources in antiquity.

L. MARTINES, *Power and Imagination: City States in Renaissance Italy* (1980). Stimulating account of cultural and political history.

E. PANOFSKY, *Meaning in the Visual Arts* (1955). Eloquent treatment of Renaissance art.

J. H. PARRY, *The Age of Reconnaissance* (1964). A comprehensive account of exploration in the years 1450 to 1650.

I. A. RICHTER (ed.), *The Notebooks of Leonardo da Vinci* (1985). The master in his own words.

Q. SKINNER, *The Foundations of Modern Political Thought; I: The Renaissance* (1978). Broad survey, including every known political theorist.

Chapter 11

The Age of Reformation

KEY TOPICS

- The social and religious background to the Reformation
- Martin Luther's challenge to the church and the course of the Reformation in Germany
- The Reformation in Switzerland, France, and England
- Transitions in family life between medieval and modern times

In the second decade of the sixteenth century a powerful religious movement began in northern Germany. Protestant reformers, attacking what they believed to be burdensome superstitions that robbed people of money and peace of mind, led a revolt against the medieval church. The Protestant Reformation opposed aspects of the Renaissance, especially the optimistic view of human nature that humanist scholars derived from classical literature. But the Reformation embraced some Renaissance ideas—particularly educational reform and training in ancient languages that equipped scholars to go to the original sources of important texts. Protestant challenges to Catholic practices originated in the study of the Hebrew and Greek Scriptures.

Society and Religion

A struggle between two political foes set the stage for the Reformation: the monarchies that were centralizing governments of nation-states, and the towns and regions that were fighting to preserve their traditional autonomy. Since the fourteenth century, the king's law and custom had been superseding local law and custom almost everywhere. Many townspeople and village folk viewed religious revolt as a part of a wider fight to limit this encroachment on their liberties.

The Reformation began in the free cities of Germany and Switzerland. There were about sixty-five of them, most of which developed Protestant movements even if they did not ultimately come under Protestant control. These cities were troubled by more than a desire to defend themselves against intervention by princes. They suffered deep internal social and political divisions, and some of their factions favored the Reformation more than others. Guilds whose members were prospering and rising in social status were often in the forefront of the Reformation, but less distinguished groups were also attracted to the Protestant revolt. People who felt pushed around by either local or distant authorities tended, at least initially, to find an ally in the Protestant movement. The peasants on the land responded as much as the townsfolk, for their freedoms, too, were eroded by princely governments.

For many converts to Protestantism, religion and politics seemed to be two sides of the same coin. When Protestant preachers scorned the authority of ecclesiastical landlords and ridiculed papal laws as arbitrary human inventions, they raised issues of political as well as religious liberty. An attack on the legitimacy of the one kind of authority translated easily into a critique of the other.

Popular Religious Movements and Criticism of the Church

The Protestant Reformation was, in part, a response to the crises that afflicted the late medieval church: the papacy's "exile" in Avignon, the Great Schism, the conciliar movement, and the flagrant worldliness of the Renaissance popes. These things led many clergy and laity to become increasingly critical of the traditional teaching and spiritual practice of the church. The late Middle Ages were marked by calls for reform and by widespread experimentation with new religious practices.

The laypeople of the late medieval period were less subservient to the clergy than their ancestors. The residents of cities had grown increasingly knowledgeable about the world and politics. As soldiers, pilgrims, explorers, and traders, they traveled widely. The establishment of postal systems and printing presses increased the information at their disposal. Improved access to books and libraries raised the rate of literacy among them and heightened their curiosity. Education equipped them to take the initiative in shaping the cultural lives of their communities.

The lay religious movements that preceded the Reformation all advocated religious simplicity in imitation of Jesus. They were inspired by an ideal of apostolic poverty that they saw in the Gospels' descriptions of the lives of Jesus and his disciples. They wanted a more egalitarian church that gave a voice to its members, not just its head. They wanted a more spiritual church, one that emulated the New Testament model.

THE MODERN DEVOTION   One of the most constructive lay religious movements of the period was led by the Brothers of the Common Life, advocates for the "Modern Devotion." The brothers urged ordinary people to adapt for their own uses the spiritual disciplines of monasticism.

They took no formal vows and held no church offices. They supported themselves by working at secular jobs.

After Gerard Groote (1340–1384) began the movement in the Netherlands, the brother and (less numerous) sister houses spread rapidly throughout northern Europe. The Modern Devotion brought clerics and laity together to share a common life that stressed individual piety and practical religion. Thomas à Kempis (d. 1471) summarized the philosophy of the movement in what became the most popular devotional tract of the period, the *Imitation of Christ.* This guide to the inner life was intended primarily for monks and nuns, but it spoke also to the many laity who sought spiritual growth through the practice of ascetic disciplines.

The Brothers of the Common Life flourished during an age in which the laity wanted instruction from good preachers and were even taking the initiative to create endowments to provide this service. The brothers served the public's desire for better education by opening schools, working as copyists, sponsoring publications, and running hospices for poor students. Some famous scholars, such as Erasmus and Reuchlin, began their training with the brothers.

The Modern Devotion has been credited with inspiring humanist, Protestant, and Catholic reform movements in the sixteenth century, but it was actually a very conservative movement. By integrating traditional clerical doctrines and values with an active common life, the brothers met the need of late medieval people for a more personal religion and a better-informed faith. The Modern Devotion helped laypersons develop fuller religious lives without turning their backs on the world.

LAY CONTROL OVER RELIGIOUS LIFE The medieval papacy's successful campaign to win control over the appointment of candidates to church offices did not improve the administration of the church. The popes sold ecclesiastical posts to the highest bidders. The purchasers were entitled to the income from their offices, but they were not required personally to carry out the duties attached to the offices they bought. They hired inexpensive, often poorly trained and motivated substitutes to do their work while they resided elsewhere. Rare was the late medieval German town that did not complain about clerical malfeasance or dereliction of duty.

City governments sometimes took the initiative in trying to improve religious life by endowing preacherships. These positions provided for well-trained, dedicated pastors who could provide regular preaching and pastoral care superior to the perfunctory services offered by other clergy. In many instances these preacherships became platforms for Protestant reformers.

Because medieval churches and monasteries were holy places, they had been exempted from secular taxes and laws. It was also considered inappropriate for holy persons (clergy) to do "dirty jobs" such as military service, compulsory labor, standing watch at city gates, and other obligations of citizenship. Nor was it thought right that the laity, of whatever rank, should sit in judgment over God's priestly intermediaries. On the eve of the Reformation, however, secular governments were beginning to take steps to curtail clerical privileges that seemed undeserved.

Long before 1520, when Luther published a famous summary of economic grievances (*Address to the Christian Nobility of the German Nation*), communities were loudly protesting the financial abuses of the medieval church. Prominent among these was the sale of indulgences (i.e., papal letters that guaranteed sinners released time from purgatory). If rulers and magistrates were given a share of the profits, they usually did not object. But it was a different matter if local revenues were siphoned off for projects far from home. The state did not join the campaign against financial exactions such as indulgences until rulers recognized how they themselves might profit from religion. The financial appeal of Protestantism lay in its rationale for the state's dissolution of monasteries and confiscation of ecclesiastical properties.

Martin Luther and German Reformation to 1525

The kings of France and England were able to limit ecclesiastical taxation and papal jurisdiction over their churches. But Germany lacked the political unity needed to enforce "national" religious reforms. The restraints imposed on the church on a universal level in England and France were enacted locally and piecemeal in Germany as popular resentment of ecclesiastical abuses spread. By 1517 mass discontent was pervasive enough to win Martin Luther a widespread, sympathetic audience.

Luther (1483–1546) was the son of a successful Thüringian miner. He received his early education in a school run by the Brothers of the Common Life. Between 1501 and 1505, he attended the University of Erfurt where the nominalist teachings of William of Ockham and Gabriel Biel (d. 1495) prevailed. After receiving his master of arts degree in 1505, Luther obeyed his parents and registered with the law faculty. But he never began the study of law. To the disappointment of his family, he entered the Order of the Hermits of Saint Augustine in Erfurt on July 17, 1505. This decision was an attempt to resolve a long-standing spiritual struggle. It came to a head during a lightning storm in which a terrified Luther promised Saint Anne, the patron of travelers in distress, that he would enter a monastery if he escaped death.

Luther was ordained in 1507 and led a conventional monastic life. In 1510 he went to Rome on business for his order and saw firsthand some of the things that were raising doubts about the church. In 1511 he moved to the Augustinian monastery in Wittenberg. A year later, he earned his doctorate in theology from Wittenberg's university and joined its faculty.

Justification by Faith Alone

Reformation theology was a response to the failure of traditional medieval religion to provide many laypeople and clergy with personal or intellectual satisfaction. Luther was especially plagued by his inability to achieve the perfect righteousness that medieval theology taught that God required for salvation. The church's teachings and sacrament of penance failed to console Luther and give him hope. The church seemed to demand of him a perfection he knew neither he nor any other human being could achieve.

The study of St. Paul's letters eventually brought Luther an insight into the process of salvation that quieted his fears. Luther concluded from his reading of the Scriptures that the righteousness that God demanded was not the product of religious works and ceremonies. It was a gift God gives to those who believe and trust in Jesus Christ—who alone is perfectly righteous. To believe in Christ meant to stand before God clothed in Christ's righteousness—to be justified solely by faith in him, not by confidence in one's record of good works.

The Attack on Indulgences

The doctrine of justification by faith was incompatible with the church's practice of issuing indulgences, which remitted the obligation to perform a "work of satisfaction" for a sin. According to medieval theology, after the priest absolved a penitent of guilt, the penitent still had to pay the penalty for sin. The penitent could discharge the penalty here and now by prayers, fasting, almsgiving, retreats, and pilgrimages. But penitents whose works of satisfaction were inadequate could expect to suffer for them in purgatory.

Indulgences had originally been devised for Crusaders who fell in battle with the enemies of the church without an opportunity to do penance for their sins. Gradually, they were offered to laypeople who were anxious about the consequences of neglected penances or unrepented sins. In 1343 Pope Clement VI (1342–1352) declared the existence of a "treasury of merit," an infinite reservoir of excess good works that the saints had earned and that the pope could appropriate for others. Papal "letters of indulgence" were drafts on this treasury to cover the works of satisfaction owed by penitents. In 1476 Pope Sixtus IV (1471–1484) greatly expanded the market for these letters by proclaiming the church's power to grant indulgences not only to the living but also to souls in purgatory.

Originally, indulgences had been granted only for significant services to the church, but by Luther's day their price had been significantly discounted to encourage mass marketing. Pope Julius II (1503–1513) excited considerable interest by declaring a special Jubilee indulgence (to be sold in 1517) to raise funds for rebuilding Saint Peter's in Rome. In 1517 Archbishop Albrecht of Mainz was in debt to the Fugger bank of Augsburg for a loan he had taken out to pay the pope for permission to ignore church law and hold three profitable ecclesiastical offices—the archbishoprics of Mainz and Magdeburg and the bishopric of Halberstadt. In exchange for Albrecht's help in promoting sale of the Jubilee indulgence, Pope Leo X agreed to share the proceeds. A famous preacher, John Tetzel (d. 1519), was sent to drum up business in Luther's neighborhood.

Johannes Tezelius Dominicaner Münch/mit sei-
nen Römischen Ablaßkram/welchen er im Jahr Christi 1517. in Deutsch-
landen zu marckt gebracht/wie er in der Kirchen zu Pirn in seinem
Vaterland abgemahlet ist.

O ihr deutschen mercket mich recht/
   Des heiligen Vaters Papstes Knecht/
Bin ich/vnd vr in euch jtzt allein/
   Zehn tausent vnd neun hundert carein/
Gnad vnd Ablaß von einer Sünd/
   Vor euch/ewer Elter n/Weib vnd Kind/
Sol ein jeder gewehret sein
   So viel jhr leg t ins Kästelein/
So bald der Gülden im Becken klingt/
   Im huy die Seel im Himel springt/

A contemporary caricature depicts John Tetzel, the famous indulgence preacher. The last lines of the jingle read: "As soon as gold in the basin rings, right then the soul to Heaven springs." It was Tetzel's preaching that spurred Luther to publish his ninety-five theses.
Courtesy Stiftung Luthergedenkstaten in Sachsen-Anhalt/Lutherhalle Wittenberg

According to tradition, Luther posted his ninety-five theses opposing the sale of indulgences on the door of Castle Church in Wittenberg on October 31, 1517. Luther especially protested Tetzel's insinuation that indulgences remitted sins and released the dead from punishment in purgatory. Luther believed Tetzel's claims went far beyond traditional practice and made salvation something that could be bought and sold.

Election of Charles V

The ninety-five theses made Luther famous overnight and prompted official proceedings against him. In April 1518, he was summoned to appear before the general chapter of his order in Heidelberg, and the following October he was called to Augsburg to be examined by the papal legate and general of the Dominican Order, Cardinal Cajetan. Then the death of the Holy Roman Emperor Maximilian I on January 12, 1519, diverted attention from Luther's case to the contest for a new emperor.

Charles I of Spain, a youth of nineteen, succeeded his grandfather and became Emperor Charles V. But the electors, who constantly sought to enhance their power, exacted a price for the office. They forced Charles to agree to consult with a diet of the empire on all major domestic and foreign issues. This ruled out unilateral imperial action in Germany—something for which Luther was soon to be thankful.

Luther's Excommunication and the Diet of Worms

While the imperial election was being held, Luther was in Leipzig (June 27, 1519) to debate an Ingolstadt professor, John Eck. This contest led Luther to question the infallibility of the pope and the inerrancy of church councils and, for the first time, to appeal to the Scripture as the sole authority governing faith.

In 1520 Luther described his position in three famous pamphlets. His *Address to the Christian Nobility of the German Nation* urged the German princes forcefully to reform the Roman

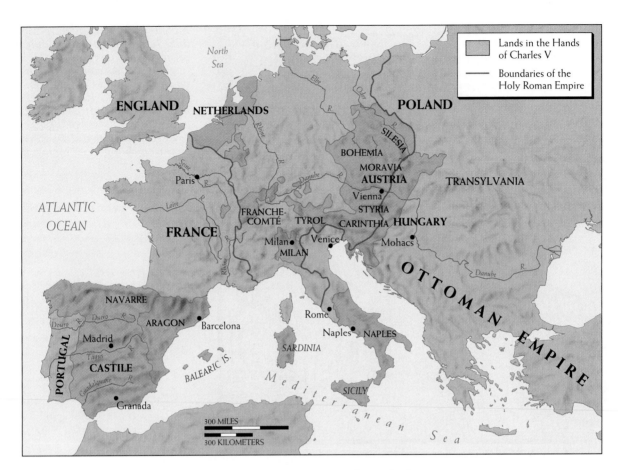

MAP 11–1   THE EMPIRE OF CHARLES V   *Dynastic marriages and simple chance delivered large, if scattered, portions of Europe (as well as Spain's overseas possessions) into Charles's hands. Election as emperor increased his responsibilities.*

Catholic Church and curtail its political and economic power. *The Babylonian Captivity of the Church* examined the sacraments, arguing that only two of the church's seven (Baptism and the Eucharist) were authentic. The pamphlet also claimed that the Scriptures, decrees of church councils, and decisions of secular princes were superior to the authority of a pope. The eloquent *Freedom of a Christian* explained Luther's key theological insight, salvation by faith alone.

On June 15, 1520, a papal bull, *Exsurge Domine,* condemned Luther for heresy and gave him sixty days to retract. The final bull of excommunication, *Decet Pontificem Romanum,* was issued on January 3, 1521. In April of that year, Luther appeared before a diet of the empire in Worms (over which the newly elected Charles V presided). Ordered to recant, Luther refused, for such an act, he claimed, would violate Scripture, reason, and conscience. On May 26, 1521, Luther was placed under the imperial ban. This meant that his heresy became a crime punishable by the state. Friends

protected Luther by hiding him in Wartburg Castle. The year (April 1521 to March 1522) he spent in seclusion was put to good use. At Wartburg Luther produced one of the essential tools of Reformation: a German translation of Erasmus's Greek text of the New Testament.

Imperial Distractions: France and the Turks

Charles V was too preoccupied with military ventures to pay much attention to the Reformation that erupted in Wittenberg following Luther's trial. France wanted to move into Italy to drive a wedge through Charles's empire, and the Ottoman Turks were advancing on eastern Europe. Charles needed friendly relations with the German princes in order to recruit German troops for his armies.

In 1526 the Turks overran Hungary at the Battle of Mohacs, and in western Europe the French organized the League of Cognac in preparation for the second of four wars between the Habsburg and Valois dynasties (1521–1559). Thus preoccupied, the emperor, at the Diet of Speyer (1526), granted each German prince the right to deal as he saw fit with the situation Luther had created. This cleared the way for the Reformation to put down roots in places where the princes sympathized with it, and it inaugurated a tradition of princely control over religion that was to be enshrined in law by the Peace of Augsburg in 1555.

How the Reformation Spread

In the 1520s and 1530s, leadership of the Reformation passed from theologians and pamphleteers to magistrates and princes. City governments acted on the proposals of Protestant preachers and their growing flocks and mandated religious reforms. Reform ceased to be a matter of slogans and passed into law binding on all a town's residents. Like urban magistrates, some regional princes (e.g., the elector of Saxony and the prince of Hesse) implemented the reform in large states. They recognized political and economic advantages to themselves in the overthrow of the Roman Catholic Church and urged their neighbors to join them. Powerful alliances were negotiated, and Protestant leaders prepared for war with their Catholic emperor.

The Peasants' Revolt

In its first decade the Protestant movement suffered more from internal division than from imperial interference. By 1525, Luther had become as controversial a figure in Germany as the pope, and many of his early supporters had broken with him. Germany's peasants, who had welcomed Luther as an ally, had a particular reason for losing faith in him. Since the late fifteenth century, their leaders had been struggling to prevent the territorial princes from ignoring traditional restraints and imposing new regulations and taxes. Many peasants saw Luther's proclamation of Christian freedom and criticism of monastic landowners as a declaration of support for their cause.

Luther and his followers sympathized with the peasants, but Lutherans were not social revolutionaries. Luther's freedom of the Christian individual was an inner release from guilt and anxiety, not a restructuring of society by violent revolution. When the peasants rebelled against their masters from 1524 to 1525, Luther condemned them in the strongest possible terms and urged the princes to crush the revolt. Tens of thousands of peasants (possibly 100,000) died in the struggle. Had Luther supported the Peasants' Revolt, he would have contradicted his own teaching and would also probably have ended any chance for his reform to survive beyond the 1520s.

The Reformation Elsewhere

Luther was the first to rebel against the church, but independent reform movements soon developed in France and Switzerland.

Zwingli and the Swiss Reformation

Switzerland's political environment was as favorable to the success of a religious revolt as Germany's. Switzerland was a loose confederacy of thirteen autonomous cantons (states) and allied areas. Some (e.g., Zurich, Bern, Basel, and Schaffhausen) became Protestant, some (especially in the heartland around Lucerne) remained Catholic, and a few effected a compromise. Two developments prepared the ground for the Swiss Reformation: (1) a growth of national sentiment created by opposition to the practice of impressing Swiss soldiers into mercenary service outside their homeland, and (2) an interest in church reform that had been stimulated by the convocation of famous church councils in the Swiss cities of Constance (1414–1417) and Basel (1431–1449).

THE REFORMATION IN ZURICH Ulrich Zwingli (1484–1531), the leader of the Swiss Reformation, received a humanist education and credited Erasmus for sparking his interest in reform. He was chaplain to Swiss mercenaries in Italy in 1515, and his experiences at a disastrous battle at Marignano prompted him to become an ardent critic of mercenary service. By 1518 he was also widely known for opposing the sale of indulgences and for denouncing religious superstitions.

In 1519 Zwingli applied for the post of people's priest in Zurich's main church. His fitness was questioned because of his acknowledged fornication with a barber's daughter. Many of

Art & the West

A Royal Stag Hunt

Lucas Cranach, German, 1472–1553. *Hunting Near Hartenfels Castle*, 1540. Oil on wood, 116.8 × 170.2 cm. © The Cleveland Museum of Art, 2001, John L. Severance Fund, 1958.425.

*L*ucas Cranach the Elder (1472–1553), court painter to the Elector of Saxony, was a close friend of Martin Luther. His employer was one of the most powerful noblemen in Germany, and Cranach was responsible for making sure that the elector's residences reflected his status. He painted interiors and exteriors for five of his lord's dozen residences. He outfitted rooms with portraits, tapestries, furniture, and utensils. He designed decorations for celebrations and even provided tailors with sketches of clothing to be worn at court.

Royal hunts were important social and political occasions, and Cranach's paintings of them were popular. Depicted here is a hunt that took place at Castle Torgau in 1540. Hunts were carefully choreographed. The animals to be hunted were kept in pens until it was time to drive them toward the places where the hunters had stationed themselves. Cranach's picture depicts three hunts: stags in the foreground, a bear in the upper left, and a boar in the upper right. The Elector John Frederick is shown, dressed in green and arming a crossbow, near the center of the painting's bottom edge.

Source: *Lucas Cranach: Ein Maler-Unternehmer aus Franken*, ed. by Claus Grimm, et al. (Verlag Friedrich Pustet, Regensburg, 1994), pp. 311–313.

his contemporaries, however, sympathized with the plight of celibate clergy, and Zwingli defended himself forcefully. Later he led the fight to abolish clerical celibacy and to establish the right of clergy to marry.

Zwingli's post as the people's priest in Zurich gave him a pulpit from which to campaign for reform. His reform program was simple: Whatever lacked literal support in Scripture was to be neither believed nor practiced. Application of that standard led him, as it did Luther, to question many traditional teachings and practices: fasting, transubstantiation, the worship of saints, pilgrimages, purgatory, clerical celibacy, and some of the sacraments. A public debate, held on January 29, 1523, ended with the city government endorsing Zwingli's ideas. Zurich took the lead in the Swiss Reformation and pioneered the kind of Protestantism that came to be called "puritanical."

THE MARBURG COLLOQUY Landgrave Philip of Hesse (1504–1567) believed that Protestants had to cooperate if they hoped to fend off attacks from Catholics, and he tried to unite the Swiss and German reformations. He brought Luther and Zwingli together in his castle in Marburg in early October 1529. But theological disagreements over the nature of Christ's presence in the Eucharist prevented the two leaders from forming a political alliance. Luther concluded that Zwingli was a dangerous fanatic, and Zwingli believed that Luther was irrationally in thrall to medieval ideas.

The disagreement splintered the Protestant movement. Separate credal statements were issued, and separate defense leagues were formed. Semi-Zwinglian views were embodied in the *Confessio Tetrapolitana* prepared by the Strasbourg reformers Martin Bucer and Caspar Hedio. In 1530 this was presented to the Diet of Augsburg as an alternative to the *Augsburg Confession*, which the Lutherans proposed as a basis for unity.

SWISS CIVIL WARS. As Protestants and Catholics divided up the Swiss cantons, civil wars began. There were two major battles—both at Kappel (one in June 1529, the second in October 1531). The first was a clear victory for the Protestants. The Catholic cantons were forced to repudiate their foreign alliances and recognize the rights of Protestants. The second battle cost Zwingli his life, but the treaty that ended the fighting confirmed the right of each canton to determine its own religion. Thereafter, things settled down. Heinrich Bullinger (1504–1575), Zwingli's protégé, assumed leadership of the Swiss Reformation and guided it toward the status of an established religion.

Anabaptists and Radical Protestants

The seeming failure of the Lutheran and Zwinglian reformations to elevate standards of ethical conduct and the slow pace of change discontented many people. Those who wanted a more rapid and thorough restoration of "primitive Christianity" (the church described in the New Testament) accused the reformers of going only halfway. These people formed radical Protestant movements, chief among which was that of the Anabaptists (among whom were the founders of the Mennonite and Amish communities). The Anabaptists ("rebaptizers") took their name from their rejection of infant baptism and their insistence on rebaptizing adults who had been baptized as infants.

Conrad Grebel (1498–1526) symbolically inaugurated Anabaptism by performing the first adult rebaptism in Zurich in January 1525. In October 1523, Grebel's passion for biblical literalism had caused him to break with his mentor, Zwingli. He opposed Zwingli's support for the government's plea to proceed slowly in altering traditional religious practices. In 1527 Grebel's followers, the Swiss Brethren, published a statement of their principles, the *Schleitheim Confession*. They practiced adult baptism, opposed the swearing of oaths, committed themselves to pacifism, and refused to condone secular governments. Anabaptists literally withdrew from society to be free to live as they believed the first Christians had lived. State authorities interpreted their conduct as an attack on society's bonds.

THE ANABAPTIST REIGN IN MÜNSTER Lutherans and Zwinglians joined Catholics in persecuting the Anabaptists. In 1529 rebaptism became a capital offense throughout the Holy Roman Empire, and from 1525 to 1618 somewhere between 1,000 and 5,000 people were executed for undergoing rebaptism. Brutal punishments for nonconformists increased after state authorities witnessed the behavior of a group of Anabaptist extremists who took over the German city of Münster in 1534 to 1535.

Anabaptists converted the majority of the citizens of Münster and set up a town government that forced Lutherans and Catholics to convert or emigrate. Münster became an Old Testament theocracy—replete with charismatic leaders and the practice of polygamy. The latter was an attempt to provide for the women (widowed or deserted) who greatly outnumbered the men of the city.

The outside world was shocked, and Protestant and Catholic armies united to crush the radicals. After this bloody episode, Anabaptism reasserted its commitment to pacifism, and the movement spread largely among rural populations. Later Anabaptist leaders—such as Menno Simons (1496–1561), the founder of the Mennonites—were moderates.

OTHER NONCONFORMISTS   The Anabaptists were not the only Protestant radicals. The Spiritualists were extreme individualists who believed that the only religious authority one ought to obey was the voice of God's spirit in one's heart. Thomas Müntzer (d. 1525), an early convert to Lutheranism and a leader of a peasants' revolt, belonged to this camp—as did Sebastian Franck (d. 1541), a freelance critic of all dogmatic religion, and Caspar Schwenckfeld (d. 1561), a prolific author for whom the tiny Schwenckfeldian denomination is named.

At the other extreme, the Reformation's critique of religious superstition led some people to embrace rationalism. The most prominent exponents of commonsense, rational, ethical religion were the Antitrinitarians. Their most famous spokesman, a Spaniard named Michael Servetus (1511–1553), was executed by the Protestant government of Geneva for rejecting the doctrine of the Trinity. Italian reformers, Lelio (d. 1562) and Faustus Sozzini (d. 1604), founded Socinianism, a humanistic faith that opposed the emerging Protestant orthodoxies and advocated religious toleration.

John Calvin and the Genevan Reformation

In the second half of the sixteenth century Calvinism replaced Lutheranism as the domi-

A portrait of the young John Calvin.   Bibliotheque Publique et Universitaire, Geneva

nant Protestant force in Europe. Although Calvinists believed strongly in divine predestination, they also believed that Christians ought to reorder society according to God's plan. They were zealous reformers who used the machinery of government to compel men and women to live according to codes of conduct that they believed were set forth in the Scriptures.

Calvinism's founder, John Calvin (1509–1564), was the son of a well-to-do secretary to the bishop of Noyon in Picardy. The church *benefices* the boy was given at age twelve paid for the excellent education he received at Parisian colleges and the law school at Orléans. Young Calvin associated with a group of Catholic humanists (led by Jacques Lefèvre d'Étaples and Marguerite d'Angoulême, the queen of Navarre) who advocated reform. Calvin eventually concluded that these people were ineffectual, but they helped awaken his interest in the Reformation.

It was probably in the spring of 1534 that Calvin converted to Protestantism, an experience he described as God's making his "long stubborn heart . . . teachable." In May 1534, he dramatically surrendered the *benefices* that had long supported him and joined the Reformation.

POLITICAL REVOLT AND RELIGIOUS REFORM IN GENEVA In Luther's Saxony, religious reform paved the way for political revolution. In Calvin's Geneva, political revolution awakened an appetite for religious reform. The Genevans, assisted by the city-states of Fribourg and Bern, won their independence from the House of Savoy in 1527 and drove out their resident prince-bishop. The city councils assumed his legal and political powers. Late in 1533 Bern sent the Protestant reformers Guillaume Farel (1489–1565) and Antoine Froment (1508–1581) to Geneva. In the summer of 1535, after much internal turmoil, the Genevans discontinued the traditional Mass and other Catholic religious practices. On May 21, 1536, Geneva officially joined the Reformation.

Calvin arrived in Geneva in July 1536. He had been forced to flee France to avoid persecution for his religious beliefs, and he was intending to seek refuge in Strasbourg. The third Habsburg-Valois war forced him to detour to Geneva, where Farel persuaded him to stay. Before a year had passed, Calvin had drawn up articles for the governance of Geneva's new church as well as a catechism to guide its people. Both were presented for approval to the city councils in early 1537. Because of the strong measures they proposed for governing the moral conduct of Genevans, the reformers were accused of creating a "new papacy." Both within Geneva and outside it, opponents attacked the attempt to impose a new orthodoxy. Bern, which had adopted a more moderate Protestant reform, pressured Geneva to restore ceremonies and holidays that Calvin and Farel opposed. In February 1538, the four syndics (the leading city magistrates) turned against the reformers and drove them out.

Calvin went to Strasbourg to became pastor to a group of French exiles. During his long stay in Strasbourg, he wrote a second edition of his masterful *Institutes of the Christian Religion.* Many scholars consider this to be the definitive theological explication of Protestant faith. Calvin married, took part in ecumenical discussions, and learned important lessons in practical politics from the Strasbourg reformer Martin Bucer.

CALVIN'S GENEVA In 1540 Geneva elected syndics who were eager to establish the city's independence from Bern. They believed that Calvin would be a valuable ally and invited him to return. Within months of his arrival in September 1540, the city implemented new ecclesiastical ordinances. Civil magistrates were pledged to work with the clergy to maintain discipline within the city.

The church Calvin designed was administered by four kinds of officials: (1) five presiding pastors; (2) various teachers or doctors who handled religious instruction; (3) twelve elders, laymen chosen by and from the Genevan councils to "oversee the life of everybody"; and (4) deacons, also laymen, who managed the church's charitable disbursements. Calvin believed that a strong church government was needed to maintain the highest moral standards for the community, for no Christian city could tolerate conduct that was not pleasing to God. The consistory, a committee composed of the elders and the pastors of the church and presided over by one of the four syndics, was given this responsibility. It meted out punishments for a broad range of moral and religious transgressions—from missing church services (a fine of 3 sous) to fornication (six days on bread and water and a fine of 60 sous). The making of statements critical of Calvin and the consistory was listed among the sins meriting punishment. Calvin branded his opponents wanton "Libertines" and showed them little mercy. His most prominent victim was the Antitrinitarian Michael Servetus. Servetus fled to Geneva in 1553, seeking refuge from the Spanish Inquisition—only to be indicted by Calvin for heresy and burned at the stake.

After 1555 the city's syndics were all solidly behind Calvin, and he began to attract disciples from across Europe. Geneva welcomed the thousands of Protestants who were driven out of France, England, and Scotland, and at one point more than a third of the population of the city consisted of refugees (over 5,000 of them). They were utterly loyal to Calvin, for in their experience Geneva was Europe's only "free" city. Whenever they were allowed to return to their homes, they ardently championed Calvinistic reforms.

Political Consolidation of the Lutheran Reformation

By 1530 the Reformation had become irreversible, but it took several decades for that fact to be accepted throughout Europe.

The Expansion of the Reformation

Charles V, who spent most of his time in Spain and Italy, visited the empire in 1530 to convene a diet at Augsburg. The purpose of the meeting was to resolve the religious conflicts that had developed following Luther's break with the papacy in 1520. Charles adjourned the meeting with a blunt order to all Lutherans to revert to Catholicism.

The Reformation was too far advanced by that time to be halted by such a peremptory gesture. The emperor's mandate only served to persuade Lutherans that they needed to form a defensive alliance, which they called the Schmalkaldic League. The league endorsed a common statement of faith, the *Augsburg Confession*, and followed this in 1538 with Luther's more strongly worded *Schmalkaldic Articles*. Regional consistories (i.e., judicial bodies composed of theologians and lawyers) were set up by Lutheran governments to replace the bishops who had formerly administered their churches. Charles was prevented from doing much about this by the outbreak of new hostilities with France and with the Turks. Consequently, the league's leaders, Landgrave Philip of Hesse and Elector John Frederick of Saxony, were, for the time being, able to hold him at bay as Lutheranism spread.

Christian II (r. 1513–1523) introduced Lutheranism to Denmark, where it became the state religion. In Sweden in 1527, Gustavus Vasa (r. 1523–1560) persuaded a Swedish nobility that was eager to confiscate church property to embrace the reform. Poland, primarily because of the absence of a central political authority, became a model of religious pluralism and toleration. In the second half of the sixteenth century, it sheltered Lutherans, Anabaptists, Calvinists, and even Antitrinitarians.

Reaction and Resolution

In 1547 the armies of Charles V crushed the Schmalkaldic League, and the emperor issued the *Augsburg Interim*. It ordered Protestants to return to Catholic beliefs and practices but made a few concessions to Protestant tastes. Clerical marriage was permitted in individual cases when the pope approved, and laypeople were allowed to receive both the bread and the wine at communion. Many Protestant leaders chose exile rather than comply with the terms of the *In-*

terim, and the Reformation was too entrenched by 1547 to be ended by such an imperial fiat.

Maurice of Saxony, whom Charles V handpicked to replace Elector John Frederick as ruler of Saxony, recognized the inevitable and shifted his allegiance to the Protestants. Wearied by three decades of war, the emperor, too, finally surrendered his lifelong quest for the restoration of religious unity in Europe. In 1552 Charles reinstated John Frederick and Philip of Hesse and issued the Peace of Passau (August 1552), guaranteeing religious freedom for Lutherans. The Peace of Augsburg in September 1555 made the division of Christendom permanent. It legalized a principle well established in practice: *cuius regio, eius religio*—meaning that the ruler of a land determines the religion of that land. A subject who was discontented with the religion chosen by his ruler was permitted to migrate to a district that practiced his preferred faith, but diverse faiths were not permitted within a state.

The English Reformation to 1553

The king of England was the only major European monarch to break with the papacy, but England's Reformation owed more to nationalism than to sympathy with Lutheran or Calvinistic theology.

The Preconditions of Reform

England had a long history of maintaining the rights of the crown against the pope. Edward I (d. 1307) defeated Pope Boniface VIII's attempt to deny kings the right to tax their clergy. In the mid-fourteenth century, the English Parliament passed the first Statutes of Provisors and *Praemunire*. These curtailed the right of the pope to appoint candidates to church offices in England, limited the amount of money that could be sent out of England to Rome, and restricted the number of court cases that could be appealed to Rome from English jurisdictions.

In the late Middle Ages, Wycliffe and the Lollards fanned anticlerical sentiment among the English of all classes, and by the early 1520s advocates of reform were smuggling Lutheran writings into England. From 1524 to 1525 William Tyndale (ca. 1492–1536) translated the New Testament into English and had it published in Cologne and Worms. It began to circulate in England in 1526. Access to a Bible in the language of the people became the centerpiece of the English Reformation.

The King's Affair

Henry VIII (r. 1509–1547), the king who severed England's ties with the papacy, initially opposed the Reformation. When Luther's ideas began to circulate, Henry's chief ministers, Cardinal Thomas Wolsey (ca. 1475–1530) and, later, Sir Thomas More (1478–1535), urged him to rush to the pope's defense. Henry declared his Catholic convictions by publishing a treatise justifying the seven sacraments. It earned him a contemptuous response from Luther and the grant of a title, "Defender of the Faith," from Pope Leo X.

It was the king's unhappy marriage, not his doubts about theology, that allowed the seeds of reform to take root in English soil. Henry had married Catherine of Aragon (d. 1536), daughter of Ferdinand and Isabella of Spain and the aunt of Emperor Charles V. By 1527 the union had produced only one surviving child, a daughter, Mary. Since the precedent for women rulers was weak and the practice controversial, Henry feared that civil war would break out if he left his throne to a daughter.

Henry had wed Catherine in 1509 under unusual circumstances that had required a papal dispensation. Catherine had been the wife of Henry's elder brother, Arthur, the heir to their father's throne. When Arthur died, Catherine was betrothed to Henry, the new heir. This preserved England's alliance with Spain. Catherine's numerous miscarriages and stillbirths convinced Henry that their union, despite papal permission, had been a sin and had violated God's prohibition of incest in Leviticus 18:16, 20:21.

By 1527, Henry was thoroughly enamored of Anne Boleyn, one of the aging Catherine's young ladies in waiting. In order to wed Anne, who he believed would be a more fruitful mate, he needed a papal annulment of his marriage to Catherine. Legally, it would have been difficult for the pope to justify an annulment of a marriage that had been approved by a papal dispensation, and in practical terms it was impossible. The soldiers of the Holy Roman Empire had just mutinied and sacked Rome, and Pope Clement VII was a prisoner of Catherine's nephew, Charles V.

Cardinal Wolsey, Henry's Lord Chancellor and a papal legate who had aspirations to become pope, was given the job of securing the annulment. After two years of profitless diplomatic maneuvering, Henry concluded that Wolsey had failed and dismissed him in disgrace (1529). Thomas Cranmer (1489–1556) and Thomas Cromwell (1485–1540), both of whom harbored Lutheran sympathies, then became the king's chief advisers. They proposed a different course: Why not simply declare the king supreme in England's spiritual affairs as he was in England's temporal government? Once that was done, no foreign permission would be needed to legalize a new marriage for the king.

The "Reformation Parliament"

In 1529 Parliament convened for a seven-year session and began to issue a flood of legislation to establish the king's authority over the clergy. In January 1531, Convocation (a legislative assembly representing the English clergy) recognized Henry as head of the church in England "as far as the law of Christ allows." In 1532 Parliament passed a decree (the Submission of the Clergy) that gave the king jurisdiction over the clergy and canon law. Another act (the Conditional Restraint of Annates) recognized the king's power to withhold from Rome the payment of dues traditionally owed the pope.

In January 1533, Thomas Cranmer secretly wed Henry to the pregnant Anne Boleyn. In February 1533, Parliament's Act for the Restraint of Appeals forbade appeals from the king's courts to those of the pope. In March 1533, Cranmer became archbishop of Canterbury, England's primate (i.e., highest-ranking clergyman) and declared that the king had never been validly married to Catherine. In 1534 Parliament ended all payments by the English clergy and laity to Rome and gave Henry sole jurisdiction over high ecclesiastical appointments. The Act of Succession in the same year declared Anne Boleyn's children legitimate heirs to the throne, and the Act of Supremacy proclaimed Henry "the only supreme head on earth of the Church of England." In 1536 the first Act for Dissolution of Monasteries closed the smaller houses, and three years later all English monasteries were shut and their endowments confiscated by the king.

Not all of Henry's subjects approved of the nationalization of their church, but Henry encouraged compliance by making examples of two of his most prominent critics. When Thomas More and John Fisher, bishop of Rochester, refused to accept the Act of Succession and the Act of Supremacy, Henry had them executed.

Wives of Henry VIII

Henry was more successful as a politician than as a husband. In 1536 Anne Boleyn, who had disappointed Henry by bearing him another daughter (Elizabeth), was executed for alleged treason and adultery. Henry married four more times. His third wife, Jane Seymour, died in 1537, shortly after giving birth to the long-desired male heir, Edward VI. Henry then wed Anne of Cleves as part of a plan that Cromwell promoted to forge an alliance among Protestant princes. Neither the alliance nor Anne—whom Henry found to have a remarkable resemblance to a horse—proved worth the trouble. The marriage was annulled by Parliament, and Cromwell was executed. Catherine Howard, Henry's fifth wife, was beheaded for adultery in 1542. His last wife, Catherine Parr, was a patron of humanists and reformers. Henry was her third husband, and she survived him to marry a fourth time.

The King's Religious Conservatism

Henry was far bolder in politics than in piety. Except for his break with Rome and his approval of the use of English Bibles in English churches, Henry opposed changes in doctrine and practice. The Ten Articles of 1536, a program for England's nationalized church, made only mild concessions to Protestant tenets. In 1539 the king issued the Six Articles, which were intended to stem a rising tide of enthusiasm for Protestantism. These reaffirmed transubstantiation, denied the Eucharistic cup to the laity, preserved mandatory celibacy for the clergy, authorized private masses, and ordered the continuation of auricular confession. England had to await Henry's death before it could become a genuinely Protestant country.

The Protestant Reformation Under Edward VI

When Henry died, his son, Edward VI (r. 1547–1553), was only ten years old. The young king's regents gave him a Protestant education—enlivened by correspondence with John Calvin. Edward's pro-Protestant government repealed Henry's Six Articles and laws against heresy, and it sanctioned clerical marriage and lay communion with both cup and bread. In 1547 the chantries, endowments supporting priests who said masses for the dead, were dissolved. In 1549 the Act of Uniformity imposed Thomas Cranmer's *Book of Common Prayer* on all English churches, and a year later images and altars were ordered removed from churches.

The Second Act of Uniformity, passed in 1552, revised the *Book of Common Prayer* and published a forty-two-article confession of faith written by Thomas Cranmer. The confession endorsed the Protestant doctrines of justification by faith and supremacy of Holy Scripture. It recognized only two sacraments and rejected transubstantiation—although it affirmed the real presence of Christ in the Eucharistic elements.

The turn toward Protestantism that took place during Edward's reign was reversed by his heir, Catherine of Aragon's fervently Catholic daughter, Mary. In 1553 Mary succeeded her teenaged half-brother and made it her mission, as queen, to restore England to the Catholic community. Despite a bloody persecution of Protestants, she was unable completely to undo the work her father and brother had begun. When she died childless in 1558, Anne Boleyn's daughter, Elizabeth (d. 1603), inherited her throne and engineered a religious compromise. The Elizabethan "settlement" left England with a stable, moderately Protestant national church.

Catholic Reform and Counter-Reformation

Before Luther spoke out, proposals had already been made for reforming the Roman Catholic Church. One of the boldest came on the eve of the last church council that met before the Reformation, the Fifth Lateran Council (1513–1517). But the pope, remembering how the councils of Constance and Basel had usurped the authority of his predecessors, squelched the initiative.

Sources of Catholic Reform

The Modern Devotion inspired many of the Catholic laity and clergy who pushed for reform.

The Ecstasy of Saint Teresa of Avila, *by Gianlorenzo Bernini (1598–1680). Mystics like Saint Teresa and Saint John of the Cross helped revive the traditional piety of medieval monasticism.* S. Maria della Vittoria, Rome. Scala/Art Resource, NY

In 1517 it prompted the foundation of a new kind of religious organization in Rome, the Oratory of Divine Love. The Oratory encouraged cooperation among learned laity and clergy who were deeply committed to the cultivation of inner piety, the promotion of Christian living, and the reform of the church.

The fervent Catholic faith of the sixteenth century generated many new religious orders. The Theatines were founded in 1524 to groom devout, reform-minded leaders for the higher levels of the church hierarchy. The Capuchins were established in 1528 to minister to ordinary people by returning to the ideals of Saint Francis. The Somaschi, in the mid-1520s, and the Barnabites, in 1530, dedicated themselves to caring for the residents of war-torn areas of Italy. The Ursulines, founded in 1535, undertook the religious education of girls from all social classes.

The Oratorians, established in 1575, promoted religious literature and church music—the great hymnist and musician Giovanni Palestrina (1526–1594) was one of them. And, thanks to the inspiration of the Spanish mystics, Saint Teresa of Avila (1515–1582) and Saint John of the Cross (1542–1591), older monastic orders also underwent renewal.

Ignatius of Loyola and the Jesuits

The most influential of the new orders, the Society of Jesus, was organized in the 1530s by Ignatius of Loyola (1491–1556). Ignatius, a dashing courtier and *caballero*, began his spiritual pilgrimage in 1521 when he was seriously wounded in battle. He passed a lengthy and painful convalescence reading Christian classics and studying the techniques developed by the church's saints for overcoming mental anguish and pain. A dramatic conversion experience determined him to do whatever was necessary to become a "soldier of Christ." The lessons Ignatius learned from his struggles with himself evolved into a program for personal individual renewal. Ignatius believed that a person could create a new self through study and discipline, and he wrote a devotional guide (*Spiritual Exercises*) to teach techniques for achieving spiritual self-mastery.

The Protestant reformers of Ignatius's day made a virtue of opposing the authority of the traditional church. Ignatius, however, urged Catholics to deny themselves and submit without question to the church. Perfect discipline and self-control were to be cultivated—as were enthusiasm for traditional spirituality, mystical experience, and willingness to subordinate all personal goals to those of the church. People imbued with these qualities were well equipped to counter the Reformation. Within a century the ten original "Jesuits" were joined by more than 15,000 ardent recruits. They recovered districts initially lost to Protestantism in Austria, Bavaria, and the Rhineland, and staffed missions as far afield as India, Japan, and the Americas.

The Council of Trent (1545–1563)

Pope Paul III (1534–1549), in response to pressure from Emperor Charles V, finally called a general council to address the crisis created by the Reformation. The commission, appointed by the pope to prepare for the council, was chaired by

Caspar Contarini (1483–1542), a member of the Oratory of Divine Love. Contarini was such an advocate of reform that his critics branded him a "semi-Lutheran." The report he presented to the pope in February 1537 was so blunt an indictment of the papal curia that Protestants circulated it to justify their break with the papacy.

The opening of the council, which met in Trent in northern Italy, was delayed until 1545, and its three sessions spread over eighteen years (1545–1563). Long interruptions were caused by war, plague, and politics. Unlike the late medieval councils, Trent was strictly under papal control—and dominated by Italian clergy. Only high-ranking churchmen could vote. Theologians from the universities, the lower clergy, and laypersons did not have a voice in the council's decisions.

The council focused on the restoration of internal church discipline. It curtailed the selling of church offices and other religious goods. It ordered bishops who resided outside their dioceses

MAP 11–2   THE RELIGIOUS SITUATION ABOUT 1560   *By 1560 Luther, Zwingli, and Loyola were dead, Calvin was near the end of his life, England had separated from Rome, and the last session of the Council of Trent was about to assemble. The religious fragmentation of Europe was well underway.*

to return home and to take steps to elevate the conduct of their charges. Bishops were enjoined to preach and to conduct frequent tours of inspection of the clergy. Trent also sought to increase respect for the parish priest by requiring him to be neatly dressed, better educated, strictly celibate, and active among his parishioners. To achieve these ends Trent called for the construction of a seminary in every diocese.

Trent made no doctrinal concessions to Protestantism. On the contrary, it ringingly affirmed most of the things to which Protestants objected: traditional scholastic education; the role of good works in salvation; the authority of tradition; the seven sacraments; transubstantiation; the withholding of the Eucharistic cup from the laity; clerical celibacy; purgatory; indulgences; and the veneration of saints, relics, and sacred images.

Trent was not designed to heal the rifts that had developed within Christendom but to strengthen the Roman Catholic Church in opposition to Protestantism. Some secular rulers were initially leery of Trent's assertion of papal authority, but they were reassured as the new legislation took hold and parish life revived under the guidance of a devout and better-trained clergy. The increasing religious polarization of Europe was, however, a source for anxiety.

The Church in Spanish America

The Roman Catholic priests who accompanied the expeditions that explored and conquered the Americas were imbued with the Christian humanism that flourished in sixteenth-century Spain. They wanted to convert the Indians not only to Christianity but to European civilization as well.

The early Spanish conquerors and the mendicant friars who worked among the Indians were often at odds. Many priests believed that conquest was a necessary prerequisite for the conversion of the Indians, but they deplored exploitation of native peoples and tried to defend them. Bartolomé de Las Casas, a Dominican, contended that conquest was not necessary for conversion. The campaign he began in 1550 for royal legislation to regulate conquest was successful, but his rhetoric encouraged the growth of the "Black Legend"—a condemnation of all Spanish colonists for inhumanity toward the In-

Significant Dates from the Period of the Protestant Reformation	
1517	Luther posts ninety-five theses against indulgences
1519	Charles V becomes Holy Roman Emperor
1521	Diet of Worms condemns Luther
1524–1525	Peasants' Revolt in Germany
1527	The Schleitheim Confession of the Anabaptists
1529	Marburg Colloquy between Luther and Zwingli
1529	England's Reformation Parliament convenes
1531	Formation of Protestant Schmalkaldic League
1533	Henry VIII weds Anne Boleyn
1534	England's Act of Supremacy
1534–1535	Anabaptists take over Münster
1536	Calvin arrives in Geneva
1540	Jesuits, founded by Ignatius of Loyola, recognized as order by pope
1546	Luther dies
1547	Armies of Charles V crush Schmalkaldic League
1547–1553	Edward VI, king of England
1555	Peace of Augsburg
1553–1558	Mary Tudor, queen of England
1545–1563	Council of Trent
1558–1603	Elizabeth I, queen of England; the Anglican settlement

dians. Although the "Black Legend" contained elements of truth, it exaggerated the case against Spain. The Aztec demands for human sacrifice prove that Indian rulers could also be exceedingly cruel. Had the Aztecs discovered Spain and won the upper hand, they would have dealt with Europeans much as Spaniards dealt with Indians.

By the end of the sixteenth century, the church in Spanish America had made peace with colonialism. On numerous occasions, individual priests defended the rights of Indian tribes, but the church also profited from the growing prosperity of the Spanish colonists. As a great landowner with a stake in the colonial status quo, it did not challenge Spanish domination or any but the most extreme modes of economic exploitation. By the time the colonial era drew to a close in the late eighteenth century, the Roman Catholic Church had become one of the strongest and most conservative institutions in Latin America.

The Social Significance of the Reformation in Western Europe

Luther, Zwingli, and Calvin believed that Christians were called not to separate themselves from the world but to take up their Christian duties as citizens of the state. Consequently, they have been called "magisterial reformers," meaning not only that they were leaders of major Protestant movements but also that they were willing to use the magistrate's sword to advance their causes.

To some modern observers this looks like a compromise of the highest religious principles, but the reformers did not see it that way. They assumed that their reforms had to conform to the realities of the societies of which they were members. The reformers were so sensitive to what they believed was politically and socially possible that some scholars claim that they encouraged acceptance of the status quo. But despite this political conservatism, the Reformation, in some places, contributed to radical changes in traditional religious practices and institutions.

The Revolution in Religious Practices and Institutions

RELIGION IN FIFTEENTH–CENTURY LIFE   On the eve of the Reformation, the clergy and the religious made up 6 to 8 percent of the total population of the central European cities that were about to become Protestant. In addition to their spiritual authority, they exercised considerable political power. They legislated, taxed, tried cases in special church courts, and enforced laws with threats of excommunication. The church calendar regulated the daily life of the city. About one-third of the year was given over to some kind of religious observance, fast, or celebration. Cloisters, which educated the children of prominent citizens and enjoyed the patronage of powerful aristocratic families, had great influence. There was booming business at religious shrines, where

pilgrims gathered by the hundreds or thousands. Begging friars constantly worked the streets, and several times each year special preachers arrived to sell letters of indulgence.

The conduct of many of the religious was a source of concern. Despite the fact that clergy were sworn to celibacy and forbidden legal marriages, many had concubines and children. Society's response to these relationships was mixed, but the church tolerated them upon payment of penitential fines. Everywhere there were complaints about the clergy's exemption from taxation and immunity from prosecution in civil courts, and people grumbled about having to support church offices whose occupants lived and worked elsewhere.

RELIGION IN SIXTEENTH-CENTURY LIFE   The Reformation made few changes in the politics or class structures of the cities where it triumphed. The same aristocratic families governed as before, and the same people were rich and poor. The Reformation did, however, have a profound impact on the clergy. Their numbers fell by two-thirds; religious holidays shrank by one-third. Monasteries and nunneries nearly disappeared—transformed into hospices or educational institutions. Parish churches were reduced in number by at least one-third. Worship was conducted in the vernacular. In some places, particularly those influenced by the Zwinglian reform, the walls of sanctuaries were stripped bare and whitewashed.

The laity observed no obligatory fasts. Local shrines were closed down, and anyone found venerating saints, relics, and images was subject to punishment. Copies of Luther's translation of the New Testament or excerpts from it could be found in private homes. Instead of controlling access to the Scriptures, the new clergy encouraged laypersons to study them. Protestant clergy could marry, and many did. They paid taxes and were punished for their crimes in civil courts. The moral life of the community was supervised by committees composed of equal numbers of laity and clergy, and secular magistrates had the last word in resolving disputes. Not all Protestant clergy were enthusiastic about lay authority in religion. The laity complained about "new papists" among the Protestant preachers—men who sought the strict control over the lives of the laity that the Catholic clergy enjoyed.

The laity themselves were no less ambivalent about certain aspects of the Reformation, and they could be just as reactionary as some clergy. Over half of the original converts returned to the Catholic fold before the end of the sixteenth century.

The Reformation and Education

The Reformation's implementation of humanistic educational theories in new Protestant schools and universities had significant cultural impact. Even when the reformers' views on doctrine and human nature separated them from the humanists, they shared the humanists' belief in the unity of wisdom, eloquence, and action. The humanist program of study, which emphasized language skills and a reliance on original sources, was essential for the practice of a Protestant faith that acknowledged no authority higher than that of Scripture.

When, in August 1518, Philip Melanchthon (1497–1560), a young professor of Greek, joined Luther at the University of Wittenberg, his first act was to champion humanist curricular reforms. In his inaugural address, *On Improving the Studies of the Young,* Melanchthon defended classical studies against medieval scholasticism, and he and Luther completely restructured the University of Wittenberg's program of study. Canon law and commentaries on Lombard's *Sentences* were dropped. Old-fashioned scholastic lectures on Aristotle were replaced by a straightforward historical approach. Students read primary sources directly, not as interpreted by scholastic commentators. Candidates for theological degrees relied on exegesis of the Bible, not the citation of "authorities," to defend their theses. New chairs of Greek and Hebrew were created. Luther and Melanchthon also pressed for universal compulsory education so that both boys and girls could learn to read the Bible in vernacular translation.

In Geneva, John Calvin and his successor, Theodore Beza, founded an academy that developed into the University of Geneva. Their school, which concentrated on training Calvinist ministers, developed a program similar to the one designed by Luther and Melanchthon. Calvinist refugees trained in the academy carried Protestant educational reforms to France, Scotland, England, and the New World. Thanks to them, a working knowledge of Greek and Hebrew became commonplace in educated circles in the sixteenth and seventeenth centuries.

Some contemporaries complained that the original humanist program narrowed its focus as Protestants took it over, but humanist culture and learning profited from the Reformation. Protestant schools and universities consolidated and preserved for the modern world many of the basic pedagogical achievements of humanism.

The Reformation and the Changing Role of Women

The Protestant reformers rejected ascetic disciplines, such as celibacy, as vain attempts to earn salvation, and they urged clergy to marry to dispel the belief that the lives of clergy were spiritually more meritorious than those of laypersons. The development of a more positive attitude toward marriage translated into a more positive attitude toward women.

Medieval thinkers often degraded sexually active women as temptresses (such as Eve) and exalted virginal women as saints (such as Mary). Protestants praised woman in her own right but especially in her biblical vocation as mother and housewife. The reformers acknowledged the contribution their wives made to their ministries, and Protestants stressed as no religious movement before them had the sacredness of home and family. The ideal of companionate marriage—that is, of husband and wife as coworkers in a special God-ordained community of the family—greatly improved women's legal status. Since Protestant marriage was not a sacrament, divorce was easier, and women had the right to leave husbands who flagrantly violated marriage contracts. Although from a modern perspective, Protestant women remained subject to men, new marriage laws gave them greater security and protection.

Because they wanted women to become pious housewives modeling their lives on biblical precepts, Protestants encouraged vernacular literacy for girls. Some women became authors and contributed to the literature of the Reformation. Many, in the course of their studies, pondered the significance of biblical passages that suggested they were equal to men in the presence of God. The discussion of the role of women that Protestant theology encouraged inched society marginally closer to the emancipation of women.

Family Life in Early Modern Europe

Many changes took place in the sixteenth and seventeenth centuries in the customs influencing marriage and family life. The Reformation was only one of many factors shaping these developments.

Later Marriages

Men and women began to delay first marriages to later ages than they had in previous centuries. Grooms tended to be in their mid- to late twenties rather than in their late teens and early twenties, and brides in their early to mid-twenties rather than in their teens. The church-sanctioned minimum age for marriage remained fourteen for men and twelve for women. Betrothal could still occur at these young ages if parents approved.

Later marriages were a reflection of the difficulty couples encountered in amassing enough capital to establish an independent household. Family size and population increased in the fifteenth and early sixteenth centuries. That meant that property tended to be divided among more heirs, and an average couple had to work longer to prepare materially for marriage. Many—possibly 20 percent of all women in the sixteenth century—never married. Single women often grew increasingly impoverished as they aged without the support of a husband or children.

Arranged Marriages

Marriages tended to be "arranged" in the sense that the male heads of two families met and discussed the terms of a marriage before they informed the prospective bride and bridegroom. It was rare, however, for the two people involved not to know each other in advance or to have no prior relationship. Children had a legal right to protest and resist an unwanted marriage. A forced marriage was, by definition, invalid, and no one believed an unwanted marriage would last. The best marriage was one desired by both parties and approved by their families.

Later marriages to older partners shortened the length of the average marriage and elevated the rate of remarriage. Maternal mortality increased with late marriage and, as the rapid growth of orphanages and foundling homes between 1600 and 1800 testifies, so did out-of-wedlock pregnancies.

Family Size

The early modern family was conjugal or nuclear. It consisted of a father and a mother and an average of two to four surviving children. A wife endured a pregnancy about every two years. About one-third of the children born died by age five, and one-half were gone by age twenty. Rare was the family at any social level that did not suffer the loss of children. Martin Luther fathered six children, two of whom died—one at eight months and another at thirteen years.

Birth Control

Birth control methods of limited effectiveness had been available since antiquity: acidic ointments, sponges, and *coitus interruptus.* The church's growing condemnation of contraception in the thirteenth and fourteenth centuries suggests that its use was increasing. St. Thomas Aquinas defended the church's position by asserting that a natural act, such as sex, was moral only when it served the end for which it was created—in this case, the production of children and their subsequent rearing to the glory of God. Christian moral teachings may, however, have increased some couples' use of contraception by encouraging husbands to empathize with the burden frequent pregnancies placed on their wives.

Wet Nursing

Theologians and physicians joined in condemning the widespread custom of putting newborn children out to wet nurses. Wet nurses were mothers who made money by suckling other women's children. Wet nursing often exposed an infant to great risks from disease or neglect, but nursing a child was a chore many upper-class women found distasteful. Husbands also disliked it, for the church forbade sexual intercourse while a woman was lactating on the theory that sexual intercourse spoiled a woman's milk. Nursing also has a contraceptive effect, and there is evidence that some women prolonged nursing to fend off new pregnancy. For wealthy burghers and noblemen who wanted an abundance of male heirs, time spent nursing was time wasted.

Loving Families?

In addition to wet nursing, other practices common to early modern families cause them to appear cold and unloving. A child who spent the first year of his life with a wet nurse might, between the ages of nine and fourteen, find himself sent away from home again for an apprenticeship or employment. Also, the gap in ages between husband and wife was often great, and a widower or widow sometimes remarried very quickly.

The forms love and affection take, however, are as relative to time and culture as other values. Depending on the options that are available, a kindness in one historical period can seem a cruelty in another. Primitive living conditions, which made single life difficult, necessitated quick remarriages. A competitive economic environment with limited opportunities for vocational education encouraged early apprenticeships if children were to have jobs. There is no convincing evidence that people of the Reformation era were less capable of loving one another than modern people are.

Literary Imagination in Transition

As Europe approached the seventeenth century, it was no longer medieval, but it was also not yet modern. The intellectual life of the period may have been so remarkably rich and vital because it issued from the interplay of both points of view. The great literary figures of the era were capable of defending traditional values while exploring alternatives that encouraged people to develop a fresh perspective on life's potentials.

Miguel de Cervantes Saavedra: Rejection of Idealism

There was religious reform in Spain but no Protestant Reformation. The Spanish state empowered the Inquisition to enforce uniformity of opinion in Spain, and the religion of which the state approved was the mystical, ascetic piety of the early Middle Ages. It was this that colored Spain's literature.

For centuries Spain had been a nation of crusaders, and the union of Catholic piety with sec-

Miguel de Cervantes Saavedra (1547–1616), the author of Don Quixote, *considered by many to be Spain's greatest writer.* Art Resource, NY

ular power, which is characteristic of a crusade, shaped a culture based on the ideals of medieval chivalry—particularly, honor and loyalty. The novels and plays of the period are almost all devoted to stories in which these virtues are tested.

Miguel de Cervantes Saavedra (1547–1616), who is generally acknowledged to be the greatest writer Spain has produced, devoted himself to exploring the strengths and weaknesses of religious idealism. Cervantes was self-educated—reading widely and immersing himself in the "school of life." As a youth, he worked in Rome for a Spanish cardinal. He entered the army and was decorated for gallantry in the Battle of Lepanto (1571). He was also captured by pirates and enslaved in Algiers for five years. He later found work as a tax collector and was imprisoned for padding his accounts. It was in prison in 1603 that he began to write his most famous work, *Don Quixote.*

Cervantes set out to satirize the chivalric romances popular in Spain in his day, but he developed a deep affection for Don Quixote, the deluded knight whose story he tells. *Don Quixote* is satire only on the surface. The work raises serious questions about the things that give meaning to human lives. Cervantes's Don Quixote is a none-too-stable, middle-aged man who is driven mad by reading too many chivalric romances. He aspires to become the knight of his own imagination and sets out to prove his worthiness by performing brave deeds. He dedicates himself as a courtly lover to the service of Dulcinea, a quite unworthy peasant girl whom he imagines to be a refined and noble lady. Sancho Panza, a clever, worldly-wise peasant, accompanies him as his squire and watches with bemused skepticism as the Don repeatedly makes a fool of himself. The story ends tragically when a well-meaning friend tries to restore Don Quixote's reason by defeating him in battle and forcing him to renounce his quest for knighthood. Stripped of the delusion that gave meaning to his life, the Don returns to his village to die a shamed and broken-hearted old man.

Don Quixote examines side by side the modern realism of Sancho Panza and the old-fashioned religious idealism of the Don. It comes to the conclusion that both are respectable and both are necessary for human fulfillment.

William Shakespeare: Dramatist of the Age

Little is known about William Shakespeare (1564–1616), the greatest playwright in the English language. He married young (at age eighteen), and by 1585 he and his wife, Anne Hathaway, had three children. He may have worked for a time as a schoolteacher. The wide but erratic knowledge of history and classical literature that informs his plays suggests that he was not schooled as a professional scholar.

Once he could afford it, Shakespeare chose to live the life of a country gentleman. He entered eagerly into the commercialism and the bawdy pleasures of the Elizabethan Age, and his work shows no trace of Puritan anxiety about worldliness. He was radical in neither politics nor religion, and his few allusions to Puritans are more critical than complimentary. By modern standards he was a political conservative, accepting the social rankings and the power structure of his day and demonstrating unquestioned patriotism.

Shakespeare experienced every aspect of life in the theater—as playwright, actor, and owner-producer. He wrote and performed for a famous company of actors, the King's Men, and, between 1590 and 1610, many of his plays were staged at Elizabeth's court. Although the French drama of the period was dominated by classical models, the Elizabethan audience that Shakespeare wanted to please welcomed a mixture of styles: classical comedies and tragedies, medieval morality plays, and contemporary Italian short stories.

Shakespeare wrote all kinds of plays that synthesized the best from the past and from the work of his contemporaries. The most original of Shakespeare's tragedies may be *Romeo and Juliet* (1597), but four of his greatest were the products of one short period in his career: *Hamlet* (1603), *Othello* (1604), *King Lear* (1605), and *Macbeth* (1606). Shakespeare also wrote comedies and plays based on real historical events. The latter were strongly colored by the propaganda that served the Tudor monarchy, but almost all of Shakespeare's plays have demonstrated a remarkable ability to transcend the limits of the world for which they were written. Their keen analyses of human motivation, stirring evocations of human emotion, and stunning poetry keep them alive and capable of filling theaters.

In Perspective

The Lutheran Reformation, which made pluralism a fact of Western religious life, was the product of an age of widespread discontent. People at all levels of society had come to resent a church that failed to hold clergy accountable for their spiritual conduct while exempting them from many burdens imposed on the laity. Spiritual and secular grievances combined to fuel a revolution that restructured both the church and the state.

Luther's declaration that Scripture was the only authority governing faith opened a Pandora's box, for people proved to have very different ideas about what Scripture taught. Lutheran, Zwinglian, Anabaptist, Spiritualist, Calvinist, and Anglican versions of biblical religion appeared in rapid succession, and Protestants had difficulty containing their revolution.

A move to reform the Catholic church was underway long before the Reformation broke out in Germany, but, lacking papal support, it made little progress until the mid-sixteenth century. Catholic reform, when it came, was doctrinally reactionary but administratively and spiritually innovative. The church demanded strict obedience and conformity, but it also provided the laity with a better-educated and disciplined clergy. The result was a smaller but more vigorous church, prepared to fight for its place in an increasingly pluralistic culture.

REVIEW QUESTIONS

1. What were the main problems of the church that contributed to the Protestant Reformation? Why was the church unable to suppress dissent as it had earlier?
2. On what did Luther and Zwingli agree? On what did they disagree? What about Luther and Calvin? Did differences and splits within the ranks lessen the effectiveness of the Protestant movement?
3. Why did the Reformation begin in Germany? How did the political context Germany provided for a reform movement differ from the situation in France or Italy?
4. What was the Catholic Reformation? What were the major reforms instituted by the Council of Trent? Did the Protestant Reformation have a healthy effect on the Catholic church?
5. Why did Henry VIII break with the Catholic church? Did he establish a truly Protestant religion in England? What problems did his successors face as a result of his religious policies?
6. What impact did the Reformation have on women in the sixteenth and seventeenth centuries? What new factors and pressures affected relations between men and women, family size, and child care during this period?

SUGGESTED READINGS

HAROLD BLOOM, *Shakespeare: The Invention of the Human* (1998). A modern master's complete analysis of the greatest writer in the English language.

W. BOUWSMA, *John Calvin: A Sixteenth Century Portrait* (1988). Interpretation of Calvin against the background of Renaissance intellectual history.

J. DELUMEAU, *Catholicism Between Luther and Voltaire: A New View of the Counter Reformation* (1977). Programmatic essay on a social history of the Counter-Reformation.

A. G. DICKENS, *The English Reformation* (1974). The best one-volume account.

M. DURAN, *Cervantes* (1974). Detailed biography.

H. O. EVENNETT, *The Spirit of the Counter Reformation* (1968). Essay on the continuity of Catholic reform and its independence from the Protestant Reformation.

B. GOTTLIEB, *The Family in the Western World* (1992). Accessible overview, with up-to-date annotated bibliographies.

R. HOULBROOKE, *Death, Religion and Family in England, 1480–1758* (1998). How death was met in the early modern English family.

J. L. IRWIN, ed., *Womanhood in Radical Protestantism, 1525–1675* (1979). Sources illustrating images of women in sectarian Protestant thought.

S. MARSHALL, ed., *Women in Reformation and Counter Reformation Europe: Private and Public Worlds* (1989). Lucid and authoritative presentations.

J. F. MCNEILL, *The History and Character of Calvinism* (1954). The most comprehensive account, and very readable.

H. A. OBERMAN, *Luther: Man Between God and the Devil* (1989). Perhaps the best account of Luther's life, by a Dutch master.

J. O'MALLEY, *The First Jesuits* (1993). Extremely detailed account of the creation of the Society of Jesus and its original purposes.

S. OZMENT, *The Age of Reform, 1250–1550: An Intellectual and Religious History of Late Medieval and Reformation Europe* (1980). A broad survey of major religious ideas and beliefs.

S. OZMENT, *Flesh and Spirit: Private Life in Early Modern Germany* (1999).

D. STARKEY, *The Reign of Henry VIII* (1985). Portrayal of the king as in control of neither his life nor his court.

F. WENDEL, *Calvin: The Origins and Development of His Religious Thought*, trans. by Philip Mairet (1963). The best treatment of Calvin's theology.

Chapter 12

The Age of Religious Wars

KEY TOPICS

- The war between Calvinists and Catholics in France
- The Spanish occupation of the Netherlands
- The struggle for supremacy between England and Spain
- The devastation of central Europe during the Thirty Years' War

Political rivalries and religious conflicts combined to make the late sixteenth and the early seventeenth centuries an "age of religious wars." The era was plagued both by civil conflicts within nations and by battles among nations. Catholic and Protestant factions struggled for advantage within France, the Netherlands, and England. The Catholic monarchies of France and Spain attacked Protestant regimes in England and the Netherlands. Ultimately, every major nation in Europe was drawn into a conflict that devastated Germany, the Thirty Years' War (1618–1648).

Renewed Religious Struggle

During the first half of the sixteenth century, religious war was confined to central Europe—to parts of the empire where Lutherans fought for recognition. In the second half of the sixteenth century, the battles shifted to western Europe (France, the Netherlands, England, and Scotland) as Calvinists struggled for their cause.

The Peace of Augsburg (1555) ended the first phase of the war in central Europe by granting each ruler of a region of the empire the right to determine the religion of his subjects. The only kind of Protestantism that Augsburg recognized, however, was Lutheranism. Lutherans and Catholics joined forces to oppose Anabaptists and other sectarians, and Calvinists were not yet strong enough to demand legal standing.

By the time the Council of Trent adjourned in 1563 the Roman Catholic Church had been reinvigorated, and the Jesuits were spearheading a counteroffensive to recover regions lost to Protestantism in western Europe. John Calvin, who died in 1564, made Geneva both a refuge for Protestants fleeing persecution and a school to equip them to meet the Catholic challenge.

Genevan Calvinism and Tridentine Catholicism were equally dogmatic and aggressive—and mutually incompatible. Calvinism mandated a presbyterian organization that distributed authority among local governments. Boards of presbyters (elders), composed of both clergy and laity and representing individual congregations, set policy for the church at large. The Roman Catholic Church was, by contrast, a centralized, hierarchical system that stressed absolute obedience to the pope. The pope and bishops ruled supreme without the necessity of consulting with the laity. Calvinism attracted people who favored the decentralization and distribution of political power and who opposed authoritarian rule, whereas Catholicism was preferred by advocates of absolute monarchy—those who favored "one king, one church, one law."

As religious wars engulfed Europe, intellectuals perceived the wisdom of religious pluralism and toleration. Skepticism, relativism, and individualism in religion increasingly came to be seen as virtues. Valentin Weigel (1533–1588), a Lutheran who surveyed a half-century of religious strife in Germany, spoke for many when he advised people to look within themselves for religious truth and not to churches and creeds.

Politicians were slower than intellectuals to embrace principles of toleration. The rulers who succeeded best at holding religious strife and civil war in check were those who did so—the *politiques*, pragmatic monarchs such as Elizabeth I of England who urged moderation and compromise in religious matters. Governments led by people who took religion with utmost seriousness (e.g., Mary I of England, Philip II of Spain, and England's Oliver Cromwell) failed to maintain stability.

The French Wars of Religion (1562–1598)

Anti-Protestant Measures and the Struggle for Political Power

In the 1520s Lutheran ideas began to circulate in Paris and to excite the suspicions of the French government. French Protestants were dubbed "Huguenots"—after Besançon Hugues, the leader of the revolt that won Geneva its freedom at that time.

In 1525, when Emperor Charles V captured King Francis I of France at the Battle of Pavia, the French authorities began actively to prosecute Protestants. They hoped that by cooperating with Charles's anti-Protestant campaign they might win favorable terms for the king's release. A second crackdown followed a decade later. It was a response to a major Protestant publicity campaign that (on October 18, 1534) plastered Paris and other cities with anti-Catholic placards. The government's reaction convinced some that the monarchy was committing itself to exterminating Protestantism, and John Calvin and other members of the French reform decided to leave France.

Hostilities between the French and the empire (the Habsburg-Valois wars) ended with the Treaty of Cateau-Cambrésis in 1559. The treaty marked a shift in the European balance of power from France to Spain, and it was a prelude to an outbreak of civil conflict within France. Both these developments began with an accident. In 1559 the French king, Henry II, was mortally wounded in a tournament, and his sickly fifteen-year-old son, Francis II, ascended the throne. The queen mother, Catherine de Médicis, governed France as the boy-king's regent. The weakness of her administration tempted three powerful families to struggle for leadership of France: the Bourbons, whose power lay in the south and west; the Montmorency-Chatillons, who controlled the center of France; and the Guises, whose lands were in the east.

The Guises were initially the strongest, and they dominated the young king. Francis, duke of Guise, had commanded Henry II's army, and his brothers, Charles and Louis, were cardinals of the church. They arranged for their niece, Mary Stuart, Queen of Scotland, to marry Francis II. Since the Guise family championed a militant, reactionary Catholicism, France's Protestants rallied behind its opponents—the Bourbon prince of Condé,

Warring Architectural Styles: Baroque vs. Plain Churches

Interior of "Asamkirche," *Asam Cosmas Damian (1686–1739). Saint Nepomit Church in Munich designed by the brothers Cosmas Damian and Egid Quirin Asam in 1733. The church stands next to the house the brothers built for themselves. Asamkirche (St. Johann-Nepomuk).* Erich Lessing/Art Resource, NY

Art and architecture reflect religious beliefs as clearly as creeds and laws. Congregations that embraced the Reformed Protestant doctrines of Calvin and Zwingli and the various nonconformist sects (e.g., Anabaptists and Quakers) believed that traditional ecclesiastical art and music—which Lutherans as well as Catholics endorsed—distracted worshipers from the Word of God. Finding no biblical support for the use of ornament in worship, these groups stripped their sanctuaries bare and confined music to the chanting of psalms. In Catholic districts the Counter-Reformation encouraged the opposite tendency, that is, reliance on an exuberant baroque style of art and architecture that was meant to be emotionally overwhelming. It strove to appeal to worshipers' senses and fill them with awe and wonder at the power of faith. In the hands of the Jesuits, baroque art was an effective tool for strengthening the Catholic community and reclaiming people who had been lost to Protestantism. Both the plain and baroque traditions inspired great artists. The painter Peter Paul Rubens (1571–1640) and the sculptor Gianlorenzo Bernini (1598–1680) were Catholics, but Protestantism could boast artists of equal stature: for example, the architect Christopher Wren (1632–1723) and the painter Rembrandt van Rijn (1606–1669).

Temple de Lyon. Bibliotheque Publique et Universitaire, Geneve

The interiors of the churches from Munich and Lyon, which are depicted here, dramatically illustrate the contrast between the baroque and Protestant Reform styles. The former dazzles, explodes with energy, and urges worshipers to emotional flights of self-transcendence. The latter removes all distraction, creates an atmosphere conducive to quiet introspection, and assists worshipers in reflecting on God's Word and their individual spiritual lives.

227

Louis I (d. 1569), and the Montmorency-Chatillons admiral, Gaspard de Coligny (1519–1572).

Appeal of Calvinism

Ambitious aristocrats and discontented towns-people had different reasons for joining Calvinist churches in opposing the Guise-dominated French monarchy. Although there were more than 2,000 Huguenot congregations in France by 1561, Huguenots were a majority of the population in only two regions: Dauphiné and Langue-doc. Huguenots made up only about one-fifteenth of France's population, but they controlled important districts and were heavily represented among the more powerful segments of French society. Over two-fifths of the country's aristocracy became Huguenots. Many probably saw Protestantism as a way to strengthen their authority over their domains. They hoped to establish within France a principle of territorial sovereignty akin to that endorsed for the Holy Roman Empire by the Peace of Augsburg.

The military organization of Condé and Coligny progressively merged with the Huguenot churches. Each side had much to gain from the other. Calvinism provided both a theological justification and a practical motive for political resistance to the Catholic monarchy. Armed strength was essential if Calvinism hoped to become a viable religion in France, but the confluence of secular and religious motives cast suspicion on the sincerity of some Calvinist leaders. Religious conviction was neither the only nor always the main reason for their conversion to Protestantism.

Catherine de Médicis and the Guises

Francis II died in 1560, but his mother, Catherine de Médicis, continued to rule France as regent for her second son, Charles IX (r. 1560–1574). Catherine's first concern was always to preserve the monarchy. Hoping to balance the power of the Guises, she sought allies among the Protestants. In 1562, after conversations with Coligny and Theodore Beza, Calvin's successor, she issued the January Edict. This granted Protestants freedom to hold public worship services outside towns—but only private meetings within them. Royal efforts to promote toleration ended abruptly in March 1562, when the duke of Guise massacred a Protestant congregation at Vassy and began a war with the Huguenots.

Had Condé and the Huguenot armies rushed immediately to the queen's side after this attack, they might have secured an alliance with Catherine, who feared the powerful Guises. But the Protestant leaders hesitated, and the Guises won control of the young king and his mother.

THE PEACE OF SAINT-GERMAIN-EN-LAYE During the first French war of religion (April 1562 to March 1563), the duke of Guise was assassinated. A brief resumption of hostilities from 1567 to 1568 was followed from September 1568 to August 1570 by the bloodiest phase in the conflict. Condé was killed, and Huguenot leadership passed to Coligny, who was far the better military strategist. He negotiated the Peace of Saint-Germain-en-Laye in 1570, which won Huguenots religious freedoms within their territories and the right to fortify their cities.

Queen Catherine tried to survive by balancing the fanatical Huguenot and Guise extremes. Like the Guises, she preferred a Catholic France and tolerated Protestants only as a counter to Guise domination of the monarchy. But after the Peace of Saint-Germain-en-Laye strengthened the Huguenots, Catherine switched sides. She began to plot with the Guises to prevent the Protestants from winning over her son. Catherine had reason to fear Coligny. He was on the verge of persuading the young king to invade the Netherlands to help the Dutch Protestants against their Catholic Habsburg ruler. Such a move would have set France on a collision course with Spain, and Catherine knew that France stood little chance in such a contest.

THE SAINT BARTHOLOMEW'S DAY MASSACRE On August 18, 1572, the French nobility gathered in Paris for the wedding of the king's sister, Marguerite of Valois, to Henry of Navarre, a Huguenot leader. Four days later an attempt was made on Coligny's life. Catherine had apparently been party to a plot by the Guises to eliminate Coligny, and when it failed, she panicked. She feared both the king's reaction to her complicity with the Guises and what the Huguenots and Coligny might do in seeking revenge. In desperation she convinced Charles that a Huguenot coup was afoot and that only the swift execution of the Protestant leaders could save the crown.

On Saint Bartholomew's Day, August 24, 1572, Coligny and 3,000 fellow Huguenots were ambushed in Paris and butchered. Within three

The massacre of worshiping Protestants at Vassy, France (March 1, 1562), which began the French wars of religion. An engraving by an unidentified seventeenth-century artist. The Granger Collection

days an estimated 20,000 Huguenots were executed in coordinated attacks throughout France. Protestants across Europe were horrified, while Pope Gregory XIII and Philip II of Spain greeted the news of the Protestant deaths with special religious celebrations.

Catholics came to regret the slaughter of the French Protestants, for Saint Bartholomew's Day changed the nature of the struggle between Protestants and Catholics everywhere. The disastrous outcome of France's internal squabbling over political power and religious freedom convinced Protestants in many lands that they were engaged in an international war for survival—a fight to the death with an adversary whose cruelty justified any means of resistance.

PROTESTANT RESISTANCE THEORY At the start of the Reformation, Protestants tried to honor the biblical mandate (in Romans 13:1) that directed subjects to obey the rulers God placed over them. Luther only grudgingly approved resistance to Charles V after the emperor ordered Protestants to return to Catholicism in 1530. Calvin, secure in his control of Geneva, had always condemned willful disobedience and rebellion against lawfully constituted governments. But he also taught that lower magistrates, as part of legally

constituted governments, had the duty to oppose higher authorities if these became tyrannical.

An early Calvinist rationale for revolution was developed by John Knox, a Scot driven into exile by the Catholic regent for Scotland, Mary of Guise. Knox's *First Blast of the Trumpet Against the Terrible Regiment of Women* (1558) declared that the removal of a heathen (i.e., Catholic) tyrant was not only permissible but a Christian duty. The Saint Bartholomew's Day massacre persuaded other Calvinists to adopt a similar point of view. François Hotman's *Franco-Gallia* (1573) argued that France's representative assembly, the Estates General, was an authority superior to the crown. Theodore Beza's *On the Right of Magistrates over Their Subjects* (1574) justified the overthrow of tyrants by lower authorities. And Philippe du Plessis Mornay's *Defense of Liberty Against Tyrants* (1579) urged princes, nobles, and magistrates to cooperate in rooting out tyranny in any land where it appeared.

The Rise to Power of Henry of Navarre

Henry III (r. 1574–1589), the last of Henry II's sons to wear the French crown, was caught between the vengeful Huguenots and the radical Catholic League formed in 1576 by Henry of Guise. Like his mother Catherine, Henry sought a middle course and appealed to the neutral Catholics and Huguenots who put the political survival of France above its religious unity. In May 1576, Henry, in the Peace of Beaulieu, promised the Huguenots almost complete religious and civil freedom. The move was premature, for the Catholic League was able to force Henry to reverse himself. In October 1577, the Edict of Poitiers again restricted Huguenots to limited areas.

By the mid-1580s the Catholic League, with Spanish help, was supreme in Paris. In 1588 Henry III launched a surprise attack (known as the "Day of the Barricades") to rout the league. The coup failed, and the king had to flee. News of the English victory over the Spanish Armada then emboldened him to order the assassinations of both the duke and the cardinal of Guise. These murders enraged the Catholic League, which was led by another Guise brother, Charles, duke of Mayenne. By April 1589, the king was left with no choice but to seek an alliance with the Protestant leader, Henry of Navarre, the Bourbon heir to his throne.

As the two Henrys prepared to attack the Guise stronghold in Paris, a fanatical Jacobin friar assassinated Henry III and cleared the way for Henry of Navarre to become King Henry IV (r. 1589–1610) of France. Pope Sixtus V and King Philip II of Spain were aghast at the prospect of France suddenly becoming a Protestant nation. Philip dispatched troops to support the Catholic League and to claim the throne of France for his daughter, Isabella, Henry II's granddaughter.

The threat of Spanish intervention in their affairs rallied the people of France to Henry IV's side and strengthened his hold on the crown. Henry was a popular man who had the wit and charm to neutralize any enemy in a face-to-face meeting. He was also a *politique*, a leader who considered religion less important than peace. Henry concluded that since most of his subjects were Catholics, he could best rule as a Catholic who was committed to protecting Protestants. Consequently, on July 25, 1593, he embraced Catholicism—reputedly claiming that "Paris is worth a Mass." The Huguenots were horrified, and Pope Clement VIII remained skeptical. But the majority of the French people, both clergy and laity, were relieved. They had had enough of war.

The Edict of Nantes

On April 13, 1598, Henry issued the Edict of Nantes to end the civil wars of religion, and on May 2, 1598, the Treaty of Vervins made peace between France and Spain. The Edict of Nantes confirmed a promise of toleration that Henry IV had made the Huguenots at the start of his reign. By granting some religious rights to a dissenting Protestant minority within what was to remain an officially Catholic country, Nantes came close to creating a state within a state. It designated certain towns and territories as places where Huguenots, who by this time numbered well over a million, could openly conduct worship, hold public offices, enter universities, and maintain forts. Nantes was a truce more than a peace. It turned a hot war into a cold one—a war that eventually claimed Henry IV as a victim. In May 1610, he was assassinated by a Catholic fanatic.

Imperial Spain and the Reign of Philip II (r. 1556–1598)

Pillars of Spanish Power

Philip II of Spain dominated international politics for much of the latter half of the sixteenth century.

Bitter experience had led his father, Charles V, to conclude that the Habsburg family lands were too extensive to be governed by one man. He, therefore, divided them between his son and his brother. Philip inherited the intensely Catholic and militarily supreme western half. The eastern portion (Austria, Bohemia, and Hungary) went to Philip's uncle, Emperor Ferdinand I. The imperial title, thereafter, remained with the Austrian Habsburgs.

Philip was a reclusive man who preferred to rule as the remote executive manager of a great national bureaucracy. His character is reflected in the unique residence he built outside Madrid, the Escorial. A combination palace, church, tomb, and monastery, it was a home for a monkish king. Philip was a learned and pious Catholic, a regal ascetic with a powerful sense of duty to his office. He may even have arranged the death of his son Don Carlos (1568), when he concluded that the prince was too mad and treacherous to be entrusted with the power of the crown.

NEW WORLD RICHES Philip's home base was Spain's populous and prosperous district of Castile. The wealth of the New World that flowed through the port of Seville gave Philip great sums with which to fight wars and underwrite international intrigues. Despite this flood of bullion, Philip's expenses exceeded his income. Near the end of his life he destroyed one of Europe's great banks, the house founded by the Fuggers of Augsburg, by defaulting on his loans.

The American wealth that entered Europe through Spain had a dramatic impact on society. Increased prosperity led to increased population. By the early seventeenth century, the towns of France, England, and the Netherlands had tripled and quadrupled in size, and Europe's population had reached about 100 million. Growth in wealth and numbers of consumers triggered inflation—a steady 2 percent a year rise in prices. More people with more currency to spend meant more competition for food and jobs, and that caused prices to double and triple while wages stagnated. This was especially the case in Spain, where the new wealth was concentrated in the hands of a few. Nowhere did the underprivileged suffer more than in Spain. The Castilian peasants, the backbone of Philip II's great empire, were the most heavily taxed people in Europe.

SUPREMACY IN THE MEDITERRANEAN At the start of Philip's reign, his attention focused al-naval battle of the sixteenth century and a clear victory for the Christians. Thirty thousand Turks died and over one-third of the Turkish fleet was sunk or captured. The Mediterranean, for the moment, belonged to Spain.

In 1580 Philip confirmed his dominance of the south by annexing Portugal. This augmented Spanish sea power and brought the magnificent Portuguese overseas empire in Africa, India, and the Americas into the Spanish orbit.

The Revolt in the Netherlands

Philip was far less successful in northern Europe than he was in the Mediterranean, and a rebellion in the Netherlands, the richest district in Europe, set in motion a chain of events that ended Spain's dreams of world empire. The Netherlands was governed for Philip by his half-sister, Margaret of Parma. She was assisted by a council headed by Cardinal Granvelle (1517–1586). Granvelle hoped to check the advance of Protestantism in the Netherlands by promoting church reform. He also planned to reduce the autonomy of the seventeen Netherlands provinces and to create a centralized royal government directed from Madrid. The merchant towns of the Netherlands were, however, accustomed to their independence, and many, such as magnificent Antwerp, had become Calvinist strongholds. Two members of the royal council opposed their Spanish overlords: the Count of Egmont (1522–1568) and William of Nassau, the Prince of Orange (1533–1584), surnamed "the Silent" because of his small circle of confidants.

William of Orange was a *politique* who placed the political autonomy and well-being of the Netherlands above religious creeds. In 1561 he married Anne of Saxony, the daughter of the Lutheran Elector Maurice and the granddaughter of the late Landgrave Philip of Hesse, but he remained a Catholic until his conversion to Lutheranism in 1567. After the Saint Bartholomew's Day massacre in 1572, Orange became a Calvinist.

In 1561 Cardinal Granvelle began an ecclesiastical reorganization of the Netherlands that was intended to tighten the Catholic hierarchy's control over the country and to accelerate its assimilation as a Spanish dependency. Orange and Egmont, with the support of the Dutch nobility, succeeded in engineering Granvelle's removal from office in 1564. But when the aristocrats who took Granvelle's place proved inept at running the government, popular unrest mounted.

Titian's portrait of Philip II of Spain (r. 1556–1598), the most powerful ruler of his time. Alinari/Art Resource, NY

most exclusively on a struggle with the Turks in the Mediterranean. During the 1560s, the Turks had advanced deep into Austria, and their fleets had spread out across the Mediterranean. Between 1568 and 1570, armies under Philip's half-brother, Don John of Austria, the illegitimate son of Charles V, suppressed and dispersed the Moors in Granada. In May 1571, Spain, Venice, and the pope formed the Holy League—again under Don John's command—to counter Turkish maneuvers in the Mediterranean. On October 7, 1571, Don John's fleet engaged the Ottoman navy under Ali Pasha off Lepanto in the Gulf of Corinth. The result was the largest

In 1564 Philip unwisely insisted that the decrees of the Council of Trent be enforced throughout the Netherlands. Opposition materialized under the leadership of William of Orange's younger brother, Louis of Nassau, who had been raised a Lutheran. The Calvinist-inclined lesser nobility and townspeople joined him in a national covenant, the *Compromise*, a solemn pledge to oppose Trent and the Inquisition. In 1566, when Margaret's government spurned the protesters as "beggars," Calvinists rioted, and Louis called for help from French Huguenots and German Lutherans. A full-scale rebellion against the Spanish regency seemed about to erupt.

THE DUKE OF ALBA   A revolt failed to materialize, for the Netherlands' higher nobility were repelled by the behavior of Calvinist extremists and unwilling to join their rebellion. Philip dispatched the duke of Alba to restore order and make an example of the would-be revolutionaries. In 1567 an army of 10,000 was transferred from Milan, and responsibility for the Netherlands was delegated to a special tribunal, the Council of Troubles (as Spain called it) or the Council of Blood (as it was known in the Netherlands). The new government inaugurated a reign of terror. It executed the counts of Egmont and Horn and several thousand suspected heretics, and it imposed high taxes to force the Netherlanders to pay the costs for the suppression of their revolt. Persecution and taxation drove tens of thousands of refugees from the Netherlands during Alba's cruel six-year rule, and the duke came to be more hated than Granvelle or the radical Calvinists.

RESISTANCE AND UNIFICATION   William of Orange, who was an exile in Germany during these turbulent years, now emerged as the leader of an independence movement in the Netherlands. The northern, Calvinist-inclined provinces of Holland, Zeeland, and Utrecht, of which Orange was the *stadholder* (i.e., governor), became his base. Here, as elsewhere, a fight for political independence was combined with a struggle for religious liberty.

The uprising in the Netherlands was a true popular revolt that enlisted all kinds of people. William even endorsed the raids of the "Sea Beggars," an international group of anti-Spanish exiles and criminals who were brazen pirates. In 1572 the Beggars captured Brill and other seaports in Zeeland and Holland. They incited the native popula-

tion to join the rebellion, and resistance spread steadily southward. In 1574 the people of Leiden heroically withstood a long Spanish siege, and the Dutch opened the dikes and flooded their country to repulse the hated Spanish. The faltering Alba had by that time ceded power to Don Luis de Requesens, who replaced him as commander of Spanish forces in the Netherlands in November 1573.

The greatest atrocity of the war followed Requesens's death in 1576. Leaderless and unpaid Spanish mercenaries ran amok in Antwerp on November 4, 1576. Seven thousand people lay dead in the streets as a result of what came to be called "the Spanish Fury." This brief event did more to unify the Netherlanders than all previous appeals to religion and patriotism. The ten largely Catholic southern provinces (approximating modern Belgium) joined the seven largely Protestant northern provinces (roughly the modern Netherlands) in opposing Spain.

The Pacification of Ghent declared the unification of the Netherlands on November 8, 1576. The Netherlanders resolved religious differences by agreeing to a territorial settlement such as the one that the Peace of Augsburg had defined for the Holy Roman Empire in 1555. In January 1577, the last four provinces joined the all-embracing Union of Brussels, and for the next two years the Spanish faced a unified and determined Netherlands.

In November 1576, Don John, the victor over the Turks at Lepanto, took command of Spain's land forces and promptly suffered his first defeat. In February 1577, he signed the Perpetual Edict, a humiliating treaty that promised the removal of all Spanish troops from the Netherlands within twenty days.

The Spanish were, however, nothing if not persistent. The nobility's fear of Calvinist extremism caused a breakup of the Union of Brussels, and Don John and Alessandro Farnese of Parma, the regent Margaret's son, reestablished Spanish control in the southern provinces. In January 1579, the southern provinces formed the Union of Arras and made peace with Spain. The northern provinces responded by organizing the Union of Utrecht.

NETHERLANDS' INDEPENDENCE   Seizing the opportunity to break the back of the Netherlands' resistance, Philip II declared William of Orange an outlaw and placed a bounty of 25,000 crowns on his head. This stiffened the resistance of the northern provinces, and in a famous speech to the Estates General of Holland in December 1580 (the *Apology*),

Orange denounced Philip as a heathen tyrant whom the Netherlands need no longer obey.

On July 22, 1581, most of the northern provinces belonging to the Union of Utrecht formally repudiated Philip's authority and pledged themselves to the French duke of Alençon, Catherine de Médicis's youngest son. Alençon was seen as a compromise between the extremes of Spanish Catholicism and Calvinism, and he was expected to aspire to nothing more than titular authority over the provinces. When he rashly attempted to impose his will on them in 1583, he was deposed and sent back to France.

When William of Orange was assassinated in July 1584, his son, Maurice (1567–1625), became leader of the Dutch resistance. Fortunately for him and his cause, Philip II overextended himself by meddling in the affairs of France and England. Spain's power waned after England defeated Philip's great Armada in 1588. By 1593 the northern provinces had driven out all Spanish soldiers, and in 1596 France and England formally recognized the independence of these provinces. Peace with Spain was concluded in 1609, and full international recognition came in the Peace of Westphalia in 1648.

England and Spain (1553–1603)

Mary I

In an effort to protect England's Reformation, Edward VI (d. 1553) sought to disinherit his Catholic half-sister, Mary Tudor (r. 1553–1558). As heir to his throne he named, not his sister, but his cousin— Lady Jane Grey, a grandniece of Henry VIII's. The people of England felt, however, that Mary was clearly the rightful heir, and they rose up to support her. Jane Grey lost both the crown and her head.

As queen, Mary exceeded the worst fears of the Protestants. Her Parliaments repealed Edward's Protestant statutes and reverted to the strict Catholic religious practice of her father, Henry VIII. She executed as heretics the great Protestant leaders who had served her brother: John Hooper, Hugh Latimer, and Thomas Cranmer. The names of 282 Protestants whom she burned at the stake are recorded. Many others avoided martyrdom by fleeing to the continent. These "Marian exiles" settled in Germany and Switzerland, where they established communities of worship, wrote tracts justifying armed resistance, and waited for the

time when a Protestant counteroffensive could be launched in their homelands. Many absorbed religious beliefs that were much more radical than those they had brought from England.

In 1554 Mary chose a highly unpopular husband, Prince Philip (later King Philip II) of Spain. She favored him because he was the leader of the militant Catholicism that Mary hoped to establish in England, but many of Mary's subjects feared that the marriage would lead to Spain's dominance of England. The politically troublesome marriage was childless, and Mary died knowing that her half-sister, Elizabeth, the daughter of her father's first Protestant marriage, would follow her to the throne.

Elizabeth I

Elizabeth I (r. 1558–1603), the daughter of Henry VIII and Anne Boleyn, was perhaps the most astute politician of the sixteenth century. Assisted by a shrewd adviser, Sir William Cecil (1520–1598), she built a true kingdom on the ruins of Mary's reign. Between 1559 and 1563, she and Cecil guided a religious settlement through Parliament. It merged a centralized episcopal system, which the queen controlled, with broadly defined Protestant doctrine and traditional Catholic ritual. The resulting Anglican church avoided inflexible religious extremes and spared England the religious conflicts that were bloodying continental nations.

CATHOLIC AND PROTESTANT EXTREMISTS   Religious compromises were unacceptable to zealots of both persuasions, and subversive groups worked to undermine Elizabeth. When she ascended the throne, most of her subjects were Catholics. The extremists among them, encouraged by the Jesuits, plotted to replace her with Mary Stuart, Queen of Scots. Unlike Elizabeth, whose father had declared her illegitimate, Mary Stuart had an unblemished claim to the throne inherited from her grandmother Margaret, sister of Henry VIII. Elizabeth responded swiftly to Catholic assassination plots but rarely let emotion override her political instincts. Despite proven cases of Catholic treason and even attempted regicide, she executed fewer Catholics during her forty-five years on the throne than Mary Tudor had executed Protestants during her brief five-year reign.

Elizabeth dealt cautiously with the extreme Protestants—the "Puritans" who wanted to "purify" the national church of every vestige of

Elizabeth I (r. 1558–1603) standing on a map of England in 1592. An astute politician in both foreign and domestic policy, Elizabeth was perhaps the most successful ruler of the sixteenth century. National Portrait Gallery, London

"popery." The Puritans had two major grievances: (1) the retention of Catholic ceremony and vestments within the Church of England, which made it appear to the casual observer that no Reformation had occurred, and (2) the continuation of the episcopal system of governance, which enabled the queen to take the pope's place in dominating the church.

The more extreme Puritans, the Congregationalists, wanted every congregation to be autonomous, a law unto itself, with neither higher episcopal nor presbyterian control. But most sixteenth-century Puritans were not separatists. They campaigned in Parliament for an alternative national church of semiautonomous congregations governed by representative presbyteries (hence, their name "Presbyterians"). Their model was the system Calvin had established in Geneva. Elizabeth conceded nothing that lessened the hierarchical unity of the Church of England and her control over it. The Conventicle Act of 1593 gave separatists

the option of either conforming to the practices of the Church of England or facing exile or death.

DETERIORATION OF RELATIONS WITH SPAIN   Despite the sincerest desires on the part of both Philip II and Elizabeth to avoid a direct confrontation, events led inexorably to war between England and Spain. In 1567, when the Spanish duke of Alba marched his army into the Netherlands, many in England feared that Spain intended to use the Netherlands as a base for an invasion of England. In 1570 Pope Pius V (1566–1572) branded Elizabeth a heretic and proposed a military expedition to recover England for Catholicism. His mischievous act only complicated a difficult situation.

Following Don John's demonstration of Spain's awesome sea power at the battle of Lepanto in 1571, England signed a mutual defense pact with France. Throughout the 1570s, Elizabeth's famous seamen, John Hawkins (1532–1595) and Sir Francis Drake (1545?–1596), preyed on Spanish shipping in the Americas. Drake's circumnavigation of the globe between 1577 and 1580 was one in a series of dramatic demonstrations of England's growing ascendancy on the high seas.

The Saint Bartholomew's Day Massacre forced a change in Elizabeth's foreign policy. Protestants in France and the Netherlands appealed to her as their only protector. In 1585 she signed the Treaty of Nonsuch, which sent English soldiers to the Netherlands. Funds she had previously funneled covertly to Henry of Navarre's army in France now flowed openly. These developments strained relations between England and Spain, but the event that brought on war was Elizabeth's decision to execute Mary, Queen of Scots (1542–1587).

MARY, QUEEN OF SCOTS   Mary Stuart, the daughter of King James V of Scotland and Mary of Guise, had resided in France from the time she was six years old—training for her role as the future wife of King Francis II. The death of her young husband in 1561 sent Mary back to Scotland to rule a land she barely knew. A year earlier, a fervent Protestant Reformation had won legal recognition in the Treaty of Edinburgh. Mary, who had been raised a Catholic in France, had no sympathy with Scotland's new religion or with its dour morality. She wanted to replicate in Scotland the gaiety and sophistication of French court life.

John Knox, the leader of the Scottish Reformation, railed openly about the queen's private Mass and Catholic practices (which Scottish law made capital offenses for everyone else). Although Queen Elizabeth personally despised Knox, she recognized that his defense of Protestantism served her foreign policy. It limited Mary's ability to persuade the Scots to cooperate with France against England.

In 1568 a scandal cost Mary her throne. Mary had married Lord Darnley, a youth with connections to the royal houses of both England and Scotland. She had a son by him (the James who was eventually to inherit both Scotland and England), but Darnley proved an impossible husband. Mary reputedly took the earl of Bothwell as her lover, and he, allegedly, murdered Darnley. Acquitted of this crime, Bothwell abducted Mary and married her. This amounted to usurpation of the throne. Outraged Protestant nobles forced Mary to abdicate in favor of her infant son and to flee Scotland.

Mary unwisely entered England seeking refuge from her cousin Elizabeth. Elizabeth distrusted Mary, for in the opinion of Catholics, Mary had the superior claim to the English throne. Elizabeth, therefore, held Mary under house arrest—for nineteen years. In 1583 Elizabeth's vigilant secretary, Sir Francis Walsingham, uncovered a plot against Elizabeth involving the Spanish ambassador Bernardino de Mendoza. In 1586 Walsingham exposed still another Spanish scheme to unseat Elizabeth, and this time he had proof of Mary's involvement. Elizabeth was loath to execute Mary. She feared that such an act would diminish the aura of divine right that was one of the props of monarchy, and she knew that it would raise a storm of protest among Catholics. In the end, however, she concluded that she had no choice, and Mary was beheaded on February 18, 1587. Mary's death dashed Catholic hopes for a bloodless reconversion of England and persuaded Philip II that the time had come for a military assault on the Protestant nation.

THE ARMADA   Spain's preparations for war were interrupted in the spring of 1587 by the successful raids Sir Francis Drake led on the port city of Cadiz and the coast of Portugal. These strikes forced Philip to postpone his invasion of England until the spring of 1588.

On May 30, 1588, the ill-fated armada of 130 ships, bearing 25,000 sailors and soldiers under the command of the duke of Medina-Sidonia, set to sea. The barges that were to transport Spanish soldiers from their galleons onto England's shores were prevented from leaving Calais and Dunkirk to rendezvous with the fleet. While the Spanish vessels waited, an "English wind" sprang up and helped the swifter English and Dutch ships scatter the Spanish forces.

Spain never fully recovered from this defeat, and by the time of Philip's death on September 13, 1598, its armies had suffered reversals on all fronts. Philip's successors, Philip III (r. 1598–1621), Philip IV (r. 1621–1665), and Charles II (r. 1665–1700), were all inadequate men. They allowed the French to emerge as the leading continental power and the Dutch and English to nibble away at Spain's empire.

When Elizabeth died on March 23, 1603, she left behind a strong nation poised on the brink of acquiring a global empire. Since Elizabeth had never married (choosing instead to use the hope of winning her hand as a tool for English diplomacy), her death ended the Tudor dynasty. Ironically, her heir, James I of England, was Mary's son, James VI of Scotland.

The Thirty Years' War (1618–1648)

The Thirty Years' War in the Holy Roman Empire was the last and most destructive of the wars of religion, and it was unusually devastating. Religious passions escalated to the point where the combatants seemed willing to sacrifice everything in pursuit of victories that were increasingly less worth winning. Virtually every major European land was drawn into the conflict. When the hostilities ended in 1648, the agreements among the victorious nations shaped the map of northern Europe as we know it today.

Preconditions for War

FRAGMENTED GERMANY   In the second half of the sixteenth century, Germany was a collection of about 360 autonomous political entities: secular principalities (duchies, landgraviates, and marches), ecclesiastical principalities (archbishoprics, bishoprics, and abbeys), free cities, and regions dominated by knights with castles. The Peace of Augsburg (1555) had given each a degree of sovereignty within its borders. Since each levied its own tolls and tariffs and coined its own money, travel and trade were difficult. Many little states also had pretensions that exceeded their powers.

During the Thirty Years' War, Germany, which was Europe's crossroads, became Europe's stomping ground. The great conflict had many causes. Most stemmed from a fear of German unification. The Council of Trent raised Protestant suspicions about an imperial-papal conspiracy to use the Holy Roman Empire to restore Catholic dominance throughout Europe. The imperial diet, which was controlled by the German magnates, was leery of any attempt to consolidate the empire at the expense of the liberties of the territorial princes. It countered every move by the emperor to impose his will in the empire, and individual German rulers called on allies outside of Germany for help in defending their rights. Allies were eager to help, for even the Catholic nations of Europe feared what might happen to the balance of power if Germany was brought under the control of a Catholic emperor.

RELIGIOUS DIVISION   By 1600, there may have been slightly more Protestants than Catholics in the Holy Roman Empire. The territorial principle proclaimed by the Peace of Augsburg in 1555 was designed to freeze Lutherans and Catholics in place by forcing each territory to declare its faith. But as time passed, there were troublesome shifts of jurisdiction. Lutherans gained control in some Catholic areas and Catholics in a few places designated as Lutheran. Lutherans were more suc-

cessful in securing rights to worship in Catholic lands than Catholics were in securing such rights from Lutherans. Catholic rulers who had been weakened by the Reformation had no choice but to make concessions to Protestant communities within their territories, and these Protestant enclaves became constant sources of tension. Protestants were also reluctant to enforce the "Ecclesiastical Reservation" provision of the Peace of Augsburg, which called for the restoration to Catholic control of ecclesiastical property in places where rulers converted to Protestantism.

Protestant and Catholic antipathies were not the only sources of religious strife. Warring factions emerged among Protestants in the second half of the sixteenth century. Liberal and conservative branches of Lutheranism opposed each other, and Calvinists failed to come to terms with either of these.

Calvinism had not been recognized as a legal religion by the Peace of Augsburg, but it won a foothold in the empire when Frederick III (r. 1559–1576), Elector Palatine (ruler within the Palatinate), made it the official religion of his domain. His royal city of Heidelberg became the German "Geneva," an intellectual center for Calvinism and a staging area for Calvinist penetration of the empire. The Lutherans came to fear the Calvinists almost as much as they did the Catholics, for the bold missionary forays of the Palatine Calvinists threatened

MAP 12–1   RELIGIOUS DIVISIONS ABOUT 1600   *By 1600, with the exception of Spain and southern Italy, which remained thoroughly Catholic, large religious minorities had rooted themselves in almost every European state.*

to undo what the Peace of Augsburg had done to stabilize the empire. Some Lutherans were also shocked by outspoken Calvinist criticism of their doctrines (e.g., Lutheran faith in Christ's real presence in the Eucharist).

Like the Calvinists, the Jesuits also undermined the Peace of Augsburg. Catholic Bavaria, led by Duke Maximilian and supported by Spain, did for the Counter-Reformation what the Palatinate did for Calvinism. Jesuit missionaries, operating from Bavaria, returned major cities (e.g., Strasbourg and Osnabrück) to the Catholic fold. In 1609 Maximilian organized a Catholic League to counter a Protestant alliance formed in the same year by the Calvinist Elector Palatine, Frederick IV (r. 1583–1610). The army the league assembled under the command of Count Johann von Tilly tipped Germany into war.

Four Periods of War

THE BOHEMIAN PERIOD (1618–1625)

The war broke out in Bohemia after the ascent to the Bohemian throne in 1618 of Ferdinand, Habsburg archduke of Styria and heir to the empire. Ferdinand, who had been educated by Jesuits, was determined to restore Catholicism to the Habsburg lands. No sooner had he become king of Bohemia than he revoked the religious freedoms of Bohemia's Protestants. The Protestant nobility responded in May 1618 by literally throwing his regents out a window—an event known as the "defenestration of Prague." A year later, when Ferdinand (II) became Holy Roman Emperor, the Bohemians refused to recognize his jurisdiction and declared their allegiance to the Calvinist Elector Palatine, Frederick V (r. 1616–1623).

The Bohemian revolt escalated into an international war. Spain, Maximilian of Bavaria, and the Lutheran Elector John George I of Saxony (r. 1611–1656)—who saw a chance to expand his domains at the expense of the Calvinist Elector Palatine—sided with Ferdinand. Tilly, the empire's general, routed Frederick V's troops at the Battle of White Mountain in 1620, and by 1622 Ferdinand had subdued Bohemia and conquered the Palatinate. As the remnants of Frederick's army retreated north, Duke Maximilian of Bavaria followed—claiming land as he went.

THE DANISH PERIOD (1625–1629)

Maximilian's forays into northwestern Germany raised fears of a Catholic consolidation of the empire. Christian IV (r. 1588–1648), the Lutheran king of Denmark and duke of the German duchy of Holstein, was urged by the English, French, and Dutch to undertake the defense of Protestantism. He invaded Germany in 1626 but was quickly forced to retreat by Duke Maximilian.

Fearing Maximilian's growing power, Emperor Ferdinand turned the conduct of the war over to a mercenary whom he had employed against the Bohemians, Albrecht of Wallenstein (1583–1634). A brilliant and ruthless military strategist, Wallenstein became a law unto himself, but he so effectively broke the back of Protestant resistance that Ferdinand was able to issue an Edict of Restitution in 1629. It outlawed Calvinism and ordered

The horror of the Thirty Years' War is captured in this painting by Jan Brueghel (1568–1625) and Sebastien Vranx (1573–1647). During the breaks in fighting, marauding armies ravaged the countryside, destroying villages and massacring the rural population. Kunsthistorisches Museum, Vienna

MAP 12–2 THE HOLY ROMAN EMPIRE ABOUT 1618 *On the eve of the Thirty Years' War, the empire was thoroughly fragmented. Lutherans dominated the north, Catholics the south, and Calvinists controlled the United Provinces, the Palatinate, Brandenburg, and parts of Switzerland.*

the surrender to Catholics of all church lands acquired by the Lutherans since 1552. Compliance would have meant Protestant concession of sixteen bishoprics and twenty-eight cities and towns to Catholic governors. The edict struck panic in the hearts of the Habsburgs' opponents and reignited resistance.

THE SWEDISH PERIOD (1630–1635) Gustavus Adolphus of Sweden (r. 1611–1632), a deeply pious Lutheran monarch and a military genius, took up the gauntlet for Protestantism. He was handsomely bankrolled by two very interested bystanders: Cardinal Richelieu, the minister of the Catholic king of France who wanted to prevent a powerful Habsburg empire from materializing on France's border; and the Dutch—long-standing Protestant opponents of the Habsburgs. The Swedish king won a stunning victory at Breitenfeld in 1630 that suddenly reversed the course of the war. The battle was significant, but far from final–and the Protestant cause faltered when Gustavus Adolphus died fighting Wallenstein's forces at the Battle of Lützen in November 1632. Two years later Ferdinand arranged for Wallenstein, who had outlived his usefulness, to be assassinated. The German Protestant states then reached a compromise agreement with Ferdinand (the Peace of Prague of 1635). But when the Swedes (with encouragement

from France and the Netherlands) refused to join them, hostilities resumed.

THE SWEDISH-FRENCH PERIOD (1635–1648) The French openly entered the war in 1635 and prolonged it for thirteen more years. French, Swedish, and Spanish soldiers looted the length and breadth of Germany. The Germans, who were too disunited to repulse the foreign armies, simply watched and suffered. By the time peace talks began in the Westphalian cities of Münster and Osnabrück in 1644, an estimated one-third of the German population had died. It was the worst catastrophe in Europe since the Black Death of the fourteenth century.

The Treaty of Westphalia

The Treaty of Westphalia ended hostilities in 1648 by ensuring the continued fragmentation of Germany. The territorial principle proclaimed by the Peace of Augsburg in 1555 was reasserted to confirm rulers in their right to determine the religions of their subjects. Calvinism was added to the list of legal religious options, and the German princes were acknowledged supreme over their principalities. Bavaria was elevated to the rank of an elector state, and Brandenburg-Prussia emerged as the most powerful north German

Legend:
- Swedish Dominions
- Brandenburg Prussia
- Spanish Monarchy
- Austria Habsburg
- Church Lands
- Boundary of the Empire

MAP 12–3 EUROPE IN 1648 At the end of the Thirty Years' War, Spain still had extensive possessions, Austria and Brandenburg-Prussia were prominent, the United Provinces and Switzerland were recognized as independent, and Sweden held important north German ports.

239

principality. The independence of the Swiss Confederacy and of the United Provinces of Holland, long a fact, was proclaimed in law. France also acquired considerable territory.

War between France and Spain continued outside the empire until 1659, when the French forced the Spanish to accept the humiliating Treaty of the Pyrenees. Germany's fragmentation and Spain's humbling left victorious France the dominant power in Europe. The competitive nationalisms of the modern world are rooted in these religious conflicts of the seventeenth century.

In Perspective

Politics, as well as religion, contributed to the great conflicts of the Age of Religious Wars: France's civil strife, Spain's struggle with the Netherlands, England's resistance to Spain, and the devastation of Germany by a consortium of European powers. But neither religion nor politics alone explains the course of the wars. The religious differences that occasioned a war were sometimes ignored in pursuit of political objectives shared by Catholics and Protestants, and wars ended with agreements to disagree—with the recognition of minority religious rights and a guarantee of the traditional boundaries of political sovereignty. The result was that at midcentury Europe had a real but unsustainable peace.

REVIEW QUESTIONS

1. What part did politics play in the religious positions adopted by France's leaders? How did the French king (or his regent) decide which side to favor? What led to the infamous Saint Bartholomew's Day Massacre? What did it achieve?
2. How did Spain acquire the dominant position in Europe in the sixteenth century? What were its strengths and weaknesses as a nation? What were Philip II's goals? Which did he fail to achieve? Why?
3. What made a leader a *politique?* How well does the term describe Henry of Navarre (Henry IV of France), Elizabeth I, and William of Orange?
4. What changes occurred in the religious policies of England's government in the process of establishing the Anglican church? What were Mary I's political objectives? What was Elizabeth I's "settlement"? How was it imposed on England? Who were her opponents? What were their criticisms of her?
5. Why was the Thirty Years' War fought? Could matters have been resolved without war? To what extent did politics determine the outcome of the war? What were the terms and objectives of the Treaty of Westphalia?
6. Was, as some have claimed, the Thirty Years' War "the outstanding example in European history of meaningless conflict"?

SUGGESTED READINGS

F. BRAUDEL, *The Mediterranean and the Mediterranean World in the Age of Philip the Second*, vols. 1 and 2 (1976). Widely acclaimed work of a French master historian.

R. DUNN, *The Age of Religious Wars, 1559–1689* (1979). Excellent brief survey of every major conflict.

P. GEYL, *The Revolt of the Netherlands, 1555–1609* (1958). The authoritative survey.

J. GUY, *Tudor England* (1990). A standard history and good synthesis of recent scholarship.

C. HAIGH, *Elizabeth I* (1988). Elizabeth portrayed as a magnificent politician and propagandist.

J. LYNCH, *Spain under the Hapsburg I: 1516–1598* (1964). Political narrative.

G. PARKER, *Europe in Crisis, 1598–1648* (1979). The big picture at a gallop.

J. H. M. SALMON, *Society in Crisis: France in the Sixteenth Century* (1976). Standard narrative account.

K. THOMAS, *Religion and the Decline of Magic* (1971). Provocative, much-acclaimed work focused on popular culture.

J. WORMALD, *Mary, Queen of Scots: A Study in Failure* (1991). Mary portrayed as a queen who did not understand her country and was out of touch with the times.

Chapter 13
Paths to Constitutionalism and Absolutism: England and France in the Seventeenth Century

KEY TOPICS

- The factors behind the divergent political paths taken by England and France in the seventeenth century
- The conflict between Parliament and the king over taxation and religion in early Stuart England, the English Civil War, and the abolition of the monarchy
- The Restoration of the English monarchy and the development of Parliament's supremacy over the throne after the "Glorious Revolution"
- The establishment of an absolutist monarchy in France under Louis XIV
- Religious policies of Louis XIV
- The wars of Louis XIV

During the seventeenth century, England and France evolved contrasting political systems. England became a parliamentary monarchy with a policy of religious toleration. France developed an absolutist, highly centralized monarchy that enforced religious conformity. Both systems defy simple description. English monarchs did not share all power with Parliament, and the kings of France were not free of all institutional or customary restraints on their authority.

Two Models of European Political Development

In the second half of the sixteenth century, changes in military technology sharply increased the cost of warfare and forced governments to look for new sources of revenue. Monarchs who, like France's kings, developed sources of income that were not controlled by nobles or by assemblies representing their wealthy subjects achieved absolute power. In places such as England, where rulers had insufficient funds and limited powers of taxation, royal authority was compromised. Kings had to negotiate policy with groups on which they depended for financial support.

The contrast between the French and English political systems was visible by the end of the seventeenth century, but not in 1603 when England's Elizabeth I died. The much revered queen had broad support, and Parliaments met during her reign only to approve taxes. The Stuart kings who succeeded to Elizabeth's throne had a different experience. They pursued fiscal and religious policies that alienated their nation's propertied classes and united them against the crown.

Elizabeth's contemporary, Henry IV (r. 1589–1610) of France, struggled with a divided nation emerging from the turmoil of religious war. His successor, Louis XIII (r. 1610–1643), began to reassert the crown's authority, and in the second half of the seventeenth century, Louis XIV brought the French nobles under control. The aristocratic *Parlement* of Paris won the right to register royal decrees to give them the authority of law, and the king allowed regional *parlements* considerable latitude to deal with local issues. But when the nobles discovered that a strong king was a source of patronage and a guardian of their privileged place in society, they lost interest in organizing anything resembling England's Parliament. An Estates General had developed in France in the late Middle Ages, but once the monarchy won control over taxation, there was little reason for it to meet. No sessions were held from 1614 until the eve of the French Revolution in 1789.

Constitutional Crisis and Settlement in Stuart England

James I

When the childless Elizabeth died in 1603, no one contested the right of James VI of Scotland (the son of Mary Stuart, Queen of Scots) to claim her throne and become James I of England. But a formidable task lay ahead of him. As a Scot, James was an outsider who had no native constituency to help him deal with England's religious factions and substantial national debt. James's advocacy of the divine right of kings, a subject on which he had written a book *(A Trew Law of Free Monarchies)* in 1598, also set him on a collision course with English tradition.

England's Parliament, the country's chief check on royal power, met only when summoned by the monarch to authorize tax levies. James hoped to develop alternative resources that would enable him to fund his government without calling Parliament. Relying on the authority of ill-defined privileges that he alleged were royal prerogatives, James created new customs duties called *impositions*. Members of Parliament resented these, but they preferred to wrangle and negotiate behind the scenes rather than risk serious confrontation.

Religious problems added to political tensions during James's reign. Puritans within the Church of England had hoped that James's upbringing as a Scottish Presbyterian would dispose him to support the reformation of the English church. They wanted to eliminate elaborate priestly rituals and end government of the church by bishops—establishing in their places simple services of worship and congregations run by presbyters elected by the people. James, however, had no intention of using his national church to promote representative government, which he regarded as an infringement on the divine right of kings.

In January 1604, James responded to a list of Puritan grievances (the so-called Millenary Petition) by pledging to maintain and even enhance the Anglican episcopacy. As he explained: "A Scottish presbytery agreeth as well with monarchy as God and the devil. No bishops, no king." James did, however, accept the Protestant demand for the use of vernacular Scriptures, and in 1611 the royal commission he appointed issued an eloquent new translation of the Bible. For generations the Authorized (i.e., King James) Version remained the standard English text.

James had no sympathy with the moral agenda implicit in English Puritanism. The recreations and sports of which the Puritans disapproved were, to the king, innocent activities that were good for people. James also believed that Puritan rigidity about such things discouraged Roman Catholics from converting to the Church of England. Consequently, in l618 James tried to force a change by ordering the clergy to read his *Book of Sports*—a royal decree that legalized playing games on Sunday—from their pulpits. When they refused, he backed down.

James's lifestyle also seemed designed to give offense to the Puritans, for the royal court was a center of scandal and corruption. James was strongly influenced by a few court favorites, the most powerful of whom, the duke of Buckingham, was rumored to be the king's homosexual lover. Buckingham controlled royal patronage and openly sold peerages and titles to the highest bidders. There had always been royal favorites, but never before had a single person so controlled access to England's monarch.

Disappointment and disgust with James led some Puritans voluntarily to leave England for the New World. In 1620 Puritan separatists founded Plymouth Colony in Cape Cod Bay. Later in the same decade another larger and better-financed group founded the Massachusetts Bay Colony.

In addition to James's domestic policy, his conduct of foreign affairs also roused opposition. James preferred peace to war, for he feared that wars would generate debts that would force him to beg assistance from Parliament. The treaty he signed with Spain in 1604 was long overdue, but some of his subjects viewed it as evidence of his pro-Catholic sentiments. Their suspicions increased when the king tried unsuccessfully to relax the penal laws against Catholics. The situation further deteriorated in 1618, when James wisely hesitated to rush English troops to the aid of German Protestants in the Thirty Years'

War—and when he suggested that his son Charles marry the Infanta, the daughter of the king of Spain.

As James aged and his health failed, the reins of government passed to Charles (and to Buckingham), and parliamentary opposition and Protestant sentiment combined to undo his pro-Spanish foreign policy. The marriage alliance was rejected, and in 1624, shortly before James's death, Parliament pushed England into a war with Spain.

Charles I governed England from 1625 to 1649. His attempts to establish an absolutist government in matters of both church and state provoked clashes with the English Parliament and the outbreak of the Civil War in 1642. He was executed in 1649. Daniel Mytens/The Granger Collection

Charles I

Although Parliament supported war with Spain, distrust of Buckingham undercut its willingness to finance the venture. This forced Charles I (r. 1625–1649), with the help of the unpopular Buckingham, to pursue the same fiscal strategy as his father. Without consulting parliament, he imposed new tariffs and duties, collected discontinued taxes, and subjected people of property (under threat of imprisonment) to the "forced loayn"—a tax that the government, theoretically, was supposed eventually to refund. Soldiers in transit to war zones were also quartered in English homes.

When Parliament met in 1628, its members were furious. They refused to acquiesce to the king's request for funds unless he agreed to abide by terms they set forth in a Petition of Right: (1) no more forced loans or taxation without the consent of Parliament, (2) no imprisonment of citizens without due cause, and (3) an end to billeting troops in private homes. Though Charles promised what was demanded, Parliament did not trust him to keep his word.

YEARS OF PERSONAL RULE In August 1628, Buckingham, Charles's chief minister, was assassinated. Although his death caused some rejoicing, it was not enough to reconcile king and Parliament. In January 1629, Parliament issued more decrees critical of the king. The levying of taxes without parliamentary consent and Charles's high-church policies were declared acts of treason. Charles responded by dissolving Parliament, and it did not reconvene until a war with Scotland created a fiscal crisis in 1640.

Without funds from Parliament, Charles could not continue his foreign wars. But when he made peace with France in 1629 and Spain in 1630, some of his subjects accused him of wanting to strengthen his ties with Roman Catholic nations. Many Protestant leaders feared that Catholics were establishing ascendancy over their king. Charles had wed a French princess whose marriage contract gave her the right to hear Mass daily at the English court. Charles also favored a movement within the Church of England (the Arminians) that opposed some Puritan doctrines and advocated elaborate services of worship.

To allow Charles to rule without having to negotiate with Parliament for money, the king's chief minister, Thomas Wentworth, earl of Stafford (after 1640), instituted the policy of *thorough*. This was a plan to establish absolute royal control over England by promoting strict efficiency and administrative centralization. Toward this end, Charles's men exploited every legal fund-raising device. They enforced previously neglected laws and extended existing taxes into new areas. Charles won challenges to his policies in the courts but at the cost of alienating the propertied men who would sit in any future Parliament he might be forced to call.

During his years of personal rule, Charles lived expensively. He surrounded himself with an elaborate court and patronized some of the greatest artists of the day. Like his father, he sold titles of nobility to raise money—and to diminish the prestige of the aristocracy. Nobles and great landowners, who saw their fortunes, their local influence, and their social standing diminishing, began to fear that Charles would avoid ever having to call another Parliament.

Charles might have ruled indefinitely without Parliament had he not departed from the tolerant example set by his father and tried to impose religious conformity within England and Scotland. William Laud (1573–1645), Charles's religious adviser and archbishop of Canterbury (after 1633), encouraged the king's preference for high-church Anglicanism. This "Anglo-Catholicism" favored a state-supported church with a powerful episcopacy and elaborate liturgies instead of the preaching-centered worship of the Puritans. In 1637 Charles and Laud, over objections by English Puritans and the Scots, attempted to impose the English episcopal system and prayer book on Scotland. The Scots rebelled, and Charles, having insufficient resources for a war, had to convene Parliament.

The members of Parliament were in the peculiar position of wanting to oppose their king's policies while crushing the rebellion against him. Led by John Pym (1584–1643), they refused to discuss funding for the war until Charles agreed to redress their list of grievances. The king responded by dissolving what came, for obvious reasons, to be known as the Short Parliament (April–May 1640). However, when the Presbyterian Scots invaded England and defeated an English army at the Battle of Newburn in the summer of 1640, Charles had no choice but to recall Parliament on its own terms for a long, fateful session.

THE LONG PARLIAMENT   The landowners and the merchant classes whom Parliament represented resented the king's financial exactions and paternalistic rule. Those who were Puritans also disliked his religious policies. The Long Parliament (1640–1660), therefore, enjoyed support from many important factions.

The House of Commons began by impeaching the king's chief advisers, the earl of Stafford and Archbishop Laud. (Stafford was executed for treason in 1641 and Laud in 1645.) Parliament then abolished the instruments the king used to implement the political and religious policy of *thorough,* the Court of Star Chamber and the Court of High Commission. The levying of new taxes without consent of Parliament was declared illegal, and Parliament declared itself a permanent branch of England's government. It claimed that it could not be dissolved without its own consent and that no more than three years could elapse between its meetings.

Members of Parliament were united on the subject of curtailing the powers of the monarchy but divided on the issue of religious reform. Moderate Puritans (Presbyterians) and extreme Puritans (Independents) wanted to abolish the episcopal system and end use of the *Book of Common Prayer.* The Presbyterian majority also hoped to impose a Calvinist system in which the church would be governed by presbyteries, committees composed of representatives from local congregations. The Independents wanted a radical decentralization of the church that would allow each congregation to govern itself. A considerable number of conservatives in both houses of Parliament, however, did not want any changes at all.

These divisions intensified in October 1641, when a rebellion erupted in Ireland and Parliament was asked to raise funds for a royal army to suppress it. Pym and his followers argued that Charles could not be trusted with an army and that Parliament should take command of England's armed forces. Conservatives in Parliament were appalled at the thought of such a radical departure from tradition.

ERUPTION OF CIVIL WAR   Charles saw the division within Parliament as a chance to regain the upper hand. On December 1, 1641, Parliament presented him with the Grand Remonstrance, a summary of over 200 grievances against the crown. In January 1642, he responded by sending soldiers into Parliament to arrest Pym and other leaders. When they escaped, Charles withdrew from London and began to raise an army against Parliament. The House of Commons hastened to pass the Militia Ordinance, giving Parliament authority to raise its own army, and for the next four years (1642–1646) civil war engulfed England.

The royal forces, the Cavaliers, were based in the northwestern half of England. They fought for a strong monarchy and an Anglican church presided over by bishops. Their parliamentary opponents, the Roundheads (so-called from their unfashionable short haircuts), had their stronghold in the southeastern half of the country. They wanted parliamentary government and a decentralized church with a presbyterian government.

Oliver Cromwell and the Puritan Republic

Two things contributed to Parliament's victory. The first was an alliance struck between Parliament and Scotland in 1643. It was made possible by Parliament's acceptance of the Scots' presbyterian system of church government. The second was the reorganization of the parliamentary army under Oliver Cromwell (1599–1658), a middle-aged country squire who favored the Independents. Cromwell and his "godly men" wanted neither the king's episcopal system nor the presbyterian organization endorsed by Parliament's Solemn League and Covenant with Scotland. The only established state church they would accept was one that granted freedom of worship to Protestant dissenters.

In 1644 Parliament won the largest engagement of the war, the Battle of Marston Moor, and in June 1645, Cromwell's newly reorganized and fanatical forces, the New Model Army, defeated the king at Naseby. Charles tried to exploit the divisions within Parliament by winning the Presbyterians and the Scots over to his side, but Cromwell foiled him. In December 1648, Colonel Thomas Pride used Cromwell's soldiers to prevent the Presbyterians, who had a majority in Parliament, from taking their seats. After "Pride's Purge," only a "rump" of fewer than fifty members remained. This Rump Parliament was dominated by Independents who did not shy away from bold action. On January 30, 1649, after trial by a special court, the Rump Parliament executed the king and abolished the monarchy, the House of Lords, and the Anglican Church. Civil war had become revolution.

From 1649 to 1660 England was officially a Puritan republic. In reality, Cromwell ruled. On the military front, his achievements were impressive. His army conquered Ireland and Scotland and unified what we know today as Great Britain. Cromwell was, however, a much better general than a politician. He was easily frustrated by the necessity of working with the dawdling members of Parliament. When in 1653 the House of Commons entertained a motion to disband his expensive army of 50,000 men, he marched in and disbanded Parliament.

Calling himself "Lord Protector," Cromwell established a military dictatorship that had minimal popular support. His army and foreign ad-

ventures cost taxpayers three times what they had owed to Charles's government, and he was still unable to prevent near chaos from erupting in many parts of England. Commerce suffered, and people chafed under Cromwell's rigorous enforcement of Puritan codes of conduct. The Lord Protector was as intolerant of Anglicans as the king had been of Puritans.

Cromwell failed to build a political system that provided a workable alternative to the monarchy and Parliament. He tried various arrangements, none of which succeeded. By the time he died in 1658, a majority of the English were ready to end the Puritan republican experiments and return to traditional institutions of government. In 1660 the exiled Charles II (r. 1660–1685), son of Charles I, was invited home to restore the Stuart monarchy.

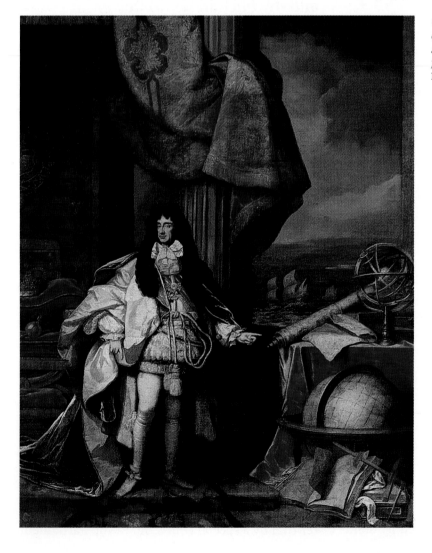

Charles II (r. 1660–1685) was a person of considerable charm and political skill. Here he is portrayed as the founder of the Royal Society. Robert Harding Picture Library

Charles II and the Restoration of the Monarchy

Charles II, a man of considerable charm and political skill, ascended the throne amid great rejoicing, and England returned to the institutions it had abandoned in 1642: a hereditary monarchy that had no obligation to consult with Parliaments, and an Anglican Church with bishops and an official prayer book. Since Charles had secret Catholic sympathies, he favored a policy of religious toleration—which was the best that Catholics could hope for in England. Few in Parliament, however, believed that patriotism and religion could be separated. Between 1661 and 1665, Parliament enacted the Clarendon Code, which excluded Roman Catholics, Presbyterians, and Independents from religious and political offices. Penalties were also imposed for attending non-Anglican worship services. Adherence to the *Book of Common Prayer* and the *Thirty-nine Articles* (the Anglican Church's statement of faith) was demanded, and oaths of allegiance to the Church of England were required of persons who wished to serve in local government. Charles also tried to tighten his grip on the rich English colonies in North America and the Caribbean, many of which had been developed by separatists who wanted independence from English rule.

Charles's foreign policy was dominated by a series of naval wars with Holland that were caused by England's Navigation Acts. These acts required that goods brought to England be carried either in English ships or in ships registered to the country in which their cargo originated. Since Dutch vessels carried goods from many nations, this was a direct attack on Holland's shipping industry. In 1670 Charles allied with the French, who were also at war with Holland, and received French aid to underwrite the cost of his campaign. In exchange for the promise of a substantial subsidy from Louis XIV of France, Charles also secretly pledged to announce, at some propitious moment, his conversion to Catholicism. The time to fulfill that pledge never came.

To unite the English people behind the war with Holland and to show good faith with Louis XIV, Charles issued a Declaration of Indulgence (1672) that suspended all laws against Roman Catholics and Protestant nonconformists. But again, Parliament blocked the king's efforts to promote religious tolerance by refusing to grant money for the war until Charles rescinded the Declaration. Parliament then passed the Test Act, which excluded Roman Catholics from public office by requiring all royal officials to swear an oath repudiating the doctrine of transubstantiation.

The Test Act was aimed in large measure at the king's brother, James, duke of York, heir to the throne and a recent, devout convert to Catholicism. In 1678 a notorious liar, Titus Oates, accused Charles's Catholic wife of plotting with Jesuits and Irishmen to kill her husband and bring his Catholic brother to the throne. Parliament was caught up in the hysteria of Oates's alleged "Popish Plot." Several people were executed, and a faction in Parliament, the Whigs, nearly won passage for a bill excluding James from the succession.

Chronically short of money and having little hope of adequate grants from Parliament, Charles II increased customs duties and extracted more financial aid from Louis XIV. This allowed him to avoid convening a Parliament after 1681. By the time of his death in 1685 (following a deathbed conversion to Catholicism), he had cowed his opponents and positioned James to call a Parliament filled with royal friends.

James II and Renewed Fears of a Catholic England

James II (r. 1685–1688) did not know how to use his opportunities. He alienated Parliament by insisting on the repeal of the Test Act. When Parliament balked, he dissolved it and flaunted the Test Act by openly appointing known Catholics to high offices. In 1687 he issued a Declaration of Indulgence that suspended religious tests and permitted free worship. Candidates for Parliament who opposed the Declaration were evicted by the king's soldiers and replaced by Catholics. In June 1688, James imprisoned seven Anglican bishops who had refused to publicize his suspension of laws against Catholics.

James's policy of toleration was actually a drive to bring England under tighter royal control. His goal was absolutism, and even conservative, loyalist "Tories" (as the monarchy's allies were called) could not abide this. The English had reason to fear that James hoped to establish in England the kind of monarchy that Louis XIV had created in France. (In the year James came to the throne Louis had revoked the Edict of Nantes and used soldiers to suppress Protestant worship in France.)

A birth galvanized James's enemies into action against him. They had hoped that he would die without a male heir and that the throne would pass to Mary, his eldest daughter. She was a Protestant and the wife of William III of Orange, *stadtholder* of the Protestant Netherlands, great-grandson of William the Silent, and the leader of the European states that were threatened by Louis XIV's plots to expand France's power. On June 20, 1688, James's second wife alarmed England's Protestants by giving birth to a son, a Catholic heir to their throne. Within days of the boy's birth, Whig and Tory members of Parliament had agreed to invite William and Mary to invade England to preserve "traditional liberties."

The "Glorious Revolution"

When the English people failed to oppose the landing that William of Orange's army made in November 1688, James accepted defeat and fled to France. Parliament completed the bloodless "Glorious Revolution" by declaring the throne vacant and proclaiming William and Mary its heirs. They, in turn, issued a Bill of Rights that limited the powers of the monarchy and guaranteed the civil liberties of England's privileged classes. Henceforth, the English monarch would be subject to law and would govern with the consent of a Parliament that met regularly. The Bill of Rights also prohibited Roman Catholics from occupying the English throne. The Toleration Act of 1689 legalized all forms of Protestantism—save those that denied the Trinity—and outlawed Roman Catholicism.

In 1701 the Act of Settlement closed the "century of strife" (as the seventeenth century came to be known in England) by providing for the English crown to go to the Protestant House of Hanover in Germany if none of the children of Queen Anne (r. 1702–1714), the second daughter of James II and the last of the Stuart monarchs, survived her. Since she did outlive her children, the Elector of Hanover became King George I of England and the third foreigner to occupy the English throne in just over a century.

Although the "Glorious Revolution" of 1688 was not a popular revolution such as those that erupted in America and France a hundred years later, it established a framework for a government by and for the governed—a permanent check on monarchical power by the classes represented in Parliament. English philosopher John Locke's *Second Treatise of Government* (1690), which was written prior to the revolution, came to be read as a justification for the new system. Locke claimed that the relationship between a king and his people was a bilateral contract. If the king broke that contract, the people (by whom Locke meant those with property) had the right to depose him. Locke's political theory and England's parliamentary monarchy were destined to have wide appeal.

Rise of Absolute Monarchy in France

In seventeenth-century France, unlike England, absolute monarchy established itself, limited the freedom of the nobility, and enforced religious conformity. The dictum of Louis XIV (r. 1643–1715) was "one king, one law, one faith."

Louis's predecessors had provoked a rebellion among the nobles by trying to impose direct rule on the nation at all levels. Louis chose, instead, to work through established social and political institutions rather than to destroy them. His genius lay in his ability to make the monarchy the most powerful political institution in France while assuring the nobles and other wealthy groups that it posed no threat to their private power bases and their standing. Once nobles understood that the king would protect their local authority, they supported his central authority. The king and the nobles agreed that they needed each other but that Louis XIV was the senior partner in the relationship.

Henry IV and Sully

Louis XIV learned much from his predecessors. Henry IV (r. 1589–1610), who came to the throne at the end of the French wars of religion, had tried to rein in the French nobility—particularly the provincial governors, the regional *parlements*, and the powerful *Parlement* of Paris. These groups were divisive elements within the state, for their chief interest was the protection of their privileges. Since the war-weary French were eager for the restoration of order, Henry and his finance minister, the duke of Sully (1560–1641), were able to expand governmental authority. They established royal monopolies on gunpowder, mines, and salt. They began construction of a canal system that linked France's rivers to create a waterway from the Atlantic to the Mediterranean. They introduced the *corvée*, a labor tax that drafted workers to build and maintain roads. Sully even dreamed of joining the whole of Europe in a kind of common market.

Louis XIII and Richelieu

Henry IV was assassinated in 1610, and the following year Sully retired. Louis XIII (r. 1610–1643), Henry's son, was only nine years old at the time, so the task of governing fell to the queen mother, Marie de Médicis (d. 1642). Sensing a lack of support from the French nobility, Marie sought to make a friend of France's archrival, Spain. In 1611 she negotiated the Treaty of Fontainebleau. It provided for a ten-year mutual defense pact and for marriage alliances between the royal houses of the two nations. Louis XIII was to wed the Spanish Infanta, and his sister, Elizabeth, was engaged to the heir to the Spanish throne. The queen's best move was the appointment of Cardinal Richelieu (1585–1642) as the king's chief adviser. The loyal, shrewd Richelieu was the architect of the success the French monarchy enjoyed in the first half of the seventeenth century.

Richelieu was a devout Catholic, but he believed that France's interests were best served by curbing the power of the Catholic Habsburgs. Although he endorsed the queen's treaty with Catholic Spain and encouraged conformity to Catholic practices in France, Richelieu was determined to contain Spain—even if that meant aiding Protestants. In the Thirty Years' War, Richelieu helped to fund the Protestant army of Gustavus Adolphus. His influence with Sweden saved Catholic Bavaria from attack and won freedom of religion for Catholics in places his Protestant allies conquered. Thanks to Richelieu, France emerged from the war with substantial gains in land and political influence.

At home, Richelieu implemented a rigorous centralization of royal government. Supported by a king, who let him make most decisions of state, Richelieu stepped up the campaign Henry IV had begun against separatist provincial governors and *parlements*. He appointed civil servants called *intendants* to guard against abuses in the sale of royal privileges—such as the right to collect taxes or sell licenses. He made it clear to everyone that there was only one law in France. If noblemen disobeyed the king's edicts, they were imprisoned or executed. Such treatment of the nobility won Richelieu much enmity—even from his patron, the queen mother.

In 1629 Richelieu began a campaign against the Huguenots. Royal armies occupied important Huguenot cities and imposed the Peace of Alais. It truncated the Edict of Nantes by denying Protestants the right to maintain garrisoned cities, separate political organizations, and independent law courts. Richelieu was prevented from doing more to limit religious freedoms by France's alliances with Protestant powers in the Thirty Years' War. But in 1685 Louis XIV completed his work by revoking the Edict of Nantes.

Richelieu was a modern politician in the sense that he understood the use of propaganda and the importance of mobilizing popular support for government policies. He employed the arts and the printing press to defend his actions and to persuade the French people to accept things done for *raisons d'état* ("reasons of state"). Louis XIV's masterful use of propaganda to develop royal power was a tribute to Richelieu's example.

Young Louis XIV and Mazarin

Louis XIII survived Richelieu by only five months. Since his heir, Louis XIV (r. 1643–1715), was five years old, the son's reign began, as the father's had, with a regency government. The queen mother, Anne of Austria (d. 1666), entrusted the monarchy to Cardinal Mazarin (1602–1661), Richelieu's protégé.

Since many members of the aristocracy and the wealthy commercial classes had deeply resented Richelieu's efforts to build a strong, centralized monarchy, Mazarin was confronted by a violent political backlash. From 1649 to 1652, there were widespread rebellions, which are known collectively as the *Fronde* (after the name of a slingshot used by street ruffians). The uprisings were exploited by nobles and townspeople who wanted to reverse the drift toward absolute monarchy and to preserve local autonomy.

When the *Parlement* of Paris initiated the *Fronde* in 1649, "the many" (i.e., the nobles) briefly triumphed over "the one" (i.e., the king). Mazarin released some aristocratic prisoners in February 1651, and he and Louis XIV went briefly into exile. (Mazarin left France and Louis fled Paris.) When the nobles failed to restore order and near anarchy ensued, support for the young king materialized and Louis and Mazarin returned in October 1652. The *Fronde* convinced most French people that a strong king was preferable to the chaos created by many competing regional powers. On the other hand, Louis XIV and his later advisers concluded that heavy-handed policies (such as those of Richelieu and Mazarin) might endanger the monarchy.

The Years of Louis's Personal Rule

On the death of Mazarin in 1661, Louis XIV assumed personal control of the government. Unlike his royal predecessors, he appointed no single chief minister. This had the advantage of making revolt more difficult to rationalize. Rebellious nobles could no longer claim that they were opposing their king's wicked ministers but not the crown itself. Mazarin had prepared Louis well for the duties of government, and the young king's experiences during the *Fronde* had stiffened his resolve to be a strong ruler. Louis wrote in his memoirs that the *Fronde* caused him to loathe "kings of straw."

Louis devised two successful strategies for enhancing the power of the monarchy. First, he became a master of propaganda and political image-making. Louis never missed an opportunity to remind the French people of the grandeur of the crown. Second, Louis made sure that the French nobles and other major social groups benefitted from the growth of his authority. Although he maintained control over foreign affairs, he usually conferred informally with regional *parlements* before making rulings that would affect them. Likewise, he rarely enacted economic regulations without consulting local opinion, and local *parlements* were given considerable latitude in regional matters.

King by Divine Right

Reverence for the king, the personification of government, had been nurtured in France since Capetian times, and it was widely accepted that the king's wish was the law of the land. Louis XIV transformed this traditional respect for the crown into a belief in the king's divine right to absolute authority.

Bishop Jacques-Bénigne Bossuet (1627–1704), the king's tutor, provided the theoretical rationale for Louis's concept of the royal office. Bossuet was an ardent champion of the so-called "Gallican liberties," traditional exemptions the French clergy claimed from interference in their affairs by the papacy. (The theory of the "divine right of kings" that Bossuet outlined gave kings spiritual legitimacy as caretakers of national churches.) Bossuet based his theory of monarchy on the example set by the rulers in the Old Testament who had been appointed by and were answerable only to God. Just as medieval popes had insisted that only God could judge a pope, so Bossuet argued that none save God could judge a king. Kings were duty-bound to honor God's will, but as God's regents on earth they were not accountable to mere princes and *parlements*. A king could claim, as Louis was alleged to, *"L'état, c'est moi"* ("I am the state").

Versailles

One of the most successful instruments of Louis XIV's propaganda was the splendid palace he built to house his court at Versailles on the outskirts of Paris (1682). Versailles was a temple to royalty and a proclamation of the glory of France's "Sun King." It was also home to Louis and thousands of his subjects: France's more important nobles and numerous royal officials and servants. The maintenance of Versailles and its expansion and elaboration, which continued throughout Louis's lifetime, consumed over half the royal income. The political dividends Versailles paid, however, proved well worth the investment.

By organizing life at court around his personal routine, Louis demonstrated that he alone was the sole source of power and privilege in France. Nobles scrambled for the honor of being present at intimate moments in the king's day—his rising,

Versailles, as painted in 1668 by Pierre Patel the Elder (1605–1676). The central building is the hunting lodge built for Louis XII earlier in the century. The wings that appear here were some of Louis XIV's first expansions. Pierre Patel, *Perspective View of Versailles*, Chateau, Versailles, France. Giraudon/Art Resource, NY

dressing, or retiring—in hopes of having a chance to whisper special requests in his ear. Like menial servants, the most distinguished of aristocrats fought for the privilege of holding the king's candle or assisting him with the left sleeve of his nightshirt. These duties were choreographed by an extraordinarily elaborate court etiquette, which was designed to domesticate and trivialize the nobility. Barred by law from high government positions, the nobles were kept busy with ritual and play that left them little time to plot revolt. Luxurious dress codes and high-stakes gambling drove them into debt and financial dependency on the king. Members of the court spent the afternoons hunting, riding, or strolling about the lush gardens of Versailles. Evenings were given over to plays, concerts, gambling, and the like—followed by supper at 10:00 P.M.

The real business of government was handled by Louis and members of councils charged with responsibility for foreign affairs, domestic relations, and the economy. The chief ministers of these councils were talented self-made men or members of families with long histories of loyal service to the crown. Louis trusted them with power, for, unlike the nobility, they had no independent bases in the provinces and relied solely on the king for their places in government and society.

Suppression of the Jansenists

Like Richelieu before him, Louis believed that political stability required religious conformity. The first deviant religious groups to attract his attention were not Protestants but Roman

Rigaud's Louis XIV: The State Portrait

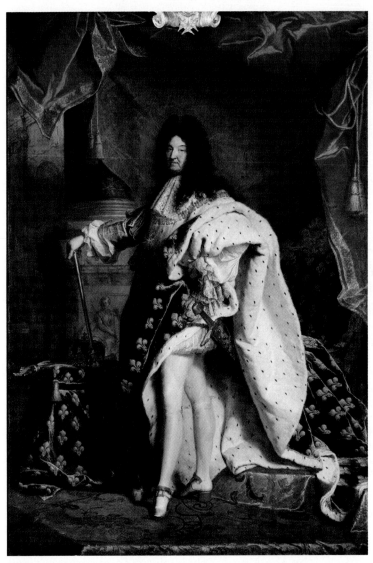

Hyacinthe Rigaud, *Louis XIV*, 1701. Giraudon/Art Resource, NY

Sources: Peter Burke, *The Fabrication of Louis XIV* (New Haven, CT: Yale University Press, 1992); Daniel Roche, *France in the Age of the Enlightenment* (Cambridge, Ma: Harvard University Press, 1998), pp. 273–277; Germain Bazin, *Baroque and Rococo Art* (New York: Praeger, 1966); Marilyn Stockstad, *Art History* (New York: Harry N. Abrams, Inc., and Prentice Hall, Inc., Publishers, 1999), pp. 750–751.

The portrait that Hyacinthe Rigaud painted of the sixty-three-year-old Louis XIV in 1701 broke new ground. The many previous likenesses of the king had placed him in allegorical or historical settings that equated him with mythical heroes and Roman emperors. This picture cloaked the king in images of his own majesty and thereby established the model for what came to be regarded as "the state portrait."

A mature Louis is depicted in coronation robes decorated with the *fleurs-de-lis* symbols of his dynasty. The crown rests beside him, and the throne is in the background. He holds the royal scepter, the staff with which he maintains the social order, and the sword of state, the symbol of his military might and a reminder of his many wars, hangs half concealed at his side. A figure representing justice ornaments the base of the column that rises behind the crown and scepter.

As was the custom, the painting magnified its subject without resorting to absurd flattery. The king's face reflects something of the wisdom (and burden) of his years, but his athletic legs and luxuriant wig imply a youthfulness and vigor that the aging, gout-afflicted monarch may not have felt. The portrait's air of gravity suited a man who was growing more devout, conservative, and restrained in his personal life as he aged. So well did Louis believe that the portrait captured his spirit that he had it copied for distribution and even sent it to represent the crown at council and ministerial meetings he could not attend in person.

Catholics called Jansenists. Catherine de Médicis had prevented the Catholic Jesuits from working in France because of their close connections to Spain, but following Henry IV's conversion to Catholicism, this ban was lifted (1603). Jesuits who swore an oath of allegiance to the king and acquired special licenses were permitted to set up a limited number of colleges and conduct various public activities. The Jesuits soon became the royal confessors and dominated the education of the upper classes. Their commitment was to the enforcement of the decrees of the Council of Trent throughout France.

Jansenism, which appeared in the 1630s, was a Catholic movement named for a Flemish theologian and bishop who was critical of the Jesuits, Cornelius Jansen (d. 1638). Jansenists followed the teachings of Saint Augustine, who emphasized the role divine grace played in human salvation. They objected to the Jesuits' emphasis on free will and good works, for they believed with Saint Augustine that original sin so corrupted humankind that individuals could do nothing good nor secure their own salvation without divine grace. Jansenist emphasis on salvation by grace led the Jesuits to accuse the Jansenists of being crypto-Protestants.

The fight between the Jansenists and the Jesuits had political as well as theological dimensions. Jansen had ties with a prominent Parisian family, the Arnaulds, who, like many others in France, believed that the Jesuits had arranged the assassination of Henry IV in 1610. The Arnaulds dominated Jansenist communities at Port-Royal and Paris during the 1640s. In 1643 a book *(On Frequent Communion)* by Antoine Arnauld attracted attention by charging that the Jesuits' use of the confessional allowed people easily to escape responsibility for their sins.

On May 31, 1653, Pope Innocent X declared that five Jansenist theological propositions concerning grace and salvation were heresies. In 1656 the pope banned a book by Cornelius Jansen (*Augustinus*, 1640), and the Sorbonne censured Antoine Arnauld. In the same year Antoine's friend, Blaise Pascal (d. 1662), published a defense of Jansenism, the first of his *Provincial Letters.* Pascal was a deeply religious man who objected to Jesuit moral theology not only because it was lax, but also because its rationalism failed to do justice to the profound mysteries of religious experience.

In 1660 Louis banned Jansenism and closed down the Port-Royal community. This drove Jansenism underground, where it apparently continued to thrive. In 1710 Louis ordered a more thorough purge of Jansenist sympathizers. His suppression of Jansenism, which was a kind of Catholicism broad enough to appeal to Huguenots, eliminated the best hope for peacefully unifying France's religions.

Government Geared for War

Louis saw himself as a warrior king, and his many campaigns led his neighbors to fear French aggression and form coalitions against him. He, however, probably did not aspire to European domination but only to the defense of what he regarded as France's interests. These centered on achieving a secure northern border (with the Spanish Netherlands, the Franche-Comté, Alsace, and Lorraine), frustrating the ambitions of the Habsburgs, and dealing with problems of succession to the thrones of various states.

COLBERT AND THE FRENCH ECONOMY The economy of France was overwhelmingly agrarian, as was true of other nations in Louis's day. But Jean-Baptiste Colbert (1619–1683), Louis's brilliant financial adviser, managed it so skillfully that France was able to support a huge standing army. Colbert centralized the French economy just as Louis centralized French government. The kind of economic policy Colbert instituted has been called *mercantilism.* Its aim was to maximize exports, minimize imports, and thus conserve the bullion foreign sales brought to an exporting nation. Colbert relied on state supervision of industries and tariffs to regulate the flow of imports and exports. He established new national industries and imposed a strict regimen for workers in state-run factories. He simplified the administrative bureaucracy; reduced the number of tax-exempt nobles; and increased the *taille,* the direct tax on the peasantry that provided much of the king's income.

LOUVOIS, VAUBAN, AND THE FRENCH MILITARY Thanks to Colbert, Louis was able to afford an army of about 250,000 men. It was created for him by a father-son team of war ministers: Michel Le Tellier (minister to 1666) and Tellier's son, the marquis of Louvois (minister from 1667 to his death in 1691). Before Louvois, the French army had been an amalgam of local companies of recruits and mercenaries who supplemented their irregular pay by pillaging the countryside. Louvois made soldiering a respectable profession. He improved discipline, established a system of promotion by merit, restricted enlistment to single men, and paid them well. The conduct of the military at all levels was also monitored by civil servants.

New technology was provided for Louvois's new army by a brilliant military engineer, Sebastien Vauban (1633–1707). He perfected the arts of fortifying and besieging towns, invented trench warfare, and developed the concept of the defensive frontier—an idea that remained basic to military tactics through World War I.

Louis's Early Wars

THE WAR OF DEVOLUTION   Louis's first great foreign adventure was the War of Devolution (1667–1668). Like the later War of the Spanish Succession, it was fought to press a claim Louis's wife, Marie Thérèse (1638–1683), had to Spain's Belgian provinces. In 1659 Marie had surrendered her place in the line of succession to the Spanish throne in exchange for a huge dowry to be paid to Louis. The dowry was never paid, but Philip IV of Spain, who died in September 1665, left a will disinheriting Marie in favor of a sickly four-year-old son by a second marriage, Charles II (r. 1665–1700). Louis decided to contest the will, and the legal grounds he chose gave the war its name. Louis argued that in certain regions of Brabant and Flanders, which were part of Philip's estate, property "devolved" to the children of a first marriage rather than to those of a second. Therefore, Marie had a better claim to these districts than Charles. In 1667 Louis sent his armies into Flanders and the Franche-Comté, and England, Sweden, and the United Provinces of Holland reacted by forming the Triple Alliance. In 1668 Louis signed the Treaty of Aix-la-Chapelle and agreed to a peace that gave him control of some towns bordering the Spanish Netherlands.

INVASION OF THE NETHERLANDS   In 1670 France persuaded England to join an alliance against the Dutch. The Triple Alliance crumbled, and in 1672 Louis struck directly at Holland, the power that had organized the Triple Alliance. Without neutralizing Holland, Louis knew he could make no progress in the Spanish Netherlands, nor could he fulfill his dream of winning European hegemony. Louis's attack on the United Provinces of Holland was countered by the young Prince of Orange, the future William III of England. Orange was the great-grandson of William the Silent, the native leader who had repulsed Philip II and established the independence of Holland. Orange persuaded the Holy Roman Emperor, Spain, Lorraine, and Brandenburg to join him in stopping the "Christian Turk," the voracious French king who was becoming a menace to the whole of western Europe. In 1676 a victory over the Dutch fleet gave France control of the Mediterranean. The United Netherlands, however, lost no territory, and the war ended in 1679 with no clear winner.

Revocation of the Edict of Nantes

Following the Peace of Nijmwegen, which ended the war in the Netherlands and halted (for the moment) France's aggression in Europe, Louis imposed religious conformity on his subjects. The Edict of Nantes of 1598 had established a legal Protestant minority in France, but the Huguenots' relations with the Catholic majority (nine-tenths of the French population) were never good. The French Catholic Church denounced Calvinists as heretics and traitors and declared their persecution a pious, patriotic duty.

Louis hounded the Huguenots from public life by banning them from government office and excluding them from the professions. He raised their taxes, quartered his troops in their towns, and in October 1685, he outlawed their faith by revoking the Edict of Nantes. Protestant churches and schools closed. Protestant clergy went into exile. Nonconverting laity were enslaved on the galleys, and Protestant children were turned over to Catholic priests for baptism.

Louis's flaunting of religious intolerance was a major blunder, for it persuaded Protestant countries that he had to be stopped at all costs. More than a quarter-million French people fled their homeland to stiffen opposition to France in England, Germany, Holland, and the New World. Many of the Huguenots who remained in France formed guerilla bands to fight the king. But Louis, to his death, was persuaded that the revocation of Nantes was his most pious act—one that put God in his debt.

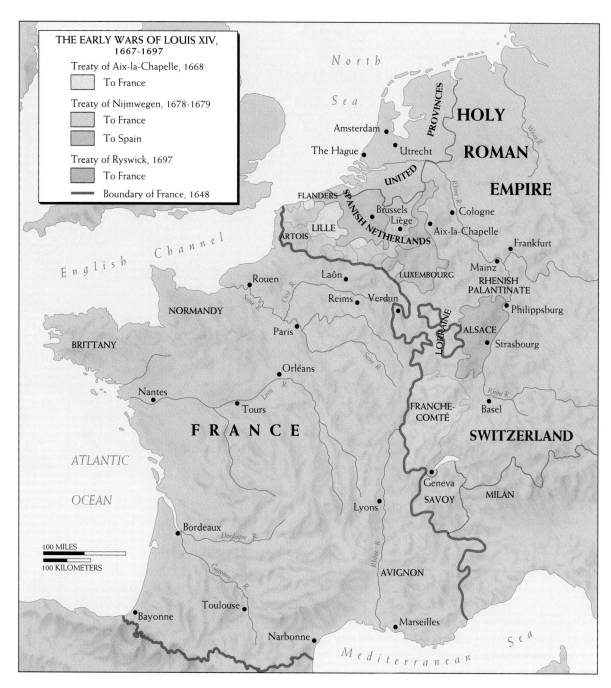

MAP 13–1 THE WARS OF LOUIS XIV *This maps illustrates the territorial changes that resulted from Louis's first three major wars prior to the War of the Spanish Succession.*

Louis's Later Wars

THE LEAGUE OF AUGSBURG AND THE NINE YEARS' WAR In 1681 Louis's forces conquered the free city of Strasbourg, prompting new defensive coalitions to form against him. One of these, the League of Augsburg, expanded to include England, Spain, Sweden, the United Provinces, the electorates of Bavaria, Saxony, and the Palatinate, and the Emperor Leopold. From 1689 to 1697, the league and France fought the Nine Years' War, while in North America England and France fought King William's War, a struggle for the colonies. In 1697 mutual exhaustion forced an interim settlement, the Peace of Ryswick. The treaty was a triumph for William of Orange,

The foreign policy of Louis XIV brought warfare to all of Europe. This eighteenth-century painting by Benjamin West memorializes the British victory over France in the battle of La Hogue in 1692. © 1778, oil on canvas, 1.527 × 2.143 (60 1/8 × 84 3/8); framed: 1.803 × 2.410 (71 × 94 7/8). Andrew W. Mellon Fund. © Board of Trustees, National Gallery of Art, Washington.

now William III of England, and the Emperor Leopold. It secured Holland's borders and thwarted Louis's expansion into Germany.

WAR OF THE SPANISH SUCCESSION: TREATIES OF UTRECHT AND RASTADT   Louis tried a fourth time to win dominance over Europe. Charles II of Spain (surnamed "the Sufferer" because of his genetic deformities and lingering illnesses) died on November 1, 1700. Louis and the Austrian Emperor Leopold each claimed the Spanish inheritance for a grandson. Louis's grandson, Philip of Anjou, had the better claim, for his grandmother, Marie Thérèse was the older sister of the Spanish princess, Margaret Thérèse, who had married Leopold. But Marie Thérèse had renounced her right to the Spanish throne when she married Louis.

Louis feared that the Habsburgs would dominate Europe if they ruled both Spain and the Holy Roman Empire. Most of the nations of Europe, however, feared France more than the Habsburgs. As a result, even before Charles II died, international negotiations were underway to partition his inheritance in a way that would preserve the balance of power. Charles II upset these negotiations by bequeathing his estate to Philip of Anjou. Louis, finding himself the unexpected winner, ignored partition agreements, sent his grandson to Madrid to become Philip V of Spain, and invaded Flanders. In September 1701, England, Holland, and the Holy Roman Empire formed the Grand Alliance. They hoped to secure Flanders as a neutral barrier between Holland and France and to gain a share of the Spanish inheritance for the Habsburgs. The result was the War of the Spanish Succession (1701–1714), another total war enveloping all of western Europe.

In this campaign the French army was poorly financed, poorly equipped, and poorly led. England, on the other hand, had advanced weaponry, superior tactics, and a splendid general—John Churchill, the duke of Marlborough. Marlborough routed French armies in two decisive engagements: Blenheim in August 1704, and Ramillies in 1706. From 1708 to 1709 famine and excessive taxation spawned revolts that tore France apart, and Louis wondered aloud how God could forsake a king who had done so much for Him.

Louis could not bring himself to accept the stiff terms the alliance demanded for peace, and hostilities continued. A clash at Malplaquet (September 1709) created carnage unsurpassed until mod-

ern times. France and England finally declared an armistice at Utrecht in July 1712 and in March 1714 came to an agreement with Holland and the emperor (the Treaty of Rastadt). Philip V remained king of Spain, but England won Gibraltar and a chance to become a Mediterranean power. Spain continued to decline following the war because Philip was distracted by efforts to secure thrones in Italy for the sons of his second wife, Elizabeth Farnese. The sixteenth century had belonged to Spain and the seventeenth to France, but England was to have the eighteenth.

MAP 13–2 **Europe in 1714.** *Although France and Spain remained separate countries, the War of the Spanish Succession established Bourbon kings on both their thrones. It also cost Spain its non-Iberian possessions.*

Louis XIV's Legacy

Louis XIV left France a mixed legacy. Although the monarchy was still strong when he died, it was more feared than admired. Its finances were insecure, and its debts great. Its tightly centralized control of political and economic life had suppressed the development of representative institutions, and its use of Versailles to trivialize the lives of aristocrats had diminished their capacity to provide the nation with effective leadership. Louis's wars had also imbued the army and the aristocracy with a thirst for military glory, and the wars that France continued to fight during the eighteenth century doomed efforts to put the government on a sound financial footing.

On the positive side, Louis erected magnificent buildings, provided patronage for important artists, and brought a new majesty to France. He skillfully handled the fractious French aristocracy and bourgeoisie. He appointed talented ministers, councillors, and *intendants.* And he created a French empire by expanding trade with Asia and by colonizing North America.

The Sun King's rule was not so absolute as to oppress the daily lives of his subjects. Louis's France was not a modern police state. His interests were those that traditionally had been assumed to be the responsibilities of kings: the making of war and peace, the regulation of religion, and the oversight of economic activity. Even at the height of his power, local elites enjoyed considerable independence so long as they did not interfere with his plans on the national level. The French people showed little interest in pursuing a more representative form of government until a severe financial crisis revealed the impotency of their monarchy at the end of the eighteenth century.

In Perspective

In the seventeenth century, England and France developed divergent forms of government: parliamentary monarchy in England and absolute monarchy in France. The politically active nobility and wealthy commercial classes of England struggled throughout the century to limit the authority of their rulers. They were not advocates of democracy or religious freedom in a modern sense, but they did establish representative government in England and extend legal recognition to a variety of religious beliefs. In France, the monarchy remained supreme. Although the king had to mollify local elites, France developed no national institution such as the English Parliament. Louis XIV was able, on his own, to build the largest army in Europe and to crush religious dissent. The model of effective centralized monarchy he created had great appeal to later generations of European rulers.

REVIEW QUESTIONS

1. What similarities and differences do you see between the systems of government and religious policies in place in England and France

Significant Dates from the Seventeenth Century	
1603	James I, king of England
1611	Authorized, or King James, Version of the Bible
1625	Charles I, king of England
1642	Outbreak of the English Civil War
1643	Louis XIV, king of France
1648	Treaty of Westphalia
1649	Charles I executed
1649–1652	The *Fronde*
1649–1660	England, Puritan Commonwealth
1660	Charles II restores the English monarchy
1667–1668	War of Devolution
1685	James II, king of England
1685	Louis XIV revokes Edict of Nantes
1688	England's "Glorious Revolution"
1689	William and Mary rule England
1689–1697	Nine Years' War
1701	Act of Settlement, the Hanoverian Succession
1701–1714	War of the Spanish Succession
1702	Queen Anne, the last of the Stuarts
1714	Death of Queen Anne of England
1715	Death of Louis XIV of France

at the end of the seventeenth century? What accounts for the path each nation took?

2. Why did the English king and Parliament come into conflict in the 1640s? Does one of them bear more responsibility than the other for the war that broke out? What role did religion play in the struggle?

3. What was the "Glorious Revolution"? Why did it take place? What were James II's mistakes? What were the issues involved in the events of 1688? What kind of settlement emerged from the revolution? How did England in 1700 differ from England in 1600?

4. By what stages did absolutism develop in France? How did the policies of Henry IV and Louis XIII contribute to the creation of absolute monarchy?

5. How did Louis XIV consolidate his monarchy? What limits were there on his authority? What was Louis's religious policy?

6. How successful was Louis XIV's foreign policy? What were its aims? Were they realistic? To what extent were they attained?

SUGGESTED READINGS

R. ASHTON, *Counter-Revolution: The Second Civil War and Its Origin, 1646–1648* (1995). A major examination of the resumption of civil conflict in England that ended with the abolition of the monarchy.

W. BEIK, *Absolutism and Society in Seventeenth-Century France* (1985). An important study that questions the extent of royal power.

R. BONNEY, *Political Change in France Under Richelieu and Mazarin, 1624–1661* (1978). A careful examination of the manner in which these two cardinals laid the foundation for Louis XIV's absolutism.

G. BURGESS, *Absolute Monarchy and the Stuart Constitution* (1996). A new study that challenges traditional interpretations.

P. BURKE, *The Fabrication of Louis XIV* (1992). Examines the manner in which the public image of Louis XIV was forged in art.

P. COLLINSON, *The Religion of Protestants: The Church in English Society, 1559–1625* (1982). The best recent introduction to Puritanism.

T. ERTMAN, *Birth of the Leviathan: Building States and Regimes in Medieval and Early Modern Europe* (1997). An extensive survey by a sociologist.

R. HUTTON, *Charles the Second, King of England, Scotland, and Ireland* (1989). Replaces all previous biographies.

P. K. MONOD, *The Power of Kings: Monarchy and Religion in Europe, 1589–1715* (1999). An innovative examination of the roots of royal authority.

C. RUSSELL, *The Causes of the English Civil War* (1990). A major revisionist account, which should be read with Stone below.

L. STONE, *The Causes of the English Revolution, 1529–1642* (1972). Brief survey stressing social history and ruminating over historians and historical method.

D. J. STURDY, *Louis XIV* (1998). An excellent overview.

D. UNDERDOWN, *Revel, Riot, and Rebellion* (1985). On popular culture and the English civil war.

J. B. WOLF, *Louis XIV* (1968). Very detailed political biography.

Chapter 14
New Directions in Thought and Culture in the Sixteenth and Seventeenth Centuries

KEY TOPICS

- The astronomical theories of Copernicus, Brahe, Kepler, Galileo, and Newton, and the emergence of the scientific worldview
- Impact of the new science on philosophy
- Social setting of early modern science
- Women and the Scientific Revolution
- Approaches to science and religion
- Witchcraft and witch hunts

During the sixteenth and seventeenth centuries, science created a new view of the universe that challenged many previously held beliefs. Earth moved from the center of things to become only one of several planets orbiting a sun that was only one of countless stars. This new cosmology forced people to rethink humanity's place in the larger scheme of things. Traditional religion and the new science came into an apparent conflict that raised questions about the received grounds for faith and morality. Europeans discovered that the world was a much more complex place than their ancestors had imagined. The telescope opened the heavens to them while the microscope disclosed the exis-

tence of a realm of microorganisms. A spate of scientific discoveries added to the intellectual dislocation that had already been created by the Reformation (which challenged many medieval religious and social institutions) and contact with the New World (which confronted Europeans with places, things, and peoples they had never known to exist).

The Scientific Revolution

The intellectual breakthroughs of the sixteenth and seventeenth centuries have been described as the Scientific Revolution, but that metaphor may be misleading if it is assumed to imply a rapid, widespread transformation of culture. The development of science was a slow process that never involved more than a few hundred people. These pioneers thought of themselves as "natural philosophers," not *scientists*—a term that was not invented until the 1830s. Progress in science depended on the inventiveness of artisans and craftspeople as well as a few brilliant minds. Some individuals worked at universities or had the patronage of kings, but many pursued their studies informally from their homes or private workshops. It was not until the second half of the seventeenth century that learned societies and academies were established to promote research.

Despite this rather casual approach to scientific work, by the end of the seventeenth century the new scientific concepts and methods that were emerging were so impressive that they were setting the standard for assessing the validity of all knowledge in the West. Science was already achieving the cultural supremacy over other forms of intellectual activity that it still enjoys and was establishing itself as one of the defining characteristics of modern Western civilization. The discipline that did most to initiate these developments was astronomy.

Nicolaus Copernicus Rejects an Earth-centered Universe

Nicolaus Copernicus (1473–1543), a respected Italian-educated Polish astronomer, had a reputation as a fairly conventional thinker until he published, in the year of his death (1543), a book entitled *On the Revolutions of the Heavenly Spheres*. The book did not so much create a revolution as lay the groundwork for one by providing Copernicus's successors with an intellectual springboard for a criticism of the previously accepted view of the position of Earth in the universe.

THE PTOLEMAIC SYSTEM The maps of the universe commonly accepted in Copernicus's day were variants of one found in the ancient Greek astronomer Ptolemy's *Almagest* (c. 150 C.E.). They assumed that Earth was the center point of a ball-shaped universe composed of concentric, rotating crystalline spheres to which the heavenly bodies were attached. At the outer regions of these spheres lay the realm of God and the angels. The assumptions about the laws of physics, which the Greek philosopher Aristotle had popularized, lay behind Ptolemy's model. Earth was at the center of the universe because it was presumed to be the heaviest of objects. Since rest was thought to be the natural state of all objects, an explanation had to be proposed for the motion of the heavenly bodies. They were said to be attached to invisible rotating spheres that transferred motion down from the highest level where a "prime mover" imparted motion to the system. Christians, of course, identified Aristotle's "prime mover" with God.

Medieval astronomers were aware of problems with Ptolemy's system. Chief among these was the fact that the planets did not appear to move in circular orbits. Sometimes they actually seemed to go backward. Ptolemy and his disciples explained this by advancing a theory of epicycles, that is, planets moving in short circular cycles which travel the orbits of much larger cycles. This accounted fairly well with what astronomers observed, but it produced a very cluttered model for the universe.

COPERNICUS'S UNIVERSE Copernicus's *On the Revolutions of the Heavenly Spheres* was meant not to refute Ptolemy's theory but to propose a refinement that would provide a more elegant solution to some of the mathematical problems it raised. Copernicus suggested that if Earth were assumed to rotate about the sun in a circular orbit, the epicycles could be—if not eliminated—at least reduced in size and the apparent retrograde motion of the planets could be explained as an illusion created by astronomers viewing them from a planet that was itself in motion. Except for modifying the position of Earth, Copernicus maintained most of the other assumptions of Ptolemaic astronomy (e.g., circular orbits, epicycles, etc.), and his system was no more accurate than older ones in predicting the movements of the planets. The Copernican model of the universe was, therefore, slow to attract adherents, and the importance of his work originally lay primarily in the encouragement it gave people to think in new ways about scientific problems.

Tycho Brahe and Johannes Kepler Make New Scientific Observations

Tycho Brahe (1546–1601), a Danish astronomer, spent most of his life trying to refute Copernicus and defending a revised version of Ptolemy's Earth-centered model for the universe. He thought that the moon and the sun revolved around Earth and that the other planets revolved around the sun. To make his case, Brahe collected the most accurate astronomical data that had ever been acquired by observation with the naked eye.

When Brahe died, his astronomical tables passed to Johannes Kepler (1571–1630), a German astronomer and a convinced Copernican. After much work, Kepler discovered that if the planets were described as moving in elliptical, not circular, orbits, Brahe's data supported the Copernican theory that Earth revolved about the sun. Kepler published his findings in 1609 in a book entitled *The New Astronomy*, but their acceptance was hampered by the fact that no one could explain why planets were locked in orbits of any shape rather than spinning out into space. The solution to that puzzle had to await Isaac Newton and his theories about gravitation.

Galileo Galilei Argues for a Universe of Mathematical Laws

By Kepler's day little was known about the universe that could not have been known to Ptolemy, for all data had been gathered with the naked eye. But in the year that Kepler published his work, an Italian scientist, Galileo Galilei (1564–1642), turned a Dutch invention called a telescope on the heavens and saw things that had never been seen before. Unknown stars appeared, mountains were discovered on the moon, spots passed across the face of the sun, and moons

The telescope with which Galileo worked after 1609. He observed Earth's moon and the cyclical phases of the planet Venus and discovered the most prominent moons of Jupiter. These observations had revolutionary intellectual and theological implications in the seventeenth century. Muséo della Scienza, Florence, Italy. Scala/Art Resource, NY

were seen to orbit the planet Jupiter. Galileo argued that a Copernican model of the universe provided the simplest explanation for much of what the telescope revealed.

Galileo did not pursue science in the seclusion of an ivory tower. He worked at the court of the Medici Grand Duke of Tuscany, and his livelihood depended on promoting his discoveries in ways that enhanced the reputation of his noble patron. Galileo, therefore, publicized his findings in literate, accessible treatises. This made him appear to be the leading advocate for the Copernican model of the universe and caused problems for him with the Roman Catholic Church (discussed later).

Galileo not only popularized Copernicanism, he also fostered belief in a universe governed by rational laws stated in mathematical formulas. The mathematical regularity that Copernicus saw in the heavens, Galileo believed, was characteristic of all nature. This conviction encouraged scientists to look for explanations for things by focusing primarily on phenomena that could be quantified. They sought mathematical models to account for qualities such as color, beauty, and taste—and even to explain such things as social relationships and political systems. When viewed from this perspective, nature appeared to be a cold, mechanistic system. Only things that were mathematically measurable seemed real and of lasting significance. This attitude portended a major intellectual shift for Western civilization.

Isaac Newton Discovers the Laws of Gravitation

The puzzle that Copernicus, Kepler, and Galileo left unsolved was why the heavenly bodies moved in the orderly fashion described by the new astronomy. It was an interest in the mystery that lay behind the laws of planetary motion that led Isaac Newton (1642–1727), an English mathematician, to make the discoveries that established a basis for physics that endured for over two centuries.

In 1687 Newton published *The Mathematical Principles of Natural Philosophy* (or *Principia Mathematica*, its Latin title). Newton shared Galileo's faith that reality could be described mathematically, and he was influenced by Galileo's theory of inertia. Earlier scientists had assumed that rest (motionlessness) was an object's natural state and that movement had to be explained. Galileo proposed instead that what the physicist ought to ask is not why there is motion instead of rest, but why there is a change in an existing state—be it rest or movement.

Newton theorized that the revolutions of the heavenly bodies were controlled by gravity, a pull that every physical object exerts on the objects around it. Since the strength of this attrac-

Sir Isaac Newton discovered the mathematical and physical laws governing the force of gravity. Newton believed that religion and science were compatible and mutually supportive, and that the study of nature gave one a better understanding of the Creator. This portrait of Newton is by Sir Godfrey Kneller. Sir Godfrey Kneller, *Sir Isaac Newton.* Bildarchiv Preussicher Kulturbesitz

tion is proportional to the mass and proximity of each object, the order that exists among the planets can be explained as the balance they have achieved among their mutual forces. Newton demonstrated the effects of gravity mathematically, but he made no attempt to explain what gravity was in itself.

Newton believed that mathematics held the key to understanding nature, but, like the other advocates of the new science, he also believed that the ultimate test of a theory was its ability to explain empirical data and observation. The final test of any hypothesis was whether it described what could be observed. Science began and ended with empirical observation of what was actually in nature, not with a rational argument about what ought to be there. Consequently, religious dogma could not dictate conclusions to science.

Philosophy Responds to Changing Science

The revolution taking place in science prompted a major rethinking of the Western philosophical tradition. The religious beliefs of the medieval Scholastics were abandoned in favor of a world described in terms of mechanical metaphors and the language of machinery. The new model for the universe was to imagine it not as a living thing but as a kind of gigantic clock. This dispelled much of the mystery of existence and reduced God to the role of an observer—a great mechanic who had constructed the machinery of the universe but did not participate in its operation. Philosophers had previously assumed that an understanding of the natural order would reveal divine mysteries and yield transcendent insights, but now they concluded that knowledge of nature revealed nothing beyond itself. Such knowledge might lead to physical improvements for living beings, but it could not disclose a divine purpose for life.

Francis Bacon: The Empirical Method

Francis Bacon (1561–1626), the English lawyer, statesman, and author who is often honored as the father of the scientific method of research, was not himself a scientist. His contribution to science was to help create an intellectual climate conducive to its growth. In books such as *The Advancement of Learning* (1605), the *Novum Organum* (1620), and the *New Atlantis* (1627), Bacon attacked medieval Scholasticism's reverence for authority, that is, its belief that most truth had already been discovered and only needed to be explicated. He urged his contemporaries to strike out on their own to search for a new understanding of nature. Bacon was a leader among the early European writers who defended the desirability of innovation and change.

Bacon believed that knowledge was not just an end in itself but that it should produce useful results. It should improve the human condition. He claimed that Scholasticism had nothing more to contribute toward this end, for its practitioners did nothing but rearrange old ideas. If any real progress was to be made, philosophers had to go back and reexamine the foundations of their thought. If they relied on empirical observation more than logical speculation, Bacon promised that they would discover new information that would open new possibilities for humankind.

Bacon's rejection of past methods of inquiry sprang from his awareness that the world was becoming a much more complicated place than it had been for his medieval forebears. Like Columbus, and partially because of him, Bacon claimed that he had to chart a new route to intellectual discovery. The new territories that were being explored on the globe were opening new vistas for the mind. Most people in Bacon's day assumed that the best era in human history lay in antiquity, but Bacon disagreed. He anticipated a future of material improvement and more effective government achieved through the empirical examination of nature.

René Descartes: The Method of Rational Deduction

René Descartes (1596–1650), the gifted French mathematician who invented analytic geometry, popularized a scientific method that relied more on deduction than empirical observation and induction. Thinkers all over Europe eagerly applied his techniques to all kinds of subject matters.

Descartes's *Discourse on Method* (1637) tried to put all human thought on a secure mathematical footing. In order to arrive at truth, Descartes said that it was necessary to doubt all ideas except those that were clear and distinct. An idea was worthy of trust not because some authority vouched for it but because all rational beings could intuit its validity for themselves. Descartes began his search for truth by seeing if he had any ideas he could not doubt, that is, any ideas that were self-substantiating. He concluded that it was not possible to question his own act of thinking without assuming that he existed. To doubt doubting, one could not doubt the existence of the doubter. With this clear and distinct idea as his premise, Descartes was able to construct arguments deducing the existence of God and a real world external to the human mind.

Descartes divided existing things into two basic categories: things in thought and things in space. Thinking was characteristic of the mind, and extension (i.e., things occupying space) of the body. Since space was measurable by mathematical means, mathematical laws governed the world of extension. Its laws were discoverable by reason, for mathematical truths form coherent systems in which each part can be deduced from some other part. Spirits, divinities, or immaterial things have no place in the world of extension. That realm belongs exclusively to the scientist who explains it by using mathematical reason to discover the mechanical properties of matter.

Natural scientists eventually abandoned Descartes's deductive method for induction, the process of formulating a hypothesis by generalizing from discrete bits of empirical data. Deduction, however, remained popular with people who pondered subjects for which little empirical data was available, for example, political theory, psychology, ethics, and theology.

Thomas Hobbes: Apologist for Absolutism

Nowhere did the new science have a greater impact on political thought than in the work of Thomas Hobbes (1588–1679), the most original political philosopher of the seventeenth century. Hobbes was an urbane and much-traveled man who enthusiastically supported the new scientific movement. He visited Paris and made Descartes's acquaintance. He spent time in Italy with Galileo, and he was interested in the work of William Harvey (1578–1657), the man who discovered that blood circulated through the human body. Hobbes was also a superb classicist. His translation of Thucydides' *History of the Peloponnesian War*, the first in English, is still read, and his dark view on human nature probably owed something to Thucydides.

The English Civil War made Hobbes a political philosopher and inspired him in 1651 to publish a book entitled *Leviathan*. It offered a thoroughly materialistic, mechanistic explanation for human behavior. Hobbes theorized that all psychological processes derive from sensation and that all motivations are egoistical. The driving force in each human life is to increase pleasure and minimize pain. Human beings exist for no higher spiritual ends and serve no great moral purpose. They simply strive to meet the needs of daily life,

and to do so they have to form a government. A sovereign commonwealth is all that prevents a society of egotists from tearing itself apart.

The key to Hobbes's political philosophy is found in a brilliant myth he devised to explain humanity's original state. Hobbes claimed that nature inclines people to a "perpetual and restless desire" for power. Because all people want, and in the state of nature possess, a right to everything, their equality breeds enmity, competition, diffidence, and perpetual quarreling—"a war of every man against every man." Whereas earlier and later philosophers saw the original human condition as a paradise from which people had fallen, Hobbes described it as a corrupt environment from which people could be delivered only by the establishment of a politically organized society. Unlike Aristotle and Christian thinkers such as Thomas Aquinas, Hobbes did not believe human beings were naturally sociable. He claimed that they were self-centered beasts who were utterly without discipline unless it was imposed on them by force.

People escape their terrible natural state by entering a social contract, that is, by agreeing to live in a commonwealth ruled by law. It is their desire for "commodious living" and their fear of death that drive them to accept the constraints of communal life. The social contract obliges every person, for the sake of peace and self-defense, to agree to set aside his or her right to all things and be content with as much liberty against others as he or she would allow others against himself or herself. Because words and promises are insufficient to guarantee this agreement, the social contract also authorizes the coercive use of force to compel compliance.

Believing the dangers of anarchy to be greater than those of tyranny, Hobbes thought that rulers should have unlimited power. He did not think that it mattered much what form governments took (e.g., monarchies or legislative bodies). The crucial factor was that there could be no challenge to their authority. There is little room in Hobbes's political philosophy for protest in the name of individual conscience or for a spiritual authority distinct from secular government. Both Catholics and Puritans criticized these features of *Leviathan*, but Hobbes insisted that loss of rights for some individuals was clearly preferable to the suffering everyone experienced in a civil war.

John Locke: Defender of Moderate Liberty and Toleration

The most influential critic of political absolutism was another Englishman, John Locke (1632–1704). Locke's sympathies were with the leaders of popular revolutions. His father fought with the parliamentary army during the English Civil War, and in 1682 Locke himself joined a rebellion against Charles II led by Anthony Ashley Cooper, the earl of Shaftesbury. Its failure forced him to seek asylum in Holland.

During the reign of Charles II, Locke wrote two *Treatises of Government.* The first was a devastating critique of the traditional arguments for absolutism. These tried to justify the power of rulers by comparing it to the role fathers play in patriarchal families. Locke argued that both fathers and rulers are bound by the law of nature that creates everyone equal and independent. In his *Second Treatise of Government* he made the case for government's obligation to be responsive to the wishes of the governed. He disagreed with Hobbes's assumption that people were driven only by passion and selfish interests and argued that they were endowed by nature with reason and goodwill. They are able to cooperate and live together in peace on their own, but they established governments to solve problems and facilitate social life. Governments are based on social contracts that are meant to protect the liberty of the state of nature, not restrain it. Rulers who fail to honor the terms of such contracts can legitimately be replaced by their subjects.

Locke believed that governments should limit themselves to protecting property and should not make religious decisions for their people. In his *Letter Concerning Toleration* (1689) he argued that each individual was responsible for working out his or her own salvation. Differences of opinion were likely, but uniformity could not be imposed because faith was a matter of conscience. Locke denied religious liberty to two groups—to atheists on the ground that their oaths (lacking any divine sanction) could not be trusted, and to Roman Catholics on the ground that they were pledged to serve a foreign prince (i.e., the pope).

Locke's most immediately influential book was his *Essay Concerning Human Understanding* (1690). It offered a scientific explanation for human psychology. Locke claimed that the mind of a newborn was a blank tablet on which no ideas had yet been inscribed. No knowledge was innate. It all came from sensory experience. This meant that human beings were products of their environments and that they could be reformed and perfected by transforming the world that shaped them. Locke claimed that religious knowledge was acquired like other kinds of knowledge. It came from studying the Scriptures and observing the natural order, not from private revelations. These, he believed, were the source of fanaticism and superstition.

The New Institutions of Expanding Natural Knowledge

Medieval scholars assumed that learning was a process of recovering what had already been discovered by ancient philosophers (such as Aristotle) or revealed to the authors of the Bible and the founders of the church. Even the Protestant reformers saw themselves only as restoring the original Christian message and not as discovering something new in it. As science took root, however, confidence grew that genuinely new discoveries about nature and humanity were possible. Learning could advance by creating new knowledge.

The new intellectual faith that science fostered had wide-ranging social implications. The universities, where traditional scholastic and Aristotelian modes of thought were deeply entrenched, became a frequent target of criticism by advocates of the new science. This was not always entirely fair, for the new ideas did penetrate the universities and some of them provided support for natural philosophers (e.g., Newton). The slowness of the schools to assimilate scientific advances, however, persuaded scientists that they needed to establish new kinds of institutions to advance their work.

Most prominent among these was the Royal Society of London, which was founded in 1660 to promote research and the sharing of scientific information. Similar organizations on both the local and national level sprang up in most European countries. Members of these societies met to hear papers and witness experiments. The high social standing of many society "fellows" lent credibility to reports of scientific discoveries, and their polite exchange of ideas helped promote a culture of civility that elevated science above the religious and political conflicts of the day.

The sixteenth and seventeenth centuries saw Europeans expanding their knowledge into the ancient past, into the New World, and into the starry heavens. In this painting, The Sciences and the Arts, *the artist depicts recent paintings that connect contemporary culture with the ancient world and the Bible. In the same room, he sets globes depicting the New World and astronomical instruments used by natural philosophers exploring the heavens, according to the theories of Copernicus, Kepler, and Galileo. Yet throughout all of the expansion of mind and geographical knowledge, women were generally excluded as they are in this painting. For example, only on the rarest occasion were women permitted to visit the Royal Society of London.* Adriaen Stalbent, *The Sciences and the Arts.* Wood, 93 × 114 cm. Inv. 1405. Museo del Prado, Madrid, Spain. Erich Lessing/Art Resource, NY

Members of these societies were drawn from the intellectual elite, but their interests led them to cooperate with laborers, craftspersons, and sailors whose skills, work experience, and travels made them invaluable sources of aid and information. Learned societies were eager to demonstrate what science could do to solve practical problems—and, thus, to advance the aims of government and enrich economic life. Persons who had ideas for improvements in things such as navigation, agriculture, engineering, and military technology turned to the societies for support, and the patrons of the new science sought to apply knowledge to practical ends, to urge religious toleration, and to promote political liberty. They were the harbingers of a confident, optimistic future.

Women in the World of the Scientific Revolution

Traditions that had long excluded women from intellectual activities continued to block them from doing scientific work. With a very few exceptions, women were not admitted to medieval or early modern universities—a situation that prevailed until the end of the nineteenth century. Women were also not welcomed into the new scientific societies and academies. A few women from the noble and artisan classes managed, however, with the help of male members of their families, to do some scientific work.

Margaret Cavendish (1623–1673), Duchess of Newcastle, was introduced by her husband to a circle of natural philosophers where she debated the theories of Descartes and Hobbes and criticized the Royal Society for doing too little to explore the practical applications of science. She was the only woman allowed to attend a meeting of the society. Her most important scientific publications were *Observations upon Experimental Philosophy* (1666) and *Grounds of Natural Philosophy* (1668). She also wrote a text intended primarily to introduce women to the study of science: *Description of a New World, Called the Blazing World* (1666). A few men similarly wrote popularizations of scientific theories for female audiences.

Women from the artisan classes had more opportunities to pursue science than other females, for they were traditionally trained to work in their families' businesses. Several German astronomers were assisted by their wives and daughters, and some of these women (e.g., Maria Cunitz, Elisabetha Hevelius, and Maria Winkelmann) wrote books or made notable discoveries on their own. After the death of her husband in 1710, Maria Winkelmann (who had discovered a comet in 1702) applied to the Berlin Academy of Sciences for permission to continue her husband's work. She was denied on the basis of her gender. Years later she tried to return as an assistant to her son, but she was ultimately forced to abandon astronomy.

In the 1730s the French philosopher Voltaire relied on the mathematical expertise of Emilie du Châtelet for help in writing a book on Newton, but few women were admitted to the fields of science and medicine before the late nineteenth century. Allegedly scientific arguments were even developed to explain how differences between male and female brains made women intellectual inferiors who were incapable of scientific work. The pursuit of natural knowledge was said to be a male vocation.

The New Science and Religious Faith

Many people believed that the new science posed a challenge to religion. Three issues were most troublesome: (1) disagreements between the biblical descriptions of the heavens and scientific discoveries, (2) the relative authority of clergymen versus scientists, and (3) the tendency of science to promote an exclusively materialistic view of the universe.

The Case of Galileo

The Roman Catholic Church was going through a particularly difficult period in its history when, in 1633, it took the infamous step of condemning the Copernican theory and Galileo. The Council of Trent asserted that the church alone had the authority to interpret the Bible, and in order to counter Protestant accusations that Catholicism had strayed from the Scriptures the church's interpretations had become narrowly literal. Galileo's views on biblical interpretation, which he published in 1615 (*Letter to the Grand Duchess Christina*), sounded suspiciously Protestant to some Catholic leaders, and the astronomer's discoveries seemed to support the Copernican view of the universe, which the church officially condemned as unbiblical in 1616.

Galileo apparently won the church's permission to write about Copernicanism so long as he did not assert its truthfulness but only entertained it as a theoretical possibility. In 1623 a new pope, who was an acquaintance of Galileo's, took office and allowed him to publish his research. The result was a book, *Dialogue on the Two Chief World Systems* (1632), which clearly asserted the correctness of the Copernican model of the heavens. Pope Urban VIII felt betrayed and mocked by Galileo's work and ordered it investigated. Galileo was forced to repudiate his theories, and he spent the last nine years of his life under house arrest. The incident cast a shadow that troubled the relationship between science and Catholic faith for a very long time. Pope John II eventually reopened the case, and in 1992 the church admitted that errors had been made.

Blaise Pascal: Reason and Faith

Blaise Pascal (1623–1662), a French mathematician and physical scientist, made the most influential attempt to reconcile faith with the new science. Pascal was a deeply religious man who surrendered his wealth to pursue a life of austerity, but he opposed the religious dogmatism of people such as the Jesuits as much as the skepticism of atheists and rationalists. Personally, he sided with the Jansenists, the French Catholics who endorsed the Augustinian doctrines of original sin, predestination, and total dependence on grace for salvation and knowledge of God. Unfortunately, he was never able to turn his insights into a fully integrated system. Instead, he published them as a collection of provocative reflections on the human condition, which he entitled *Pensées.*

Pascal believed that reason could reveal humanity's utter corruption, but that it was too weak to resolve the problems of human nature or disclose the meaning of human life. For these purposes, religion was required, and religion operated outside the domain of reason. It required a "leap of faith" that accepted one's total reliance on divine grace. Pascal proposed an ingenious "wager" to demonstrate the unreasonableness of skepticism. He noted that it is a better bet to believe that God exists than to doubt. If God does exist, the believer wins everything. If it turns out that God does not exist, the believer has not lost much by believing. Furthermore, Pascal argued that religious faith is valuable in and of itself apart from the issue of God's existence. It provides motivation for self-discipline and strengthens moral character. Pascal urged people to pursue self-awareness through "learned ignorance" (i.e., through contemplation of the significance of human limitations). This, he hoped, would counter what he saw as the false optimism promoted by the new scientific rationalism.

The English Approach to Science and Religion

Francis Bacon sought to reconcile religion and science by suggesting that the Bible and nature were both sources of divine revelation. Since both were created by God, it was logical to assume that the knowledge they produced would ultimately be discovered not to be incompatible with itself. One could be expected to illuminate the other.

As science promoted a progressively mechanistic view of the universe, men such as Newton came to believe that the rational laws that governed nature implied that nature's Creator was also characterized by rationality. To study nature was to study the Creator and to move gradually from knowledge of phenomena to knowledge of their ultimate cause. Such faith promoted a popular ideology called *physico-theology.* At a time when Europeans were tiring of wars sparked by religious disputes, it held out the hope that science might end such conflicts by developing a new understanding of God on which all parties could agree. Faith in a rational God also encouraged faith in human rationality and humanity's ability to overcome the errors of its past. The new way of life that began to emerge from the new science was increasingly justified as part of a divine plan. It seemed obvious that God had placed rational beings in a rational world so that they should master it. Scientific advance and economic enterprise, thus, became religious missions.

Continuing Superstition

Despite the optimistic confidence certain European intellectuals had in the ultimate triumph of reason, many Europeans of the sixteenth and seventeenth centuries continued to believe in magic and the occult. Almost all Europeans believed to some degree in the Devil and the power of his demons.

Witch Hunts and Panic

Loss of faith in traditional certainties drove some thinkers to seek a new grounding for truth in reason and science, but there was a darker alternative. Many people responded to the intellectual challenges of the age with fear and suspicion, and in their desperate search for security, they crossed the line that divides religion from superstition. This was as true for the learned as for the less educated. Between 1400 and 1700, an estimated 70,000 to 100,000 people were sentenced to death in the West for practicing harmful magic (*maleficium*) and diabolical witchcraft. Between episodes of persecuting their neighbors, witches were said to fly off to conventions called *sabbats* where they engaged in sexual orgies with the Devil and practiced every indecency imaginable. The Reformation may have unintentionally contributed to this development by emphasizing the power of demons and the Devil while eliminating many of the traditional sacraments and rituals that had once offered a defense against these powers of darkness.

Vermeer's The Geographer and The Astronomer: *Painting and the New Knowledge*

The Netherlands stood at the center of the developments that were transforming the intellectual life of Europe in the sixteenth and seventeenth centuries. Dutch opticians and metal workers produced the instruments used in the new science, and Dutch sailors plied the shipping lanes that flooded Europe with information about areas of the world that had previously been unknown to the West. Furthermore, a tradition of religious tolerance, open immigration, and freedom of the press created an atmosphere in the Netherlands that stimulated intellectual activity.

Two paintings by the Dutch artist Jan Vermeer (1632–1675) illustrate the spirit that pervaded the Netherlands. They were intended to be hung side by side and to give meaning to each other. Their subjects, astronomy and geography, were important to the sea-faring Dutch because of the contributions these disciplines made to techniques of navigation. The new maps of the geographer, who gazes out his window onto a world of increasing wonder, acquainted ordinary Europeans with dis-

tant, exotic locales and enabled sailors to conduct the trade on which Dutch prosperity depended. The astronomer contemplates a globe that depicts the constellations of the night sky. A chart containing additional astronomical information hangs on his wall, and an instrument for observing the heavens lies on his table. Plainly working with the data of observation and mathematical theorizing was as important to him as peering at the heavens. The most curious element in the picture is the painting that hangs on the wall at the astronomer's back. It depicts the finding of the infant Moses, a subject that symbolizes God's divine providence. Vermeer may have included it to suggest that the new natural knowledge was a part of God's providential plan for humanity.

Mariet Westermann, *A Worldly Art: The Dutch Republic 1585–1718* (New York: Prentice Hall/Abrams, 1996); Arthur K. Wheelock, Jr., *Vermeer and the Art of Painting* (New Haven: Yale University Press, 1995); J. M. Montias, *Vermeer and His Milieu: A Web of Social History* (Princeton: Princeton University Press, 1989); Arthur K. Wheelock, Jr., *Perspective, Optics, and Delft Artists Around 1650* (New York: Garland Press, 1997)

Vermeer van Delft, Jan, *The Geographer* (1668–1669). Oil on canvas. Staedelsches Kunstinstitute, Frankfurt am Main. The Granger Collection

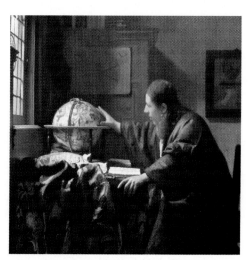

Vermeer van Delft, Jan (1632–1675), *The Astronomer* (1668). Oil on canvas 31.5 × 45.5 cm. Louvre, Dep. des Peintures, Paris, France. Erich Lessing, Art Resource, NY

Three witches suspected of practicing harmful magic are burned alive on a pyre in Bade. On the left, two of them are shown feasting and cavorting with demons at a Sabbat. Bildarchiv, Preussischer Kulturbesitz

Village Origins

Belief in witchcraft pervaded elite as well as popular cultures, but it had deep roots in rural areas. Village societies have customarily dealt with the threats and terrors of life by turning for help to "cunning folk," to people who are believed to have special powers to avert or mitigate natural disasters and ease problems caused by disease and infertility. The witch cultures of medieval and early modern village societies also probably thrived as a form of peasant self-assertion. If they perpetuated ancient, pre-Christian religious practices, their devotees may have seen them as a means for rebelling against the oppressive authority of urban Christian society.

Since a reputation for possession of magical powers gave a person standing in a village society, such claims were often made by people who were most in need of influence—the elderly, the impoverished, and single or widowed women. Should any of their neighbors claim, however, that they used their powers for evil rather than good, they were also the element in society least able to defend itself.

Influence of the Clergy

Widespread faith in magic was the essential precondition for the great witch hunts of the sixteenth and seventeenth centuries, and such belief was not limited to ordinary people. It was shared by intellectuals and the Christian clergy whose sacramental powers were a form of magic. The church promoted fear of demons and the Devil in its efforts to persuade people to accept its discipline, and exorcism of demons was a traditional function of priests.

In the late thirteenth century the church declared that its priests were the only possessors of legitimate magical power. Inasmuch as such power was not human, theologians reasoned that it had to come either from God or from the Devil. Since the only people empowered to act for God were the church's priests, it followed that all other wonder workers must have made pacts with the Devil in order to acquire their magic. The church sincerely believed that it was its duty to root out the servants of the Devil, but by destroying the "cunning folk" it also cleansed village communities of the people who competed with its priests for spiritual authority.

Why Women?

A good 80 percent of the victims of witch hunts were women, most of whom were single and between forty-five and sixty years of age. It is possible that persecution of witches provided a male-dominated society with a means for ridding itself of unconventional women who were not under some man's control. Or it may simply be that older single women were attacked not because of their gender but because they were perceived to be, with other poor people, burdens on society. Some female professions, such as midwifery and nursing, exposed women to suspicion of malfeasance by associating them with mysterious deaths. Economic need may also have driven more women than men to take the risk of claiming supernatural powers as healers and casters of spells.

End of the Witch Hunts

The great witch panics occurred in the second half of the sixteenth and early seventeenth centuries. They were, in part, a response to the suffering caused by the religious divisions and wars that ravaged European society at that time. Increasing levels of violence exacerbated fear and hatred and inspired a search for scapegoats on which to vent these emotions. Witch hunts also helped church and state enforce conformity and eliminate competition for the loyalty of their subjects.

By the end of the seventeenth century, however, authorities began to fear that things were getting out of hand. When it became evident that witch hunting was doing more to destabilize society than to impose order and unanimity, the witch trials ceased. The emergence of the new scientific worldview also undercut belief in witches, and improvements in things such as medicine gave people greater confidence in their ability to solve problems without supernatural assistance. The Reformation may also have helped to end the witch craze by ridiculing the sacramental magic of the old church and by preaching faith in a God who was absolutely sovereign. Ultimately, for Protestants, God was the only significant spiritual force in the universe, and his freely offered grace, not magic, was the only defense against the power of evil.

In Perspective

The Scientific Revolution and the thought of writers whose work was contemporaneous with it mark a major turning point in history. During the seventeenth century, many of the fundamen- *tal premises of the medieval worldview were abandoned. The earth was displaced from the center of the universe, and the universe seemed much larger and more complex than had previously been imagined. New knowledge of the physical universe called into question dogmas that rested on the authority of the church and Scripture. Theology and metaphysics yielded to mathematics as the preferred discipline for exploring nature. Political thought became much less concerned with religious issues and much less in awe of traditional authorities. Arguments were developed to promote greater freedom of religious and political expression. People began to comprehend the influence of environment on human character and action. Life on Earth became the chief preoccupation of Western intellectuals, and they demonstrated greater self-confidence in their capacity to realize its potentials.*

REVIEW QUESTIONS

1. What contributions to the Scientific Revolution were made by Copernicus, Brahe, Kepler, Galileo, and Newton? What did Bacon contribute to the foundation of scientific thought? Who do you think made the most important contribution? Why?

2. Was the Scientific Revolution truly a revolution? Which has a greater impact on history, a political or an intellectual revolution?

3. How do the political philosophies of Hobbes and Locke compare? How did each view human nature? Would you rather live under a government designed by Hobbes or by Locke? Why?

4. What prevented women from playing a greater role in the development of the new science? How did family connections enable some women to contribute to the advance of natural philosophy?

5. What things account for the church's condemnation of Galileo? How did Pascal try to reconcile faith and reason? How did English natural theology encourage economic expansion?

6. How do you explain the fact that witchcraft and witch hunts flourished during an age of scientific enlightenment? Why did the witch panics occur in the late sixteenth and seventeenth centuries? How might the Reformation have affected them?

SUGGESTED READINGS

R. ASHCRAFT, *Revolutionary Politics and Locke's Two Treatises of Government* (1986). The most important study of Locke to appear in recent years.

J. BARRY, M. HESTER, and G. ROBERTS, eds. *Witchcraft in Early Modern Europe: Studies in Culture and Belief* (1998). A collection of recent essays.

H. BUTTERFIELD, *The Origins of Modern Science, 1300–1800* (1949). A classic survey.

H. F. COHEN, *The Scientific Revolution: A Historiographical Inquiry* (1994). Supplants all previous discussions of the history and concept of the Scientific Revolution.

M. A. FINOCCHIARO, *The Galileo Affair: A Documentary History* (1989). A collection of all the relevant documents and introductory commentary.

S. GAUKROGER, *Descartes: An Intellectual Biography* (1995). A major work that explores both the science and philosophy in Descartes's work.

A. GOLDGAR, *Impolite Learning: Conduct and Community in the Republic of Letters, 1680–1750* (1995). A lively survey of the structure of the European intellectual community.

I. HARRIS, *The Mind of John Locke: A Study of Political Theory in Its Intellectual Setting* (1994). The most comprehensive recent treatment.

A. JOHNS, *The Nature of the Book: Print and Knowledge in the Making* (1998). A brilliant study of the role of printing in the intellectual life of early modern Europe.

R. KIECKHEFER, *European Witch Trials: Their Foundations in Popular and Learned Culture, 1300–1500* (1976). Excellent background for understanding the great witch panic.

T. S. KUHN, *The Copernican Revolution* (1957). A scholarly treatment.

B. LEVACK, *The Witch Hunt in Early Modern Europe* (1986). Lucid up-to-date survey of research.

D. LINDBERG and R. L. NUMBERS, eds., *God and Nature: Historical Essays on the Encounter Between Christianity and Science* (1986). An excellent collection of essays.

L. PYENSON and S. SHEETS-PYENSON, *Servants of Nature: A History of Scientific Institutions, Enterprises, and Sensibilities* (1999). A history of the settings in which the creation and diffusion of scientific knowledge have occurred.

E. REEVES, *Painting the Heavens: Art and Science in the Age of Galileo* (1997). An exploration of the impact of Galileo's thought on the visual arts.

L. SCHIEBINGER, *The Mind Has No Sex: Women in the Origins of Modern Science* (1989). A major study of the subject.

S. SHAPIN, *The Scientific Revolution* (1996). The best brief introduction.

K. THOMAS, *Religion and the Decline of Magic* (1971). Provocative, much-acclaimed work focused on popular culture.

R. TUCK, *Philosophy and Government 1572–1651* (1993). A continent-wide survey.

R. S. WESTFALL, *Never at Rest: A Biography of Isaac Newton* (1981). An important major study.

P. ZAGORIN, *Francis Bacon* (1998). A comprehensive treatment.

Chapter 15
Successful and Unsuccessful Paths to Power (1686–1740)

KEY TOPICS

- The Dutch Golden Age
- French aristocratic resistance to the monarchy
- Early eighteenth-century political stability
- The efforts of the Habsburgs to secure their holdings
- The emergence of Prussia as a major power under the Hohenzollerns
- The efforts of Peter the Great to transform Russia into a powerful, centralized nation along Western lines

The late seventeenth and early eighteenth centuries witnessed significant shifts of power within Europe. Great Britain, France, Austria, Russia, and Prussia emerged as the dominant states, while Spain, the United Netherlands, Poland, Sweden, and the Holy Roman and Ottoman empires declined. The most successful countries were those that developed strong central governments. During the seventeenth century, the turmoil created by the English civil wars and the Fronde in France had impressed people with the value of a monarch as a guarantor of domestic tranquility. On the continent, this created support for the kind of absolutist government pioneered by France's Louis XIV. The path a nation took was often a function of the character, personality, and energy of its ruler.

The Maritime Powers

Spain and the United Netherlands had been major powers during the sixteenth and seventeenth centuries, but during the eighteenth century they became politically and militarily marginal as England and France took the lead. Both, however, retained considerable economic power and influence.

The Netherlands: Golden Age to Decline

The seven provinces that became the United Provinces of the Netherlands formed the only genuinely new state to appear in Europe during the early modern period. They first asserted their independence in a revolt against Spain in 1572. In the 1580s they won recognition from the other European powers, and Spain acknowledged their autonomy in 1609 and their formal independence in 1648.

While rising powers such as France and England chose to develop strongly centralized governments, the Dutch opted for a republic in which each of their provinces retained considerable authority. The States General, the central government seated in the Hague, tended to be dominated by the prosperous, populous province of Holland. From time to time when war demanded a more powerful executive, the Dutch would permit a member of the noble House of Orange to assume leadership. William III, the *stadtholder* of Holland, led a European coalition against Louis XIV of France and ultimately shared the throne of England with his wife, Mary. Following his death in 1702 and the conclusion of peace with France in 1714, the Dutch returned to republican government.

The official church of the Netherlands stood in the Calvinist Reform tradition, but allegiance to it was not enforced. The population remained religiously mixed, and the Netherlands enjoyed a reputation for tolerance that made it a haven for Jews driven out of other countries. Tolerance proved a workable policy that spared the Netherlands the internal strife that plagued so many other European states.

URBAN PROSPERITY The Dutch were remarkable to their contemporaries as much for their prosperity as their spirit of tolerance. While other states squandered resources on religious wars, the Dutch concentrated on economic development. They transformed agriculture, promoted trade and finance, and built an overseas commercial empire. The Netherlands became the most urbanized region in Europe, boasting a percentage of urban dwellers in its population that other countries did not reach until the industrial era.

The concentration of the Dutch in cities was made possible by innovations in agriculture that were copied throughout Europe. During the seventeenth century Dutch farmers drained and reclaimed a great deal of land from the sea. Since Dutch shipping dominated trade with the Baltic, the Netherlands was able to feed itself with cheap grain from that region. This enabled Dutch farmers to devote their land to more profitable cash crops (e.g., dairy products, meat, and even tulip bulbs). Dutch fishing fleets supplied much of the

In the mid-eighteenth century, when this picture of the Amsterdam Exchange was painted, Amsterdam had replaced the cities of Italy and south Germany as the leading banking center of Europe. Amsterdam retained this position until the late eighteenth century. Painting by Hiob A. Berckheyde, *The Amsterdam Exchange.* Canvas 85 × 105 cm. Coll. Museum Boijmans Van Beuningen, Rotterdam, The Netherlands herring (a major source of inexpensive protein) consumed on the continent, and Dutch mills provided textiles to many parts of Europe. Dutch ships were found in every European port transporting all kinds of goods, and ship building itself constituted a highly profitable industry for the Netherlands. Profits from these enterprises provided capital for banks, and the Dutch boasted the most advanced financial system of their day. Shareholders funded ventures such as the Dutch East Indies Company, which won control of the East Asian spice trade from the Portuguese. The Netherlands retained a colonial presence in Indonesia until after World War II.

ECONOMIC DECLINE   For a variety of reasons, the Dutch economy began to weaken in the eighteenth century. After the death of William III in 1702, the provinces blocked the rise of another powerful *stadtholder* who could provide unified political leadership. Naval supremacy began to pass to England, the fishing industry declined, and the Dutch lost the technological lead in shipbuilding. Countries developed their own fleets to carry their own goods rather than relying on Dutch shipping, and Dutch manufacturing began to stagnate. The absence of vigorous leadership handicapped efforts to confront these challenges, but the Netherlands still managed to retain considerable influence thanks to its banks and stock exchange.

France after Louis XIV

France, although less strong in 1715 than in 1680, was still a great power. It had a large population, an advanced economy, and a highly developed administrative structure. Its resources were drained by the last of Louis XIV's wars, but these conflicts had similarly debilitated the other major European states. All that France needed in order to recover economically was intelligent leadership and a less ambitious foreign policy.

France did begin to recover, but not because of an improvement in the quality of its leadership. The prestige of the monarchy was already faltering when Louis XIV passed the crown to his five-year-old great-grandson Louis XV (r. 1715–1774). The young king's regent—his uncle, the duke of Orléans—made a deteriorating situation worse. Orléans was a gambler who turned over the financial management of the government to a Scottish speculator, John Law (1671–1729). Law believed

that an increase in the money supply would stimulate postwar economic recovery, so he established a bank to issue paper money. Law transferred responsibility for managing the national debt that this money represented to the Mississippi Company, a corporation that had a monopoly on trading privileges with France's Louisiana colony in North America. The company issued shares of its stock in exchange for government bonds and relied on profits from stock speculation to redeem those bonds. Initially the price of the stock rose handsomely, but smart investors took their profits and exchanged the paper currency from Law's bank for gold. Since the bank lacked sufficient bullion to back up the money it printed, in February 1720, the government had to halt gold trading in France. Law fled the country, and the "Mississippi Bubble" (as the affair was called) burst. The fiasco brought disgrace on the government and cast a shadow over economic activity in France for the rest of the century.

RENEWED AUTHORITY OF THE *PARLEMENTS*   The duke of Orléans further weakened the monarchy by trying to recreate a role for the French nobility in the decision-making processes of the government. Louis XIV had filled governmental offices with commoners and kept aristocrats distracted and competing for meaningless honors at Versailles. The regent was pressured by the aristocrats to restore their influence, and he set up a system of administrative councils on which nobles served with bureaucrats. The experiment failed, for the nobles, whom Louis had thoroughly domesticated, lacked both the talent and the will to govern.

The great French families were not, however, prepared to yield ground in their ancient fight to limit the power of the monarchy over their landed domains. Their most effective weapons in this struggle were the *parlements*, the aristocratically dominated courts. The French *parlements* were different from the English Parliament. They did not have the power to legislate, but as courts that enforced the law, their formal approval was required to make a royal law valid. Louis XIV had curtailed the authority of stubborn, uncooperative *parlements*, but the duke of Orléans restored their right to register laws. For the rest of the century, until the revolution that overthrew the monarchy in 1790, the aristocrats used the *parlements* to resist royal authority.

Rachel Ruysch, Flower Still Life: Flowers, Commerce, and Morality

*P*aintings often contain symbols that give them a deeper meaning than is apparent to the casual observer. This is most obvious when a painter develops an allegorical scene employing mythological figures, but it can also be a characteristic of a still life—a painting of objects. Rachel Ruysch (1664–1750), a female artist working in Amsterdam, chose elaborate floral arrangements as her favorite subject. Several decades before Ruysch completed this painting (*Flower Still Life*) a peculiar mania had swept Holland for wild financial speculation in rare tulip bulbs. This picture and the hundreds of similar ones that were produced in the seventeenth and eighteenth centuries would have reminded people of that event. Flowers represented work and commerce, not just the aesthetic beauties of nature. Commercial growers dealt in exotic plants brought to the Netherlands from its overseas empire, and they symbolized the country's global trade. The flowers depicted here were valuable varieties, not humble blooms. As such, they were emblematic of wealth and abundance.

Paintings such as this one helped the Dutch reconcile life in Europe's richest society with the frugality and abstinence that were the values of their Calvinistic faith. The melancholy atmosphere that hovers over these lush blossoms reminds the viewer that all rare and lovely things soon decay. Shadows surround the flowers' riotous display of beauty, and the empty snail shells on the table hint at death and the transitory nature of existence. The artist's extraordinary attention to detail witnesses, however, to the interests of a scientifically inclined age in accurately describing and cataloguing the transitory things of this world. She probably worked from botanical manuals rather than

Rachel Ruysch, Dutch, 1664–1750, *Flower Still Life* (1956.57). The Toledo Museum of Art, Toledo, Ohio. Purchased with funds from the Libbey Endowment, Gift of Edward Drummond Libbey

from real floral arrangements, for the flowers she depicts did not all bloom in the same season.

Sources: Norman Bryson, *Looking at the Overlooked: Four Essays on Still Life Painting* (Cambridge, MA: Harvard University Press, 1990); Mariët Westermann, *A Worldly Art: The Dutch Republic, 1585–1718* (Upper Saddle River, NJ and New York: Prentice Hall Publishers, Inc., and Harry N. Abrams, Inc., 1990); Marilyn Stokstad, *Art History*, rev. ed. (Upper Saddle River, NJ and New York: Prentice Hall Publishers, Inc., and Harry N. Abrams, Inc., 1999), pp. 798–801.

ADMINISTRATION OF CARDINAL FLEURY   After 1726 things briefly improved for the monarchy thanks to a seventy-three-year-old churchman, Cardinal Fleury (1653–1743), who became the king's chief minister. Like his seventeenth-century predecessors, the cardinals Richelieu and Mazarin, Fleury was a political realist who understood that the nobles were both politically ambitious and irresponsible. He believed that steps had to be taken to enable France to recover economically. To this end, he avoided expensive military ventures, repudiated part of the national debt, built roads and bridges, and encouraged the growth of new industries. He was never able, however, to impose sufficient taxes on the nobles or the church to put the state on a stable financial footing.

Following Fleury's death in 1743, his work was speedily undone. Despite the cardinal's best efforts to train Louis XV for the responsibilities of office, the king possessed all the vices and none of the virtues of his great-grandfather. He wanted absolute power but would not work the long hours required to use it. He became a pawn of the intrigues of his court, and his personal life was scandalous. Louis XV was too mediocre a man to be evil, but in a monarch mediocrity could do as much damage as wickedness.

Despite its lack of able leadership, France remained a major power. At midcentury its army was still the largest and strongest on the continent. Its commerce and production were expanding. Its colonies were producing wealth and spurring the growth of domestic industries. France had great potential, but it lacked a head capable of exploiting its opportunities.

Great Britain: The Age of Walpole

THE HANOVERIAN DYNASTY   The British monarchy was not as degraded as the French, but it was not entirely stable. In 1701 Parliament's Act of Settlement had positioned the German house of Hanover to inherit the throne. But a challenge was mounted to the ascension of the first member of the dynasty, George I (r. 1714–1727). In December 1715, James II's son, James Edward, the "Stuart pretender" (1688–1766), landed in Scotland and began to rally an army. His men were soon dispersed, but the experience alerted the new dynasty to the necessity of consolidating its position.

WHIGS AND TORIES   During the seventeenth century, England had been one of the most politically restive countries in Europe, and as Queen Anne's reign (1702–1714) came to a close, there were sharp clashes between political factions called Whigs and Tories. Neither group was organized like a modern political party. Each was a network of like-minded local politicians whose points of view were articulated by a few national spokesmen. The Tories favored a strong monarchy, low taxes for landowners, and the Anglican Church. The Whigs believed that the monarchy should acknowledge the sovereignty of Parliament. They defended urban commercial interests and rural landowners, and they advocated religious toleration for Protestant nonconformists. Both groups were conservative in that they defended the status quo.

The Tories wanted peace with France, but the Elector of Hanover, who was to succeed Queen

Madame de Pompadour (1721–1764) was the mistress of Louis XV. She exercised considerable political influence at the court and was a notable patron of artists, craftspeople, and writers. This 1763 portrait is by Hubert Drouais (1727–1775).   Liaison Agency, Inc.

Anne as George I, believed that it was in Hanover's interest to keep France at war. The Whigs sought his support, and in the final months of Anne's reign, some Tories opened channels of communication with the Stuart pretender. Given this, it was little wonder that the Whigs won the confidence of the new king. For the forty years following his succession, the chief difference between Whigs and Tories was that the former were given public offices and patronage and the latter were not.

THE LEADERSHIP OF ROBERT WALPOLE English politics remained in a state of flux until Robert Walpole (1676–1745) persuaded the king to redesign the nation's government. Walpole, a Norfolk squire, had been active in the House of Commons and had served as a cabinet minister. A British financial scandal similar to France's Mississippi Bubble scheme brought him to the king's attention.

Management of Britain's national debt had been assigned to the South Sea Company. The company exchanged government bonds for its stock, and, as in the French case, the price of its stock soared until speculators began to sell their holdings. Parliament intervened in 1720 to prevent a crash and, under Walpole's leadership, adopted measures to honor the national debt. Walpole's contemporaries credited him with saving the financial integrity of the nation.

Walpole has often been described as the first prime minister of Great Britain. He originated England's system of administration by a cabinet of ministers—each of whom had responsibility for a separate branch of government. But unlike a modern prime minister, he was not chosen by the House of Commons. His power depended on his ability to manipulate the House while retaining the favor of his kings, George I and George II (r. 1727–1760).

Walpole's slogan, "Let sleeping dogs lie," summarized his policy of maintaining peace abroad while promoting the status quo at home. Corruption was the glue that held his government together, for politicians quickly learned that to oppose him was to risk the almost certain loss of government patronage for self, family, and friends.

THE STRUCTURE OF PARLIAMENT The eighteenth-century British House of Commons was neither a democratic nor a representative body. Members of Parliament were chosen by property owners and expected to protect their economic and social interests. Each county elected two members. But if the more powerful landed families in a county agreed on the candidates, there was no contest. Other members were chosen by units called boroughs. A few boroughs were large enough to hold truly democratic elections, but most boroughs had a very small number of electors. A rich family could buy up most of the property to which the votes of a borough were attached and, in effect, own a seat in Parliament.

Members of Parliament did not pretend to represent the people at large, but they provided England with unified government. Owners of property were suspicious of the bureaucrats who worked for the crown and preferred to bear the burdens of local administration themselves (e.g., as judges, militia commanders, tax collectors). In this sense Britain's nobles and substantial landowners governed the nation. Since Parliament represented their interests, they acknowledged its sovereignty as a central political authority. Parliament, thus, provided Britain with the kind of unity that was possible elsewhere in Europe only under an absolutist monarchy.

Parliament also provided the British government with a sound financial base. Continental kings could impose taxes unilaterally, but the British monarch could do so only with the consent of Parliament. Since the property owners represented in Parliament levied taxes on themselves, in England, unlike France, there were virtually no exemptions from taxation. Consequently, vast sums could be raised to fight the wars that Parliament endorsed. By 1693, when the Bank of England was set up to regulate credit, financial policies were in place that enabled Britain to become a great power.

The British people enjoyed more political freedom than the citizens of continental states. Patronage did not stifle divergent points of view among members of the government. Newspapers and public debate flourished. Free speech and freedom of association were possible, and there was no standing army to intimidate the populace. Rights that the English regarded as traditional raised a real barrier to the government's arbitrary use of power. If public outcry was loud enough, Parliament would rescind unpopular measures or allow itself to be persuaded to begin or end wars. Despite manifest corruption, Britain became a European power of the first order with a form of government and an economy that inspired progressive thinkers across Europe.

Central and Eastern Europe

The maritime nations of western Europe had well-defined borders and strong central governments. Their battles were more often fought on the high seas and in their overseas empires than on European territory. East of the Elbe River, however, political organization was "soft." Economies were largely agrarian. Serfdom persisted. Cities were few. No states had overseas empires or much overseas trade. Wars were fought out at home rather than abroad and accustomed people to frequently shifting political loyalties. The rulers of the region's numerous small states and principalities resisted the development of any centralized monarchy.

In the last half of the seventeenth century, political and social institutions emerged that were to characterize eastern and central Europe for the next 200 years. Following the Peace of Westphalia, the Austrian Habsburgs resigned themselves to the weakness of Germany's Holy Roman Empire and turned their attention to developing a base of power farther east. At the same time in northern Germany, Prussia evolved

as a challenger to Habsburg domination. By the start of the eighteenth century, Russia, too, was becoming a major military power. As Sweden, Poland, and the Ottoman Empire faded, Austria, Prussia, and Russia began to flourish.

Sweden: The Ambitions of Charles XII

Sweden had seized the opportunity of the Thirty Years' War to make a bid for empire. During the seventeenth century, it won control of the Baltic and permitted Russia and Germany access to the sea only on its terms. Sweden's economy was not strong enough, however, to sustain its political success.

In 1697 a headstrong (possibly insane) king, Charles XII (r. 1697–1718), ascended Sweden's throne. Three years later Russia launched the Great Northern War (1700–1721) to win a foothold on the Baltic. Charles XII fought vigorously and often brilliantly, but he mismanaged the campaign. After an initial victory and a distracting foray into Poland, he invaded Russia. His army bogged down in the brutal winter weather and suffered decisive defeat at Poltava in 1709. The war ended in 1721, when Sweden ran out of resources. Russia occupied a large section of the eastern Baltic coast and broke Sweden's monopoly of the sea. After Charles XII's death, the Swedish nobles limited the

William Hogarth produced a series of etchings to satirize the notoriously corrupt English electoral system. In this one he shows voters being offered bribes and free gin before they headed off to the polls. Voting was public, for the secret ballot was not introduced in England until 1872. William Hogarth, *An Election Entertainment,* Print. The Metropolitan Museum of Art, Harris Brisbane Dick Fund, 1932. 32.35(212)

power of the monarchy, and Sweden abandoned foreign adventures.

The Ottoman Empire

The Ottoman Empire was the chief barrier to expansion of Europe's major southeastern states: the Austrian Habsburg domain and Russia. Late in the seventeenth century the Ottomans still controlled most of the Balkan peninsula and the entire coastline of the Black Sea.

Although officially Islamic, the Ottoman Empire contained an ethnically and religiously diverse population. Its government worked through religiously defined political entities called *millets*. Laws and regulations applied to people according to the *millets* to which they belonged rather than to the districts in which they lived. The non-Islamic residents of the empire (the *zimmis*) could practice their faiths, but they were second-class citizens who could not rise in the service of the empire. This arrangement limited interaction among—and integration of—people of different faiths.

From its beginnings in the fifteenth century, the Ottoman Empire had been an aggressive power pressing westward from Istanbul (Constantinople) into Europe. By 1683 it was besieging the city of Vienna and forcing Christians in the Balkan peninsula and on the islands of the eastern Mediterranean to convert to Islam. Many of these people had previously been compelled by the Venetians to accept Roman Catholicism, and they welcomed the Turks as liberators.

By the end of the seventeenth century, the Ottomans were overextending themselves. Since military campaigns left Ottoman sultans little time to attend to civilian affairs, political factions in the capital acquired considerable independence. They resisted attempts to strengthen the central government, and rivalries among them weakened the effectiveness of the empire's administration. Control of distant provinces came to depend on the goodwill of native rulers, and commercial agents representing foreign nations dominated the empire's trade and its economy.

By the early eighteenth century, the weakness of the Ottoman Empire was creating a political vacuum on the southeastern perimeter of Europe. For the next two centuries European states probed and appropriated parts of the empire. In 1699 the Turks surrendered Hungary, Transylvania, Croatia, and Slavonia to the Habsburgs. Russia also moved into Ottoman territory, and early in the nineteenth century many of the peoples who lived in the Balkans and around the Black Sea launched campaigns to establish independent states. The result was political and ethnic turmoil that has yet to end.

Poland: Absence of Strong Central Authority

In no other part of Europe was the failure to maintain a competitive political position so complete as in Poland. The fault lay with the Polish nobility, who defeated all attempts to establish an effective central government—even one of their own making.

The Polish monarchy was elective, and divisions among the noble families prevented them from choosing one of their own to be king. Most of Poland's monarchs, therefore, were outsiders and puppets of foreign powers. The Polish nobles belonged to a central legislative body called the *Sejm* (i.e., Diet). It was an aristocratic assembly that excluded representatives from corporate bodies, such as towns. The Diet was virtually powerless. Its rule of *liberum veto* permitted any one of its members unilaterally to disband its meetings—a practice known as "exploding" the Diet. The need to achieve unanimity on every issue made it extremely difficult for the Diet to do much. Government as it was developing elsewhere in Europe simply was not tolerated in Poland. Consequently, during the last half of the eighteenth century, Poland disappeared from the map of Europe.

The Habsburg Empire and the Pragmatic Sanction

The Thirty Years' War was a turning point for the Austrian Habsburgs. It ended their dream of winning control over Germany and returning it to the Catholic fold. The decline of the Spanish branch of the family freed the Austrian Habsburgs to strike out in a new direction of their own.

The Treaty of Westphalia had legalized Protestantism and recognized the autonomy of more than 300 political entities within the Holy Roman Empire. The Habsburg family retained its hold on the imperial title, but the effectiveness of the title depended on the emperor's ability to

MAP 15–1   THE AUSTRIAN HABSBURG EMPIRE, 1522–1772   *The empire's three chief units were Austria, Bohemia, and Hungary. Expansion was mainly eastward, acquiring East Hungary from the Ottomans in the seventeenth century and Galacia from Poland in 1772. Silesia was lost, but the imperial title preserved some influence for the Habsburgs in Germany.*

elicit cooperation from the members of the imperial Diet. Although the post-Westphalian Holy Roman Empire resembled Poland in its lack of central authority, the Diet (which met at Regensburg from 1663 until its final dissolution in 1806) achieved some coordination of economic and political interests. The Habsburgs' domains and the emerging Prussian state also helped stabilize Germany.

CONSOLIDATION OF AUSTRIAN POWER   The Habsburgs began by consolidating their power within their hereditary possessions. These consisted of the Crown of Saint Wenceslas (i.e., the kingdom of Bohemia in what was until recently Czechoslovakia and the duchies of Moravia and Silesia) and the Crown of Saint Stephen (i.e., Hungary, Croatia, and Transylvania). In the early eighteenth century the family acquired the former Spanish (thereafter Austrian) Netherlands, Lombardy in northern Italy, and, for a brief time, the Kingdom of Naples in southern Italy. For most of the eighteenth and nineteenth centuries, the Habsburgs' power derived from lands outside Germany.

The Habsburgs' possessions were extremely difficult to rule. The various properties that composed the empire were held by different titles, and in most areas the Habsburgs could govern only with the cooperation of the local nobles. Geographical barriers and differences of language and custom prevented the Habsburgs' subjects from developing a common identity. Even the Habsburg zeal for Roman Catholicism was no bond for unity, for many of the Magyar nobles of Hungary were zealous Calvinists. The Habsburgs tried to chart common policies for their far-flung domains, but they repeatedly found it necessary to make concessions to nobles in one part of Europe to maintain their position in another.

Despite these difficulties, Leopold I (r. 1657–1705) was able to keep both the Turks and France's Louis XIV at bay. In 1699 the Ottomans recognized his sovereignty over Hungary, and Leopold's increasing strength in the East enhanced his political leverage in Germany. He began to bring his Magyar subjects under control and to extend his reach into the Balkan peninsula and western Romania. These new possessions

MAP 15–2   EXPANSION OF BRANDENBURG-PRUSSIA   *Brandenburg-Prussia expanded during the seventeenth century by acquiring dynastic titles to geographically separated lands. In the eighteenth century it resorted to aggression, seizing Silesia in 1740 and parts of Poland in 1772, 1793, and 1795.*

made it possible for him to turn the port of Trieste into a base for Habsburg power in the Mediterranean.

THE HABSBURG DYNASTIC PROBLEM   Leopold was succeeded by Joseph I (r. 1705–1711) and Charles VI (r. 1711–1740). Charles, who had no male heir, feared that after his death the European powers would intervene in the Austrian Habsburg lands just as they had in the Spanish Habsburgs' domains in 1700. To prevent this and to provide his realm with a semblance of legal unity, he devoted most of his reign to winning the approval of his family, the various diets representing his subjects, and Europe's chief nations for a document called the Pragmatic Sanction. It recognized a single line of inheritance for the Habsburg dynasty through Charles VI's daughter Maria Theresa (r. 1740–1780).

Charles succeeded in establishing a clear line of succession and a basis for legal bonds among the Habsburg holdings, but he could not prevent other nations from attacking his daughter. Less

than two months after his death, the fragility of his foreign agreements became clear. In December 1740, Frederick II of Prussia invaded the Habsburg province of Silesia, and Maria Theresa had to fight to defend her inheritance.

Prussia and the Hohenzollerns

Like the Habsburgs, the Hohenzollerns of Prussia held a scattered collection of lands by a variety of different feudal titles. But the Hohenzollerns were more successful than the Habsburgs in forging their diverse properties into a centrally administered state. They constructed a powerful bureaucratic machine to mobilize every social class and most economic pursuits in support of the institution on which the state was founded: the army. As a result, *Prussian* has become synonymous with administrative rigor and military discipline.

A STATE OF DISCONNECTED TERRITORIES   The Hohenzollern family rose to prominence in 1417 as rulers of the German territory of Brandenburg. To this they added the duchy of Cleves and the counties of Mark and Ravensburg in 1609, the duchy of East Prussia in 1618, and the duchy of Pomerania in 1637. At Westphalia in 1648 the Hohenzollerns lost part of Pomerania to Sweden but were compensated by the grant of three bishoprics and the promise of the archbishopric of Magdeburg (1680). By the late seventeenth century the scattered Hohenzollern holdings constituted a block of territory within the Holy Roman Empire second in size only to that of the Habsburgs.

Despite its size, the Hohenzollern conglomerate was weak. Except for Pomerania, none of the new acquisitions was contiguous with the home base in Brandenburg. All were exposed to foreign aggression. All were poor in natural resources. Many had been devastated during the Thirty Years' War. Each was dominated by a native aristocracy that limited the power of the Hohenzollern ruler. They shared no single concern that might encourage their unification.

FREDERICK WILLIAM, THE GREAT ELECTOR Frederick William (r. 1640–1688), "the Great Elector," transformed this unlikely mix of possessions into a powerful modern state. His instruments were a tightly centralized bureaucracy and a rigorously disciplined army. The threat of invasion by Sweden or Poland helped persuade his subjects to cooperate in the creation of these institutions.

The army with which Frederick William began his reign was too small to intimidate his neighbors. In 1655, when the Brandenburg estates refused his request for taxes to finance a larger force, he used the soldiers at his disposal to collect the money he needed to employ more. He also skillfully co-opted potential opponents. In exchange for supporting the Hohenzollerns, the Prussian nobles, the Junkers, were granted complete control over the serfs on their estates. Frederick William also used the Junkers to collect his taxes, which fell most heavily not on the nobility, but on the peasants and the urban classes. The privilege of joining the army officer corps became an honor reserved to men of aristocratic lineage.

Since the army was the one institution that drew members from all the Hohenzollern territories and all its soldiers and civilian personnel took an oath of loyalty to the elector, the army defined the state. Total mobilization of the state's resources enabled Frederick William to build a military machine far larger than that usually sustained by a small country. Prussia, thus,

became a power with which other (and larger) nations had to reckon.

FREDERICK WILLIAM I, KING OF PRUSSIA The house of Hohenzollern had created a nation, but it did not yet possess a crown. The acquisition of a royal title was the achievement of the Great Elector's son, Frederick I (r. 1688–1713). Frederick was the least "Prussian" member of his family. He built palaces, founded Halle University (1694), supported the arts, and lived luxuriously. In 1700, when the War of the Spanish Succession broke out, he made a deal with the Holy Roman Emperor. In exchange for the use of the Prussian army, the emperor permitted Frederick to assume the title "King in Prussia."

Frederick's heir, Frederick William I (r. 1713–1740), was both the most eccentric and the most effective of the Hohenzollern monarchs. After giving his father a funeral that would have pleased the luxury-loving Frederick I, Frederick William I imposed policies of strict austerity. He increased the size of the army and consolidated an obedient, compliant bureaucracy. He ruled alone without the assistance of ministers. His officials submitted reports in writing to him in his office, his *Kabinett*. Then he alone studied the papers, made decisions, and issued orders.

Frederick William's civilian bureaucrats worked under military discipline. All departments were centrally managed by the General Directory, the *General-Ober Finanz-Kriegs-und-Domänen- Direktorium*. The nobility were subjected to taxation, and most remaining feudal dues were transformed into money payments. Service to the state and the monarch became an automatic impersonal reflex—a mechanical and unquestioning recognition of a duty to a public office, not a loyalty engendered by any feeling for the unique qualities of the individual who held that office.

THE PRUSSIAN ARMY Frederick William was a near fanatic where his army was concerned. He required each district in his kingdom to provide him with a certain number of men. They were trained with rigorous discipline, and a show regiment composed of the tallest men in Europe was recruited. There were different laws for soldiers and for civilians, and royal patronage made the officer corps society's highest class. Frederick William merged the army, the Junker nobility, and the monarchy into a single political entity.

In 1725 he began the practice of always appearing in military uniform in order to publicize his concept of the state. Frederick William's military force grew from about 39,000 in 1713 to over 80,000 in 1740. Prussia was only the thirteenth most populous nation in Europe, but it fielded Europe's third or fourth largest army. Military priorities and values dominated Prussian government, society, and daily life as no place else in Europe. Other nations possessed armies, but Prussia was possessed by its army.

Having built the best army in Europe, Frederick William avoided using it. He enjoyed drilling his soldiers but not sending them into battle. He was capable of terrorizing his family and associates—occasionally knocking out teeth with his walking stick. But he did not pursue aggressive foreign policies. He regarded the army as a symbol of Prussian power and unity, not an instrument to be used for foreign adventures.

Frederick II, "the Great" (r. 1740–1786) inherited his father's superb military machine, but not his father's self-restraint. He celebrated his ascension to the throne by invading Silesia and challenging Austria for control of Germany. The struggle dominated central European affairs for over a century.

Russia Enters the European Political Arena

The rise of Prussia and the consolidation of the Austrian Habsburg domains doubtless seemed to many at the time only one more shift in the ancient game of German politics. But the entrance of Russia into European affairs was something wholly new. Russia had long been considered a part of Europe only by courtesy. Hemmed in by Sweden on the Baltic and by the Ottoman Empire on the Black Sea, it had no warm-water ports. Archangel, a port on the White Sea, was its chief outlet to the West, but it was closed by ice during part of the year. Russia was a land of vast but unfocused potential.

Birth of the Romanov Dynasty

The reign of Ivan IV, "the Terrible" (1533–1584), the first Muscovite prince to use the title "Tsar of Russia," was followed by a period of anarchy and civil war. In 1613 an assembly of nobles tried to end the confusion of this "Time of Troubles" by recognizing the seventeen-year-old Michael Romanov (r. 1613–1654) as their tsar. He founded the dynasty that ruled Russia until 1917.

Michael Romanov and his two successors, Alexis I (r. 1654–1676) and Theodore III (r. 1676–1682), stabilized Russia's government, but their nation remained weak and poor. Russia's administrative bureaucracy was dominated by the old nobility (the *boyars*), and it was only barely capable of maintaining order. The chief sources of instability were peasant revolts, raids by cossacks (horsemen who lived on the steppe frontier), and the potentially mutinous *streltsy*, Moscow's garrison.

Peter the Great

In 1682 two boys ascended Russia's fragile throne: Peter I, "the Great" (r. 1682–1725), and Ivan V. The succession was bloodily disputed, and the *streltsy* decided the outcome. Sophia, the boys' elder sister, served as regent until Peter's followers overthrew her in 1689. Peter then ruled personally, although in theory he shared the crown with the sickly Ivan until Ivan's death in 1696.

Like Louis XIV of France, whose youthful development had also been shaped by the experience of social upheaval, Peter resolved to establish a strong central monarchy. For ideas about how this could be done, he turned to the West. Products and workers from the West had filtered into Russia, and Europe's culture, particularly its military science, intrigued Peter.

In 1697 Peter made a famous tour of Europe. For convenience, he traveled officially incognito rather than as a head of state. (This minimized ceremonial functions.) The European leaders whom he visited found their almost seven-foot-tall guest both crude and rude. But Peter was thoroughly at home in their shipyards and munitions factories. They offered him what he had come to find.

Peter returned to Moscow determined to Westernize Russia. He set himself four objectives that he pursued ruthlessly: taming the *boyars* and the *streltsy*, extending royal authority over the church, reorganizing governmental administration, and developing the economy. Policy in each of these areas was intended to strengthen the military power of the nation and the authority of the monarchy.

TAMING THE *BOYARS* AND *STRELTSY*   In 1698, immediately on his return from abroad, Peter launched an attack on the *boyars*. He personally shaved their long beards and sheared off the dangling sleeves of their shirts and coats—Russian peculiarities that western Europeans mocked. More important, he pressed the *boyars* into government service. In 1722 he published a Table of Ranks that pegged a person's social status to his position in the bureaucracy or the army. This induced boyars to submit to the service of the state, but the Russian nobility was never as thoroughly domesticated as the Prussian aristocracy.

The *streltsy* fared less well than the *boyars.* They rebelled while Peter was on his European tour. When he returned, he brutally suppressed their revolt and executed about 1,200 of them. Their corpses were publicly displayed to demonstrate the consequences of disloyalty to the tsar.

ACHIEVING SECULAR CONTROL OF THE CHURCH
Peter was similarly ruthless in his dealings with the Russian Orthodox Church, which was firmly opposed to westernization. In 1667 Patriarch Nikon had attempted to reform the church by introducing some changes into its texts and ceremonies. Since the Russian church had always claimed to be the protector of the most ancient and authentic Christian rituals, these reforms met with a great deal of resistance. A group known as the Old Believers refused to accept the patriarch's mandates, and late in the century thousands of them committed suicide rather than submit to the new liturgies. The tragedy dissuaded the church hierarchy from making any further substantial moves toward modernization. To ensure that the clergy did not blunder into an-

other Old Believer schism or organize to oppose westernization, Peter abolished the office of patriarch in 1721 and ceded its power over the church to a synod headed by a layman, the Procurator General. This was the most radical of Peter's breaks with tradition.

REORGANIZING DOMESTIC ADMINISTRATION Peter modeled his domestic administration on Sweden's government. Rather than set up departments under a single minister to handle things such as tax collection, foreign affairs, wars, and the economy, he established "colleges" with numerous members. In 1711 Peter created a central senate of nine members who were to run the government when the tsar was in the field with the army. The chief purpose of Peter's reforms, like those of Prussia's kings, was to construct a bureaucracy that would support an efficient army.

DEVELOPING THE ECONOMY AND WAGING WAR
The economic projects Peter sponsored were those that served the military. To get the men needed to staff them, young Russians were sent abroad for training and western European craftsmen were invited to immigrate. Although few of Peter's enterprises met with much success, the iron industry he began in the Ural Mountains had by midcentury made Russia the largest iron producer in Europe.

Peter believed that Russia's economic development and its future political power depended on the acquisition of warm-water ports that

Peter the Great built Saint Petersburg on the Gulf of Finland to provide Russia with better contact with western Europe. He moved Russia's capital there from Moscow in 1703. This is an eighteenth-century view of the city. The Granger Collection

would allow Russia to communicate with the West. To acquire these, the tsar built Russia's first navy and went to war with the Ottoman Empire in the Black Sea and with Sweden in the Baltic. In 1696 he drove the Turks from Azov on the Black Sea but held this prize only until 1711.

Achievements on the Swedish front were more lasting. In 1700 Russia invaded Swedish territory on the Baltic. When Charles XII, the erratic king of Sweden, failed to follow up a victory over Peter at Narva, Peter was able to regroup. In 1709 Charles renewed the war, and Peter defeated him at the Battle of Poltava. In 1721 the Peace of Nystad ended the Great Northern War and confirmed Russia's conquest of Estonia, Livonia, and part of Finland. By 1720 the Russian fleet was larger than those of Sweden and Denmark, and Russia's newly won ports were giving it access to the markets and capitals of western Europe. By then Peter had also assembled an army of about 300,000 men and established a College of War to maintain westernized military discipline.

Peter moved the capital of Russia to a new city he built on the Gulf of Finland, Saint Petersburg. Like other monarchs of his day, he followed the example of Louis XIV and constructed a kind of Versailles. The Russian aristocrats were compelled to move to Saint Petersburg so that the tsar could keep an eye on them. The city filled with lavish buildings modeled on those that housed the courts of western Europe. It was intended to stake Russia's claim to a place among Western nations. But since it looked so different from Russia's other cities, many Russians viewed it as a western intrusion that symbolized Peter's assault on their traditions.

Despite Peter's determination to strengthen the Russian monarchy, he could not bring himself to secure its future. After he quarreled with his only son Alexis, the heir to the throne died mysteriously in his father's prison. Although Peter claimed the right to name a successor, he had not done so by the time he died in 1725. Consequently, for the next thirty years soldiers and nobles struggled to thrust their candidates onto the throne. Peter had made Russia a modern state but not a stable one.

Events and Reigns

1533–1584	Ivan the Terrible
1584–1613	Time of Troubles
1613	Michael Romanov becomes tsar
1640–1688	Frederick William, the Great Elector
1648	Independence of the Netherlands recognized
1682–1725	Peter the Great
1683	Turkish siege of Vienna
1688–1713	Frederick I of Prussia
1697	Peter the Great's European tour
1700–1721	The Great Northern War
1703	Saint Petersburg founded
1711–1740	Charles VI, the Pragmatic Sanction
1713	War of the Spanish Succession ends
1713–1740	Frederick William I of Prussia
1714	George I founds the Hanoverian dynasty
1715	Louis XV becomes king of France
1720–1742	Robert Walpole dominates British politics
1726–1743	Cardinal Fleury
1727	George II
1740	Maria Theresa succeeds to the Habsburg throne
1740	Frederick II invades Silesia

In Perspective

By the second quarter of the eighteenth century, the major European powers were not yet nation-states in which citizens were united by a shared sense of community, culture, language, and history. They were still monarchies in which the cohesion of the state was a function of the personality of the ruler and personal relationships among great noble families. Monarchs had generally grown stronger, but nobles were still able to resist or obstruct the policies of their rulers.

In foreign affairs there were two long-term conflicts. In central Europe, Austria and Prussia contested leadership of Germany. In western Europe, France and Great Britain fought on two fronts. During the reign of Louis XIV, the French bid for dominance in Europe was at the heart of the struggle. But throughout the eighteenth century, their duel was for control of overseas commerce.

These wars were accompanied by economic and social developments that, in the long run, made more significant contributions to the transformations that were taking place in Europe.

REVIEW QUESTIONS

1. Why did Britain and France remain leading powers while the United Netherlands declined?
2. How did the structure of British government change under the political leadership of Walpole? What were the chief sources of Walpole's political strength?
3. How was the Hohenzollern family able to forge a conglomerate of diverse land holdings into the state of Prussia? Who were the major personalities involved in this process, and what were their individual contributions? Why was the military so important in Prussia?
4. How do the Hohenzollerns and the Habsburgs compare with respect to their approach to dealing with the problems that confronted their domains? Which family was more successful? Why? Why were the rulers of Sweden, the Ottoman Empire, and Poland less successful?
5. How did Russia become a great power? Why? How would you describe the character of Peter the Great? What were Russia's domestic problems before he came to power? What were his methods of reform? To what extent did he succeed? How were his reforms related to his military ambitions?

SUGGESTED READINGS

J. BLACK, *Eighteenth Century Europe, 1700–1789* (1990). An excellent survey.

C. R. BOXER, *The Dutch Seaborne Empire* (1965). Remains the best treatment of the subject.

J. BREWER, *The Sinews of Power: War, Money and the English State, 1688–1783* (1989). An extremely important study of the financial basis of English power.

F. L. CARSTEN, *The Origins of Prussia* (1954). Discusses the groundwork laid by the Great Elector in the seventeenth century.

J. C. D. CLARK, *English Society, 1688–1832: Social Structure and Political Practice During the Ancien Regime* (1985). An important, controversial work that emphasizes the role of religion in English political life.

A. COBBAN, *A History of Modern France*, 2nd ed., vol. 1 (1961). A lively and opinionated volume.

N. DAVIS, *God's Playground*, vol. 1 (1991). Excellent on prepartition Poland.

W. DOYLE, *The Old European Order, 1660–1800* (1992). The most thoughtful treatment of the subject.

R. J. W. EVANS, *The Making of the Habsburg Monarchy, 1550–1700: An Interpretation* (1979). Places much emphasis on intellectual factors and the role of religion.

F. FORD, *Robe and Sword: The Regrouping of the French Aristocracy After Louis XIV* (1953). An important book for political, social, and intellectual history.

L. HUGHES, *Russia in the Age of Peter the Great* (1998). Will likely stand for some time as the standard work.

C. J. INGRAO, *The Habsburg Monarchy, 1618–1815* (1994). The best recent survey.

J. I. ISRAEL, *The Dutch Republic, Its Rise, Greatness, and Fall, 1477–1806* (1995). The major survey of the subject.

R. A. KANN and Z. V. DAVID, *The Peoples of the Eastern Habsburg Lands 1526–1918* (1984). A helpful overview of the subject.

R. K. MASSIE, *Peter the Great: His Life and His World* (1980). A good popular biography.

D. McKAY and H. M. SCOTT, *The Rise of the Great Powers, 1648–1815* (1983). Now the standard survey.

J. H. PLUMB, *The Growth of Political Stability in England, 1675–1725* (1969). An important interpretive work.

S. SCHAMA, *An Embarrassment of Riches: An Interpretation of Dutch Culture in the Golden Age* (1987). Lively and controversial.

P. F. SUGAR, *Southeastern Europe Under Ottoman Rule, 1354–1804* (1977). An extremely clear presentation.

Glossary

absolutism   Term applied to strong centralized continental monarchies that attempted to make royal power dominant over aristocracies and other regional authorities.

Acropolis (ACK-row-po-lis)   The religious and civic center of Athens. It is the site of the Parthenon.

Act of Supremacy   The declaration by Parliament in 1534 that Henry VIII, not the Pope, was the head of the Church in England.

agape (AG-a-pay)   Meaning "love feast." A common meal that was part of the central ritual of early Christian worship.

Agricultural Revolution   The innovations in farm production that began in the eighteenth century and led to a scientific and mechanized agriculture.

Albigensians (Al-bi-GEN-see-uns)   Thirteenth-century advocates of a dualist religion. They took their name from the city of Albi in southern France. Also called Cathars.

Anabaptists   Protestants who insisted that only adult baptism conformed to Scripture.

anarchism   The theory that government and social institutions are oppressive and unnecessary and that society should be based on voluntary cooperation among individuals.

Anschluss (AHN-shluz)   Meaning "union." The annexation of Austria by Germany in March 1938.

anti-Semitism   Prejudice, hostility, or legal discrimination against Jews.

appeasement   The Anglo-French policy of making concessions to Germany in the 1930s to avoid a crisis that would lead to war. It assumed that Germany had real grievances and that Hitler's aims were limited and ultimately acceptable.

Areopagus   The governing council of Athens, originally open only to the nobility. It was named after the hill on which it met.

Arete (AH-ray-tay)   Manliness, courage, and the excellence appropriate to a hero. It was considered the highest virtue of Homeric society.

Arianism (AIR-ee-an-ism)   The belief formulated by Arius of Alexandria (ca. 280–336 C.E.) that Jesus was a created being, neither fully man nor fully God, but something in between. It did away with the doctrine of the Trinity.

aristocratic resurgence   Term applied to the eighteenth-century aristocratic efforts to resist the expanding power of European monarchies.

Arminians (are-MIN-ee-ans)   A group within the Church of England who rejected Puritanism and the Calvinist doctrine of predestination in favor of free will and an elaborate liturgy.

Asia Minor   Modern Turkey. Also called Anatolia.

asiento (ah-SEE-ehn-tow)   The contract to furnish slaves to the Spanish colonies.

assignants (as-seen-YAHNTS)   Government bonds based on the value of confiscated Church lands issued during the early French Revolution.

Atomists   School of ancient Greek philosophy founded in the fifth century B.C.E. by Leucippus of Miletus and Democritus of Abdera. It held that the world consists of innumerable, tiny, solid, indivisible, and unchangeable particles called atoms.

Attica (AT-tick-a)   The region of Greece where Athens is located.

Augsburg (AWGS-berg) **Confession**   The definitive statement of Lutheran belief made in 1530.

Augustus (AW-gust-us)   The title given to Octavian in 27 B.C.E. and borne thereafter by all Roman emperors. It was a semireligious title that implied veneration, majesty, and holiness.

Ausgleich (AWS-glike)   Meaning "compromise." The agreement between the Habsburg Emperor and the Hungarians to give Hungary considerable administrative autonomy in 1867. It created the Dual Monarchy or Austria-Hungary.

autocracy (AW-to-kra-see)   Government in which the ruler has absolute power.

Axis   The alliance between Nazi Germany and Fascist Italy. Also called the Pact of Steel.

banalities   Exactions that the lord of a manor could make on his tenants.

baroque (bah-ROWK)   A style of art marked by heavy and dramatic ornamentation and curved rather than straight lines that flourished between 1550 and 1750. It was especially associated with the Catholic Counter-Reformation.

beguines (bi-GEENS)   Lay sisterhoods not bound by the rules of a religious order.

benefice   Church offices granted by the ruler of a state or the Pope to an individual. It also meant "fief" in the Middle Ages.

bishop   Originally a person elected by early Christian congregations to lead them in worship and supervise their funds. In time bishops became the religious and even political authorities for Christian communities within large geographical areas.

Black Death   The bubonic plague that killed millions of Europeans in the fourteenth century.

blitzkrieg (BLITZ-kreeg)   Meaning "lightning war." The German tactic early in World War II of employing fast-moving, massed armored columns supported by airpower to overwhelm the enemy.

Bolsheviks   Meaning the "majority." Term Lenin applied to his faction of the Russian Social Democratic Party. It became the Communist Party of the Soviet Union after the Russian Revolution.

boyars   The Russian nobility.

Bronze Age   The name given to the earliest civilized era, c. 4000 to 1000 B.C.E. The term reflects the importance of the metal bronze, a mixture of tin and copper, for the peoples of this age for use as weapons and tools.

Bund   A secular Jewish socialist organization of Polish Jews.

Caesaro-papism (SEE-zer-o-PAY-pi-zim)   The direct involvement of the ruler in religious doctrine and practice as if he were the head of the Church as well as the state.

cahiers de doleances (KAH-hee-ay de dough-LAY-ahnce)   Meaning "lists of grievances." Petitions for reforms submitted to the French Crown when the Estates General met in 1789.

caliphate (KAH-li-fate)   The true line of succession to Muhammad.

capital goods   Machines and tools used to produce other goods.

carbonari (car-buh-NAH-ree)   Meaning "charcoal burners." The most famous of the secret republican societies seeking to unify Italy in the 1820s.

categorical imperative   According to Emmanuel Kant (1724–1804), the internal sense of moral duty or awareness possessed by all human beings.

Catholic Emancipation   The grant of full political rights to Roman Catholics in Britain in 1829.

catholic   Meaning "universal." The body of belief held by most Christians enshrined within the Church.

censor   Official of the Roman Republic charged with conducting the census and compiling the lists of citizens and members of the Senate. They could expel senators for financial or moral reasons. Two censors were elected every five years.

Chartism   The first large-scale European working-class political movement. It sought political reforms that would favor the interests of skilled British workers in the 1830s and 1840s.

chiaroscuro (kyar-eh-SKEW-row)   The use of shading to enhance naturalness in painting and drawing.

civic humanism   Education designed to promote humanist leadership of political and cultural life.

civilization   A form of human culture marked by urbanism, metallurgy, and writing.

classical economics   The theory that economies grow through the free enterprise of individuals competing in a largely self-regulating marketplace with government intervention held to a minimum.

clientage (KLI-ent-age)   The custom in ancient Rome whereby men became supporters of more powerful men in return for legal and physical protection and economic benefits.

Cold War   The ideological and geographical struggle between the United States and its allies and the USSR and its allies that began after World War II and lasted until the dissolution of the USSR in 1989.

collectivization   The bedrock of Stalinist agriculture, which forced Russian peasants to give up their private farms and work as members of collectives, large agricultural units controlled by the state.

coloni (CO-loan-ee)   Farmers or sharecroppers on the estates of wealthy Romans.

Commonwealthmen   British political writers whose radical republican ideas influenced the American revolutionaries.

Concert of Europe   Term applied to the European great powers acting together (in "concert") to resolve international disputes between 1815 and the 1850s.

Conciliar Theory   The argument that General Councils were superior in authority to the Pope and represented the whole body of the faithful.

condottieri (con-da-TEE-AIR-ee)   Military brokers who furnished mercenary forces to the Italian states during the Renaissance.

Congress System   A series of international meetings among the European great powers to promote mutual cooperation between 1818 and 1822.

conquistadores (kahn-KWIS-teh-door-hez)   Meaning "conquerors." The Spanish conquerors of the New World.

conservatism   Support for the established order in church and state. In the nineteenth century it implied support for legitimate monarchies, landed aristocracies, and established churches. Conservatives favored only gradual, or "organic," change.

Consulate   French government dominated by Napoleon from 1799 to 1804.

consuls (CON-suls)   The two chief magistrates of the Roman state.

consumer revolution   The vast increase in both the desire and the possibility of consuming goods and services that began in the early eighteenth century and created the demand for sustaining the Industrial Revolution.

containment   The U.S. policy during the Cold War of resisting Soviet expansion and influence in the expectation that the USSR would eventually collapse.

Convention   French radical legislative body from 1792 to 1794.

Corn Laws   British tariffs on imported grain that protected the price of grain grown within the British Isles.

corporatism   The planned economy of fascist Italy that combined private ownership of capital with government direction of Italy's economic life and arbitration of labor disputes. All major areas of production were organized into state-controlled bodies called corporations, which were represented in the Chamber of Corporations that replaced the Chamber of Deputies. The state, not consumers and owners, determined what the economy produced.

corvée (cor-VAY)   A French labor tax requiring peasants to work on roads, bridges, and canals.

Council of Nicaea (NIGH-see-a)   The council of Christian bishops at Nicaea in 325 C.E. that formulated the Nicene Creed, a statement of Christian belief that rejected Arianism in favor of the doctrine that Christ is both fully human and fully divine.

Counter-Reformation   The sixteenth-century reform movement in the Roman Catholic Church in reaction to the Protestant Reformation.

coup d'état (COO DAY-ta)   The sudden violent overthrow of a government by its own army.

creed   A brief statement of faith to which true Christians should adhere.

creoles (KRAY-ol-ez)   Persons of Spanish descent born in the Spanish colonies.

Crusades   Religious wars directed by the church against infidels and heretics.

culture   The ways of living built up by a group and passed on from one generation to another.

cuneiform (Q-nee-i-form)   A writing system invented by the Sumerians that used a wedge-shaped stylus, or pointed tool, to write on wet clay tablets that were then baked or dried ("cuneus" means wedge in Latin). The writing was also cut into stone.

Curia (CURE-ee-a)   The papal government.

Cynic (SIN-ick) **School, The**   A fourth-century philosophical movement that ridiculed all religious observances and turned away from involvement in the affairs of the *polis*. Its most famous exemplar was Diogenes of Sinope (ca. 400–325 B.C.E.).

deacon   Meaning "those who serve." In early Christian congregations, deacons assisted the presbyters, or elders.

deism   A belief in a rational God who had created the universe, but then allowed it to function without his interference according to the mechanisms of nature, and a belief in rewards and punishments after death for human action.

Delian (DEE-li-an)   An alliance of Greek states under the leadership of Athens that was formed in 478–477 B.C.E. to resist the Persians. In time the league was transformed into the Athenian Empire.

deme (DEEM)   A small town in Attica or a ward in Athens that became the basic unit of Athenian civic life under the democratic reforms of Clisthenes in 508 B.C.E.

demesne (di-MAIN)   The part of a manor that was cultivated directly for the lord of the manor.

divine right of kings   The theory that monarchs are appointed by and answerable only to God.

Domesday (DOOMS-day) **Book**   A detailed survey of the wealth of England undertaken by William the Conqueror between 1080 and 1086.

domestic system of textile production   Method of producing textiles in which agents furnished raw materials to households whose members spun them into thread and then wove cloth, which the agents then sold as finished products.

Donatism   The heresy that taught that the efficacy of the sacraments depended on the moral character of the clergy who administered them.

Duma (DOO-ma)   The Russian parliament, after the Revolution of 1905.

electors   Nine German princes who had the right to elect the Holy Roman Emperor.

émigrés (em-ee-GRAYS)   French aristocrats who fled France during the Revolution.

empiricism (em-PEER-ih-cism)   The use of experiment and observation derived from sensory evidence to construct scientific theory or philosophy of knowledge.

enclosure   The consolidation or fencing in of common lands by British landlords to increase production and achieve greater commercial profits. It also involved the reclamation of waste land and the consolidation of strips into block fields.

encomienda (en-co-mee-EN-da)   The grant by the Spanish Crown to a colonist of the labor of a specific number of Indians for a set period of time.

ENIAC   Electronic Numerical Integrator and Computer. The first genuine modern digital computer, developed in the 1940s.

Enlightenment   The eighteenth-century movement led by the philosophies that held that change and reform were both desirable through the application of reason and science.

Epicureans (EP-i-cure-ee-ans)   School of philosophy founded by Epicurus of Athens (342–271 B.C.E.). It sought to liberate people from fear of death and the supernatural by teaching that the gods took no interest in human affairs and that true happiness consisted in pleasure, which was defined as the absence of pain. This could be achieved by attaining *ataraxia,* the freedom from trouble, pain, and responsibility produced by withdrawing from business and public life.

equestrians (EE-quest-ree-ans)   Literally "cavalrymen" or "knights." In the earliest years of the Roman Republic those who could afford to serve as mounted warriors. The equestrians evolved into a social rank of well-to-do businessmen and middle-ranking officials. Many of them supported the Gracchi.

Estates General   The medieval French parliament. It consisted of three separate groups, or "estates:" clergy, nobility, and commoners. It last met in 1789 at the outbreak of the French Revolution.

Etruscans (EE-trus-cans)   A people of central Italy who exerted the most powerful external influence on the early Romans. Etruscan kings ruled Rome until 509 B.C.E.

Eucharist (YOU-ka-rist)   Meaning "thanksgiving." The celebration of the Lord's Supper. Considered the central ritual of worship by most Christians. Also called Holy Communion.

Euro   The common currency created by the EEC in the late 1990s.

European Economic Community (EEC)   The economic association formed by France, Germany, Italy, Belgium, the Netherlands, and Luxembourg in 1957. Also known as the Common Market.

European Union (EU)   The new name given to the EEC in 1993. It included most of the states of Western Europe.

excommunication   Denial by the church of the right to receive the sacraments.

Existentialism   The post–World War II Western philosophy that holds that human beings are totally responsible for their acts and that this responsibility causes them dread and anguish.

Fabians   British socialists in the late nineteenth and early twentieth centuries who sought to achieve socialism through gradual, peaceful, and democratic means.

family economy   The basic structure of production and consumption in preindustrial Europe.

fascism   Political movements that tend to be antidemocratic, anti-Marxist, antiparliamentary, and often anti-Semitic. Fascists were invariably nationalists and exalted the nation over the individual. They supported the interests of the middle class and rejected the ideas of the French Revolution and nineteenth-century liberalism. The first fascist regime was founded by Benito Mussolini (1883–1945) in Italy in the 1920s.

fealty   An oath of loyalty by a vassal to a lord, promising to perform specified services.

feudal (FEW-dull) **society**   The social, political, military, and economic system that prevailed in the Middle Ages and beyond in some parts of Europe.

fief   Land granted to a vassal in exchange for services, usually military.

foederati (FAY-der-ah-tee)   Barbarian tribes enlisted as special allies of the Roman Empire.

folk culture   The distinctive songs, sayings, legends, and crafts of a people.

Fourteen Points   President Woodrow Wilson's (1856–1924) idealistic war aims.

Fronde (FROHND)   A series of rebellions against royal authority in France between 1649 and 1652.

Gaul (GAWL)   Modern France.

German Confederation   Association of German states established at the Congress of Vienna that replaced the Holy Roman Empire from 1815 to 1866.

ghetto   Separate communities in which Jews were required by law to live.

glasnost (GLAZ-nohst)   Meaning "openness." The policy initiated by Mikhail Gorbachev (MEEK-hail GORE-buh-choff) in the 1980s of permitting open criticism of the policies of the Soviet Communist Party.

Glorious Revolution   The largely peaceful replacement of James II by William and Mary as English monarchs in 1688. It marked the beginning of constitutional monarchy in Britain.

gold standard   A monetary system in which the value of a unit of a nation's currency is related to a fixed amount of gold.

Golden Bull   The agreement in 1356 to establish a seven-member electoral college of German princes to choose the Holy Roman Emperor.

Great Depression   A prolonged worldwide economic downturn that began in 1929 with the collapse of the New York Stock Exchange.

Great Reform Bill (1832)   A limited reform of the British House of Commons and an expansion of the electorate to include a wider variety of the propertied classes. It laid the groundwork for further orderly reforms within the British constitutional system.

Great Schism   The appearance of two and at times three rival popes between 1378 and 1415.

Green Movement   A political environmentalist movement that began in West Germany in the 1970s and spread to a number of other Western nations.

grossdeutsch (gross-DOYCH)   Meaning "great German." The argument that the German-speaking portions of the Habsburg Empire should be included in a united Germany.

guild   An association of merchants or craftsmen that offered protection to its members and set rules for their work and products.

hacienda (ha-SEE-hen-da) A large landed estate in Spanish America.

Hegira (HEJ-ear-a) The flight of Muhammad and his followers from Mecca to Medina in 622 C.E. It marks the beginning of the Islamic calendar.

heliocentric (HE-li-o-cen-trick) **theory** The theory, now universally accepted, that the Earth and the other planets revolve around the Sun. First proposed by Aristarchos of Samos (310–230 B.C.E.). Its opposite, the geocentric theory, which was dominant until the sixteenth century C.E., held that the Sun and the planets revolved around the Earth.

helots (HELL-ots) Hereditary Spartan serfs.

heretic (HAIR-i-tick) A person whose beliefs were contrary to those of the Catholic Church.

hieroglyphics (HI-er-o-gli-phicks) The complicated writing script of ancient Egypt. It combined picture writing with pictographs and sound signs. Hieroglyph means "sacred carvings" in Greek.

Holocaust The Nazi extermination of millions of European Jews between 1940 and 1945. Also called the "final solution to the Jewish problem."

Holy Roman Empire The revival of the old Roman Empire, based mainly in Germany and northern Italy, that endured from 870 to 1806.

home rule The advocacy of a large measure of administrative autonomy for Ireland within the British Empire between the 1880s and 1914.

Homo sapiens (HO-mo say-pee-ans) The scientific name for human beings, from the Latin words meaning "Wise man." *Homo sapiens* emerged some 200,000 years ago.

honestiores (HON-est-ee-or-ez) The Roman term formalized from the beginning of the third century C.E. to denote the privileged classes: senators, equestrians, the municipal aristocracy, and soldiers.

hoplite phalanx (FAY-lanks) The basic unit of Greek warfare in which infantrymen fought in close order, shield to shield, usually eight ranks deep. The phalanx perfectly suited the farmer-soldier-citizen who was the backbone of the *polis*.

hubris (WHO-bris) Arrogance brought on by excessive wealth or good fortune. The Greeks believed that it led to moral blindness and divine vengeance.

Huguenots (HYOU-gu-nots) French Calvinists.

humanism The study of the Latin and Greek classics and of the Church Fathers both for their own sake and to promote a rebirth of ancient norms and values.

humanitas (HEW-man-i-tas) The Roman name for a liberal arts education.

humiliores (HEW-mi-lee-orez) The Roman term formalized at the beginning of the third century C.E. for the lower classes.

Hussites (HUS-Its) Followers of John Huss (d. 1415) who questioned Catholic teachings about the Eucharist.

iconoclasm (i-KON-o-kla-zoom) A heresy in Eastern Christianity that sought to ban the veneration of sacred images, or icons.

id, ego, superego The three entities in Sigmund Freud's model of the internal organization of the human mind. The id consists of the amoral, irrational instincts for self-gratification. The superego embodies the external morality imposed on the personality by society. The ego mediates between the two and allows the personality to cope with the internal and external demands of its existence.

Iliad (ILL-ee-ad) **and the *Odyssey*** (O-dis-see), The Epic poems by Homer about the "Dark Age" heroes of Greece who fought at Troy. The poems were written down in the eighth century B.C.E. after centuries of being sung by bards.

imperator (IM-per-a-tor) Under the Roman Republic it was the title given to a victorious general. Under Augustus and his successors it became the title of the ruler of Rome meaning "Emperor."

imperialism The extension of a nation's authority over other nations or areas through conquest or political or economic hegemony.

imperium (IM-pear-ee-um) In ancient Rome the right to issue commands and to enforce them by fines, arrests, and even corporal and capital punishment.

indulgences Remission of the temporal penalty of punishment in purgatory that remained after sins had been forgiven.

Industrial Revolution Mechanization of the European economy that began in Britain in the second half of the eighteenth century.

insulae (IN-sul-lay) Meaning "islands." The multistoried apartment buildings of Rome in which most of the inhabitants of the city lived.

intendents (in-TEN-duhnts) Royal officials under the French monarchy who supervised the provincial governments in the name of the king.

Intolerable Acts Measures passed by the British Parliament in 1774 to punish the colony of Massachusetts and strengthen Britain's authority in the colonies. The laws provoked colonial opposition, which led immediately to the American Revolution.

Investiture Struggle The medieval conflict between the church and lay rulers over who would control bishops and abbots, symbolized by the ceremony of "investing" them with the symbols of their authority.

Ionia (I-o-knee-a) The part of western Asia Minor heavily colonized by the Greeks.

Islam (IZ-lahm)   Meaning "submission." The religion founded by the prophet Muhammad.

Italia Irredenta (ee-TAHL-ee-a ir-REH-dent-a)   Meaning "unredeemed Italy." Italian-speaking areas that had been left under Austrian rule at the time of the unification of Italy.

Jacobins (JACK-uh-bins)   The radical republican party during the French Revolution that displaced the Girondins.

jacquerie (jah-KREE)   Revolt of the French peasantry.

Jansenism   A seventeenth-century movement within the Catholic Church that taught that human beings were so corrupted by original sin that they could do nothing good nor secure their own salvation without divine grace. (It was opposed to the Jesuits.)

Judah (JEW-da)   The southern Israelite kingdom established after the death of Solomon in the tenth century B.C.E.

Julian calendar   The reform of the calendar by Julius Caesar in 46 B.C.E. It remained in use throughout Europe until the sixteenth century and in Russia until the Russian Revolution in 1917.

July Monarchy   The French regime set up after the overthrow of the Bourbons in July 1830.

junkers (YOONG-kerz)   The noble landlords of Prussia.

jus gentium (YUZ GEN-tee-um)   Meaning "law of peoples." The body of Roman law that dealt with foreigners.

jus naturale (YUZ NAH-tu-rah-lay)   Meaning "natural law." The Stoic concept of a world ruled by divine reason.

Ka'ba (KAH-bah)   A shrine in the city of Mecca that became Islam's holiest place.

Keynesian economics   The theory of John Maynard Keynes (CANES) (1883–1946) that governments could spend their economies out of a depression by running deficits to encourage employment and stimulate the production and consumption of goods.

kleindeutsch (kline-DOYCH)   Meaning "small German." The argument that the German-speaking portions of the Habsburg Empire should be excluded from a united Germany.

Kristallnacht (KRIS-tahl-NAHKT)   Meaning "crystal night" because of the broken glass that littered German streets after the looting and destruction of Jewish homes, businesses, and synagogues across Germany on the orders of the Nazi Party in November 1938.

kulaks (koo-LAKS)   Prosperous Russian peasant farmers.

Kulturkampf (cool-TOOR-cahmff)   Meaning the "battle for culture." The conflict between the Roman Catholic Church and the government of the German Empire in the 1870s.

laissez-faire (lay-ZAY-faire)   French phrase meaning "allow to do." In economics the doctrine of minimal government interference in the working of the economy.

latifundia (LAT-ee-fun-dee-a)   Large plantations for growing cash crops owned by wealthy Romans.

Latium (LAT-ee-um)   The region of Italy in which Rome is located. Its inhabitants were called Latins.

League of Nations   The association of sovereign states set up after World War I to pursue common policies and avert international aggression.

Lebensraum (LAY-benz-rauhm)   Meaning "living space." The Nazi plan to colonize and exploit the Slavic areas of Eastern Europe for the benefit of Germany.

levée en masse (le-VAY en MASS)   The French Revolutionary conscription (1792) of all males into the army and the harnessing of the economy for war production.

liberal arts   The medieval university program that consisted of the trivium (TRI-vee-um): grammar, rhetoric, and logic, and the quadrivium (qua-DRI-vee-um): arithmetic, geometry, astronomy, and music.

liberalism   In the nineteenth century, support for representative government dominated by the propertied classes and minimal government interference in the economy.

Lollards (LALL-erds)   Followers of John Wycliffe (d. 1384) who questioned the supremacy and privileges of the Pope and the church hierarchy.

Lower Egypt   The Nile delta.

Luftwaffe (LUFT-vaff-uh)   The German air force in World War II.

Magna Carta (MAG-nuh CAR-tuh)   The "Great Charter" limiting royal power that the English nobility forced King John to sign in 1215.

Magna Graecia (MAG-nah GRAY-see-a)   Meaning "Great Greece" in Latin, it was the name given by the Romans to southern Italy and Sicily because there were so many Greek colonies in the region.

Magyars (MAH-jars)   The majority ethnic group in Hungary.

mandates   The assigning of the former German colonies and Turkish territories in the Middle East to Britain, France, Japan, Belgium, Australia, and South Africa as de facto colonies under the vague supervision of the League of Nations with the hope that the territories would someday advance to independence.

mannerism   A style of art in the mid- to late sixteenth century that permitted the artist to express his or her own "manner" or feelings in contrast to the symmetry and simplicity of the art of the High Renaissance.

manor Village farms owned by a lord.

Marshall Plan The U.S. program named after Secretary of State George C. Marshall of providing economic aid to Europe after World War II.

Marxism The theory of Karl Marx (1818–1883) and Friedrich Engels (FREE-drick Eng-ulz) (1820–1895) that history is the result of class conflict, which will end in the inevitable triumph of the industrial proletariat over the bourgeoisie and the abolition of private property and social class.

Mein Kampf (MINE KAHMFF) Meaning "my struggle." Hitler's statement of his political program published in 1924.

Mensheviks Meaning the "minority." Term Lenin applied to the majority moderate faction of the Russian Social Democratic Party opposed to him and the Bolsheviks.

mercantilism Term used to describe close government control of the economy that sought to maximize exports and accumulate as much precious metals as possible to enable the state to defend its economic and political interests.

Mesopotamia (MEZ-o-po-tay-me-a) Modern Iraq. The land between the Tigris and Euphrates Rivers where the first civilization appeared around 3000 B.C.E.

Messiah (MESS-eye-a) The redeemer whose coming Jews believed would establish the kingdom of God on earth. Christians considered Jesus to be the Messiah (Christ means Messiah in Greek).

Methodism An English religious movement begun by John Wesley (1703–1791) that stressed inward, heartfelt religion and the possibility of attaining Christian perfection in this life.

millets Administrative units of the Ottoman Empire that were not geographic but consisted of ethnic or religious minorities to whom particular laws and regulations applied.

Minoans (MIN-o-ans) The Bronze Age civilization that arose in Crete in the third and second millenia B.C.E.

missi dominici (MISS-ee dough-MIN-ee-chee) Meaning "the envoys of the ruler." Royal overseers of the king's law in the Carolingian Empire.

mobilization The placing of a country's military forces on a war footing.

modernism The movement in the arts and literature in the late nineteenth and early twentieth centuries to create new aesthetic forms and to elevate the aesthetic experience of a work of art above the attempt to portray reality as accurately as possible.

moldboard plow A heavy plow introduced in the Middle Ages that cut deep into the soil.

monophysitism (ma-NO-fiz-it-ism) A Christian heresy that taught that Jesus had only one nature.

monotheism The worship of one, universal God.

Mycenaean (MY-cen-a-an) The Bronze Age civilization of mainland Greece that was centered at Mycenae.

"mystery" religions The cults of Isis, Mithra, and Osiris, which promised salvation to those initiated into the secret or "mystery" of their rites. These cults competed with Christianity in the Roman Empire.

nationalism The belief that one is part of a nation, defined as a community with its own language, traditions, customs, and history that distinguish it from other nations and make it the primary focus of a person's loyalty and sense of identity.

natural selection The theory originating with Darwin that organisms evolve through a struggle for existence in which those that have a marginal advantage live long enough to propagate their kind.

naturalism The attempt to portray nature and human life without sentimentality.

Nazis The German Nationalist Socialist Party.

Neolithic (NEE-o-lith-ick) **Revolution** The shift beginning 10,000 years ago from hunter-gatherer societies to settled communities of farmers and artisans. Also called the Age of Agriculture, it witnessed the invention of farming, the domestication of plants and animals, and the development of technologies such as pottery and weaving. The earliest Neolithic societies appeared in the Middle East about 8,000 B.C.E. "Neolithic" comes from the Greek words for "new stone."

Neoplatonism (NEE-o-play-ton-ism) A religious philosophy that tried to combine mysticism with classical and rationalist speculation. Its chief formulator was Plotinus (205–270 C.E.).

New Economic Policy (NEP) A limited revival of capitalism, especially in light industry and agriculture, introduced by Lenin in 1921 to repair the damage inflicted on the Russian economy by the Civil War and War Communism.

New Imperialism The extension in the late nineteenth and early twentieth centuries of Western political and economic dominance to Asia, the Middle East, and Africa.

nomes regions or provinces of ancient Egypt governed by officials called nomarchs.

oikos (OI-cos) The Greek household, always headed by a male.

Old Believers Those members of the Russian Orthodox Church who refused to accept the reforms of the seventeenth century regarding church texts and ritual.

Old Regime Term applied to the pattern of social, political, and economic relationships and institutions that existed in Europe before the French Revolution.

optimates (OP-tee-ma-tes)   Meaning "the best men." Roman politicians who supported the traditional role of the Senate.

orthodox   Meaning "holding the right opinions." Applied to the doctrines of the Catholic church.

Ottoman Empire   The imperial Turkish state centered in Constantinople that ruled large parts of the Balkans, North Africa, and the Middle East until 1918.

Paleolithic (PAY-lee-o-lith-ick) **Age, The**   The earliest period when stone tools were used, from about 1,000,000 to 10,000 B.C.E. From the Greek meaning "old stone."

Panhellenic (PAN-hell-en-ick) Meaning "all-Greek." The sense of cultural identity that all Greeks felt in common with each other.

Panslavism   The movement to create a nation or federation that would embrace all the Slavic peoples of eastern Europe.

papal infallibility   The doctrine that the Pope is infallible when pronouncing officially in his capacity as head of the church on matters of faith and morals, enumerated by the First Vatican Council in 1870.

Papal States   Territory in central Italy ruled by the Pope until 1870.

parlements (par-luh-MAHNS)   French regional courts dominated by hereditary nobility. The most important was the *Parlement* of Paris, which claimed the right to register royal decrees before they could become law.

patricians (PA-tri-she-ans)   The hereditary upper class of early Republican Rome.

Peloponnesian (PELL-o-po-knees-ee-an) **Wars**   The protracted struggle between Athens and Sparta to dominate Greece between 465 and Athens final defeat in 404 B.C.E.

Peloponnesus (PELL-o-po-knee-sus)   The southern peninsula of Greece where Sparta was located.

peninsulares (pen-in-SUE-la-rez)   Persons born in Spain who settled in the Spanish colonies.

perestroika (pare-ess-TROY-ka)   Meaning "restructuring." The attempt in the 1980s to reform the Soviet government and economy.

Pharisees (FAIR-i-sees)   The group that was most strict in its adherence to Jewish law.

pharoah (FAY-row)   The god-kings of ancient Egypt. The term originally meant "great house" or palace.

philosophes (fee-lou-SOPHS)   The eighteenth-century writers and critics who forged the new attitudes favorable to change. They sought to apply reason and common sense to the institutions and societies of their day.

Phoenicians (FA-nee-shi-ans)   The ancient inhabitants of modern Lebanon. A trading people, they established colonies throughout the Mediterranean.

physiocrats   Eighteenth-century French thinkers who attacked the mercantilist regulation of the economy, advocated a limited economic role for government, and believed that all economic production depended on sound agriculture.

plantation economy   The economic system stretching between Chesapeake Bay and Brazil that produced crops, especially sugar, cotton, and tobacco, using slave labor on large estates.

plebeians (PLEB-bee-ans)   The hereditary lower class of early Republican Rome.

plenitude of power   The teaching that the Popes have power over all other bishops of the church.

pogroms (PO-grohms)   Organized riots against Jews in the Russian Empire.

polis (PO-lis) (plural, poleis)   The basic Greek political unit. Usually, but incompletely, translated as "city state," the Greeks thought of the *polis* as a community of citizens theoretically descended from a common ancestor.

polytheism (PAH-lee-thee-ism)   The worship of many gods.

pontifex maximus (PON-ti-feks MAK-suh-muss)   Meaning "supreme priest." The chief priest of ancient Rome. The title was later assumed by the Popes.

Popular Front   A government of all left-wing parties that took power in France in 1936 to enact social and economic reforms.

populares (PO-pew-lar-es)   Roman politicians who sought to pursue a political career based on the support of the people rather than just the aristocracy.

Positivism   The philosophy of Auguste Comte that science is the final, or positive, stage of human intellectual development because it involves exact descriptions of phenomena, without recourse to unobservable operative principles, such as gods or spirits.

Pragmatic Sanction   The legal basis negotiated by the Emperor Charles VI (r. 1711–1740) for the Habsburg succession through his daughter Maria Theresa (r. 1740–1780).

predestination   The doctrine that God had foreordained all souls to salvation (the "elect") or damnation. It was especially associated with Calvinism.

Presbyterians   Scottish Calvinists and English Protestants who advocated a national church composed of semi-autonomous congregations governed by "presbyteries."

presbyter (PRESS-bi-ter)   Meaning "elder." A person who directed the affairs of early Christian congregations.

proconsulship (PRO-con-sul-ship)   In Republican Rome the extension of a consul's imperium beyond the end of his term of office to allow him to continue to command an army in the field.

Protestant Ethic   The theory propounded by Max Weber in 1904 that the religious confidence and self-disciplined activism that were supposedly associated with Protestantism produced an ethic that stimulated the spirit of emergent capitalism.

Ptolemaic (tow-LEM-a-ick) **System**   The pre-Copernican explanation of the universe, with the Earth at the center of the universe, originated in the ancient world.

Punic (PEW-nick) **Wars**   Three wars between Rome and Carthage for dominance of the western Mediterranean that were fought from 264 B.C.E. to 146 B.C.E.

Puritans   English Protestants who sought to "purify" the Church of England of any vestiges of Catholicism.

Qur'an (kuh-RAN)   Meaning "a reciting." The Islamic bible, which Muslims believe God revealed to the prophet Muhammad.

racism   The pseudo-scientific theory that biological features of race determine human character and worth.

raison d'état (RAY-suhn day-TAH)   Meaning "reason of state." Concept that the interests of the state justify a course of action.

realism   The style of art and literature that seeks to depict the physical world and human life with scientific objectivity and detached observation.

Reformation   The sixteenth-century religious movement that sought to reform the Roman Catholic Church and led to the establishment of Protestantism.

regular clergy   Monks and nuns who belong to religious orders.

Reichstag (RIKES-stahg)   The German parliament, which existed in various forms, until 1945.

Reign of Terror   The period between the summer of 1793 and the end of July 1794 when the French Revolutionary state used extensive executions and violence to defend the Revolution and suppress its alleged internal enemies.

relativity   The scientific theory associated with Einstein that time and space exist not separately but as a combined continuum whose measurement depends as much on the observer as on the entities that are being measured.

Renaissance   The revival of ancient learning and the supplanting of traditional religious beliefs by new secular and scientific values that began in Italy in the fourteenth and fifteenth centuries.

reparations   The requirement incorporated into the Versailles Treaty that Germany should pay for the cost of World War I.

revisionism   The advocacy among nineteenth-century German socialists of achieving a humane socialist society through the evolution of democratic institutions, not revolution.

robot (ROW-boht)   The amount of labor landowners demanded from peasants in the Habsburg Monarchy before 1848.

Romanitas (row-MAN-ee-tas)   Meaning "Romanness." The spread of the Roman way of life and the sense of identifying with Rome across the Roman Empire.

romanticism   A reaction in early nineteenth century literature, philosophy, and religion against what many considered the excessive rationality and scientific narrowness of the Enlightenment.

SA   The Nazi paramilitary forces, or storm troopers.

sans-culottes (SAHN coo-LOTS)   Meaning "without kneebreeches." The lower-middle classes and artisans of Paris during the French Revolution.

Schlieffen (SHLEE-fun) **Plan**   Germany's plan for achieving a quick victory in the West at the outbreak of World War I by invading France through Belgium and Luxembourg.

Scholasticism   The method of study based on logic and dialectic that dominated the medieval schools. It assumed that truth already existed; students had only to organize, elucidate, and defend knowledge learned from authoritative texts, especially those of Aristotle and the Church Fathers.

scientific induction   Scientific method in which generalizations are derived from data gained from empirical observations.

Scientific Revolution   The sweeping change in the scientific view of the universe that occurred in the sixteenth and seventeenth centuries. The new scientific concepts and the method of their construction became the standard for assessing the validity of knowledge in the West.

Second Industrial Revolution   The emergence of new industries and the spread of industrialization from Britain to other countries, especially Germany and the United States, in the second half of the nineteenth century.

secular clergy   Parish clergy who did not belong to a religious order.

Sejm (SHEM)   The legislative assembly of the Polish nobility.

serfs   Peasants tied to the land they tilled.

Shi-a (SHE-ah)   The minority of Muslims who trace their beliefs from the caliph Ali who was assassinated in 661 C.E.

Sinn Fein (SHIN FAHN)   Meaning "ourselves alone." An Irish political movement founded in 1905 that advocated complete political separation from Britain.

Social Darwinism   The application of Darwin's concept of "the survival of the fittest" to explain evolution in nature to human social relationships.

Sophists (SO-fists)   Professional teachers who emerged in Greece in the mid-fifth century B.C.E. who were paid to teach techniques of rhetoric, dialectic, and argumentation.

soviets   Workers and soldiers councils formed in Russia during the Revolution.

spinning jenny   A machine invented in England by James Hargreaves around 1765 to mass-produce thread.

SS   The chief security units of the Nazi state.

Stoics (STOW-icks)   A philosophical school founded by Zeno of Citium (335–263 B.C.E.) that taught that humans could only be happy with natural law. Human misery was caused by passion, which was a disease of the soul. The wise sought *apatheia*, freedom from passion.

Sturm und Drang (SHTURM und DRAHNG)   Meaning "storm and stress." A movement in German romantic literature and philosophy that emphasized feeling and emotion.

suffragettes   British women who lobbied and agitated for the right to vote in the early 20th century.

summa (SUE-ma)   An authoritative summary in the Middle Ages of all that was allegedly known about a subject.

Sunna (SOON-ah)   Meaning "tradition." The dominant Islamic group.

symposium (SIM-po-see-um)   The carefully organized drinking party that was the center of Greek aristocratic social life. It featured games, songs, poetry, and even philosophical disputation.

syncretism (SIN-cret-ism)   The intermingling of different religions to form an amalgam that contained elements from each.

syndicalism   French labor movement that sought to improve workers' conditions through direct action, especially general strikes.

Table of Ranks   An official hierarchy established by Peter the Great in Imperial Russia that equated a person's social position and privileges with his rank in the state bureaucracy or army.

tabula rasa (tah-BOO-lah RAH-sah)   Meaning a "blank page." The philosophical belief associated with John Locke that human beings enter the world with totally unformed characters that are completely shaped by experience.

taille (TIE)   The direct tax on the French peasantry.

"ten lost tribes"   The Israelites who were scattered and lost to history when the northern kingdom of Israel fell to the Assyrians in 722 B.C.E.

tertiaries (TER-she-air-ees)   Laypeople affiliated with the monastic life who took vows of poverty, chastity, and obedience but remained in the world.

tetrarchy (TET-rar-key)   Diocletian's (r. 306–337 C.E.) system for ruling the Roman Empire by four men with power divided territorially.

Thermidorean Reaction   The reaction against the radicalism of the French Revolution that began in July 1794. Associated with the end of terror and establishment of the Directory.

thesis, antithesis, and synthesis   G. W. F. Hegel's (HAY-gle) (1770–1831) concept of how ideas develop. The thesis is a dominant set of ideas. It is challenged by a set of conflicting ideas, the antithesis. From the clash of these ideas, a new pattern of thought, the synthesis, emerges and eventually becomes the new thesis.

Third Estate   The branch of the French Estates General representing all of the kingdom outside the nobility and the clergy.

Third Reich (RIKE)   Hitler's regime in Germany, which lasted from 1933 to 1945.

Thirty-nine Articles (1563)   The official statement of the beliefs of the Church of England. They established a moderate form of Protestantism.

three-field system   A medieval innovation that increased the amount of land under cultivation by leaving only one-third fallow in a given year.

transportation   The British policy from the late eighteenth to the mid-nineteenth centuries of shipping persons convicted of the most serious offenses to Australia as an alternative to capital punishment.

transubstantiation   The doctrine that the entire substances of the bread and wine are changed in the Eucharist into the body and blood of Christ.

tribunes (TRIB-unes)   Roman officials who had to be plebeians and were elected by the plebeian assembly to protect plebeians from the arbitrary power of the magistrates.

ulema (oo-LEE-mah)   Meaning "persons with correct knowledge." The Islamic scholarly elite who served a social function similar to the Christian clergy.

Upper Egypt   The part of Egypt that runs from the delta to the Sudanese border.

utopian socialism   Early-nineteenth-century theories that sought to replace the existing capitalist structure and values with visionary solutions or ideal communities.

vassal   A person granted an estate or cash payments in return for accepting the obligation to render services to a lord.

vernacular   The everyday language spoken by the people as opposed to Latin.

vingtième (VEN-tee-em)   Meaning "one twentieth." A tax on income in France before the Revolution.

Vulgate   The Latin translation of the Bible by Jerome (348–420 C.E.) that became the standard bible used by the Catholic Church.

Waldensians (wahl-DEN-see-ens)   Medieval heretics who advocated Biblical simplicity in reaction to the worldliness of the church.

War Communism   The economic policy adopted by the Bolsheviks during the Russian Civil War to seize the banks, heavy industry, railroads, and grain.

water frame   A water-powered device invented by Richard Arkwright to produce a more durable cotton fabric. It led to the shift in the production of cotton textiles from households to factories.

Weimar (Why-mar) **Republic**   The German democratic regime that existed between the end of World War I and Hitler's coming to power in 1933.

White Russians   Those Russians who opposed the Bolsheviks (the "Reds") in the Russian Civil War of 1918–1921.

Zionism   The movement to create a Jewish state in Palestine (the Biblical Zion).

Index

SINGLE PC LICENSE AGREEMENT AND LIMITED WARRANTY

READ THIS LICENSE CAREFULLY BEFORE OPENING THIS PACKAGE. BY OPENING THIS PACKAGE, YOU ARE AGREEING TO THE TERMS AND CONDITIONS OF THIS LICENSE. IF YOU DO NOT AGREE, DO NOT OPEN THE PACKAGE. PROMPTLY RETURN THE UNOPENED PACKAGE AND ALL ACCOMPANYING ITEMS TO THE PLACE YOU OBTAINED THEM.

1. GRANT OF LICENSE and OWNERSHIP: The enclosed computer programs ("Software") are licensed, not sold, to you by Prentice-Hall, Inc. ("We" or the "Company") and in consideration of your purchase or adoption of the accompanying Company textbooks and/or other materials, and your agreement to these terms. We reserve any rights not granted to you. You own only the disk(s) but we and/or our licensors own the Software itself. This license allows you to use and display your copy of the Software on a single computer (i.e., with a single CPU) at a single location for *academic* use only, so long as you comply with the terms of this Agreement. You may make one copy for back up, or transfer your copy to another CPU, provided that the Software is usable on only one computer.

2. RESTRICTIONS: You may *not* transfer or distribute the Software or documentation to anyone else. Except for backup, you may *not* copy the documentation or the Software. You may *not* network the Software or otherwise use it on more than one computer or computer terminal at the same time. You may *not* reverse engineer, disassemble, decompile, modify, adapt, translate, or create derivative works based on the Software or the Documentation. You may be held legally responsible for any copying or copyright infringement which is caused by your failure to abide by the terms of these restrictions.

3. TERMINATION: This license is effective until terminated. This license will terminate automatically without notice from the Company if you fail to comply with any provisions or limitations of this license. Upon termination, you shall destroy the Documentation and all copies of the Software. All provisions of this Agreement as to limitation and disclaimer of warranties, limitation of liability, remedies or damages, and our ownership rights shall survive termination.

4. LIMITED WARRANTY AND DISCLAIMER OF WARRANTY: Company warrants that for a period of 60 days from the date you purchase this SOFTWARE (or purchase or adopt the accompanying textbook), the Software, when properly installed and used in accordance with the Documentation, will operate in substantial conformity with the description of the Software set forth in the Documentation, and that for a period of 30 days the disk(s) on which the Software is delivered shall be free from defects in materials and workmanship under normal use. The Company does *not* warrant that the Software will meet your requirements or that the operation of the Software will be uninterrupted or error-free. Your only remedy and the Company's only obligation under these limited warranties is, at the Company's option, return of the disk for a refund of any amounts paid for it by you or replacement of the disk. THIS LIMITED WARRANTY IS THE ONLY WARRANTY PROVIDED BY THE COMPANY AND ITS LICENSORS, AND THE COMPANY AND ITS LICENSORS DISCLAIM ALL OTHER WARRANTIES EXPRESS OR IMPLIED, INCLUDING WITHOUT LIMITATION, THE IMPLIED WARRANTIES OF MERCHANTABILITY AND FITNESS FOR A PARTICULAR PURPOSE. THE COMPANY DOES NOT WARRANT, GUARANTEE OR MAKE ANY REPRESENTATION REGARDING THE ACCURACY, RELIABILITY, CURRENTNESS, USE, OR RESULTS OF USE, OF THE SOFTWARE.

5. LIMITATION OF REMEDIES AND DAMAGES: IN NO EVENT, SHALL THE COMPANY OR ITS EMPLOYEES, AGENTS, LICENSORS, OR CONTRACTORS BE LIABLE FOR ANY INCIDENTAL, INDIRECT, SPECIAL, OR CONSEQUENTIAL DAMAGES ARISING OUT OF OR IN CONNECTION WITH THIS LICENSE OR THE SOFTWARE, INCLUDING FOR LOSS OF USE, LOSS OF DATA, LOSS OF INCOME OR PROFIT, OR OTHER LOSSES, SUSTAINED AS A RESULT OF INJURY TO ANY PERSON, OR LOSS OF OR DAMAGE TO PROPERTY, OR CLAIMS OF THIRD PARTIES, EVEN IF THE COMPANY OR AN AUTHORIZED REPRESENTATIVE OF THE COMPANY HAS BEEN ADVISED OF THE POSSIBILITY OF SUCH DAMAGES. IN NO EVENT SHALL THE LIABILITY OF THE COMPANY FOR DAMAGES WITH RESPECT TO THE SOFTWARE EXCEED THE AMOUNTS ACTUALLY PAID BY YOU, IF ANY, FOR THE SOFTWARE OR THE ACCOMPANYING TEXTBOOK. BECAUSE SOME JURISDICTIONS DO NOT ALLOW THE LIMITATION OF LIABILITY IN CERTAIN CIRCUMSTANCES, THE ABOVE LIMITATIONS MAY NOT ALWAYS APPLY TO YOU.

6. GENERAL: THIS AGREEMENT SHALL BE CONSTRUED IN ACCORDANCE WITH THE LAWS OF THE UNITED STATES OF AMERICA, AND THE STATE OF NEW YORK, APPLICABLE TO CONTRACTS MADE IN NEW YORK, AND SHALL BENEFIT THE COMPANY, ITS AFFILIATES AND ASSIGNEES. THIS AGREEMENT IS THE COMPLETE AND EXCLUSIVE STATEMENT OF THE AGREEMENT BETWEEN YOU AND THE COMPANY AND SUPERSEDES ALL PROPOSALS OR PRIOR AGREEMENTS, ORAL, OR WRITTEN, AND ANY OTHER COMMUNICATIONS BETWEEN YOU AND THE COMPANY OR ANY REPRESENTATIVE OF THE COMPANY RELATING TO THE SUBJECT MATTER OF THIS AGREEMENT. If you are a U.S. Government user, this Software is licensed with "restricted rights" as set forth in subparagraphs (a)-(d) of the Commercial Computer-Restricted Rights clause at FAR 52.227-19 or in subparagraphs (c)(1)(ii) of the Rights in Technical Data and Computer Software clause at DFARS 252.227-7013, and similar clauses, as applicable.

Should you have any questions concerning this agreement or if you wish to contact the Company for any reason, please contact in writing: History Media Editor, Prentice Hall, One Lake Street, Upper Saddle River, NJ 07458.